THE WELFARE STATE

by
Clarence B. Carson

Other Books
by
Clarence Carson

The Fateful Turn
The American Tradition
The Flight from Reality
The War on the Poor
Throttling the Railroads
The Rebirth of Liberty
The World in the Grip of an Idea
Organized Against Whom? The Labor Union in America
The Colonial Experience
The Beginning of the Republic
The Sections and the Civil War
The Growth of America
The Welfare State
America: From Gridlock to Deadlock
A Teacher's Guide to A Basic History of the United States
Basic Economics
Basic Communism
Swimming Against the Tide

A Basic History of the United States
Volume Five

THE WELFARE STATE 1929-1985

by
Clarence B. Carson

Beth A. Hoffman
Editorial Consultant

American Textbook Committee
www.americantextbookcommittee.org

email Byron_Mallory@hotmail.com

Grateful acknowledgment is hereby made to Dover Publications for permission to use an extensive number of portraits from *Dictionary of American Portraits*, edited by Hayward and Blanche Cirker and published by Dover Publications, Inc.

ISBN 1-931789-24-X

Contents

Chapter 1
Introduction

A major thrust toward establishing the welfare state came swiftly in 1933. In a special session, which lasted from March 9 through June 16, 1933, Congress, prodded by the President, asserted the authority of the federal government over the American economy in an unprecedented fashion. Never before, certainly not in time of peace, had such far-reaching legislation been passed by any Congress. The swiftness of it has led some historians to ponder whether or not it was a revolution. In the traditional meaning of the term, it certainly was not a revolution. That is, it was not a successful revolt against the established authority, carried out by force of arms. If, however, the term be taken to signify a swift, as opposed to a gradual change, the change in direction was made quickly, and it did have a considerable impact on the country.

Actually, some of the central pieces of legislation to come out of the first hundred days of the New Deal were later held to be unconstitutional, and the particular approaches were abandoned. But the premise of the welfare state was vigorously asserted, and it became established. The premise of the welfare state in the United States is that the federal government is basically responsible for the material well-being of the American people. During the 1930s this premise became so well established that it had not been dislodged by the mid-1980s. President after President has affirmed the premise, and Congress and the courts have acted upon it. Grover Cleveland once asked, "If the government supports the people, who will support the government?" His meaning was this: The government is wholly dependent upon tax receipts (or occasionally other types of payments) for its revenues. It is a nonsensical reversal of roles for the people to be dependent upon the government for their material well-being. To put it yet another way, the government produces no goods; rather, it consumes some portion of the goods taken from people. It can only play a larger role by increasing the portion that it takes and thus reducing the amount available to people generally. Cleveland's question still wants a satisfactory answer, but a welfare state has been established based upon the premise that government will provide for a vast assortment of material and other needs.

The Great Depression, as it came to be called, was the occasion for the establishment of the welfare state. It served, or was used, as the catalytic agent for a massive assertion of governmental power. The economic difficulties which many Americans were experiencing gave an opportunity for the coalescing of reformers, radical and otherwise, behind the administration of President Franklin D. Roosevelt, which was bent on taking dramatic and drastic action. Since the 1890s, reformers had been beating the drums for reform, in and out of season, in good times and bad. Populists had sounded their call; Socialists had pushed for more radical change; Progressives had their heyday from around 1905 to the midst of World War I. Revolutionists, in or out of labor unions, had pressed the case for overturning the system. The alienation of many intellectuals reached its peak in the early 1930s as Hoover and the Republicans resisted drastic change and sought to bring about improvement by modest interventions. The deepening depression gave the reformers their opportunity to make drastic reforms.

Although social programs poured forth in great array in the early days of the New Deal, that is not to suggest that the welfare state was established in one great swoop. On the contrary; the welfare state was established over several decades. There were two great surges, and a goodly number of programs introduced over the years. The first surge came during the 1930s, roughly between 1933–39. Another great surge of programs came in 1965–1966, under President Lyndon Johnson. The symbolic establishment of the welfare state as a fixture, however, came in the 1950s, when the Department of Health, Education, and Welfare attained cabinet status. Not only did this signify a greater permanence to it, but since it was done under the first Republican President elected since the beginning of the New Deal, it indicated the decline of partisan opposition to it.

Not only did the welfare state entail much more government involvement in the lives of Americans but it was also brought about by major shifts in government power. Indeed, the thrust toward the welfare state was only possible by ignoring or overriding constitutional limitations on the federal government and the assumption by it of many new powers. It involved the centralization of power in the national government. This meant that powers formerly exercised by the state or local governments, if they were exercised at all, came under the direction of the central government. Presidential power was greatly increased under Franklin D. Roosevelt, and the traditional roles were almost reversed. Presidents presented programs, and Congress tended to either pass or veto them. The initiative in legislation definitely shifted toward the presidency. A vast bureaucracy was created to administer all the programs, and government became a major growth industry. In the 1960s, the Supreme Court emerged as the dominant branch of government on all those increasing number of matters on which it spoke. The federal government became involved in one way or another with virtually every facet of American lives over the years, ranging from the schools to the monitoring of the safety of lawn mowers and automobiles. Most of the states and many local governments have also enacted their own versions of welfare measures over the years.

Nor was the welfare state idea restricted to the territorial United States in its application. After World War II, the United States launched an assortment of foreign aid projects in lands around the world. The welfare state took on global dimensions. A part of the aid was military, as the United States embraced collective security by fostering and joining the United Nations, and then by fostering collective regional alliances. But much of the foreign aid was devoted to fostering welfare state projects and subsidizing socialism.

Although the welfare state is the central theme of this volume, there are many other themes as well. War and international conflict has been at the center of much American attention for many of the years covered. World War II was a cataclysmic conflict, embracing much more of the world than the first one, and leaving Europe even worse destroyed and sundered. This war was the fruit of the rise of totalitarianism and embodied mainly a clash of collectivisms. It was a titanic struggle between National Socialism in Germany and International Communism in the Soviet Union. The English-speaking peoples ranged themselves on the side of the Soviet Union, and Italy and Japan on the side of Germany. Total war was fought to obtain unconditional surrender. All the wounds have not yet healed.

The ignominious defeat of France early in World War II and the unconditional surrenders of Germany and Japan at the end of the war, plus British withdrawal from colony after colony, left huge power vacuums in the world. The situation was further aggravated by the civil war that continued in China between the Communists and the Kuomintang. International Communism, guided from Moscow, thrust into any volatile situations, moving to establish communist regimes. Eastern Europe was the first victim of this drive, aided by Soviet armies quite often, but any outpost in the world that was weak was a likely target as well.

It began to become apparent fairly early after the war that cooperation between those countries which were still actuated by the remains of Western Civilization and the Judeo-Christian heritage and the Communist bloc of countries was not possible. Indeed, a little analysis should have made that clear without the aid of experience. After all, Communism is bent on rooting out and destroying every relic of the prevailing civilization and religion. Natural law, the great philosophical underpinning of Western culture, is repudiated root and branch by Communists, except, perhaps, in mathematics, physics, and chemistry (and the technology that flows from it). In any case, a Cold War emerged between the West and Communists in the late 1940s and has continued off and on since. The victory of Mao Tse-tung's communist forces in mainland China added a huge population block, at the least, to the communist column. The temperature of this Cold War has varied so much over the years that no summary statement could capture the changes. Suffice it to say here that the contest has persisted and serves as much more than a backdrop to virtually all international relations.

Although the doings of government have assumed an ever larger role in American life over these years, there are other themes that are either not basically political or exist mainly on the periphery or exist largely in those areas free from government control. One of these is the post-World War II resurgence of industry and agriculture. In the midst of the depression which was a fixture throughout the 1930s, there was much talk among intellectuals that the age of American economic expansion had ended. This fit into the thesis that the problem of production had been solved and that the problem now was one of distribution. It fit also into the frontier thesis, that as the open frontier had come to an end, so had America as a land of opportunity. The task that lay ahead, claimed such seers, was not growth in production but conservation, restraint of output, and a better distribution of the wealth of America.

They were false prophets. Once the bulk of the controls and restraints of World War II were lifted, Americans came forth with a burst of production that continued apace almost uninterrupted from the late 1940s to the late 1960s. Though much of the government intervention which flowed from the welfare states still posed numerous obstacles to enterprise, many of these were overcome by ingenuity and technology. American farms were generally mechanized. The shift from rural to town and city living continued or accelerated. A building boom continued throughout these years, and an increasing number of Americans bought three- or four-bedroom homes with two baths and a two-car garage. Virtually every family in America had at least one car; two became much more common, and it was not unusual for a family to have three or more motor vehicles.

New and improved technology spurred and contributed to much of this economic expansion. Television joined radio and the movies as nationally produced entertainment after World War II. Automation in both factories and in the home followed the development of computers, solid state circuitry, and other electronically timed devices. Huge earth movers made building programs feasible which would have been impossible (or impractical) without them. Electrically operated devices multiplied, and even automobiles upgraded batteries from six to twelve volts. The use of chemicals in farming, along with much heavier and more delicate machinery, made possible the production of ever larger crops by fewer and fewer farmers. Repetitive tasks were more and more done by machines, and people were freed to perform those jobs requiring human dimension skills.

While this building and production was quite real and involved many accomplishments, much of it was fostered and channeled by a massive credit expansion. The national debt was the landmark of the credit expansion, as it continued to mount with year after year of government deficits and the rising cost of interest payments on the increasing amount of the principal. The value of the dollar continued to decline, and by the early 1970s the United States could no longer defend it with gold. The country was caught with a depreciated dollar, perilously rising prices, and what amounted to an inflationary depression.

The currency was not the only thing that depreciated in value over these years. Civility, morality, and public and private virtue suffered a similar decline. The crime statistics and, in the most recent decades, the dramatic increase of lawsuits and the fantastic growth in the number of lawyers gave the most readily quantifiable evidence of this decline. These things bespeak a society at odds with or contemptuous of authority. The decline was preceded and is accompanied by a massive assault on authority, on the authority of custom and tradition, the authority of home and church, and the authority of the anciently received absolutes of morality, civility, and virtue. Indeed, the assault upon authority has gone on at many levels ranging from the highest to the most vulgar. The decline of movies from polite respectability to purveyors of profanity, obscenities, and brutal assault on the institutions of society can be chronicled in the years from the early 1960s to the mid-1980s. The youth rebellion of the late 1960s and early 1970s reached a fever pitch of opposition to all received authority. These and associated developments are surely themes of these years.

One other theme of these years may bring this introduction to its appropriate close. A counter movement to these developments has been gaining ground, or at least followers, since the 1960s. It is generally known as the conservative movement, but it has many facets, and not all those who may be called conservatives have an equal concern or, for that matter, any concern about some of them. The movement includes those who are most apt to be concerned about reviving the authority of custom and tradition, the stability of the family, the freedom of enterprise, constitutionally limited government, property rights as well as the whole body of what used to be called natural rights, fiscally responsible government, sound money, traditional religion, and the like. The resurgence of those who are outspokenly concerned about these matters will conclude this work.

Chapter 2

The Great Depression

I am convinced we have now passed the worst and with continued unity of effort we shall rapidly recover. There is one certainty in the future of a people of the resources, intelligence, and character of the people of the United States—that is, prosperity.

—Herbert C. Hoover, 1930

Fifteen hundred jobless men stormed the plant of the Fruit Growers Express Company here [Indiana Harbor, Indiana], demanding that they be given jobs to keep from starving. The company's answer was to call the city police, who routed the jobless with menacing clubs.

—Federated Press, 1931

I say that . . . the Federal Government has always had and still has a continuing responsibility for the broader public welfare. It will soon fulfill that responsibility. . . . I pledge you, I pledge myself, to a new deal for the American people. . . . This is more than a political campaign; it is a call to arms. Give me your help, not to win votes alone, but to win in this crusade to restore America to its own people.

—Franklin D. Roosevelt, 1932

Chronology

June, 1929—Passage of Agricultural Marketing Act.

August, 1929—Federal Reserve raises rediscount rate.

October, 1929—Stock Market Crash.

1930—Smoot-Hawley Tariff.

1931—Trial of Scottsboro case.

January, 1932—Reconstruction Finance Corporation authorized.

March, 1932—Norris-La Guardia Act.

July, 1932—Veterans' "Bonus Army" march on Washington.

November, 1932—Roosevelt elected President.

February, 1933—20th Amendment adopted.

February–March, 1933—Banking crisis.

Since this chapter deals mainly with events and developments between 1929 and early 1933, it may be well to emphasize those are not the inclusive dates for what has come to be called the Great Depression. The depression may well have got underway in 1929, but it did not suddenly end with the inauguration of Franklin D. Roosevelt in 1933. It was a prolonged depression, from which there was no substantial recovery until 1940. Indeed, a case can be made that the depression did not end until after World War II, though it certainly changed its character during the war. Most economic indices—gross national product, employment figures, and the like—would indicate that the depression was ending in 1940 and 1941. But much of the production and employment was war production and employment for that or in the armed services. Wartime rationing and the curtailment of production for consumer use resulted in greater deprivation in some things during the war than in the 1930s for many people. However, at the least, it is well established that the depression lasted from 1929 to 1940.

It is important to emphasize the latter dates not only because they give a much more accurate impression of how prolonged the depression was, but also because Hoover's term, and his name, have been too closely associated with the depression and Roosevelt's New Deal too rarely identified with its prolongation. The blaming of the depression on President Hoover began during his term in office. Some people took the wheels off their dilapidated cars and used them on horse-drawn vehicles, dubbed "Hoover carts." Shanty towns were referred to as "Hoovervilles." The Democrats made political hay by blaming the Republicans, and Hoover in particular, for the depression. It would be twenty years before another Republican would be elected President. None of this is meant to suggest that Hoover, and other Republicans, were not in some measure responsible for the coming of the depression, nor that they did not have a hand in prolonging it, at least in the early stages. But it was the New Deal programs that prolonged the depression throughout the 1930s. That is reason enough for emphasizing its duration.

The Great Depression was a primal development for most Americans who lived through it. It left psychic wounds on many of them that have taken a long time to heal, if they ever do. As recently as 1966, an author wrote a compelling book entitled *The Invisible Scar*. It referred to those wounds made from experiencing the impact of the depression. The greatest wound, perhaps, was that many people lost confidence in their ability to provide for themselves and their families. This gave rise to fears and a sense of insecurity. There was a widespread loss of faith in the individual, the family, and the local community as the primary reliance for well-being. This set the stage for the great expansion of government activity and for people to turn to government for aid and security.

The impact of prolonged depression was heightened by an increasing dependence of so many Americans on the market. In an earlier America, even a prolonged depression would not have had so widespread and deep impact. Most people had not only been farmers but also subsistence farmers in many cases, depending hardly at all on the market. Many grew their own food, got most of their fuel for heating from cutting wood, made their own clothes, and bought only what they could not produce themselves. Even those farmers who produced primarily for the market and bought extensively in the market could, in a pinch, provide for most of their needs on their farms. By the 1930s, indeed well before, this situation had changed dramatically. A majority of Americans now lived in towns and cities, and had little or no means of providing for most of their livelihood from their own resources. A majority of the work force was now employed by others, either directly, as in self-employment, or indirectly through employers who paid them wages or salaries for what they produced. Farmers, too, had grown increasingly dependent on the market, specializing in producing one or a few goods to be sold mostly to others. Tenants were generally required by landlords to concentrate on those that could be most readily sold in the market. During World War I, Americans had been lured by high prices and government admonitions to increase their production for the market. In the 1920s, when the wartime demand declined, as many farmers as could continued to produce for the market, seeking especially to buy the new consumer wonders that were available.

Prolonged depression left many of those dependent on the market exposed, or at least revealed in an unpleasant way to them the potential difficulties attending dependence on the market. When jobs became hard to find, some were without a job, and those who still had jobs feared they would lose them. As prices declined, farming became less and less profitable. As the situation did not greatly improve and sometimes worsened from year to year, it was easy to give way to despair. Those in debt often saw little hope of paying their debts. There should be no doubt that the 1930s were hard times for many people.

There was no shortage of prophets, seers, would-be politicians, and doomsayers to put the worst face on the situation either. Indeed, radicals, promoters of panaceas, revolutionists, and reformers abounded, all too willing to apply their favorite remedies, or just to stir up trouble. Communists, of course, had a ready made explanation for the ills of America. Capitalism was in its final stage of collapse. When William Z. Foster, the head of the American Communist Party, appeared before a Congressional committee in 1930, he proclaimed:

> What is the cause of this starvation [a figment of his imagination], misery and hardship of the millions of workers in the United States? Is it because some great national calamity has destroyed the food, clothing and shelter available for the people? No, on the contrary. Millions of workers must go hungry because there is too much wheat. Millions of workers must go without clothes because the warehouses are full to overflowing with everything that is needed. Millions of workers must freeze because there is too much coal. This is the logic of capitalist system. . . .

What did Foster offer as the solution to his overdrawn picture of the problem? Communism, of course, on the Soviet model. "The Soviet Union," he told the committee, "is revolutionizing the workclass . . . by its very existence, and by the contrast which it presents to conditions of workers under capitalism."[1] He went on to present an imaginary idyllic picture of conditions in Russia as opposed to those in the United States. Moreover, he boldly declared that the workers would establish a dictatorship in America, and that "Under the dictatorship, all the capitalist parties—Republican, Democratic, Progressive, Socialist, etc.—will be liquidated."[2]

While Communist analysis had more than a little impact by way of the remedies applied in the 1930s, most of the changes were the fruit of a much less revolutionary approach. The truth was that a considerable number of reformist intellectuals had been waiting in the wings to come to the rescue of America. The prolonged depression gave them an opportunity to try their programs. Above all, they had come to believe that government action and intervention was the key to the solution. Many, perhaps most, Americans, came to believe, too, in the midst of the prolonged depression, that government had to do something about it. And, eventually the government programs were forthcoming.

For all the above reasons, it is highly important to understand both what caused the depression, what prolonged it, as well as what the impact of the government programs was.

The Coming of the Depression

The stock market crash in October of 1929 was the critical event in the beginning of the deflation which produced the depression. To understand what caused the crash provides a part of the answer to the question of what caused the Great Depression, though it will tell us very little about why the depression was so prolonged. The background to the crash is this. There had been an extensive credit expansion for most of the 1920s. The central role in this credit expansion had been played by the Federal Reserve system, particularly its rediscount and related policies. Stock prices had become highly inflated during the period 1927–1929. Much of the easy credit had been used for the purchase and speculation in stocks, as prices rose higher and higher. Indeed, the overall rise in stock prices was in many instances nothing short of spectacular between early 1928 and September, 1929, when they reached all-time highs. For example, between March 3, 1928 and September 3, 1929 the common stocks in the following corporations rose (with adjustments made for stock splits): American Can from 77 to 181⅞ per share; American Telephone & Telegraph from 179½ to 335⅝; General Electric from 128¾ to 396¼; Montgomery Ward from 132¾ to 466½; and Union Carbide & Carbon from 145 to 413⅝. During this eighteen-month period many stocks more than doubled in price, while others more than tripled.

What spurred this rising demand for stocks was not only credit expansion in general but loans to stockbrokers in particular. While many stocks were undoubtedly bought outright, the critical figures for the crash, as well as speculative fever, were stocks bought on margin. Those who buy on margin put up only a small portion of the price of the stock, while borrowing the bulk of the cost from the broker. These loans are subject to call at any time. The great advantage of buying on margin is that if the price of the stocks rises significantly, the buyer can make a large profit with a small investment. For example, suppose a marginal buyer buys 1,000 shares of a stock at $100 per share, putting up only 10 per cent of the cost, or $10,000. Suppose further, that the price of the stock doubles to $200 over the next year, and the buyer sells at that price. He will have made $100,000 on an outlay of only $10,000, plus whatever he paid in interest. On the other hand, if the stock falls below $90 per share, he will have to put up the difference or lose everything.

Marginal buying increased greatly over the period under consideration. Brokers' loans, which indicate this, rose from $3½ billion at the end of 1927 to over $6 billion in the course of 1929. Indeed, they had reached a peak of over $6.8 billion on October 2, 1929. Estimates indicate that in the summer of 1929 there were as many as a million people who held stock on margin, and the number of shares so held has been estimated at 300 million. This great speculative binge was greatly aided by the Federal Reserve credit expansion policies. The rediscount rate was lowered from 4 to 3½ per cent in August, 1927. It was, however, raised twice in the first half of 1929, first to 4 and then to 4½ per cent, but this did not appreciably alter the course of the speculative fever.

By early 1929, there were increasing worries in some circles about this ongoing bull market. Although there were setbacks from time to time, shaking out some of the marginal buyers, each time the market came back stronger than before and prices rose higher and higher. By 1929, the prices of many common stocks were so high that they bore little relationship to any profit that might come from dividends for any foreseeable future. Herbert Hoover had been worried about the heady speculation when he was in

Coolidge's cabinet, and once he became President in 1929 he determined to clamp down on it. As he later described it, he induced the "Reserve Banks to refuse rediscount to banks which were lending largely on stocks. . . ."[3] Indeed, even before the Federal Reserve Board sent this message to the banks: "The Federal Reserve Act does not . . . contemplate the use of the resources of the Federal Reserve Banks for the creation or extension of speculative credit. A member bank is not within its reasonable claims . . . when it borrows either for the purpose of making speculative loans or for the purpose of maintaining speculative loans."[4] Hoover said, "We did at one time almost secure a stranglehold on the stock market when the Reserve Banks had so tightened the call-loan situation that a moment arrived when there was no money available to the market."[5] Actually, Hoover somewhat overstated the case. It is true that there was some tightening of money temporarily for brokers' loans, and subsequent dips in the market, but there was money available from other sources, and the market bounced back from this selective effort at shutting off credit. The Federal Reserve finally authorized a raise of the rediscount rate to 6 per cent, and these and other measures may have contributed to an impact much greater than anyone expected or hoped.

At any rate, the stock market broke disastrously on October 24, 1929. Professor Murray Rothbard maintains that there was no significant increase of the money supply after the end of 1928, and that thereafter the credit contraction, deflation, and depression became inevitable. Be that as it may, the crash came with a rush in late October. More precisely, there were successive buildups to it. Following the September 3 highs, the market broke significantly. It recovered and advanced to new highs briefly later in the month, as it had been doing for several years. But then prices began to fall once again, and a considerable sell-off was underway by the beginning of October. However, as late as October 22, 1929, Charles E. Mitchell, head of the National City Bank of New York proclaimed: "I know of nothing fundamentally wrong with the stock market or with the underlying business and credit structure. . . ."[6]

What set off the wild selling and disastrous break in prices on October 24? Almost certainly, it was that the declining prices before that day had driven many stocks below the margins for many holders of stocks on margins. The brokers sent out their calls for more money to cover the loans, and many of the stocks were sold. At the same time, the banks were put under increasing pressure as deposits were withdrawn and their own loans had to be called. The market did rally before the end of the day on October 24. Representatives of the largest banks in New York City had met at J. P. Morgan and Company and pledged $240 million to try to steady the market. It worked to some extent for the remainder of that day and until the end of the week. However, wild selling began again on Monday, and on Tuesday, October 29, the bottom virtually fell out of the market. The New York Stock

Exchange was the scene of chaos; the ticker tape fell further and further behind, and no one could be sure what prices were being paid. Stocks were being offered at market, and sometimes no buyers could be found. White Sewing Machine, which had been earlier selling at 40, fell briefly to 1, when someone offered that price for some shares when there were no other offers. The confusion ended in the following days, but not the decline in prices. The lowest prices of the year were registered on November 13, 1929. By that date, approximately $30 billion in value of stocks had simply disappeared. Westinghouse which had sold at better than 289 on September 3 had fallen to 102⅝ by November 13. So it went for stock after stock. Many investors had been wiped out.

The Depression Deepens

The stock market crash signalled the onset of a vast credit contraction. It set off a liquidity crisis which continued to reverberate through the economy in the following months and years. A liquidity crisis occurs when many people are trying to turn their assets into cash. The initial impact of the stock market crash was to send margin buyers scurrying around to find cash to hold on to their stock. But the broader credit contraction made it highly desirable to have as many liquid (quickly convertible to cash) assets as possible. To put it still more generally, the credit contraction produced a great liquidation. Everything that had been buoyed up by the credit expansion of the 1920s had to contract sooner or later to confront the new reality.

A liquidation, a credit contraction, a deflation, a depression (at least one that is permitted to run its course fairly quickly),—call it what you will—is the first stage of the recovery. A credit expansion is to an economy what a fever is to the human body, or at least there are many similarities—; there is feverish activity during the boom; the cheeks of the economy are flushed, so to speak. Then there comes the crisis, and the fever breaks and begins its return to normal. Once, the fever has spent itself recovery can begin. Of course, an economy has numerous aspects and is more complex than the human body, and it is by no means easy for the fever to subside. The credit expansion of the 1920s left in its wake great debts, for after all it had been accomplished by borrowing and by expanding the debts of financial institutions. The debts proved to be the most intractable feature of the credit contraction. Beyond that, to the extent that the economy had become dependent upon credit, it was mortgaged to the future, and when the contraction came, the future was at hand. There had to be a catching up process in which people paid off their debts and accumulated a surplus if the economy was to recover. But the payment of debts is exceedingly difficult in a deflation.

The deepening of the depression 1930–1932 can be graphically shown by some statistics. Stock prices continued to decline overall from the time of the stock market crash in 1929 through much of 1932, though there were, of course, fluctuations up and down of particular stocks. American Telephone & Telegraph, for example, fell from its high mark of 304 in September, 1929 to a low of 70¼ in the course of 1932. United States Steel from 261¾ to 21¼. Twenty-five representative industrial stocks fell from 366 to a little over 96 during the same period. New capital issues of stocks and bonds were approximately $10 billion in 1929, $7 billion in 1930, and $1 billion in 1932. In short, investment capital was becoming only a trickle.

Foreign trade declined drastically as the depression deepened. The credit contraction following upon the stock market crash in the United States sent shock waves through many European countries as well. The United States had become the major creditor nation in the world in the 1920s, and much of the trade and debt payments from Europe had been fostered by credit from the United States. This dried up from 1930 onward, and by 1931 financial institutions in Europe were having grave difficulties. Ramsay MacDonald, a Labourite and socialist, headed a coalition government in Britain and took that country off the gold standard. This action, along with that of some other countries, made for increasing difficulties in making settlements in foreign trade. American exports fell from over $4½ billion in 1929 to less than $1½ billion in 1932.

The decline in industrial production in the United States and the rise in the number of unemployed give a clear enough picture of the course of the depression. By late 1930, industrial production had fallen 26 per cent below the peak in 1929, and in mid-summer of 1932 was 51 per cent below what it had been three years before. Statistics on unemployment, such as they were, were probably less reliable than those that have been gathered since the Bureau of Labor Statistics has assayed that task, and they are always more than a little suspect. At any rate, here are some estimates from that time: 3 million unemployed in April, 1930, 4 million in October, 1930, 7 million in October, 1931, 11 million a year later, and probably over 12 million in early 1933. Even if those figures are roughly accurate, they indicate that there had been a steady rise in unemployment.

In the late summer of 1932 business improved noticeably, stock prices rose tentatively, and there were a number of signs that recovery was at hand. It did not turn out that way, but the story of the new crisis had best be left for telling a little farther on.

Mr. Hoover's Dilemma

On the face of it, Herbert C. Hoover appeared to be well qualified to be President of the United States during difficult times. Certainly, he had those qualifications that were so greatly admired in the 1920s when businessmen were in the ascendant. Hoover had not only been a businessman but also an unusually successful one. If he did not literally go from rags to riches, he came close enough as to hardly qualify the phrase. His father died when he was six, his mother a few years later, and the poor boy grew up under the care of relatives. He worked his way through Stanford to become an engineer. In the two decades or so before World War I, he became a millionaire several times over as an entrepreneur and mining engineer. His greatest successes were in buying mines that had failed and making them pay. His ventures took him to many different countries and climates, and his business was headquartered in London. Hoover became well known for his venturesome flair for investment, his careful attention to detail, and his ability to work wonders in whatever he undertook.

During World War I and its aftermath, Hoover attained international recognition for his charitable work to aid the victims of the war. The war was hardly underway when he busied himself in London coming to the aid of Americans stranded there. Soon, however, he was caught up in helping those in much more desperate circumstances, the Belgians who had been overrun by the Germans and cut off from the Allies. Hoover headed the Commission for Belgian Relief and through his determined efforts those people were saved from the full effect of the suffering that would otherwise have been their lot. At the end of the war, he answered the call from leaders of the Allies to bring aid to millions in many lands threatened by pestilence and famine. As one of his biographers has said: "Hoover sent his emissaries across Europe from Belgium to Azerbaijan. . . . His wheat laden ships sailed into empty harbors all over the former War zones. . . . For eleven months Hoover did not take a day off, never went into a shop—others bought his clothes—and ate on the run, his thoughts constantly haunted by the hungry millions, particularly the pale, stunted children, their heads shaved as a precaution against lice, stretching out their tin plates in canteens and schoolhouses for stew and bread that all Europe called Hoover Lunches. In Finland a new verb came into the language: 'to hoover' meant to be kind, to help. . . . All over the world he came to be known as the Great Humanitarian, and into his offices there poured a million signatures on a hundred thousand pages, the signatures of children and their childish drawings of him as a new angel of mercy."[7]

It is one of the great ironies of history that a man of such proven charitable instincts should come to be thought as cold and hard in the face of hardship and deprivation during the depression. The truth is that Hoover was caught on the horns of a dilemma. As President of the United States he was head of the government, not theretofore thought of as a charitable organization. Nor was Hoover of a mind to try to make it into one. On the other hand, government was already involved in the economy and under pressure from various directions to become more involved. There was the national banking system, the Federal Reserve system, the more general involvement in issuing and backing money with gold, the protective tariffs, and the like.

Herbert C. Hoover (1874–1964)

Hoover was 31st President of the United States, an engineer, philanthropist, and author. He was born in Iowa of Quaker parents, educated at the newly established Stanford University, a successful mining engineer and entrepreneur. After having been deeply involved in foreign relief activities during and after World War I, Hoover decided to devote himself to public service for the remainder of his career. Thus, he served as Secretary of Commerce 1921–1929 and as President 1929–1933. The Great Depression was his undoing and he never became actively involved in politics again. He did, however, continue an active interest in public affairs, writing, charitable work, and speaking. His early evaluation of the tendencies of the New Deal appeared in 1934 in a little book entitled *The Challenge to Liberty*. In it, Hoover pointed to parallels with Italian Fascism and warned that the programs were undermining the American constitutional system and individual liberty. In 1947, President Harry Truman appointed Hoover to head a commission to investigate the structure of the Federal government and make recommendations for improvement. The findings were known as the *Hoover Commission Report* and constituted a devastating analysis of the expansion of the Federal government bureaucracy since the early 1930s. While few could find fault with his findings, they made little impact on the continued growth of government.

Republican Presidents had claimed credit for the prosperity of the 1920s; was Hoover not equally responsible for the depression?

More broadly, Hoover saw it as his task to defend the American system of freedom and individual initiative from the efforts of interventionists and people under the sway of socialist ideas to change it. He believed in what he called *American Individualism,* the title of a little book he published in 1922, that it was up to people basically to provide for themselves by their own efforts. For those in need and unable to help themselves, because of special circumstances or disability, he thought the basic reliance ought to be on private and voluntary charity, supplemented as it might be by local government. So far as intervention in the economy went, he was strongly opposed to extensive and possibly disabling intervention. Moreover, he held that "Economic depression cannot be cured by legislative action or executive pronouncements. Economic wounds must be healed by the action of the cells of the economic body—the producers and consumers themselves."[8] He strongly opposed direct relief by the federal government:

> This is not an issue [Hoover said] as to whether people shall go hungry or cold in the United States. It is solely a question of the best method by which hunger and cold shall be prevented. . . . My own conviction is strongly that if we break down this sense of responsibility of individual generosity to individual and mutual self-help in the country in times of national difficulty, and if we start appropriations of this character we have not only impaired something infinitely valuable in the life of the American people but have struck at the roots of self-government. Once this has happened it is not the cost of a few score million but we are faced with the abyss of reliance in future upon Government charity in some form or another.[9]

On the other hand, Hoover was by temperament a take charge person and a doer. He had amply demonstrated these traits in business, in European relief work during and after World War I, as Food Commissioner under Wilson, and, above all, as Secretary of Commerce under Harding and Coolidge. Those who worked under him over the years always referred to him as "the Chief," i.e., the man in charge. The taciturn Calvin Coolidge was more than a little taken aback at the energy and bounty of ideas Hoover had in cabinet meetings and for the Commerce Department. He was the first man in Commerce to really activate the department, nor did he confine himself to that department but ranged well beyond in offering advice and conceiving things to do. Moreover, he may have been bitten by the Progressive bug more effectively than most critics have thought since his presidency. He voted for Theodore Roosevelt and his New Nationalism in 1912. He showed a bent toward regulation, though not a highly controversial one during his years in the Commerce Department. Radio had only recently begun as a commercial vehicle for broadcasting when Hoover took the post. He argued that the Federal government should regulate broadcasting on the grounds that the "ether is a public medium, and its use must be for the public benefit.The dominant element for consideration in the radio field is, and always will be, the great body of the listening public. . . ."[10] Among his other proposals was one for a Federal and state program for developing waterways, and another for Federal regulation of fishing off the shores of the United States and Alaska.

Nor did Hoover simply take a hands-off position toward the depression. First and last, a goodly number of measures were taken during his administration. But he was caught in the cross currents between those who believed it was the place and responsibility of government to control the economy and provide direct aid for those who were hard hit and his most basic view that people must provide for themselves and that to intervene in the economy would be to place obstacles in the way of their doing so.

Government Response to Depression

Most of the programs during Hoover's administration were aimed at preventing the deflation and liquidation which would probably have completed its course much sooner without the intervention. It was not simply that they were half-way measures, which has often been charged, but, much more important, they were wrong-way measures. The credit expansion had ended; a contraction was occurring which might be expected to bring the fever down to normal, allowing recovery to take place. Instead, the measures taken were designed to keep the fever up. Literally, they were usually aimed to keep wages and prices from falling and adjusting to the reduced money supply. Such measures could only drag out and prolong the agony of readjustment, and that is what they did.

Even before the stock market crash, the first of these measures under Hoover was passed: the Agricultural Marketing Act. This act embodied some of the old McNary-Haugen bill, which Coolidge had repeatedly vetoed, but did not attempt to peg prices for farm products at any level or subsidize sales on the world market. It authorized a Federal Farm Board, whose purpose was to foster cooperative buying and marketing of farm products so as to maintain prices at a generally higher level. The idea was that cooperatives and other supported organizations would buy farm goods and store them at periods of glut and sell them when prices were higher. The government provided loans for these operations. The program failed. Prices were generally declining in season and out, so that organizations operating in this fashion could only lose money.

In the midst of the stock market crash, the Federal Reserve began to lower the rediscount rate and otherwise increase bank reserves. Between October and the end of 1929, rates were lowered from 6 to 4½ per cent. This effort to reinflate, or "reflate," as the current term had it, had only a temporary effect. Nor did the further reduction in the course of 1930 by the New York Federal Reserve Bank from 4½ to 2 per cent succeed in fostering any extensive credit expansion. Banks were threatened with collapse, and they tended to use the new money to increase their cash reserves rather than expand credit. Of course, these efforts of the Federal Reserve to prevent price decline did not have any long range effect.

In the hope of forestalling a general depression, Hoover called several conferences with business and labor leaders in November, 1929. This was an attempt, also, to avoid using the force of government but rather to use the position of the presidency to persuade them to follow what he believed to be the best course. Hoover asked the business leaders to continue their planned construction programs, to hold wages at the current level rather than reduce them, and to continue employment at the present level, even if it became necessary to reduce the hours of work. The business leaders generally agreed to try to hold the line, if the labor unions could be persuaded not to try to get higher wages for their members. Union leaders agreed to go along with this plan. However well meant, the approach was bound to fail, as it did ultimately. As the credit contraction proceeded, it could only lead to increasing unemployment, and it did. It was a futile attempt to hold prices up as well. Businessmen could only bankrupt their companies by paying higher wages than the market required over an extended period, and they could only do so temporarily. All this did was to delay for a time the necessary adjustments in wages and prices to the new situation.

Another measure aimed at holding prices up was the Smoot-Hawley Tariff, passed in June, 1930. In his campaign in 1928, Hoover advocated "strengthening the protective tariff . . . , not as an abstract economic theory, but as a practical and definite policy of protecting the standards of living of the American family. . . ."[11] When Congress failed to pass a new tariff in its regular 1929–1930 session, Hoover called a special session in 1930 to deal with that and other matters. By that time, it was being considered as a depression measure. One thousand members of the American Economic Association signed a petition opposing higher tariffs, but this had no impact on events. The idea of raising tariff rates at a time when world trade was already declining did not make sense to them. But Congress forged ahead to raise the rates on agricultural raw materials from 38 per cent to 49 per cent and on other goods from 31 per cent to 49 per cent. The tariff was specifically advanced as a measure to keep farm prices high. It did not do so, of course; indeed, the United States was still mainly an agricultural exporting country, and tariffs on imports, except for such products as sugar, could have no effect on prices. Indeed, farm prices declined drastically from 1929–1932: corn from $1.05 to 39 cents per bushel, cotton from 17 to 6 cents per pound, and tobacco from 19 to 10 cents per pound.

Another measure taken to halt the decline in the depression was to increase expenditures on public works projects. From the outset, Hoover encouraged states to continue their spending for public buildings, roads, and the like. From 1930 onward Federal outlay for public buildings was increased. Major buildings, such as the new building for the Supreme Court, a Senate Office Building and House Office Building, were begun during these years, as well as many Federal buildings in the states. Hoover justified these outlays on the grounds that the public buildings were a necessity and that depression was the best time because building would give a spur to the economy. Since the building would have to be paid for by taxes drawn from private sources, it is not clear that it would do anything other than shift resources from one sector of the economy to another. Moreover, this government spending had no discernible impact on the depression.

In the elections in 1930, the Democrats won control of the House of Representatives, and the Republicans maintained only a slim majority in the Senate. Since some of the Republicans were Progressives, for example, George W. Norris of Nebraska, who found it easy to align with Democrats on many issues, neither house was under the control of regular Republicans. Thereafter, Hoover was much more often at odds with Congress, vetoing various measures. The Norris-La Guardia Anti-Injunction Act of 1932, so far as it had to do with the depression at all, may have been an indirect attempt to do something about declining wages. It was the result of a campaign by labor unions to be freed from the threat of court injunctions. This act not only attempted to make it easier for labor unions to be organized but also placed great restrictions on the issuance of injunctions against unions by Federal courts. For example, in order for a court to issue an injunction it must find that "unlawful acts have been threatened and will be committed unless restrained."[12] As it turned out, this act was the opening wedge in granting a privileged status to labor unions, a movement that was greatly accelerated under the New Deal.

Both Hoover and Congress increasingly focused upon shoring up banks and other financial institutions in 1932. The depression and credit contraction produced a crisis for fractional reserve banking. The thrust for liquidity posed problems which fractional reserve banking is not equipped for, indeed, cannot be ultimately. Under this system, banks lend out a large portion of the money deposited with them, keeping only a relatively small portion in cash reserves. At any time that a large number of deposits are withdrawn, the bank will most likely have to close its doors. This stirs panics (quite understandable) among depositors in other banks, and under modern communications conditions, could force every bank to close its doors.

Bank closings increased with the onset of the depression and continued to mount in number until 1932. There had been 659 bank closings in 1929. In 1930, there were 1,352 bank failures, and the number rose to an alarming 2,294 in 1931, as the threatened collapse in Europe and widespread abandonment of the gold standard increased pressures within the United States. Hoover always maintained that the American economic system was basically sound, but after he left office he declared "that the fault lay in the singular weakness of the banking system," as "evidenced by the fact that the . . . banks which failed . . . represented 25 per cent of the number of banks."[13] He said also that Congressional investigations revealed "a rottenness far worse than even I had anticipated."[14] Undoubtedly, the banks were the weak link in the economy, but it had much less to do with any wrongdoing in the banks than with the privileged position of banks which permits them to promise to pay on demand a great deal more than they can. In short, the weakness lies in the fractional reserve system.

At any rate, the government made a large effort to keep the banks afloat as the depression deepened. As already noted, the Federal Reserve made money available by low rediscount rates to make cash available to the banks. Long-term notes, however, posed the larger problem, especially as those who had gone into debt were increasingly unable to make their payments. Hoover moved to relieve this situation by expanding government aid for farm credit and home loan credit. More direct aid was made available in 1932 by the creation of the Reconstruction Finance Corporation. Its purpose was to make "loans for income producing . . . enterprises which will increase employment. . . ."[15]

Within a few weeks of the time it was chartered, the RFC had made loans to 587 banks and trust companies, 18 building and loan associations, 13 insurance companies, 2 joint stock land banks, 3 mortgage loan companies, as well as some loans to businesses, primarily railroads, and some farm organizations. Banks and trust companies had received well over half of the money loaned. Hoover maintained that these loans were "serving to protect the credit structure of the Nation whose collapse would mean complete disaster to all and the savings of all the people that directly or indirectly are in the safekeeping of the great fiduciary institutions, savings banks, insurance companies, buildings and loan associations, that is the whole people."[16] A little later in the year, Congress authorized funds for the states to provide more direct relief.

Apparently, the aid to financial institutions did work to stem the tide of bank failures. Bank failures during 1932 dropped to 1,456, a decline of close to 40 per cent from the year before. Moreover, in August of 1932 there were increasing signs that business was improving. Hoover believed that the worst of the depression was over, and recovery was well on its way. As it turned out, it was only the lull before the storm so far as banking and credit institutions were concerned. Hoover continued to assert in the following years that what brought the downturn and crisis late in the year and in the early 1933 were fears aroused about what Roosevelt was going to do after he was elected. There is no doubt that a new panic occurred during this latter period and that it was stimulated by widespread fears. Roosevelt's election may have sparked some of these fears, but it must also be kept in mind that the contraction of credit had not been permitted to go all the way yet. Government intervention had been used to delay and hold back what may have been inevitable.

It should be clear, at the least, that the Hoover administration had taken rather extensive measures to intervene in the economy during the depression. It is true that it introduced no new programs of business regulation, did not move either to enter into business directly nor control business activity. But it had moved far toward establishing the premise of governmental responsibility for the functioning of the economy. It was, perhaps, no more than a step beyond that to government responsibility for the well-being of the people. That is not to suggest that the Hoover administration established the welfare state. It may have, however, prepared the ground for it. Almost certainly, it prolonged the readjustment to the credit contraction by programs which deferred the adjustments. There still remains, however, the discussion of the last months of Hoover's presidency, which were preceded by a significant election.

The Election of 1932

When the Republicans met in convention, they renominated Herbert Hoover as their candidate, though many were hardly enthusiastic about his prospects for re-election. The Democrats nominated Franklin D. Roosevelt, then governor of New York. Roosevelt had appeared to be launched on a national political career, though he was on a losing ticket as vice presidential candidate in 1920, when he was struck down by polio (then called infantile paralysis) in 1921. Thereafter, his legs were paralyzed and withered, and a person with less determination and drive might have spent the rest of his days as an invalid. As soon as he had made what recovery from the disease was possible, he became involved in politics once again. He was elected governor of New York in 1928, and re-elected by an impressive majority in 1930.

Indeed, politics was Roosevelt's lifeblood, and he played the game with skilled mastery. He had a sunny temperament, a buoyant personality, and great personal charm. Indeed, he appeared to be so eager to please—or to be elected, as the case might be—that he was reluctant to take a stand on issues, and early acquired the reputation of being a trimmer and a straddler of issues. The story is told that when an aide brought him two diametrically opposed positions on the tariff and asked him to choose, he suggested that the two positions be blended together. Walter Lippmann, a journalist, wrote of Roosevelt before the election of 1932: "Franklin D. Roosevelt is an amiable man with many philanthropic impulses, but he is not the dangerous enemy of anything. He is too eager to please . . . , is no crusader. . . . He is a pleasant man who, without any important qualifications for the office, would very much like to be President."[17] Actually, Roosevelt was both more devious and more tenacious in pursuing his course than that would suggest.

But in 1932, indeed even before that, he was intent on being nominated by the Democrats for President, and after that in being elected. Thus, he was cautious, seeking sometimes to appear bold yet not specific about the direction of his boldness, willing to break with tradition but only "foolish" tradition, ready to launch costly new programs but only by reducing

Franklin D. Roosevelt (1882–1945)

Roosevelt was the 32nd President of the United States. He was born in New York, graduated from Harvard, went to law school at Columbia, and began the practice of law in New York City. The law, however, was for him only a preparation for politics. In 1910, he was elected to the New York State senate, and thereafter, except for an interlude in the 1920s after his bout with polio, he was in government and politics for the rest of his life. Although he was a distant relative of Theodore Roosevelt and married his niece, Franklin was a confirmed Democrat for his whole political career. He was appointed to the Navy Department as an assistant by Woodrow Wilson and remained at that post 1913–1921. In 1920, Roosevelt was the Democratic nominee for Vice-President, but the ticket was defeated by the Republicans, his only defeat for public office. He served for two terms as governor of New York, was elected President in 1932, and was re-elected 1936, 1940, and 1944—the only man ever to run for or be elected for more than two terms as President. His presidency occurred in the midst of the two great formative events of the 20th century: the Great Depression and World War II. Under his direction, the federal government was vastly expanded, first in a massive attempt to alter the course of the depression, and then in that titanic struggle known as World War II. He instituted the Welfare State and prepared the groundwork for the extensive role of the United States in the world.

expenditures and balancing the budget. In short, he was a candidate, seeking votes, not losing them by presenting hard choices. He was ably assisted in his drive for the presidency by Louis M. Howe, a little gnome of man who had been his right-hand man for years, and James A. Farley, an indefatigable campaigner. Although Roosevelt got off to an early lead in his quest for the nomination, he still did not have the nomination locked up when the Democrats convened. Alfred Smith, the nominee in 1928, had a number of delegates, as did John N. Garner, the Speaker of the House. The Democrats still required two-thirds majorities for nomination, and Roosevelt fell well short of that on the first two ballots. However, Garner's delegates shifted to Roosevelt on the following ballot, and the Party was very nearly united in the nomination of Roosevelt for President and Garner for Vice-President.

The Democratic platform contained hardly a hint of the drastic measures to be taken during the early New Deal. It called for a reduction of expenditures and a balanced budget, the removal of government generally from private enterprise, promised a "sound currency to be preserved at all hazards," strengthening and enforcement of the antitrust laws, observance of the Constitution and amendment of it where necessary, a strong national defense, and the like. Here and there in it there was foreshadowing of at least the direction of things to come. For example, the platform called for regulation of holding companies, stock exchanges, and utility rates, the divorce of investment banking from commercial banking, enactment of "unemployment and old age insurance under state laws," and "the enactment of every constitutional measure that will aid the farmers to receive for their basic farm commodities prices in excess of cost." It was very specific in its call for the repeal of the 18th Amendment (prohibition) and alteration of the Volstead Act so as to permit the making and sale of beer. In general, though, there was certainly nothing revolutionary suggested in the platform.

Nor did Roosevelt make clear during his campaign the shape of things to come. Here and there we can catch a glimmer of the tendency of his presidency, but that is certainly enlivened for us because we are looking back with some knowledge of what did indeed occur. Prior to his nomination, Roosevelt pleaded the cause of "the forgotten man at the bottom of the pyramid," in a speech at Albany. At Oglethorpe University, he declared: "The country needs and, unless I mistake its temper, the country demands bold, persistent experimentation."[18] When he accepted the Democratic nomination, Roosevelt referred to the "new deal." There was no indication at the time that it was a loaded phrase. It is a phrase used in card playing to refer to a new shuffling and dealing of the cards. However, Stuart Chase had only recently published a book entitled *A New Deal*. Chase was a prolific writer on economic subjects, highly critical of American business, had visited the Soviet Union in the 1920s and was highly impressed with what he saw there. As for the depression in America, he thought there ought to be some kind of redistribution of the wealth that would increase the purchasing

Acme

James A. Farley (1888–1976)

Farley was an American politician and Postmaster General during the New Deal. He was born in New York, attended a commercial school, became a bookkeeper, and started his own business. His political skills, great energy, and willingness to work until he dropped were invaluable assets to Roosevelt in his campaigns in 1932 and 1936. Roosevelt appointed him Postmaster General, a position which enabled him both to maintain his political contacts and pass out rewards to the faithful by political patronage. Farley was of great help to Roosevelt in his campaigns, but he was never an ideological New Dealer. When Roosevelt decided to run for a third term, Farley had had enough, and sought the nomination for the highest office himself. When Roosevelt won despite third-term opposition, Farley retired from his post in government.

power of people generally. He held that the problem of production had been solved and that what was needed now was for government to deal with the problem of distribution. Chase also specifically advocated such things as higher taxes on large incomes, lower tariffs, higher wages and shorter work periods, public housing, and rural electrification. Whether Roosevelt or his speech writer had read the book, the New Deal certainly followed many of the recommendations of *A New Deal*.

In fact, Roosevelt had many conversations during 1932 with a group of college professors who were dubbed the Brain Trust. Samuel Rosenman, Roosevelt's attorney and later speech writer, had recommended extensive consultation with these people. Raymond Moley, a professor who would later play a key role in forging the legislation of the New Deal, may have been the most influential of this group. It included two other important reform-minded professors from Columbia: Rexford G. Tugwell and Adolph A. Berle. Berle had recently finished a book entitled *The Modern Corporation and Private Property,* in collaboration with Gardiner C. Means. They argued that much of property had been transformed by the corporation, several hundred of which held much of the productive power in America, and these were under the effective control of some 2,000 directors. The case they presented was for government intervention and control. Tugwell was a vigorous advocate of a government-planned economy. Others of more or less radical backgrounds who had an influence on Roosevelt as he moved toward the presidency were: Frances Perkins (who would become the first woman cabinet member as Secretary of Labor), Harry Hopkins, and Henry Morgenthau, Jr.

Even so, Roosevelt muted the radicalism of his advisers during the campaign. He emphasized the need for a balanced budget and even accused Hoover of recklessly expanding the power of government. "I accuse the present Administration," Roosevelt said, "of being the greatest spending Administration in peace times in all our history. It is an Administration that has piled bureau on bureau, commission on commission. . . ." Moreover, he said, "I regard reduction in Federal spending as one of the most important issues of this campaign." He did, however, leave himself an out from his severe restrictions: "If starvation and dire need on the part of any of our citizens make necessary the appropriation of additional funds which would keep the budget out of balance, I shall not hesitate to tell the American people the full truth and ask them to authorize the expenditure of the additional amount."[19] He did call attention to some of the programs he would indeed initiate, such as the development of public power in the Tennessee Valley, but there was no forewarning that he would summarily

Derso

Raymond Moley (1886–1975)

Moley was a teacher, writer, an architect of the New Deal, and held several government posts. He was born in Ohio, graduated from Baldwin-Wallace College, and became a professor of government at Columbia in the 1920s. Moley served on several commissions of the state of New York, one when Roosevelt was governor, and he was a participant in the "Brain Trust" discussions, and a speech writer for Roosevelt. In the early months of the New Deal, he played a leading role in applying policy, but he soon became disenchanted and left the government before the end of 1933 to become an editor on a weekly newsmagazine. Toward the end of Roosevelt's second term, Moley wrote a searching critique of the New Deal, entitled, *After Seven Years*.

abandon the gold standard, vastly increase government powers without benefit of constitutional amendment, and rush headlong toward the welfare state.

Roosevelt's tactics worked, so far as the election went. He won a landslide victory over Hoover and all other candidates. Roosevelt got over 27 million popular votes to less than 16 million for Hoover. He carried 42 states with an electoral vote of 472. Both houses of Congress went heavily Democratic. Judging by the campaign and the votes, there was no large sentiment for radical change. Norman Thomas, on his way to becoming a perennial candidate, got fewer than 900,000 votes, and William Z. Foster, the Communist nominee, got only slightly over 102,000.

The Banking Crisis

There was a nearly four-month interlude between Roosevelt's election November 8, 1932 and his inauguration March 4, 1933. Not only that but the old Congress held its desultory "Lame Duck" during that winter, in keeping with the Constitution. It was destined to be the last such session of Congress, and no President would again have to wait so long after election before taking office. These arrangements which made sense in view of communication and transportation at the time of the making of the Constitution had become unnecessary. Congress had sent the 20th Amendment to the

Rexford G. Tugwell (1891–1979)

Harris & Ewing

Tugwell was an American economist and public official. He was born in New York and educated at the University of Pennsylvania, where he earned the Ph.D. in economics. While he was teaching at Columbia, Tugwell became an advocate of a government-planned economy and extensive regulation and control over industry. From this background, he became a participant in Roosevelt's "Brain Trust" in 1932 and had a hand in shaping the New Deal. After Roosevelt took office, he served in the Department of Agriculture, where he was involved in an assortment of plans for reorienting farming. During World War II, he was governor of Puerto Rico, after which he returned to teaching.

states early in the year and it was ratified in 1933. In effect, it abolished the "Lame Duck" session, provided for the new Congress to meet early in January and the President to take office later in the month. But these arrangements would only prevail in later years. In late 1932 and early 1933, Congress went through the motions of holding a session while the situation worsened and the crisis mounted.

President Hoover's string had played out. Congress had lost confidence in him, and his time in office was now too short even to plan action that might bring about improvements. During that winter it became painfully apparent that all the efforts to hold back the tide of credit contraction and deflation were to no avail. The tide of liquidation which had been stemmed by first one and then another measure had returned in full force by February, 1933 and was threatening to bring down the whole banking system with it. The chickens of credit expansion were coming home to roost. The banks, which had been the instruments of the credit expansion, were finally to feel the full force of the contraction. Hoover did not stop trying, of course; he worked early and late, growing more haggard as the economy unraveled. He desperately sought to achieve the resumption of the payment of the war debts from Europe. He sought to make plans for a World Economic conference and pleaded with Roosevelt to assist him in making plans and appointments. To no avail, though Roosevelt was polite, he insisted that his responsibilities began when he took office.

Hoover was apparently convinced that uncertainty about what Roosevelt planned to do had aroused fears that produced a banking panic. Indeed, a panic was underway by mid-February, regardless of what had produced it. On February 14, the governor of Michigan ordered an eight-day banking holiday. Frederick L. Allen has given an imaginative description of how the panic spread over the country: "All over the country there began a whispering, barely audible at first, then louder and louder: 'Trouble's coming. They say there's a run on the trust company down the street. Better get your money out of the bank.' The murmur ran among the bankers: 'Trouble's coming. Better sell some bonds and get cash before it's too late. Better withdraw your balances on deposit in New York.' It ran among the men of wealth: 'Better put everything into cash. Get gold if you can. . . .' The financial machinery of the country began to freeze into ridigity, the industrial and commercial machinery to slow down. Nor was there anything that Hoover could do to stop the panic."[20]

Even so, he tried. On February 18, he dispatched a letter which was a plea for help to Roosevelt. He urged Roosevelt to clear the "public mind on certain essentials which will give renewed confidence. . . . I do not refer to action on all the causes of alarm, but it would steady the country greatly if there could be prompt assurance that there will be no tampering with inflation of the currency. . . ."[21] Roosevelt did not answer immediately, but some days later sent word by way of the man he intended to appoint to the Treasury that he would not make the desired statement. There is no good reason to doubt that Roosevelt was already full of inflationary plans which he would shortly inaugurate. Moreover, he had probably already decided to wrest from the people what control they had over the money supply by going off the gold standard. The worse the situation, the more likely it was that he could carry through such a drastic change. Rexford G. Tugwell hinted at part of this, at least, when he told Herbert Feis, a State Department official in the Hoover (and Roosevelt) administration, regarding the banks: "Let them bust—then we'll get things on a sound basis."[22] Roosevelt himself eventually replied to Hoover's urgings by pointing out that the "real trouble is that . . . very few financial institutions . . . are actually able to pay off their deposits in full, and the knowledge of this fact is widely held. Bankers with the narrower viewpoint have urged me to make a general statement, but even they seriously doubt whether it would have a definite effect."[23] Roosevelt may have been right, but Hoover must have guessed he was making a last ditch stand for something more than the banking system.

However much Hoover may have flirted with credit expansion, so far as can be told, he was firmly committed to gold and opposed to a government managed currency. The United States had a currency that could be redeemed in gold until after Roosevelt took office, and Hoover understood how that was essential to prevent full scale inflation. He said: "Currency convertible into gold of the legal specifications is a vital protection against economic manipulation by the government. As long as currencies are convertible, governments cannot easily tamper with the price of goods. . . . They cannot easily confiscate the savings of the people by manipulation of inflation and defalcation. . . ."[24] It should be emphasized, too, that as long as currency can be converted into gold, the people can call to account those who have attempted to manipulate the money supply. Hoover never made it clear, however, that the credit expansion had been a manipulation of the money supply and that the runs on the banks were ultimately attempts to reduce the currency to the gold supply. In short, the liquidation was proceeding toward the smash of the whole fractional reserve system, including that of gold. Government had watered the stock, so to speak, and the depositors were squeezing out the water.

At any rate, the banking panic spread and worsened through the last half of February and the early days of March. Federal Reserve banks generally did what the could to stop the runs, rushing armored cars first here then there where runs were developing to provide large amounts of currency. Nothing much worked. Governors in state after state called banking holidays or imposed severe restrictions on how much cash could be paid to depositors. When banks opened for business after state ordered closings, it was generally on a limited basis. The crunch finally became too great for Chicago and New York City, the great financial centers, and early on the morning of March 4, the governors of New York and Illinois proclaimed banking holidays. On Hoover's last morning in office he was dolefully informed that banking was at a virtual standstill in the country. It looked for all the world like the death knell of fractional reserve banking. It would be many a day before some would trust their money to banks.

Chapter 3

The Thrust of the New Deal

I am prepared under my constitutional duty to recommend the measures that a stricken Nation in the midst of a stricken world may require. . . . But in the event that Congress shall fail to take one of these . . . courses . . . , I shall not evade the clear course of duty that will then confront me. I shall ask Congress for the broad Executive power that would be given to me if we were in fact invaded by a foreign foe.

—Franklin D. Roosevelt, 1933

. . . Through these programs, it is intended that a large volume of new purchasing power shall be created. By these expenditures, workers are given increased power to buy. This power to buy means that the money paid out for these purposes will go directly for the purchase of goods.

—Rexford G. Tugwell, 1933

Most people function as better people in a group. Many of the higher virtues . . . grow out of group life. Government is an instrument for transferring this group achievement into the general good. . . .

Democracy mobilizes this power of association and co-operation, giving it expression in activities for human fulfillment. Government in a democracy is a service agency for these essential activities of human co-operation.

—Frances Perkins, 1934

Chronology

1933—

March 4—Inauguration of Roosevelt
March 5—Roosevelt calls Special Session for March 9
March 6—Roosevelt declares national banking holiday
March 9—Emergency Banking Relief Act
March 31—Civilian Conservation Corps authorized
May 12—Agricultural Adjustment Act
Emergency Relief Act
May 18—Tennessee Valley Authority authorized

1933—

May 27—Federal Securities Act
June 5—Gold contracts voided
June 16—Federal Deposit Insurance Corporation authorized
Farm Credit Act
National Industrial Recovery Act
November 16—Recognition of Soviet Union
December—Prohibition repealed by 21st Amendment

1934—

January—Devaluation of Dollar authorized
February 15—Civil Works Emergency Relief Act
March 24—Philippine Independence Act
April 27—Home Owners Loan Act
May 29—Abrogation of Platt Amendment

Collectivism came swiftly to the United States in the spring of 1933. It came in the wake of a spate of legislation passed by the special session of Congress which met from March 9 to June 16 of that year—often referred to as the First Hundred Days of the New Deal. Never before, not even in time of war, had such a body of far-reaching and direction-altering legislation been passed in such a brief span of time. Indeed, except for the Reconstruction legislation and constitutional amendments, it is doubtful that the legislation passed during the whole of American history to that point had such a potential impact as that passed during the First Hundred Days. In one swoop, as it were, the government asserted authority over the economy and began its move toward assuming responsibility for the well-being of the population. There had, of course, been some earlier measures in this direction, and a goodly amount of agitation for more, but none of this could compare with the comprehensive change that came with the New Deal.

Nor were Americans prepared for the drastic changes during the days and months that preceded Roosevelt's inauguration. As noted earlier, the Democratic platform of 1932 proposed some reforms and regulations, but they fell far short of what occurred almost overnight. As for Roosevelt's campaign, when he dealt with specifics, he was most likely to discuss the tariff or economy in government. Otherwise, there was no more than a hint in the generalities in which he usually spoke. During the interval between his election and inauguration, he made no unsettling announcements. Even the members of the cabinet provided no clearcut indication of the direction that was to be taken. There may have been a scent of radicalism about Henry A. Wallace at Agriculture, Frances Perkins at Labor, or Harold Ickes at Interior, but the rest were either unknown qualities or familiar political figures such as were customarily appointed to high office.

Roosevelt's Inaugural Address had both soothing elements and portents, some of them ominous, of things to come. He had a resonantly pleasing speaking voice, which came across especially well over radio, and none could surpass him either in conveying concern or assurance that he would take care of matters. "This great Nation will endure," Roosevelt said in the opening of his speech on the windy, misty 4th of March in Washington, "as it has endured, will revive and prosper." The only thing Americans had to fear, he continued, was "fear itself—nameless, unreasoning, unjustified terror. . . ." There was much more in a soothing vein in the address. He even preached a little sermonette on the superiority of higher values to material ones.

On the other hand, the tenor of what was to come was also foreshadowed in the address. There was the not much veiled assault on bankers and speculators. "The money changers," he declared, "have fled from their high seats in the temple of our civilization." Moreover, "This Nation asks for action, and action now." He promised to "recommend the measures that a stricken Nation in the midst of a stricken world may require," and likened the current situation to a "dark hour of our national life." The shades of collectivism and of the warlike character of the discipline that was needed were called up. "If I read the temper of our people correctly," he asserted, "we now realize as we have never realized before our interdependence on each other . . . ; that if we are to go forward, we must move as a trained and disciplined army willing to sacrifice for the good of a common discipline. . . ."[25]

Moreover, Roosevelt openly threatened Congress that if it did not take appropriate action he would ask for emergency powers and do so himself. Even Eleanor Roosevelt, his wife, thought there was something ominous in this, though she attributed it to the audience response rather than to what her husband had said, "because when Franklin got to that part of the speech when he said it might become necessary for him to assume powers ordinarily granted to a President in war time, he received his biggest demonstration."[26] At this very time, Adolf Hitler was moving to consolidate his dictatorial power over Germany by obtaining extraordinary emergency powers. Mussolini had done something on that order as well. It was ominous, at the least.

It probably did not strike most people that way at the time. Many people undoubtedly wanted action, and Roosevelt had promised that. Hundreds of thousands of letters poured into the White House over the next several days, many of them filled with adulation. "It was the finest thing this side of heaven," wrote one; while another proclaimed, "It seemed to give the people, as well as myself, a new hold on life."[27] Moreover, Roosevelt did not wait long to begin acting. The very next day after the inauguration, he sent out a call for a special session of Congress. The following day he proclaimed a national banking holiday to last for four days, and suspended all interbank transactions. In addition, he placed an embargo on all exports of gold, silver, or currency. In an attempt to give the color of legality to these actions, he invoked a 1917 (wartime) act dealing with trading with the enemy.

Origins of the New Deal

Before proceeding with an account of New Deal legislation, some account of the sources may help to clarify what was going on. Roosevelt pushed much of the early legislation through on the grounds that America was confronted with an emergency of unprecedented dimensions and that the people wanted action. That is, he did not identify the ideological underpinnings of what he was proposing. On the contrary, he made it appear

Eleanor Roosevelt (1884–1962)

Mrs. Roosevelt was the wife of Franklin D. Roosevelt and the niece of Theodore Roosevelt (her maiden name was Roosevelt), but emerged as a strong personality in her own right while she was in the White House. She held weekly press conferences, traveled extensively, had her own weekly radio program, and wrote a syndicated newspaper column, *My Day*. After the death of her husband, the new President, Harry S. Truman, appointed her as a delegate to the United Nations, where she served as chairman of the Commission on Human Rights. She was born in New York City, attended a finishing school for girls, was a debutante briefly, and then worked for a while in a settlement house for the poor in the city before marrying Franklin. Although she bore six children and had the duties of the wife of a prominent man, she never shook the settlement house mentality. As a President's wife for many years, she was inclined to view the whole United States as a social work project, an outlook which she had little difficulty in extending to the world from the vantage point of the United Nations.

that he was moving swiftly on many fronts in response to the situation with which he was confronted. In the argot of those times, he was being "pragmatic," i.e., experimenting, trying first this and then that, ever seeking something that would work, or work better. Undoubtedly, there was, at least on the surface, much that was experimental about New Deal measures, but they had antecedents both in ideology and programs advanced in the past. In the broadest of terms, socialism was the origin of the New Deal, but it was socialism as it had been winnowed through the minds of American radicals and reformers and hammered out as programs.

There were at least four sources of the New Deal. Roosevelt, as it turned out, was an inflationist, and this bent traces back to Populism. Populist ideas had entered the Democratic Party in 1896 with William Jennings Bryan's candidacy, and some of the silverites were still very much in evidence in the New Deal. A broader current than that was there, however, for the Populists had favored paper money as a device for inflation as well, and, as we shall see, that was used much more for inflation by the New Deal than silver.

A second stream came from Progressivism, particularly that of Theodore Roosevelt. The Progressives had, of course, been a faction within the Republican Party, still were as late as the early 1930s. But Franklin Roosevelt wooed them vigorously in his 1932 campaign and had the help of such men as George W. Norris in winning states in the trans-Mississippi West. Moreover, Roosevelt had been early influenced by his cousin Theodore. As one historian said, the much younger Franklin "looked up to Uncle Ted, and the relationship brought Franklin Roosevelt a continuous suggestion that politics was a permissible career for a patrician, that a patrician's politics should be reform, and that reform meant broad federal powers wielded by executive leadership in the pattern of the New Nationalism."[28] Another historian has said that "There are many occasions in its history when the New Deal . . . seems to stand squarely in the tradition of the New Nationalism."[29] Among his advisers, Rexford G. Tugwell was a vigorous advocate of government regulation of big businesses rather than breaking them up by applying antitrust laws. That had been very much the emphasis of Roosevelt's New Nationalism.

The term "progressive" however, was not used by New Dealers. Instead, they usually called themselves "liberals," thus borrowing a word from the 19th century and giving it a somewhat different meaning and thrust. "Liberalism" had come into widespread use in the 19th century to describe the position favoring individual liberty, free trade, national independence, expansion of the suffrage and the like. Nineteenth-century liberals were usually strongly opposed to government intervention in the economy. By contrast, 20th-century "liberals" have favored government regulation and control over the economy, been collectivists, tended to view government as a beneficial influence in all areas of life. They are distant cousins, at best, to those of the 19th century.

A third source of the New Deal was the mobilization experience during World War I. They were greatly impressed with what they conceived had been accomplished by the use of government power to control and direct economic activity. General Hugh Johnson, who headed the National Recovery Administration (NRA) in the early period of the New Deal, had been connected with the War Industries Board during World War I and was convinced that government could effectively direct the economy in peacetime as well. "If cooperation can do so much," he said, "maybe there is something wrong with the old competitive system." He was in favor, he declared, of "self-government in industry under government supervision."[30] People with experience in wartime agencies were in great demand at the beginning of the New Deal. As one historian says, "Only the veterans of the war mobilization had much experience with the kind of massive undertaking Roosevelt had inaugurated." Such people flocked to Washington in large numbers, and, as one of those there said, "One cannot go into the Cosmos Club without meeting half a dozen persons whom he knew during the war."[31]

Warlike terminology was widely used in the early days of the New Deal. Roosevelt had set the stage for this in his Inaugural Address by his references to Americans getting behind him like a disciplined army and making "a war against the emergency." None could outdo General Johnson, who even appealed to women to enlist in the cause, declaring that "this time, it is the women who must carry the whole fight of President Roosevelt's war against depression, perhaps the most dangerous war of all. It is women . . . who will . . . go over the top to as great a victory as the Argonne."[32] Just exactly how one goes about making war against emergencies or depressions no one apparently paused to ponder. After all, except as a rather doubtful figure of speech, wars are made against flesh and blood people who are usually assembled in armies and identified as the enemy. How, we are entitled to wonder, is it possible to fire cannon or launch grenades against emergencies or depression? This militant language could, however, call up a collective effort, and that was undoubtedly its purpose.

The fourth source of the New Deal was the idea of a nationally planned economy. Those who favored such government planning were given to charging that in a free and competitive economy there was waste, duplication, and chaos, that all sorts of things got out of balance and would not right themselves. Socialists, of course, had long advanced arguments such as these against any economy that was based on private ownership, but they were now entering into the general stream of thought. The prolonged depression could be interpreted in such a way as to make the idea much more attractive. There were also supposedly models for national planning in the 1920s in Fascist Italy and the Soviet Union. The full force of the totalitarianism of these systems was not yet common knowledge, and many intellectuals, especially in Europe, were quite taken with these systems. One historian even goes so far as to say "that many of the best minds of the West saw fascism and communism as the only real alternatives of their times."[33] He goes on to say that "Mussolini was widely admired in the democracies. Had he not produced an order in his nation which the democracies were incapable of producing?"[34] Although there were overtones of Italian Fascism in some of the New Deal programs, New Dealers were hardly enthusiastic about making the identification. On the other hand, many American intellectuals, some of whom served in the New Deal, visited the Soviet Union in the late 1920s and early 1930s, as chronicled earlier, and caught much of their enthusiasm for government planned economies from the communist experiment.

But wherever they contracted the contagion, the New Deal was well equipped with enthusiasts for collective planning. Rexford G. Tugwell, who had indeed made a trip to the Soviet Union, spent much of 1932 bending Roosevelt's ear to convince him of the necessity for planning. He sent the future President a memorandum in which he explained how it would work. "It is not proposed to have the government run industry," Tugwell wrote; "it is proposed to have government furnish the . . . leadership; protect our resources; arrange for national balance; secure its citizens' access to goods, employment and security; and rise to the challenge of planning that concert of interests of which I have spoken before."[35]

Others joined the chorus for planning. Senator Robert Wagner of New York said, "I do not think we will ever have industry in order until we have a nationally planned economy."[36] Donald Richberg, who followed General Johnson as head of the NRA, held that "A nationally planned economy is the only salvation of our present situation and the only hope for the future."[37] Raymond Moley declared that what was needed was "a policy of cooperative business-government planning."[38] In the Agriculture Department, Jerome Frank argued that "Just as America took an important step forward when it rejected political anarchy and integrated this continent into one nation, so it needs now to press forward to a deliberate economic integration."[39]

Roosevelt himself pushed his programs on the basis of his great electoral victories and that the President spoke for the people. Anyone who opposed his programs was, by implication, opposing the will of the people. All this, he presented as democracy, a term he used frequently to legitimize what was being done. When Jefferson and Jackson had used democracy in connection with the United States, they meant mainly people's self-government in their own affairs. The term had now taken on a governmental connotation and signified that they somehow ruled themselves collectively. Roosevelt appealed directly to the people from time to time by way of radio talks that were called "Fireside Chats." These were intimate talks and might better, perhaps, have been called bedside chats, since the relation he assumed to the

American people was that of doctor to patient, and he had a very effective bedside manner on radio.

The First Hundred Days

The power to legislate is vested by the Constitution in the Congress. Except for revenue measures, either house may originate bills. The ordinary process is that some one or more Representatives or Senators conceives a bill, has it drawn up, and places it in the legislative stream. Any bill, however it originated, is then ordinarily sent to the appropriate committee for consideration, where most bills die from lack of attention. For those bills that have widespread support, including the majority party leadership in whichever house is involved, hearings are usually held. After the appropriate committee has recommended it for approval, it is then scheduled for consideration by the house. After debate, which may be more or less extensive, a vote may be taken. The same process may then be repeated, and when both houses have approved the same measure the bill will be sent to the President for his consideration. The whole process may take weeks or months, or even be delayed from one legislative session to another. Major legislation generally undergoes careful examination and extensive hearings and debates.

The President has only a limited and largely negative role in legislation as prescribed by the Constitution. True, the President is authorized to "recommend" to the "consideration" of Congress "such measures as he shall judge necessary and expedient." Even so, 19th-century Presidents generally kept hands off the actual legislation leaving it to the motion of Congress. Otherwise, the President is authorized to veto or approve the legislation that comes to him. That had begun to change, as noted earlier, under Theodore Roosevelt and Woodrow Wilson with their advancement of Four-Year Plans.

But even Wilson's rather aggressive role in legislation was only a prelude to Roosevelt and the New Deal, and especially during the special session of 1933. The bills passed during that session were drafted in the executive department and sent over to Congress for approval, as it were. There have been whole decades in which fewer bills of significance were passed than in that hundred days, and much of the usual legislative process was shortened or simply by-passed. The tone was set on March 9, when Congress convened. The Congress was confronted with a far-reaching Emergency Banking Relief bill as soon as it was called to order. The President had sent this message, "I cannot too strongly urge upon the Congress the clear necessity for immediate action."[40] The House acted first, though copies of the bill were not even available to most members. The bill had been prepared in the executive branch, and the ink was hardly dry on it. Nonetheless, the bill was read aloud by the Chairman of the House Banking and Currency Committee, who had barely had time to examine it himself, and debate was limited to forty minutes. That was too long for some members, who began sounding the call "Vote! Vote!" even before the time had elapsed. The House had convened at 12, and a little after 4 o'clock it passed the measure unanimously without even having a roll call. The Senate took a little longer, mainly because that body decided at first to wait for copies. But when the copies were not soon there, the Senate used the House version on which to act. Senator Huey Long did have the audacity to propose an amendment, but it was shouted down without much ceremony. By 7:30 that same evening the Senate had passed the bill 73 to 7, and an hour later the President placed his signature on it, making it law.

The aggressive role of the President in legislation and the tendency of Congress to rubber stamp them prompted the satirist H. L. Mencken to include the following provision in the mock "A Constitution for the New Deal" which he devised and published a few years later:

> The Legislature of the United States shall consist of a Senate and a House of Representatives. Every bill shall be prepared under the direction of the President and transmitted to the two Houses at his order. . . . No member shall propose any amendment to a bill without permission in writing from the President. . . . In case any member shall doubt the wisdom of a bill he may apply to the President for light upon it, and thereafter he shall be counted as voting aye. In all cases a majority of members shall be counted as voting aye.[41]

Undoubtedly, Mencken somewhat overstated his case, but there is no doubt that Roosevelt was making the White House the center of power in the government—and doing so without benefit of constitutional amendment.

The special session might have been dismissed after that hurried first day. After all, it had been called to deal with the banking emergency, and Roosevelt got everything he asked for swiftly. But the New Dealers were after bigger game than that, and Roosevelt decided to strike while the iron was hot, or at least while Congress was in a compliant mood, to get much more. The pace of legislation slowed, though the emergency mood was sustained; the President's men continued to design the bills; the President continued to promote them with messages to Congress, popular appeals by well-placed Fireside Chats, speeches, and frequent press conferences.

1. Inflation

Roosevelt was bent on a course toward inflation—increasing the money supply and credit expansion—by the very first act passed in his administration. More broadly still, he was going to do what Hoover had attempted to do but failed: he was going to reinflate, raise prices and wages, and restore the fever that was supposed to be prosperity. Actually, what he was going to achieve mainly was to prolong the Great Depression for nearly a decade. If he had concentrated only on inflating, he might have succeeded in inducing that unnatural glow to the economy which can be mistaken for prosperity. But he went off in a number of different directions with an assortment of programs so that it was exceedingly difficult to decide what was doing what.

Roosevelt did not avow his intention to inflate, but he did pursue a course toward it and do it. Indeed, both the Democratic Platform and Roosevelt in 1932 denounced the Republicans for their efforts at credit expansion. Moreover, the second act passed during the hundred days was labeled an Economy Act. The first act had at least set the stage for inflation, as we shall see, and the second one appeared to be in the direction of making it unnecessary. It cut the salaries of government employees by 15 per cent, reduced pensions to veterans, and provided for government reorganization that was supposed to save money. Roosevelt pushed this measure by declaring that the government was headed toward bankruptcy by its spending practices. In view of Roosevelt's later record as the greatest peacetime deficit spender in American history to that point, either he had not yet clearly charted his course or he was deliberately sending out a false signal. Granted, he might have reduced spending for traditional government activities in order to make room for his new spending programs, but that still would not explain the talk about spending the government into bankruptcy.

In any case, Roosevelt was leaning toward inflation from the outset. His refusal to give in to Hoover's pleas to make some announcement about his intention was to keep his options open. From the outset, Roosevelt was intent on maintaining or raising prices and increasing purchasing power, or spreading it through the population. Nor is there any good reason to doubt that he meant money when he spoke of buying or purchasing power. In a campaign speech in 1932, Roosevelt had said that there was "an insufficient distribution of buying power. . . ."[42] After attending a cabinet meeting in 1933, Secretary of Interior Ickes recorded this conclusion: "We are seriously concerned with the problem of creating buying power, which in turn, will have the effect of opening factories and stimulating businesses generally."[43] Roosevelt was clearly setting his sails on an inflationary course by the summer of 1933. A World Economic Conference was meeting in London, and an American delegation was attending, including Secretary of State Cordell Hull and, for part of the time, Raymond Moley. A major problem the conference attacked was the stabilizing of foreign exchange, and there was much pressure in Europe for the United States to return to the gold standard. Roosevelt had no intention of returning to gold nor tying the United States to any sort of fixed exchange.

He sent word to the Conference that "old fetishes of so-called international bankers are being replaced by efforts to plan national currencies. . . ," to the end that the United States could have "the kind of dollar

Harold L. Ickes (1874–1952)

Ickes was in the New Deal from first to last, indeed outlasted it as Secretary of Interior, 1933–1946. He was born in Pennsylvania, graduated from the University of Chicago, worked as a reporter in that city, and afterward practiced law. He was drawn into reform politics by Theodore Roosevelt's Bull Moose campaign in 1912, but was politically a Republican of the progressive persuasion until his New Deal days. Ickes supported Roosevelt in 1932, and after his victory took the appointment to head the Department of Interior. In addition, he was Public Works Administrator from 1933–1939. In accord with his progressive background, he favored government directed conservation and the development and distribution of electricity. Ickes was a stubborn and outspoken man, but his views pleased Roosevelt, and his honesty recommended him as an administrator.

which a generation hence will have the same purchasing power and debt paying power as the dollar value we hope to attain in the near future."[44] On that vague note, the Conference broke up with nothing achieved. Whatever Roosevelt may have meant, it is clear in retrospect that he was sold on having a government "managed" currency. After Congress adjourned in June, 1933, Roosevelt took a vacation, during which he was exposed to a variety of planned currency theories, such as a book by a British author entitled *Planned Money*. From this and other sources, he was becoming convinced that the desirable thing was for the dollar to fall in value so that prices would rise. That is another way of describing a prescription for inflation.

One thing should be certain, from the first day of his administration Roosevelt was working to give the government control over the money and the money supply. By embargoing the export of gold, he removed any foreign control. He also moved to take away any control which Americans individually had over their money by demanding payment in gold. The banking crisis provided the opportunity for taking these measures. The Emergency Banking Relief Act of March 9 confirmed and gave the force of law to steps Roosevelt had already taken. It authorized the Secretary of the Treasury to call in all gold and gold certificates in the country. Subsequently, Americans had their gold taken from them and in its place they were given paper money—Federal Reserve notes. The act also provided for the reopening of banks that were declared to be sound, and for dealing with the assets of such national banks as remained closed.

The New Deal measures did save fractional reserve banking, the banking system, and probably a goodly portion of the existing banks. It did so at the expense of the control of Americans over the quality of their money. It removed a major reason for people to make runs on banks, so far as they did so to get gold. Thereafter, if people wanted to get any currency larger than a dollar, all they could get would be Federal Reserve notes, and these could be printed in large quantities by the United States Treasury. On June 16, 1933, Congress took another step in shoring up the banks by authorizing the Federal Deposit Insurance Corporation (FDIC). Bank accounts in all member banks thereafter were insured up to $5,000 per account. This would not only discourage runs on banks, but even more important at the time, it would help to persuade many people, especially small depositors, to keep their money in banks. The last step in taking all gold away from people was taken on June 5, when Congress, by joint resolution, nullified all private or governmental contracts requiring payment in gold. It would, the resolution said, be "inconsistent with declared policy of the Congress to maintain at all times the equal power of every dollar" to allow any payments to be made in gold.[45] It did not matter, presumably, that Congress lacked the power to nullify private contracts, or that Roosevelt indicated during his campaign that government promises on this matter should be honored. He said that "no responsible government would have sold to the country securities payable in gold if it knew that the promise—yes, the covenant— . . . was . . . dubious."[46]

With the difficulties in doing so out of the way the government began shoring up and expanding credit—reinflating. The emergency banking act had expanded the authority of the Hoover Reconstruction Finance Corporation. Jesse Jones, a Texas banker, now headed it, and he used funds to fuel credit expansion through existing banks. The RFC bought preferred stock of banks, thus increasing their capital base for credit expansion. The government moved quickly, too, to stop the widespread mortgage foreclosures and to rescue the banks and credit institutions from the burden of carrying them. A Home Owners Loan Corporation was authorized in June, 1933, to refinance home mortgages and make other types of homeowner loans. By the time it went out of business it had made loans on over a million mortgages. A Farm Credit Administration was set up the same month to refinance farm mortgages. These actions helped banks to expand credit in other directions. The Commodity Credit Corporation was created to make loans on crops.

The New Deal was not long in making more direct attempts to manage the currency and manipulate the value of the dollar. The monetizing of silver fit the pattern, though neither Roosevelt nor New Dealers in general may have been enthusiastic about doing it. Silverite Congressmen were still sufficiently numerous among Democrats, however, to get their way in authorizing silver purchases. There was placed in the Agricultural Adjustment Act an amendment which authorized the government to receive silver in payment of debt and to issue silver certificates, which were to be redeemable in silver.

Roosevelt was much more enthusiastic about manipulating the price the United States would pay for gold in order to alter the value of the dollar. Indeed, in October, 1933, he personally took over the task of setting the dollar amount to be paid for gold. His announced purpose was to manipulate the price of gold so as to raise prices. Roosevelt told a radio audience that "If we cannot get prices up one way we will get them up another." Thereafter, Roosevelt, along with Henry Morgenthau, Jr., Secretary of the Treasury and Jesse Jones, of the RFC, went through a daily ritual of setting the price. The process was described this way by John T. Flynn: "They gathered around Roosevelt's bed in the morning as he ate his eggs. Then 'Henny-Penny' [Morgenthau] and Roosevelt decided the price of gold for that day. One day they wished to raise the price. Roosevelt settled the point. Make it 21 cents, he ruled. That is a lucky number—three times seven. And so it was done. That night Morgenthau wrote in his diary: 'If people knew how we fixed the price of gold they would be frightened.' "[47] This playing hopscotch with the price of gold had no clearly discernible impact on prices generally.

In January, 1934, Congress passed the Gold Reserve Act empowering the President to fix the price of gold in terms of the dollar. He did so by devaluing the dollar by 40 per cent. This move greatly overvalued gold in terms of the dollar (raised the price of gold from approximately $20 to $35 per ounce). During the ensuing years, much of the gold in the world flowed into the United States. The devaluation had set the stage for expanding the currency supply, since a given amount of gold equalled a much larger reserve. Although it was not inflexibly fixed, at any given time a gold reserve still had to be held against the outstanding currency. Thus, the inflationists were fixed both to expand credit and the actual currency, as needed. Later in 1934, the amount of silver the government could purchase was expanded further increasing the amount of the currency.

The government was accused of clipping the coins (a devious device of old when governments sometimes actually clipped gold from the coins) when it devalued the dollar. In effect, that was what was done, but in a period of less than a year the government did much more. It took the (gold) coins and certificates themselves away from people, gave them mostly unredeemable paper instead, and placed the economy at the mercy of its credit and currency expanding (or contracting) ability. The government now had what has since appeared to be a perpetual motion credit expanding (inflationary) machine at its disposal. As soon as the inflationary activity began to have an unwelcome impact on prices (during World War II and since) many of those in power shifted the meaning of inflation from increasing the money supply to the rise in prices. Thus, the government was often able to avoid responsibility for what it was doing by expanding the money supply.

2. Government Planning

The New Dealers did not know how government could plan an economy. In fact, no one did—or does. The truth is that economic activities are already planned and have been from time immemorial. Usually, they are planned by those who own, manage, or operate the resources available and in terms of what these people hope to accomplish. For example, a farmer usually plans what crops he is going to raise that year, how much he is going to put into seed and fertilizer, and, so far as possible, how he will dispose his equipment and labor. So it is for all undertakings large and small. In a country the size of the United States there are millions of plans and planners in operation at any given time. Any attempt to impose an overall plan by government will inevitably run afoul or greatly alter all those individual plans. Not only will the government's plans take away some portion at least of people's own freedom to make their plans but it will also disrupt the economy, and even if the only concern were efficiency, there is no evidence that overall government plans will be more effective.

This mattered not to influential New Dealers who were aflame with the idea of a government planned economy. Decades of assault upon the alleged wastefulness of competition, the wrongdoing involved in the private seeking of profit, utopian visions of what could be achieved by common undertakings, socialist propaganda, and collectivist insinuations had prepared the way for their experiments. Many supposed, too, that the syndicalist experiments of Mussolini and the five-year plan of Stalin were achieving great results. The Great Depression provided the opportunity to attempt some of the planning, and the willingness of Congress to go along wherever the administration led freed the New Dealers from vigorous criticism at first. During the Hundred Days, then, men who had hardly found their offices in Washington worked furiously for weeks and as much as two or more months to bring forth legislation for the planning.

Actually, the banking, inflationary, and credit expansion programs were a part of this planning, for a planned currency was to be used in manipulating the economy. But aside from these measures, there were three acts passed which were the centerpieces of the effort at government planning of the economy. They were: the Tennessee Valley Authority, the National Recovery Act, and the Agricultural Adjustment Act; or, to use the acronyms used for the organizations which attempted to put the acts into effect: the TVA, NRA, and AAA.

The TVA was not national planning; it was at best some sort of planning for a narrow region. Nor did it have much to do with ending the emergency of the time or curing the ills of the depression, except by the longest stretch of the imagination. After all, it took years to build the locks and dams and impound the waters of the Tennessee, years during which many of the inhabitants of the area were much more apt to have their lives and ways disrupted rather than ordered or greatly improved. In fact, the Tennessee Valley Authority was a socialist experiment designed to prove the superiority of the government ownership and distribution of electricity. Public power had been an obsessive vision of some of the more radical of the Progressives, and TVA became the pet project of all those who believed so strongly in the beneficence of government involvement in the economy.

The government had got its foot in this particular door during World War I, when it had begun the financing of a dam on the Tennessee at Muscle Shoals, Alabama. The efforts in Congress to sell the dam to a private company in the 1920s had been ultimately thwarted by Progressives, led vigorously by Senator George W. Norris of Nebraska. Both Coolidge and Hoover vetoed efforts to have the federal government operate it. Roosevelt came out for public power projects in the campaign of 1932. It was a politically beneficial move for him, since it secured support for him in several Western states where Progressives had made public power a popular issue. The existence of a government owned dam on the Tennessee apparently made the valley of that river into the target of opportunity, though it was remote from the area where there had been much agitation for activity.

An effort was made to fit the Tennessee Valley into a framework that would justify this large government undertaking. Rexford G. Tugwell, the Brain Truster, says that at sometime before the inauguration he showed Roosevelt "a picture taken in Ducktown, Tennessee—rolling land eroded to the yellow subsoil and cut by gullies that looked like shallow canyons." As further background to the TVA idea, he indicates discussion of soil erosion in the South, and lands "exhausted by corn and tobacco after four hundred years of intensive cultivation." In short, there was an attempt to identify the region with soil exhaustion, soil erosion, and Southern poverty attendant upon it. These were stereotypes about the south generally which did not apply at all well to the Tennessee Valley, either before or since the dams were built. The picture of Ducktown revealed nothing at all about conditions generally in the valley. Ducktown is in the southeastern corner of Tennessee, a hundred miles or so from the river, and is in an area where copper has been extensively mined. The acids from the operation have killed all vegetation, hence the nude hills and great gullies from water rushing down them unimpeded by vegetation. Tugwell's estimate of the period of intensive cultivation of the region is several hundred years off the mark, unless the Indians were guilty of intensive farming. Actually, the Tennessee Valley region is, and long has been, one of the most fertile and productive farming areas in the United States. Generally, the land lies well and is not subject to a great deal of erosion. Undoubtedly, there was some washing of the soil when the river flooded low lying areas from time to time, but there was often gain from the flooding as the receding waters enriched the soil with minerals brought in from upriver. The river bottoms along the Tennessee grew fine corn until they were permanently flooded by backwaters from the TVA dams.

In sum, TVA was a product of socialist visions, political maneuvering, stereotypes about the South, and a hodge-podge of distortions and misinformation. TVA took out of cultivation some of the most fertile farming land in the country and left most of the rest very much as it had been. The government drove all privately owned electricity distributors out of a large region of Tennessee and Alabama and sold electricity mainly to municipalities and privileged cooperatives. TVA was hardly a depression remedy, and it did not remedy the depression. Some people benefited from the concentration of nationally derived tax money on the region; some were harmed. TVA was authorized on May 18, 1933, and over the following 15 years or so dams were built at virtually every feasible site on the Tennessee and its tributaries. By the time this vast building project was completed, the demands for electricity had become so great that they could not be supplied by hydroelectric power. Thereafter, TVA began to produce more and more of its power by using coal and eventually atomic energy.

The National Recovery Administration (NRA) was the most ambitious attempt at a national planned economy, though it was shortlived. It was authorized by the National Industrial Recovery Act, passed June 16, 1933. It was a prescription for collectivizing the control over the manufacture, pricing, and distribution of goods and labor in the country. It prescribed that natural competitors should now enter into collusion with and cooperate with one another, and that those who in the nature of things must cooperate with one another should compete and struggle with one another. The natural competitors are those engaged in similar businesses and producing similar products or services, as well as workers engaged in the same or similar pursuits and using similar skills. That is, such businesses are naturally competitors with one another, and such workers are in competition with one another for jobs, pay, and the like. The New Deal proposed to turn these natural economic conditions upside down and inside out. It would have employers and employees (who must cooperate to produce) to organize against one another into employer and employee groupings. That is not how it was described in the law, but that was its essence. It was a prescription for economic disaster even in prosperous times. In the midst of a prolonged depression, it compounded the difficulties of workers and businesses, and set the stage for what might be not so loosely described as industrial warfare.

The above act also conferred powers for a presidential dictatorship over American industry. Indeed, no act in American history had placed such a range of discretionary powers on the President, though some of the other hastily drawn acts of the First Hundred Days were definitely in the running. The language of the act is replete with examples of the conferring of these discretionary powers: "Upon the application to the President. . . , the President may approve a code or codes. . . ; After the President shall have approved any such code, the provisions of such code shall be the standards. . . ; . . . the President may . . . prescribe and approve a code . . . for such trade or industry. . . ; The President may suspend or revoke any such license. . . ; Any order of the President suspending or revoking any such license shall be final if in accordance with law. . . ."[49] On and on the law goes with its litany of powers vested in the President.

The purpose of the National Industrial Recovery Act, according to its anonymous authors, was to remove obstructions to the free flow of commerce, to eliminate "unfair" competition, to increase consumption by increasing purchasing power, to reduce unemployment, to rehabilitate industry, and to conserve natural resources. These things were supposed to be accomplished by industrial codes drawn for each industry in America, i.e., cotton textile, steel, furniture, and so on, and by providing for the organization of workers into labor unions. The codes were supposed to be drawn by the businesses within an industry and enforced by government. (In case an industry failed to produce such a code, the President was authorized to provide one for it.) This approach has sometimes been called industrial democracy, though in Italy, such arrangements were called syndicates and in Germany, cartels. Some writers refer to it as business "self-regulation," but since it was done under government orders and any codes drawn could be modified by government, that misstates the case somewhat.

The National Recovery Act also contained, in Section 7(a), provisions regarding employees and working conditions. Every code was to contain a commitment by employers that their employees have the right to organize into unions and bargain collectively and that they might do so without any coercion from employers. In addition, no employer was to require membership in a company union as a condition of employment or prohibit an employee from joining the union of his choice. The President was given the power either to prescribe or approve minimum wages and maximum hours of work in each industry. This section of the act was the first step of the New Deal toward the empowerment of labor unions. It would be completed in 1935 with the National Labor Relations Act.

The other major effort toward a government planned economy was the Agricultural Adjustment Act passed May 12, 1933, which established the

Agricultural Adjustment Administration (AAA). The basic aim of this act was to raise farm prices. The act even specified a level to which they were supposed to be raised. The level was called *parity*, by which was meant an equality of farm with other prices. Or, as the law said, to raise prices "to farmers at a level that will give agricultural commodities a purchasing power with respect to articles that farmers buy, equivalent to the purchasing power of agricultural commodities in the base period."[50] The base period for most commodities was 1909–1914, but for tobacco it was 1919–1929. The main approach to achieving parity was to reduce production. Farmers were to be paid to cut their acreage planted to these commodities. The money to pay them was to be paid by the the processors of particular commodities. For example, textile mills would pay a tax on their production to pay cotton farmers to reduce their acreage, and cigarette manufacturers for tobacco growers, and so on. Another approach was for farmers to borrow on their crops at harvest and sell when prices reached the desired level. That, however, was not directly provided in the Agricultural Adjustment Act.

3. Relief

Meanwhile, and at least until these assorted plans had borne fruit, the government took more direct action to provide relief or work for the unemployed or those reckoned to be in need. One of these programs was the Civilian Conservation Corps (CCC), established by an act of March 31, 1933. It was set up to provide jobs for young men between the ages of 18–25, and to give some help to their families as well. Those who joined were sent to camps, dressed in uniforms, and lived under semi-military discipline. They were paid $21 per month, a portion of which was sent home to their parents. The CCC engaged in assorted conservation projects, the prevention of soil erosion, the impounding of waters for lakes, and the like. Initially, the enrollment was limited to 250,000, but after 1935, the number rose sometimes to nearly one-half million.

More direct relief was provided at first under the Federal Emergency Relief Act. An appropriation of $500 million was authorized by the act, which was passed May 12, 1933. The act called for grants from the federal government to states and cities to carry out relief work. Harry L. Hopkins, a social worker who had worked for Roosevelt when he was governor of New York, became Federal Relief Administrator. Hopkins got his baptism by fire in social work in the slums of New York City, and thereafter he became a buzz saw of relief activities at the highest level he could reach at any time. He was lean, usually sloppily dressed, irreverent of manner, impatient of all restraints, and a born spender of other people's money. Direct relief was not his favorite variety, mainly because he thought it was demeaning to those who received it, but he moved swiftly to set up programs and get the money available to states and cities.

A Public Works Administration (PWA) was authorized under the National Industrial Recovery Act. It set up a much expanded public works program, and Congress appropriated $3.3 billion for its work. General Hugh Johnson, appointed head of NRA, conceived of public works as being an adjunct of his activities and thought that it ought to be placed under NRA. His idea was that spending for construction would give a great spur to business recovery. The President, however, placed PWA in the Interior Department under Secretary Ickes, and he shortly became its administrator

Harry L. Hopkins (1890–1946)

Hopkins was the leader in distributing relief from the federal government during the Great Depression and Roosevelt's trusted aide and representative during World War II. He was born in Iowa, graduated from Grinnell College, and was soon deeply involved in social work in New York City. His knack for prying money loose from both government and private organizations and getting programs into operation soon brought him to the fore. When the depression came, Roosevelt, as governor of New York, appointed Hopkins director of the state's relief program. When Roosevelt began the New Deal, he placed Hopkins in charge of the Emergency Relief program. Not satisfied with that approach by itself, Hopkins managed to get a Civil Works Administration established under his control. In 1935, he took over the direction of the huge Works Progress Administration (WPA). In all the programs he headed, he spent close to $10 billion on relief in the 1930s. In 1938 Roosevelt appointed him Secretary of Commerce, an unlikely post in which he lasted for two years. During World War II, Hopkins acted as Roosevelt's personal representative in Europe and also allotted war materials to American and other allied forces. When Truman became President, he sent Hopkins to Moscow to convince Stalin that the Roosevelt policies would be continued.

himself. He was a bulldog of a man, pugnacious, apt to be impertinent toward those above him, arrogant toward those lower in status, and trusted no one but himself. As administrator of PWA, he was cautious, careful, and slow to let contracts. In any case, it usually took months of planning before work could begin on projects once they had been authorized. In consequence, it soon became apparent that PWA would make little impact on the situation during what New Dealers considered a crucial winter of 1933–1934.

In consequence, Harry Hopkins, who could figure out ways to spend money quickly and had no qualms about it, moved into the work relief area. He got a Civil Works Administration (CWA) set up in the fall of 1933, and money was siphoned into it from the PWA and relief appropriations. This was Hopkins' notion of what needed doing, and during the winter of 1933–34, he spent nearly a billion dollars on 180,000 projects and provided employment for 4 million people. In February, 1934, Congress appropriated $950 million for Civil Works Emergency Relief, and this carried Hopkins into 1935.

Meanwhile, Ickes finally got the Public Works Administration off the ground, and all sorts of projects got underway. The PWA built roads, sewage systems, schools, courthouses, bridges, jails, hospitals, dams, naval vessels, and a vast assortment of other installations. Generally, the construction was let to private contractors, so that it was a boon to the construction industry as well as to construction workers. Strictly speaking, it was not relief, but neither were many of the projects ones that the United States government had customarily financed. All told, PWA spent about $6 billion in the midst of the depression.

The programs discussed above were initiated during that First Hundred Days of the New Deal, and most of the acts were passed during that period. Finally, Congress had cleared the table of an unprecedented array of measures presented to it, and both houses adjourned on June 16, 1933—if not weary of well-doing, at least weary of rubber stamping presidential legislation.

New Deal Hoopla and Harsh Reality

The New Deal gave the impression that much was going on and something was being done, especially in the early months. It was the responsibility of government to set things right, so its programs said, to rescue the banks, manage the money, organize and rehabilitate industry, put people to work, provide emergency relief, save the farmers, and put everything on an even keel. The New Deal was part bread and part circus; it was scurry, experiment, legislate, create agencies, and spend money. The motif of the New Deal was to do something even if it was wrong, but do something.

The Blue Eagle

Hugh S. Johnson (1882–1942)

Johnson was an army officer, lawyer, and administrator. He was born in Kansas, graduated from West Point, and rose to the rank of brigadier general. General Johnson served on the War Industries Board during World War I and was greatly impressed with what he took to be the effectiveness of government planning in the economy. After the war, he resigned from the army and went into business. He was the first and most enthusiastic head of the NRA, but it did not take him long to discover that a planned economy was easier to imagine than to bring into being. Thus, he resigned from his highest position in 1934 and became a newspaper columnist and radio commentator.

There was much hoopla, abundant activity, and the checks did eventually pour out from many of the newly created agencies.

Nowhere was the hoopla (making a show to generate excitement and enthusiasm) more pronounced than in the NRA. General Johnson was temperamental, in any case, melodramatic both in language and action, given to wide mood swings, more showman than steady administrator. He did busy himself first with trying to get the representatives of industries to draw up codes and put them into effect, but when only a few industries produced codes by summer of 1933 he concluded something much more dramatic must be done. He would get the public aroused behind the NRA, and that would induce businessmen to move off dead center. He would put on a show, and that he did.

What followed was part propaganda, part pep rally, part circus, and all hoopla. The NRA must have a symbol and a slogan. One was devised. It was a blue eagle against a white background, and beneath it the legend: "NRA: We do our part." All who participated or cooperated were to have one of these symbols to display in their windows. General Johnson tried to draw the whole population into collectivism with his Blue Eagle. "When every American Housewife understands that the Blue Eagle on everything that she permits to come into her home is a symbol of its restoration to security," he said, "may God have mercy on the man or group of men who attempt to trifle with this bird." As for those who failed to cooperate:

> Those who are not with us are against us, and the way to show that you are a part of this great army of the New Deal is to insist on this symbol of solidarity. . . . This campaign is a frank dependence on the power and the willingness of the American people to act together as one person in an hour of great danger.[51]

The "NRA Days" were probably the most astounding of the NRA hoopla. In large towns and small, rallies and parades, accompanied with assorted festivities, were put on. Bands marched and played; detachments of soldiers paraded; floats celebrating local produce and adorned with pretty girls moved down the streets; boys and men chased greased pigs to claim them as prizes and tried to climb greased poles to get the prize money at the top. When General Johnson reviewed the daylong parade in New York City, he said that he took care not to raise his arm lest it be interpreted as a Fascist salute. That did not keep a photograph from being published showing him in a Mussolini stance. Johnson surmised that it must have been someone else's arm.[52]

Whether as a result of cajoling, intimidation, or ballyhoo, industries did adopt NRA codes. Here and there were holdouts who would not sign the codes, such as Henry Ford, but most went at least so far as to sign on. Indeed, there were codes for all sorts of undertakings, many of which might not come readily to mind as industries. For example, "Code 450 regulated the Dog Food Industry, Code 427 the Curled Hair Manufacturing Industry and Horse Hair Dressing Industry, and Code 262 the Shoulder Pad Manufacturing Industry. In New York, I. 'Izzy' Herk, executive secretary of Code 348, brought order to the Burlesque Theatrical Industry by insisting that no production could feature more than four strip [tease acts]."[53]

The Agricultural Adjustment Administration was not so colorful, but there was hoopla of sorts in its frenzied activity. It was in the Department of Agriculture, headed by Henry Wallace. While he was less flamboyant than Hugh Johnson, he was nonetheless determined to revive the American economy by vigorous government action. The head of the AAA itself was George Peek, a crusty veteran of the push to restore agriculture by government programs. The McNary-Haugen Bill had been his sort of legislation, but he would make do with what the New Deal provided. What the New Deal provided, as those in charge of Agriculture saw it, was a mandate to reduce production and raise farm prices.

The crops for 1933 were already planted and were on their way to being grown before the AAA could get organized for action. With most of them, it might do to wait for next year to begin reductions, but the situation was reckoned to be desperate with cotton. There was a large backlog of cotton already on hand, and farmers had planted a huge crop in 1933. So, the decision was made to contract with cotton farmers to plow up a portion of their crops, and the government would pay for the loss. The cotton was plowed up, mostly in August, when the bolls were nearly ready to open. Tractors could be guided to plow up the rows, but mules and horses could hardly be made to walk on the cotton. After all, they had long been trained not to walk on the crop, and they did it only under duress. The present writer remembers, from the time when he was a small boy, seeing the strange sight of ploughed up cotton opened so that fields were nearly white, yet the cotton could not be picked.

There was talk of plowing up corn as well, but no great program was instituted. The most disheartening thing, however, was the large number of small pigs killed and wasted. The Department concluded that it would not be

Henry A. Wallace (1888–1965)

Wallace was successively Secretary of Agriculture (1933–1941), Vice-President (1941–1945), Secretary of Commerce (1945–1946), and presidential candidate of the Progressive Party (1948). He was born in Iowa, graduated from Iowa State College, and became an editor of farm magazines. Not only was he interested in farming, and what is usually referred to politically as the farm problem, but he also developed several strains of hybrid corn and marketed them through his own company. He started out as a Republican, but began to support Democratic presidential candidates in 1928. When Roosevelt appointed him to the Department of Agriculture in 1933, he was in charge of a great variety of government programs that were supposed to help farmers. Roosevelt tapped him for the vice presidency in 1940, on the way to a successful bid for a third term as President. Wallace shared Roosevelt's amiable attitude toward the Soviet Union and blindness to the oppressive character of Communism. When Truman, as President, took a stand against the spread of Communism, Wallace publicly disagreed, and Truman dropped him from the cabinet. In 1948, his unsuccessful run for the presidency as a Progressive finished his political career.

practical to wait to reduce hog production; the number had to be reduced immediately. Thus, the government purchased and killed somewhere in the vicinity of 6 million pigs in 1933. One historian reports this conversation between President Roosevelt and George Peek of the AAA while this program was being carried out: " 'How are you getting on with your wholesale murder of hogs, George? ' said Roosevelt one day at a meeting of the Executive Council. 'I think we are progressing,' Peek replied. 'Wouldn't birth control be more effective in the long run?' asked the President, no doubt with a hearty laugh. 'We think not,' said Peek, a little grimly." After 1933, the activities of the AAA were less dramatic—there was no more plowing up of crops or killing off of small animals—, but the main thrust was still to reduce acreage and raise prices by a variety of other devices as well, mainly crop loans.

Although it is too early in the account of the New Deal to make a full evaluation of the working of the programs, it can at least be pointed out that all the scurrying about and hoopla of the government did not alter much the basic realities. And some of them were harsh realities which tended to put to nought the bold pronouncements of the New Dealers. The New Dealers were trying to supplant the market's role in the economy with the power of government. They were meddling with the basic incentives of production, and the devices by which the market operates, money, prices, competition, and the decisions of those who are actually producing and purveying the goods. Their fault was not simply that they did not know how to plan and manage an economy—no one does—, or that the market cannot be manipulated—it can—, but they supposed they could improve the working of the market by government acts. They were messing with the fundamental realities of the production and distribution of goods.

The realities were not long in asserting themselves. The industrial codes prescribed by the NRA were drawn, but that was easy to do alongside trying to make them work. The industries, freed from the application of the antitrust acts, were eager enough to collaborate so as to improve their own businesses. They would have liked to divide the market among them, with each one pulling and hauling to get as much of an assigned share as possible. Some, at least would have liked to reduce production so as to raise prices. But the New Dealers did not want these consequences at all, at least not very enthusiastically. What they wanted were for consumer prices to remain low, for wages to rise, and for the prices of farmers crops to rise. This would be a prescription for disaster for businesses, so there was a great deal of evasion and foot dragging.

The NRA did not work well—that has been the conclusion of almost everyone who has examined the matter with any care. The minimum wages and maximum hours prescribed in the codes often did not help workers notably. In Detroit, for example, factory workers had been getting 35¢ an hour, but often worked as much as 60 hours per week. The NRA code raised wages to a minimum of 40¢, but reduced hours to a maximum of 40 per week. Thus, weekly pay would actually be reduced from $21 to $16. The monetary inflation made it possible to raise wages and farm prices, but the price of consumer goods and machinery also began to rise. Indeed, the codes could easily have become an instrument for keeping wages low but raising prices of consumer goods.

What was wanted in the depression was not reduction of production but for people to become more productive in meeting their own needs and, as the case may be, those of the market. All the restrictions on production and attempts to raise prices worked in the opposite direction. That, plus government make-work programs, tended to freeze the economy in the old pattern, as farmers continued to farm hoping that higher prices would somehow redeem them, and businesses to continue along the same lines. The result was continued high unemployment, even with the government employment programs. Nor did the farm programs succeed any better.

Indeed, many farmers in the western plains were soon confronted with a far more effective crop reduction phenomenon than the New Dealers ever managed. Drought came to the plains, and with it the winds, and with the winds the dust storms. Corn and wheat crops withered in the fields in 1934, as the heat and the dust took its toll. From 1928–32, the wheat crop had averaged 864 million bushels, but from 1933–35 it fell to an average of 567 million bushels. During the great wartime demand from 1917–19, crops had been extended farther and farther into the semi-arid region of the high plains. In the 1920s, the rains were unusually plentiful. In the 1930s, the drought came, and dust storms ravaged a whole region of America, and even in the East, on some days of summer, the dust brought a haze that dimmed the light from the sun.

Infestation did for cotton crops in the Southeast what drought did for corn and wheat on lands west of the Mississippi. It reduced the yields per acre even as the amount of acreage was being reduced by government control. The boll weevil had begun to take its toll in the 1920s, but the toll mounted in the 1930s. It is possible that with less cotton planted the weevils concentrated on this with more devastating results.

In any case, the combination of drought, pestilence, acreage reduction, crop loans to hold portions of crops off the market, and monetary inflation did succeed in raising the price of farm products. Some farms and farmers profited, but many did not. It did not help too much for the price to rise if the amount grown fell. For example, a farmer was hardly better off by selling six bales of cotton at 12 cents per pound than he was when he had ten bales to sell at 9 cents per pound.

None of these developments deterred Roosevelt and loyal New Dealers; they were determined to use the power of government to gain control of the economy or by some device redistribute the wealth. Some fell by the way, like Raymond Moley, to become critics of the New Deal idea. Roosevelt pressed on, spending and experimenting. Indeed, by mid-1934, it was becoming clear that the President was bent on a continued course of deficit spending. Lewis W. Douglas was Roosevelt's economy-minded Budget Director at the outset. By August, 1934, he had all of the deficit spending he could take, and resigned. He had this to say about the direction of the New Deal:

> I see Government expenditures piled upon expenditures, so that paper inflation is inevitable, with a consequent destruction of the middle class. I see efforts to make the Government the exclusive occupant of the field of credit. I see inferences that the Government proposes and intends to plan for each individual economic activity. . . . The issue, then, it seems to me, is clearly drawn—either we will change our social order and deliberately abolish all private enterprise, replacing it with Government enterprise and employment, or we must maintain the credit of the Government so that confidence may be restored. . . . This can be accomplished only by a cessation of borrowing.[55]

Roosevelt did not like to make hard choices; he preferred to blink the reality and let the bearer of ill tidings go his way.

Foreign Policy of the Early New Deal

On the face of it, Roosevelt was an isolationist during the early years of the New Deal. Although he had run on a platform as the Democratic vice presidential candidate in 1920 which favored membership in the League of Nations, he had apparently changed his mind by 1932. In a speech during the campaign, he declared that "American participation in the League would not serve the highest purpose . . . in accordance with fundamental American ideals. Because of these facts . . . I do not favor American participation."[56] Nor did he ever make any move to have the United States join the League. Moreover, he early embarked on a course that has usually been described as economic nationalism, that is, that the United States would concentrate upon developing its own economy. He left the Smoot-Hawley high tariff in place. He took the United States off the gold standard and, in effect, torpedoed the London Economic Conference. The President apparently agreed with Walter Lippmann, who said: "If the economic system is to be organized and planned and managed, it follows that the system must be protected against external forces that cannot be controlled."[57] Certainly, President Roosevelt concentrated attention on the American economy and not foreign trade.

There were signs, too, that the United States was withdrawing from involvements and entanglements with other countries. The Philippine Independence Act in 1934 provided for Philippine independence ten years after the adoption of a constitution, which was to begin later that year. The Platt Amendment to the treaty with Cuba, which had authorized American intervention in Cuba, was declared by act of Congress in 1934 to be no longer in effect, though the United States kept naval bases that had been acquired there. American forces were withdrawn from Haiti, and Roosevelt continued a nonintervention policy in Latin America that Hoover had announced. Congress passed a Neutrality Act in 1935, signed by Roosevelt, which authorized the President to embargo the shipment of war materials to nations at war and prohibited Americans to travel in war zones except at their own risk. The occasion for the passage of this measure was the invasion of Ethiopia by Italy.

On the other hand, some of the administration's acts do not fit into the isolationist pattern even in these early years. The recognition of the Soviet Union in November, 1933 appears to be in the opposite direction. Although the Soviet Union had been in existence for 15 years, no President had thus far made any serious move to recognize the country as a nation among nations. The Soviet Union had repudiated the debt of the old regime, including debts to Americans. It was an oppressive regime, and it particularly shocked sensibilities by religious oppression. Moreover, the Communist International headquartered in Moscow vigorously promoted revolution in other countries. On the whole, the Soviet Union was not a likely candidate for peaceful relations with civilized nations. Even so, the White House entered into negotiations with Maxim Litvinov, Soviet Foreign Minister, which concluded by the formal recognition of the Soviet Union by the United States. All sorts of assurances were given by Litvinov, but they did not alter Soviet practice one whit. The debts were not settled; the Comintern continued its activities as before; and the great increase in trade that had been predicted did not take place.

Also, Roosevelt inaugurated what was thereafter described as a Good Neighbor Policy toward Latin America at the Montevideo Conference in 1933. The United States agreed to the decision reached there which denied the right of any country to intervene in the internal or external affairs of another. This ran counter to the Roosevelt Corollary to the Monroe Doctrine. The emphasis throughout the 1930s was upon cooperation between countries of America and a posture of unity toward the rest of the world.

An Export-Import bank was set up by Roosevelt in 1934, under alleged presidential power granted under the acts establishing the RFC and NRA. The purpose of the bank was to foster foreign trade by the extension of credit to foreign nations and to American exporters. In effect, it was to subsidize foreign trade. The bank was established initially to extend credit to the Soviet Union, but nothing much resulted at the time, and the bank served primarily to give credit to Latin American nations. Along similar lines, Congress passed a Trade Agreements Act in March of 1934. This act authorized the President to negotiate reciprocal trade agreements with other nations and to lower tariffs as much as 50 per cent to nations who reciprocated. Secretary of State Cordell Hull favored this policy, and a goodly number of such agreements were worked out in the 1930s, especially with Latin American countries.

There is, however, a better explanation of these apparently contradictory policies than to characterize Roosevelt as either an isolationist or internationalist. The explanation fits them into his domestic approach as well as his later foreign policy, which is usually described as internationalist. In almost everything that Roosevelt did while in office, he was increasing the power of the federal government and concentrating it in his hands as President. Whether he acquired the power in order to make changes or made changes in order to get power, there is no way to know. What is certain is that he innovated, set his mark upon the whole thrust of the government, and he acquired and exercised great power. The power came from, or was taken from, the American people mainly, though some of it may have formerly been exercised by the states.

The foreign policy moves both altered the American posture toward the rest of the world and increased the role of the President personally in these relations. By going off the gold standard he was both reducing the power of foreign governments over the United States and of the American people over their own money. The reciprocal trade agreement obviously placed arbitrary power in the hands of the President. Reciprocal trade aggreements made trade depend upon government-to-government agreements, rather than something primarily between private traders. Trade with the Soviet Union could only be trade with the government, since the Soviet Union monopolized all trade. Roosevelt acted to facilitate such trade by setting up a government credit organization—the Export-Import bank. It is plausible, too, to conclude that the government was no longer going to act forcefully to defend foreign traders abroad. Thus, the decisions not to intervene in Latin America, which had often been made in defense of the property of Americans. Instead, the government was headed toward collectivist policies at home and abroad, removing the power of people to use the government in their behalf or call the government to account. A good case can be made that Roosevelt was setting the stage for government-to-government action, for restraining Americans, whether arms manufacturers or traders generally, and for asserting the power of the American government both at home and abroad. At any rate, Roosevelt was increasing his personal power and that of the federal government in both domestic and foreign policies.

Chapter 4

Toward the Welfare State

Here is the whole sum and substance of the Share Our Wealth movement:

1. Every family to be furnished by the Government a homestead allowance . . . of not less than one-third the average family wealth of the country, which means, at the lowest, that every family shall have the reasonable comforts of life. . . .

—Huey P. Long, 1935

We have undertaken a new order of things. . . . We have proceeded . . . a measurable distance on the road toward this new order. . . . In defining immediate factors which enter into our quest. . . :

1. The security of a livelihood. . . .

2. The security against the major hazards and vicissitudes of life.

3. The security of decent homes.

—Franklin D. Roosevelt, 1935

The New Deal Administration constantly seeks to usurp the rights reserved to the States and to the people.

It has insisted on the passage of laws contrary to the Constitution. . . .

It has dishonored our country by repudiating its most sacred obligations. . . .

It has created a vast multitude of new offices, filled them with its favorites, set up a centralized bureaucracy, and sent out swarms of inspectors to harass our people.

—Republican Platform, 1936

Chronology

1935—

April 8—Works Progress Administration (WPA) authorized
May 11—Rural Electrification Administration set up
May 27—*Schechter vs. United States*
June 26—National Youth Administration

1935—

July 5—National Labor Relations Act
August 14—Social Security Act

1936—

January—*United States vs. Butler*
February—Soil Conservation and Domestic Allotment Act
November—C.I.O. organized
December—Sit-down strike against General Motors

1937—

February—Roosevelt presents Judicial Reorganization plan
July—Farm Security Administration authorized
September—National Housing Act

1938—Publication of Hemingway's *To Have and Have Not*
February—Agricultural Adjustment Act of 1938
June—Fair Labor Standards Act

1939—Publication of Steinbeck's *The Grapes of Wrath*

The New Deal shifted toward more permanent legislation in 1935, legislation that began to institute the Welfare State. Some of the earlier legislation had also had a permanent cast to it, for example, the Tennessee Valley Authority and the Federal Deposit Insurance Corporation. In the main, though, the earlier legislation had been, if not temporary, at least passed under the guise of an emergency, and some had the title in the bills. Undoubtedly, too, the notion that it was the responsibility of the federal government to look after the well being of the people had underlain the earlier legislation, as well as some passed during the Hoover administration. But much of it was pushed as expedient at the moment, and this was especially so for relief measures.

The premier piece of legislation for establishing the Welfare State was the Social Security Act passed in August, 1935. So far as the act provided for retirement programs, it was clearly not temporary nor specifically an emergency or depression measure. It applied only to those who were employed, and it was as permanent in character as any legislation ever passed. So, too, were most of its other features. It was not, of course, announced or pushed as a measure to establish the Welfare State; the phrase had not even come into use at the time. Indeed, it was not even basically pushed as a welfare measure. In his State of the Union Address, Roosevelt had talked about "security," and that was the term used in the bill. Much emphasis was thereafter placed on government providing security for people.

The term "welfare" did not begin to come into use to signify government programs to provide for the well-being of people until the 1930s. Indeed, the word had no connection with relief-type programs until well into the 20th century. The word had been around for centuries, of course, but it meant, as the dictionary says, a "state of faring well; well-being." Synonyms, in this meaning, are: "prosperity, success, happiness, weal." However, the phrase "welfare-manager" appeared in print in 1904 in England. Some factories, it seems, were employing persons to assist (or give advice to) workers to improve their well-being. Thus, the London *Daily Express* declared in 1916 that "Welfare work tends to improve the condition of life for women and girls employed in factories." But the word still was not used in connection with aid to the poor or government programs.

There is good reason to believe that New Dealers made the connection in order to try to establish some constitutional basis for Social Security. Secretary of Labor Frances Perkins, who was a leading advocate along with relief administrator Harry Hopkins, told Justice Harlan Stone of the Supreme Court in 1934 that she was worried that the social security system they were devising might not pass the constitutionality test. "The taxing power of the Federal Government, my dear," Stone replied; "the taxing power is sufficient for everything you want and need."[59] This pointed clearly toward the general welfare phrase in the clause of the Constitution authorizing taxation. In the same year, Professor E. S. Corwin, a constitutional authority of some standing, maintained that the taxing and spending authority of Congress was unchecked by the constitution.

The most generous interpretation of the above ideas is that they are the result of misreading the Constitution. The phrase, "general welfare," occurs twice in the Constitution. It is in the preamble in the midst of a list of general reasons or purposes of the Constitution, but since the preamble does not grant any powers, it would have no bearing on the issue. The second is in Article I, Section 8, and the relevant clause reads: "The Congress shall have Power to lay and collect Taxes, Duties, Imposts, and Excises, to pay the Debts and provide for the common Defence and general Welfare of the United States. . . ." The meaning here is clear enough; taxes must be levied only for the *general* welfare, and other objects listed. The phrase itself is not taken to mean that a power has been granted to levy taxes for whatever object someone might conceive by some stretch of the imagination to be for the general welfare. It is restrictive. The actual grants of power are contained in the further enumeration. Regarding the general welfare phrase, James Madison addressed this question in 1817 in vetoing a bill for internal improvements. He said, "To refer the power in question to the clause 'to provide for the common defense and general welfare' would be contrary to the established and consistent rules of interpretation, as rendering the special and careful enumeration of powers which follow nugatory and improper. Such a view of the Constitution would have the effect of giving to Congress a general power of legislation instead of the limited one hitherto understood to belong to them. . . ."[60] Moreover, Social Security and other acts that heralded the coming of the Welfare State were generally for the benefit of special classes of people, not for the *general* welfare. And, the use of welfare as a term to describe relief-like measures is, in effect to change the meaning of the word.

No matter, the New Dealers pressed on with the program under the claim that it was for the general welfare. The preamble to the Social Security Act says that it is "An Act to provide for the general welfare by establishing a system of Federal old-age benefits, and by enabling the several States to make more adequate provision for aged persons, blind persons, dependent and crippled children, maternal and child welfare, public health, and the administration of their unemployment compensation laws. . . ."[61] Thereafter, states set up what were often styled county "welfare departments" to administer part (but not all) of the programs envisioned or provided for by the Social Security Act. So it was that people began to think of such programs as welfare, not because it was an apt description of what went on, but to give them a coloring of constitutionality. Hence, too, the origin of the notion that the result of the government's taking responsibility to provide with the taxpayer's for the well-being of large numbers of people as the Welfare State.

There was, of course, much more to the Welfare State than the Social Security Act, but it has been focused upon both as a crucial act and because its enactment sheds some light on how it came to be called that. Now the broader framework of the coming of the Welfare State must be dealt with in terms of the 1930s and the New Deal.

The Tenor of Life

Before doing so, however, it may shed some light on the 1930s to make some observations about the tenor of life during the decade. It is all too easy to convey the impression that Americans generally were absorbed by depression and that government and politics were dominant factors of life. While there should be no doubt that America was being increasingly politicalized, or that the depression did not have a major impact, all this can be exaggerated. Although there was considerable and widespread unemployment and much poverty as well throughout the decade, these were not such dominant features as they have often been portrayed. It is well to keep in mind that if statistics indicate that unemployment stood at 15 per cent of the work force, then 85 per cent were employed. As for poverty, it has been in greater or lesser degree the lot of the greater portion of people from time immemorial. The struggle for a livelihood has occupied much of the attention of the race throughout history, and most peoples of the world if placed in the United States in the 1930s would have been struck rather by the prosperity than the poverty. It was only in terms of the general improvement

Margaret Mitchell (1900–1949)

Miss Mitchell was a journalist, author, and history buff. She was born in Atlanta, attended Smith College, and worked as a reporter for an Atlanta newspaper. Her interest in the South, and especially the Civil War, led her to write *Gone With the Wind,* which brought her fame and nearly a fortune. It was a long novel, running to more than a thousand pages, and was one of the all-time best sellers. The book sold about one and a half million copies during the first year (1936) and won her a Pulitzer prize in 1937. The novel was made into a movie which came out in 1939; it not only set new attendance records at the time of its release but also remained a favorite in theaters and on television over the years. Miss Mitchell never wrote another novel, but died as a result of injuries when she was struck by an automobile.

in material conditions in the country from the early 20th century to 1930 (as well as rising expectations of continued improvement) that poverty and diminished expectations stood out. When the movie *The Grapes of Wrath,* which depicted the story of a migrant family from Oklahoma in its move to California, was shown in Russia, many were impressed not with the deprivation of the Joad family but by the fact that they owned a car.

In any case, life went on as before, though there were some alterations in the rhythms of the pace. People continued to get married, and some got divorces, though the rate of both declined somewhat in the 1930s over what it had been in the 1920s. Fashions in dress changed: evening dresses were much longer, and street dresses were well below the knees. The styles of automobiles changed; the old boxy style of less expensive cars gave way to aerodynamic designs, and most manufacturers began bringing out new models each year. There were powerful and elegant vehicles, such as the Lincoln Zephyr (sporting 12 cylinders) and the Packard. Movies continued much of the popularity they had gained in the late 1920s, as talking pictures became standard, and technicolor features began to be fairly common after 1935. Churchgoing was, if anything, more widespread in the 1930s than in the previous decade. Radio was more popular than ever, and the phonograph enjoyed a resurgence.

Perhaps the best evidence that neither politics nor depression were so dominant was in popular entertainment and the pastimes. The greatest cultural event of the 1930s was the appearance of the movie, *Gone With the Wind*. Margaret Mitchell's huge novel of the Civil War and Reconstruction had come out in 1936 and had been a runaway best seller for two years running. Hollywood executives made almost as much fanfare over choosing who would play the parts of Scarlett O'Hara and Rhett Butler as in advertising the movie. Clark Gable, an already established actor was chosen to play Rhett, and a much less well-known English actress, Vivien Leigh, was chosen for the role of Scarlett. The movie fully lived up to its advance billing. It was four hours long, including a brief intermission near the middle of it, done in brilliant technicolor, and it captivated the unprecedented number of people who stood in long lines to buy premium-priced tickets to see the movie.

Indeed, the 1930s was a golden age of movies. The star system was in its heyday and included such names as Gary Cooper, Claudette Colbert, the naughty Mae West, everybody's darling little girl, Shirley Temple, W. C. Fields, Frederic March, Bette Davis, and many, many others. Movies spewed forth in great numbers—varying in quality from good to bad to indifferent—enough to provide first run houses in small towns with four or five features a week. There were comedies, such as "It Happened One Night" and "The Philadelphia Story," epics such as "Mutiny on the Bounty," musicals featuring such dancers as Ginger Rogers and Fred Astaire, and a continual barrage of thrillers, westerns, and mysteries.

The best selling fiction of the 1930s hardly indicated overweening interest in economic depression and politics. For example, there was Pearl Buck's *The Good Earth* in 1931, Hervey Allen's *Anthony Adverse* in 1933, Stark Young's *So Red the Rose* in 1934, and Kenneth Roberts' *Northwest Passage* in 1937—all reflecting interest in the historical or exotic. Even at the deeper level, William Faulkner's novels about Mississippi were only superficially stories about poverty; they dealt with haunting themes with often universal application.

The 1930s was an era of the big swing band in popular music, of Glenn Miller, Tommy Dorsey, Guy Lombardo, and Benny Goodman. Radio featured comedians and variety shows as well as drama: There was Amos 'n' Andy, Jack Benny, Fred Allen, Edgar Bergen and Charlie McCarthy, and many gathered around the set to listen to Lux Theater. It was an era, too, of big, colorful, mass circulation magazines. *The Saturday Evening Post* was surely the biggest bargain of them all. It was published weekly, often ran to as much as 150 large pages, containing five or six short stories, if not a novelette, two serials, as many as six or seven articles, numerous cartoons, and even editorials as well as letters-to-the-editor. And all that could be had for only five cents. There were other large circulations weeklies, *Collier's* for example, and many lush monthlies: *Ladies' Home Journal, McCall's, American Magazine,* and *Cosmopolitan.*

If money was scarce and wages low (they often were), prices frequently matched them. Children could often get in movies for ten cents; a small child could buy enough candy with a penny to make him sick; soft drinks could be had for a nickel. Nor is life, or its quality, simply to be reckoned by prices. So far as recreation and pastime, there was much to do that cost nothing. Children could and did play games with simple devices. Conversation with friends was still important for adults in the days before television. Libraries loaned books at no charge, and none were turned away from church services, as a rule. Neither depression nor the doings of government filled people's lives in the 1930s.

The Pink Decade

There was, however, a subculture bent on dramatizing and using the prolonged depression to radicalize and change America. It was this subculture which had much to do with fastening the Welfare State upon America. It propagated the idea that people were helpless in the face of the circumstances, that they were not responsible for their condition, that only by collective action could they do anything, and that government must assume responsibility for their well-being. As Ernest Hemingway had a character say in a novel published in 1937, *To Have and Have Not,* "A man ain't got no . . . chance by himself."

Eugene Lyons, who wrote a book on this subculture in the 1930s, called it *The Red Decade.* He focused particularly on the Communist influence, hence, the "Red," from the red flag which symbolizes communism. It might be more apt, however, to refer to it as the "Pink" decade. Undoubtedly, the Communist influence was powerful within this subculture, but actual members of the Communist Party were only a small portion, so far as we can know, of those who operated within or were strongly influenced by the subculture. There were all sorts of shadings within this socialist-inclined subculture; thus, pink more aptly comprehends it. The subculture included a large number of those who, like Roosevelt, now called themselves "liberals." The subculture flourished most vigorously in New York City, Washington, and Hollywood, in labor unions, among writers, college professors, artists in general, and those with pretensions to being intellectuals. Even many of those who would have hotly denied even that they were the mildest of socialists were often tinged with what almost became a prevalent pink.

There is no reason to doubt that the American Communist Party, directed from Moscow, played a leading role in shaping the outlook of the Pink Decade. This was so even though for the first year or so of the New Deal Communists denounced Roosevelt, the New Deal, and almost every political measure taken as fascism. A major change took place in late 1934 and early 1935, however, and from that point until the late summer of 1939 the Communist party line was much more favorable to American politics and the dominant political leaders. Earl Browder, head of the American Communist Party, spent several months in Moscow in 1934. When he returned, he passed the word along to the faithful that a new era of friendship with the Western democracies was to begin. This is known as the era of "Popular Fronts" participation by Communists. The Communist position had been opposed to participation in "bourgeois" political activities or parties. Suddenly, the posture was reversed, and Communists were ordered to cooperate with, infiltrate, and even take on the national flavor of their native or adopted countries. They were encouraged to identify Communism with democracy, progressivism, reformism, and national aspirations. "We are an American party composed of American citizens," Browder told a mass meeting. The Communist Party, he declared, "by continuing the traditions of 1776 and 1861 . . . is really the only party entitled by its program and work to designate itself as 'sons and daughters of the American Revolution.' "[62]

While Communist Party membership is secret, the number of actual members has apparently always been small in the United States. It did increase, however, during the 1930s. In 1934, there were perhaps 30,000 members; the party claimed 50,000 members in 1936; at the height of its influence, it was claiming 100,000 members in 1938. But party membership was hardly an indication of Communist influence. The Communist Party had not only its own publications, organizations, and political party, but it reached out far beyond these to "front" organizations it had formed or did control, to writers and reviewers and publishing houses in which its influence was sometimes decisive. Communist front organizations, such as National Student League, American League Against War and Fascism, Congress of American Revolutionary Writers, brought tens and hundreds of thousands under their influence. In the days of the Popular Front, labor unions were an especially important means for magnifying Communist power. When John L. Lewis of the United Mine Workers broke with the AF or L, he utilized large numbers of Communists in organizing the CIO. As Lyons says, "the C.I.O. quickly became saturated with Stalinist organizers, communist ideology and Muscovite strategy." Of the role of Communists in this organizational drive, here is a reasonable estimate: "Various estimates have been made of the ultimate strength of Communists within the CIO. At minimum they controlled unions containing about 25 percent of the CIO's total membership and at maximum they wielded powerful influence in unions having another 25 percent."[64]

The discussion of the labor union movement may be a good place, too, to emphasize that there was much more at work in the Pink Decade than the acid of Communism. A goodly number of the labor union leaders of the time

Acme

Sidney Hillman (1887–1946)

Hillman was a labor union leader, a New Dealer, an organizer of the CIO, and a prominent figure in the Roosevelt administration. He was born in Lithuania, a part of the Russian Empire, trained in a seminary, and became a Marxist. At the age of 19 he fled the country to England after serving prison terms for his part in strikes. Hillman came to Chicago before World War I and was soon involved in the union movement there. In 1914, he was elected to head the Amalgamated Clothing Workers of America, a position he held for the rest of his life. He played a leading role in organizing the CIO, when the government threw its weight behind unionization with the passage of the National Labor Relations Act. In the late 1930s and early 1940s he was a confidant of President Roosevelt and served on the boards of several wartime agencies.

were deeply imbued with socialism. David Dubinsky, leader of the International Ladies Garment Workers Union, was an enthusiastic socialist before he became a union leader. He was born in Czarist Russia, made his way to the United States in 1911, and within days of his arrival joined the Socialist Party. Sidney Hillman, leader of the Amalgamated Clothing Workers and confidant of President Roosevelt, was a Russian by birth and a socialist in his early life also. Indeed, in Russia, he had been a Menshevik, the less violent of the Marxist Communist parties. Homer Martin, the president of the United Auto Workers who took the union into the CIO, was under the influence—perhaps domination would be nearer the mark—of Jay Lovestone. Lovestone was an anti-Stalinist who formed his own small Marxist party. Walter Reuther, long a leader in the UAW and CIO, was trained in socialism by his father. The CIO, formed in the mid-1930s, was honeycombed with socialists and Communists.

The important point here, however, is not whether particular people were socialists, Communists, or some other radical view, but that there existed a subculture in which these ideas and beliefs were prevalent, and that this subculture achieved considerable influence on the course of America. They spread these ideas in speeches, books and articles, plays, and even in songs and paintings. They planted certain assumptions in the minds of tens of million of people, assumptions which were crucial to the Welfare State. Among them was the notion that the "working class," particularly the industrial workers, were especially virtuous, deserving, and could do no wrong. Thus, labor unions must prevail. Another was the assumption that the "poor" are especially deserving of government aid, that they are poor through no fault of their own, but because they have been exploited. The migrant worker was particularly made into an object of such public solicitude.

A chronicler of these years notes that "The austere Marxist theory that labor is the source of all value . . . was translated into simple propositions: See how the common people suffer! Look, they've been robbed. . . . Literature discovered . . . the . . . 'little people.' Mill workers, strikers, migrant pickers, sharecroppers, soda jerkers, miners, the night shift, the unemployed. . . . A Broadway hit of 1937 was *Pins and Needles,* a musical comedy about garment workers. It was a good show, but theatergoers saw social significance in the talent it uncovered in ordinary workers." For example, "Artists and writers glorified the migrant wanderers. Artists on WPA put them on post-office walls they were commissioned to decorate. . . . Deprivation made dramatic short stories. In Steinbeck's 'Daughter,' a sharecropper shoots his daughter because he does not have anything to give her to eat. The painters documented the unemployed scrounging for food in ashcans, along railroad tracks."[65] Novelists could, and some did, depict the plight of the poor and unemployed at great length. Erskine Caldwell described degenerate and ne'er do well Southern farmers in *Tobacco Road, God's Little Acre,* and other novels. James T. Farrell chronicled the stunting impact of environment on *Studs Lonigan* in multi-volumned detail. John Steinbeck's *Grapes of Wrath* gave a graphic account of the migration of "Okies." *Tobacco Road* became a long running play on Broadway. Richard Wright's *Native Son* was a bitter portrayal of the results of being born Black.

Many writers were drawn into the radical orbit and became radicalized. For example, among the endorsers of the call for the Congress of American Revolutionary Writers, which set up the Communist front League of American Writers, were: Theodore Dreiser, Erskine Caldwell, James T. Farrell, John Dos Passos, and Richard Wright. Thus, many novels and plays were the result of this radical viewpoint and more or less deliberately set the stage for radical change.

A goodly number of the radicalized who had imbibed this subculture got into the government bureaucracy and participated in government programs. The WPA's projects for writers, artists, and the like were a haven for radicals of various stripes, and enabled them to collect materials, devise plays, and engage in other intellectual endeavors in accord with their inclinations. Some made their way into the Washington bureaucracy as well. The best known instance is that of a Communist cell in the Department of Agriculture, which included Alger Hiss, whose espionage work was revealed after World War II by Whittaker Chambers. People high in government circles were frequently involved in promoting Communist fronts, innocently or not. Among those listed as frequently engaged in these activities by Eugene Lyons were Frances Perkins, Harold Ickes, and Eleanor Roosevelt. Indeed, he observes that the First Lady was regarded by Communists "as one of the party's most valuable assets," though she was probably unaware of all that.[66]

But however high their influence reached, those who made the 1930s a Pink Decade were a subculture, distinct from the dominant American culture. Americans were not generally attracted to Communism nor much given to radicalism on the whole. Most of those who were belonged in the category commonly referred to as intellectuals, though these had their camp followers among students and unionists, for example. Many politicians and a large number of Americans generally were attracted, however, to the justifications that radicals made for government programs. Many who received government checks did accept the justification of their own helplessness and developed dependency on government programs. It was in this fashion that the Pink Decade had its impact.

The Second New Deal

Historians often distinguish between the programs of the first two years of Roosevelt's first administration and those between 1935–1939. The earlier ones are referred to as the First New Deal, and the later as the Second New Deal. The legislation of the two periods does not fit so neatly into rigid classifications, but there was a shift in emphasis in 1935 from the earlier emphasis. The shift was toward more permanent programs and away from emergency ones. The shift was toward redistribution programs and away from industrial planning. Thereafter, the emphasis was upon government regulation directly, rather than by way of industry codes. The shift was, as the title of this chapter suggests, toward the Welfare State.

The impulse to the new emphasis came from a variety of directions. The subculture of the Pink Decade was beginning to have a stronger impact. The early programs of the New Deal were not succeeding well in their object, and some of them were being successfully challenged in the courts. Roosevelt had earlier promised to do something about unemployment insurance and old age pensions, and nothing had been done. Above all, though, political challengers were coming forth with new schemes for redistributing the wealth.

One of those stirring the waters for more drastic reform was a Catholic priest, Charles E. Coughlin. He was based in Detroit, and began to build a following by way of his weekly radio program in the late 1920s. As the depression deepened, he began to advance radical reform ideas, and by the time Roosevelt became President he had a national following for his network broadcasted program. So far as the New Deal was concerned, Coughlin blew hot and cold, but he became increasingly critical. In November, 1934, he formed a National Union for Social Justice. Coughlin frequently denounced the banks and bankers, and much of his program had to do with displacing the Federal Reserve with direct government control over the money supply. The Union favored greatly increasing the supply of the currency. (His objection was not so much to the direction of the New Deal in this respect, but to the fact that the banks were being used in the effort.) In addition, the Union wanted a guaranteed annual wage, the nationalization (government ownership) of electric power, oil, and natural gas, and greater protection of organized labor. Coughlin's influence peaked in 1934–1935.

An even more direct redistribution plan was popularly advanced by Francis E. Townsend, a physician located in California. The Townsend Plan was simplicity itself. He proposed giving $200 per month as a pension to all those over 60, on the condition that they renounce all employment and spend all the money within the month they received it. Just how such a program was to be financed and administered was never very well settled. Townsend proposed such things as printing up a large supply of money initially, but he thought that in the long run it would have to be financed by a sales tax on transactions. No matter, the response to his plan was highly enthusiastic, and Townsend clubs were widely organized. Older people especially flocked to his standard by the hundreds of thousands, if not millions, and for a time in the mid-1930s he was a force to be reckoned with.

Another Californian, Upton Sinclair, a long running muckraker and socialist, entered the field of politics with his program. He contrived a plan to End Poverty in California (EPIC) and proceeded to run for Governor of the state as a Democrat. Sinclair's plan was for the poor and unemployed to take over unused land and other resources, to form cooperatives, and eventually to replace all private enterprise in California, if not the world. Although he had been a member of the Socialist Party for several decades, he abandoned that ticket in 1934 and registered as a Democrat. He won handily in the Democratic primary but lost to the Republican candidate in the general election. The EPIC movement did not survive Sinclair's defeat in the election, but it was some indication of the radicalism of the times.

Much more threatening for the Democrats nationally (and the American people generally) was Huey P. Long's Share the Wealth program. Long's program was actually no more practical than the Townsend plan or Sinclair's proposal for ending poverty in California. But Long was actually a United States Senator, a former governor of Louisiana, and he was undoubtedly the head of the Long machine which still ruled Louisiana in 1934–1935. Moreover, Long had made strides toward establishing a mini-welfare state in Louisiana. He had shown that he knew how to tax and spend: the state built new highways, schools, hospitals, provided free textbooks in the schools, provided bus transportation to schools, and provided employment for at least some of the otherwise unemployed.

Long's Share Our Wealth program might be ill conceived, but here was a man who had demonstrated that he could and would use the muscle of government for his chosen public purposes. He proposed to tax away large accumulations of wealth or income, to confiscate all income over $1 million and all inheritances over $5 million. With this he would make every man a king, even if on a small scale. Every family was to have an allowance of

---

AP

Huey P. Long (1893–1935)

Long was a politician from Louisiana, governor, Senator, and probable presidential candidate had he lived. He was born on a farm in Louisiana, attended but did not graduate from high school, was a salesman for several years, attended law school at Tulane, and was admitted to the bar. Politics, not law, was Long's interest, and he soon got himself appointed to the state railroad commission, where he gained attention for his attacks on large corporations. Long ran unsuccessfully for governor of the state in 1924, but was successful in his candidacy in 1928. As governor, he quickly moved to assert control over all branches of the government, raised taxes, initiated large construction projects, and took steps toward turning Louisiana into a mini-welfare state. In 1930, he ran for and was elected to the United States Senate, but did not take his seat until 1932. He supported Roosevelt in 1932, cooperated with him briefly, then turned against the New Deal. Roosevelt was not moving vigorously enough, he claimed, to soak the rich and share the wealth. Long gained a growing following for his Share Our Wealth Society, but was assassinated in 1935.

$5,000 to get a homestead, and an annual income of at least $2,000. In addition, Long proposed reduced hours of work for workers, to balance agricultural production with consumption, and to provide pensions for the elderly. He launched the Share Our Wealth Society in January, 1934, and by the middle of 1935 he was claiming 7 million members, though the figures were most likely inflated. But if he could have put together a coalition of Townsendites, Coughlinites, and socialists, he might have become a formidable presidential candidate in 1936. As it turned out, he was assassinated in September, 1935, but that was in the future when the Second New Deal was initiated in early 1935.

Roosevelt moved early that year to take the wind out of the sails of the peddlers of panaceas. He signaled the move in the Annual Message to Congress in January with his emphasis on government provided security. "Throughout the world," he said, "change is the order of the day. . . . In most nations social justice, no longer a distant ideal, has become a definite goal, and ancient governments are beginning to heed the call." During the First Hundred Days, as he summarized, the main emphasis had been upon recovery from the depression. Now, however, he argued that there was no point in distinguishing between recovery measures and reform; both must go on apace. Now he was clearly turning toward reform with a focus on security. Thus, he told the Congress, repeating an earlier admonition in the first sentence quoted: " 'Among our objectives I place the security of the men, women, and children of the nation first.' That remains our first and continuing task; and in a very real sense every major legislative enactment of this Congress should be a component part of it."[67]

Congress followed Roosevelt's lead and passed a barrage of new legislation in 1935. It was not done so hastily as in the early days of the New Deal, but it was nevertheless an unusual amount of major legislation. The New Deal had now largely turned away from promoting business self-regulation toward government regulation and restrictions on business. The Motor Carrier Act placed buses and trucks hauling people and goods in interstate under the Interstate Commerce Commission. They were thereafter subject to rate and other regulation. The Public Utility Holding Company Act restricted the operation of holding companies in gas and electric power operations.

Perhaps, the best indication of the new attitude of the New Deal toward private capital accumulation and wealth was in the Revenue Act of 1935. It was, on its face, a soak-the-rich-and-profitable measure. In his message to Congress asking for its passage, Roosevelt declared: "Our revenue laws have operated in many ways to the unfair advantage of the few, and they have done little to prevent an unjust concentration of wealth and economic power."[68] He proposed to remedy that. The act raised the income tax rates on all incomes above $50,000 per year and graduated upward to a maximum of 75 per cent. Estate and gift taxes were increased. The income tax on small corporations was slightly reduced, while the rates on corporations with an income of $50,000 or above were raised. An excess profits tax on corporations was also levied. For all profits above 10 per cent there was a minimum tax of 6 per cent. That rose to 12 per cent for corporate profits of 15 per cent. The act clearly owed more than a little to Huey Long's Share Our Wealth Program.

Indeed, the Second New Deal was almost entirely redistributionist in character; in general, it was an attempt to redistribute the wealth of Americans mainly to the unemployed, the poor, industrial workers, and farmers. The wealth to be distributed came from two major sources: taxation and credit expansion. The New Deal generally continued its policy of deficit spending, borrowing money to make up the difference. Much of the government borrowing was inflationary, i.e., it increased the money supply. This was a subtle tax on savings and on creditors, since it reduced the value of the currency. The redistribution can be discussed under three headings: Relief and Government Aid, Social Security, and the National Labor Relations Act.

1. Relief and Government Aid

The most massive relief program was that of the Works Progress Administration begun under the Relief Appropriation Act of 1935. The program was tailored to the ideas of Harry Hopkins, who was its head and administrator for the first three years of the organization. Hopkins had maintained all along that the best sort of relief was to put people to work and pay them for it rather than to hand them a dole. Under the new act the federal government withdrew from direct relief and engaged in indirect relief by providing employment on a host of projects. Hopkins began approving projects and hiring people in great numbers, so that by March of 1936, the WPA, as it was called, had 3,400,000 on its rolls. All told, during the eight years of its existence, WPA workers built hundreds of thousands of miles of roads, over a hundred thousand bridges and public buildings, and numerous parks and other structures. In addition to manual workers, the WPA employed writers, actors, artists, and musicians, and undertook projects in accord with their skills.

The primary task of the WPA, as Hopkins conceived it, was to put people to work and provide them with incomes. The quality of the work, the skill of the workers, or the character of the project was secondary. From the outset, many of the WPA undertakings were criticized as being make-work. Many jokes went the rounds about the laziness and shiftlessness of the workers. "Did you hear about the WPA crew that drowned in the river," one man asked another. "No," the other replied, "what happened?" "The way I heard it," he answered, "the crew was working on a project across the river and had to swim to and from the job. One day, the whistle for quitting work blew while they were in the middle of the river; all the men stopped swimming and drowned.'' Further, a Congressional investigation in 1938 revealed that there had been widespread instances in the four states examined of requiring WPA workers to make contributions to Democratic candidates in order to get or keep jobs. Whether the accomplishments of WPA and the putting of people to work somehow counterbalanced its weaknesses would be impossible to calculate. In any case, it was a redistribution program which turned funds from private undertakings to public projects.

The Rural Electrification Administration (REA) was one of the government aid programs. It was established by executive order to make loans to cooperatives which were to generate and distribute electricity in rural areas where electricity was not generally available from other sources. The loans were extended by the government on very generous terms. The REA probably did provide electricity in some areas earlier than it would have been economic to provide it. This approach did, however, promote cooperatives and redistribute from private to public agencies.

The National Youth Administration (NYA) was another government aid agency established by executive order. It was a government-financed program to provide part-time work mainly to enable young people to continue their schooling in high school or college. The recipients were usually from families on relief. In 1936, over 600,000 young people were receiving some employment by NYA. One of the strangest of the government aid programs was the Resettlement Administration, another organization created by executive order of the President. It was authorized to resettle rural and urban families on productive farms. The whole notion ran against the grain of the long-term tendency of more and more people to live in urban areas. Rexford G. Tugwell was appointed to head this outfit, and he said: ''My idea is to go just outside centers of populations, pick up cheap land, build a whole community and entice people into it. Then go back into the cities and tear down whole slums and make parks of them.''[69] In any case, the RA did not succeed very well in its undertaking; it had ''planned to move 500,000 families, actually resettled 4,441.''[70]

2. National Labor Relations Act

The National Labor Relations Act of 1935 climaxed the drive to have government empower labor unions. Unionists claimed not only the right to organize (which had never been formally denied to them) and bargain for their members but also sought to have government so weight the scales in their favor that they would ordinarily prevail in any dispute with employers. The Norris-La Guardia Act of 1932 had placed a whole series of obstacles in the way of court injunctions to restrain unions. Section 7(a) of the National Industrial Recovery Act had given strong verbal support to unionization. However, it provided no effective means for settling disputed issues, and the recovery act was held to be unconstitutional in 1935. Even before that had

Robert F. Wagner (1877–1953)

Wagner was a long-time Senator from New York and was the senatorial mainstay of the New Deal. He was born in Germany but came with his family to the United States at the age of eight. There, he later graduated from the City College of New York and attended law school. Wagner served in the New York state legislature from 1905–1919, and was a justice of the state supreme court from 1919–1926. In the latter year, he was elected to the United States Senate, in which he served until his retirement in 1949. His career reached a peak in the 1930s as he guided the New Deal legislation through the Senate. The act for which he was best known was the National Labor Relations Act, but he also had a hand in a variety of other legislation, most directly that dealing with unemployment.

occurred, Senator Robert Wagner of New York had been working on a more thorough law, and he got it passed as the National Labor Relations Act.

It may not be immediately clear why an act empowering labor unions would be for the redistribution of wealth. Granted, it does not exactly fall under the category of levying either a direct or indirect tax. But so far as labor unions succeed in getting higher compensation for their members, a redistribution of wealth takes place, whether from employers to employees or ultimately from the higher prices that consumers may pay for the union produced goods. Thus, a redistribution of wealth is at least contemplated when labor unions are empowered by government.

The main instrument for the empowerment of unions in this act was the National Labor Relations Board (NLRB) it authorized. The board, consisting of three appointed members, is vested by the act with semi-judicial powers; its decisions in labor disputes have the standing of "administrative law." It may compel witnesses, hold hearings, supervise union elections, and make decisions or rulings in labor disputes. A major device by which the act empowered unions was to set forth a series of unfair labor practices which employers may be guilty of. (None were listed for unions, so that it appeared that only employers could commit unfair practices.) By law, it became an unfair practice for employers to interfere with the unions' right to organize, bargain collectively, or engage in concerted activities (strikes, for example); to dominate, give financial support to, or interfere with the running of a labor union; to encourage or discourage membership in a labor union (''*Provided*, that nothing in this Act . . . shall preclude an employer from making an agreement with a labor organization . . . to require as a condition of employment membership therein. . . .''[71] In other words, it was all right for an employer to *require* membership in a labor union.); or to refuse to bargain collectively with a labor union.

The NLRB, which was early packed with pro-union members, made the requirement to bargain a requirement of employers to make concessions to unions. As one scholar on the subject has described the situation:

> Employers must do more than just meet with the representatives and merely go through the motions of bargaining. To satisfy the requirement of collective bargaining, an employer must bargain in ''good faith.'' In defining the term, the Board held that an employer to bargain in good faith ''must work toward a solution, satisfactory to both sides of the various proposals and other affirmative conduct. . . .'' The Board has considered counter-proposals so important an element of collective bargaining that it has found the failure to offer counter-proposals to be persuasive of the fact that the employer has not bargained in good faith.[72]

The penalty on an employer for committing one ''unfair act'' could be harsh indeed. ''If,'' for example, an employer ''committed one 'unfair' act in an attempt to operate a struck plant, they had to take back all strikers with back pay. . . .''[73]

Labor union membership increased rapidly in the 1930s under the New Deal. It rose from 2,805,000 in 1933 to 8,410,000 in 1941. This was contrary to virtually all historical experience. In view of the prolonged depression, membership should have continued to decline, as had always been the case. The major difference between the New Deal depression and earlier ones was that the government had empowered the unions and supported the unions in their determination to prevail. Indeed, as soon as the NRA was set up, many unions went on an organizational rampage, some even claiming that they were acting for the government in effect:

> A circular distributed in Kentucky . . . stated that NIRA ''recommends that coal miners . . . organize in a union of their own choosing.'' In many places, the organizers went further: ''The President wants you to join the union.'' They wanted their listeners to believe that they referred to the president of the United States; if pressed, they admitted that they referred to the president of the United Mine Workers.[74]

But the really rapid growth occurred after the passage of the National Labor Relations Act. The spearhead of this rapid growth was the newly organized C.I.O. prodded by John L. Lewis. The purpose of the C.I.O. was to form unions organized by industry, i.e., steelworkers, automakers, and the like, rather than by craft, as the American Federation of Labor had usually done. To achieve this task, the C.I.O. welcomed and used radicals and revolutionaries of every stripe. "Communists, Socialists, Trotskyites, members of Proletarian party and Revolutionary Workers League . . . , and syndicalists became involved, particularly in the centers of the new mass production industries."[75] They often succeeded in bringing in workers of major industries.

Some of the most violent and disruptive strikes in American history took place in the 1930s. It had been violent enough in 1933 and 1934, but with so many radicals pushing it, the turbulence rose to a peak in 1937, when nearly 5 million workers were involved in work stoppages. Congress declared in the preamble to the National Labor Relations Act that it was "An Act to diminish the causes of labor disputes. . . ." Which causes, according to the body of the act, are: "The denial by employers of the right of employees to organize and the refusal by employers to accept the procedure of collective bargaining lead[ing] to strikes and other forms of industrial strife or unrest. . . ."[76] In short, the act declared that employers are the cause of labor strife because of their failure to accept labor unions and collective bargaining. If that were indeed the case, labor strife should have been ended by this act, for it placed the power of government firmly behind unionization and collective bargaining. It did no such thing, of course; some of the most violent and prolonged strikes in history have occurred since its passage.

3. Social Security

Social Security turned out to be the largest redistribution or transfer of wealth program in American history. It did not start out that way, at least in what was actually done at first. The earliest levies for old age benefits and unemployment compensation were modest enough, and it was not clear that any transfer of wealth was involved in this program, except from employers to the account of employees. The initial tax was only one per cent of wages on covered employees and one per cent on employers of wages paid out to them. The rate was scheduled to increase over the years, but not steeply. Moreover, the money for old age benefits, what is nowadays referred to as Social Security, was to be placed in a reserve fund in the Treasury and an accumulation was to occur before any substantial benefits were paid out. Thus, it was not described as a redistribution or transfer program, except for that portion paid in by the employers. In later years, it was often referred to as an insurance program, about which, more shortly.

There were, however, programs in the Social Security Act which were clearly redistributionist from the outset. Not only did the act provide for old age benefits but also unemployment compensation, aid to dependent children, to maternal and child care, to crippled children, to neglected children, and for public health programs. All these programs, except for old age and survivors' benefits, were to be administered and in some measure supported by the states. The federal government made appropriations which were to induce the states to set up programs meeting Federal guidelines in all these areas. Thus, the federal government not only paid out tax money for distribution but also encouraged the states to make appropriations and set up or redesign programs that would be acceptable.

The only one of these programs that may need further comment here, except for that one generally known as Social Security, is unemployment compensation. If extended unemployment be accepted as the norm for a considerable portion of the population, it makes sense to insure against this hazard. Indeed, prudent people have long believed it wise to set something aside against a "rainy day," i.e., against some unfavorable circumstance beyond their control. When government undertakes such a program, it takes over at least a portion of the responsibility which before that fell upon the individual, family, or, perhaps, the local community or neighbors. From an economic point of view, government provided unemployment compensation amounts to paying people not to work. It is a highly uneconomic, or diseconomic, practice. This is made more impractical, if that is possible, by taking the contribution to the program from the employer and placing no penalty upon the worker while he receives the compensation. The only check on it is that the compensation must end after a specified period of time.

As for that portion of the program now known as Social Security, it has turned out to be a kind of pyramid scheme. A pyramid scheme is a plan in which the first ones to take part in the program may get a much larger return on an investment than the amount they put into it. They may be told, for example, that they can invest $100 in a plan and get back, say, $10,000 over a period of a few months. They start on their way by getting, say, 10 other people to invest $100 each; then that 10 each get 10 more and so on and on. The person who is at the top gets a percentage of what each of those down the line from him contributes. Such schemes suffer two disadvantages, aside from the fact that they are illegal if no good changes hands. So long as all efforts are voluntary, there is little likelihood that many of those in the chain will succeed in getting much by way of contributions. Even if they did, the potential pool of contributors would eventually be exhausted, and those near the bottom of the pyramid would get little or nothing by way of return.

Social Security has some advantages over private pyramid schemes. The payments made into it are a tax and are compulsory. Moreover, government can both expand the number of people covered and increase the percentage of income taxed. While there are upper limits to these, until they have been reached, in theory at least, the government can continue to pay out much larger amounts to those higher up in the pyramid than they paid in by way of taxes. Social Security need not have resembled the pyramid device at all. All resemblance to such schemes could have been avoided by having the individual's benefits tied rigorously to the amount of his contribution, plus interest. That was never more than loosely done, and Congress and Presidents have seen fit to increase benefits over the years without regard to the future. In consequence, the reserve fund was eventually used up. Since that time, payments have been made from current receipts, and Social Security taxes have gone higher and higher. Thus, Social Security has become an outfit which transfers wealth from the working to those who are no longer working. A little of the story beyond the 1930s had to be touched on to indicate something of the real nature of Social Security.

The New Deal at Bay

For the first year or so of the New Deal, the critics almost appeared to lose their tongues. In truth, a large portion of the American people were bemused by Roosevelt and the New Dealers and continued to be more or less throughout the thirties. The New Deal had been sprung on America virtually without warning, in an atmosphere of urgency imposed by the announced emergency. The intellectual fences were down, so to speak. Congress was a pliant instrument for the President through 1935. The strident calls for collective unity must surely have intimidated the timid among potential critics. Most of the early critics were advancing more radical programs than the New Deal, as, for example, Huey P. Long.

In 1934, however, some of the critics other than radicals began to find their tongues and make constitutional and traditional American arguments against the New Deal. The Liberty League was founded in that year to muster the opposition. It mustered into its ranks both disenchanted Democrats and Republicans who were neither amused nor bemused. Among those who spoke out were two former Democratic presidential candidates, John W. Davis and Alfred E. Smith. Noting the lack of effective opposition in Congress to New Deal measures, Davis warned that the Congress would soon be "little more than that of the present Congress of the Soviets, the Reichstag of Germany or the Italian Parliament." Al Smith said of the New Dealers, "It is all right with me if they want to disguise themselves as Karl Marx or Lenin or any of the rest of that bunch, but I won't stand for . . . allowing them to march under the banner of Jackson or Cleveland."[77]

The most careful of the early critical appraisals of the New Deal was made by former President Herbert Hoover. He published a book in 1934, entitled *The Challenge to Liberty,* in which he carefully assessed the

Alfred E. Smith (1873–1944)

Smith was in New York City politics, served several terms as governor of New York, was presidential candidate for the Democrats in 1928, and became an outspoken opponent of the New Deal. He was born in New York City, quit school at the junior high level, and went to work. About the time he turned 21, he became involved in local politics, and rose through the ranks over the years to the highest office in the state. Smith was a leading candidate for the Democratic nomination for President in 1924, but he was unable to get the necessary two-thirds majority in the convention. In 1928, he was nominated by the Democrats, the first Roman Catholic to be nominated by a major party, but it was a Republican year and he was defeated by Herbert Hoover. Although Smith did not like the tenor of Roosevelt's opposition to men of wealth, he supported him in 1932. He was not long, however, in breaking with the New Deal, decrying its socialistic tendencies, and becoming, in effect, a Republican.

tendencies of the New Deal. His was not a blanket denunciation of every New Deal measure; some reforms were needed, he said. But he discerned a dangerous concentration of power in the executive branch, a fearful centralization of power in Washington, and an undermining of constitutional restraints upon the general government. Beyond that, there was the assertion of the power of government in the lives of the people in ways that posed a threat to individual liberty. All these things he placed in the context of the totalitarian thrusts to power going on in Europe. "Whatever their names be," Hoover declared, "Fascism, Socialism, or Communism—they have this common result: wherever these systems have been imposed tyranny has been erected, government by the people abolished." That there were some parallels between these systems and the New Deal, whose programs he called National Regimentation, he did not doubt. "From the examples of National Regimentation we have examined," Hoover pointed out, "it is obvious that many of its measures . . . are emulating parts of some of these other systems with the hope of speeding recovery from the depression."[78] "In our blind gropings," Hoover continued:

> we have stumbled into philosophies which lead to the surrender of freedom. The proposals before our country do not necessarily lead to the European forms of Fascism, of Socialism, or of Communism, but they certainly lead definitely from the path of liberty. The danger lies in the . . . experience, that a step away from liberty itself impels a second step, a second compels a third. The appetite for power grows with every opportunity to assume it. . . . A few steps so dislocate social forces that some form of despotism becomes inevitable and Liberty dies.[79]

Hoover's was very nearly a voice crying in the wilderness, though his and others did help to start a thwarted rally among Republicans to oppose the New Deal root and branch in 1936. But the story of that must await the telling of a temporarily much more effective development.

1. Courts Block New Deal

The Federal courts did not immediately succumb to the New Deal as the Congress had done. The constitutionality of major New Deal measures became a lively issue in the mid-1930s. It was hardly surprising that this occurred. The New Dealers made the greatest reform surge in history, introducing changes for which there were often no precedents and no clear constitutional authority. As one historian of the New Deal has noted, "On the whole, the Founding Fathers sought to contain government, not promote change. It was remarkable that the New Deal was able to break through these carefully devised constitutional barriers for so long."[80] What may be equally remarkable is that all this was done without a single amendment to the Constitution being proposed or adopted. Other major reform surges had been accompanied by the adoption of several amendments. It is true that two Amendments were adopted in 1933, but they had been proposed before Roosevelt's inauguration and did not authorize New Deal programs. The 20th Amendment abolished the "Lame Duck" session of Congress and moved the presidential inauguration back to January. The 21st Amendment repealed the 18th, which had provided for national prohibition.

At any rate, the courts were not generally swayed by either the President's charm or the emergency motif from their duty to examine carefully the constitutionality of challenged New Deal measures. It takes some time, of course, for such challenges to work their way through the courts, but in 1935 and 1936 it became increasingly doubtful if the bulk of the New Deal program would survive the court tests. In the course of those years some 1600 injunctions against the application of New Deal laws were issued by lower court judges. "At no time in the country's history," the *Harvard Law Review* observed, "was there a more voluminous outpouring of judicial rulings in restraint of acts of Congress than the body of decisions in which the lower courts, in varying degree invalidated every measure deemed appropriate by Congress for grappling with the great depression." Beginning in January, 1935, the Supreme Court itself began to nullify major acts of the New Deal. In the sixteen months from the beginning of 1935, the high court entertained 10 major cases against the various laws, and in eight of them the laws were held to be unconstitutional. Among those struck down were a portion of the National Industrial Recovery Act, the National

A Constitution for the New Deal

H. L. Mencken

(In 1937, Mencken published a mock constitution in which he satirized the concentration of power in the presidency, in the portion quoted below.)

PREAMBLE

We, the people of the United States, in order to form a more perfect union, establish social justice, draw the fangs of privilege, effect the redistribution of property, remove the burden of liberty from ourselves and our posterity, and insure the continuance of the New Deal, do ordain and establish this Constitution.

Article I

The Executive

All governmental power of whatever sort shall be vested in a President of the United States. He shall hold office during a series of terms of four years each. . . .

The President shall be commander-in-chief of the Army and Navy, and of the militia, Boy Scouts, C.I.O., People's Front, and other armed forces of the nation.

The President shall have the power:

To lay and collect taxes, and to expend the income of the United States in such manner as he may deem to be to their or his advantage;

To borrow money on the credit of the United States, and to provide for its repayment or non-repayment on such terms as he may fix;

To regulate all commerce with foreign nations, and among the several states, and within them; to license all persons engaged or proposing to engage in business; to regulate their affairs; to limit their profits by proclamation from time to time; and to fix wages, prices and hours of work.

To coin money, regulate the content and value thereof, and of foreign coin, and to amend or repudiate any contract requiring the payment by the United States or by any private person, of coin of a given weight or fineness;

To repeal or amend, in his discretion, any so-called natural law, including Gresham's law, the law of diminishing returns, and the law of gravitation. . . .

Recovery Administration, the Railroad Pension Act, the Farm Mortgage law, the Agricultural Adjustment Act, the Bituminous Coal Act, and the Municipal Bankruptcy Act. Of the acts challenged all the way to the Supreme Court to this point, only the monetary acts of 1933 and TVA had survived. The acts of 1935 had not yet gone through their challenges, but it was doubtful if some, or any, of them would survive.

In nullifying the central legislation of the First New Deal, the Court resoundingly rejected the arguments of the government lawyers. In defending the NRA, the government argued that the measure was justified by the national emergency. To this point, Chief Justice Charles E. Hughes, who wrote the majority opinion, declared: "Extraordinary conditions do not create or enlarge constitutional power. The Constitution established a national government with powers deemed to be adequate . . . , but these powers of the national government are limited by the constitutional grants. Those who act under these grants are not at liberty to transcend the imposed limits because they believe that more or different power is necessary." As to the alleged voluntary character of the NRA codes Hughes pointed out that "the statutory plan is not simply one for voluntary effort. . . . It involves the coercive exercise of the lawmaking power." For basically constitutional reasons, the Court held the NRA "code provisions here in question to be invalid."[82]

In *United States vs. Butler,* which came before the Supreme Court in 1936, the Agricultural Adjustment Act was held to be unconstitutional. Associate Justice Owen Roberts, who gave the majority opinion, pointed out clearly the task of the Court when an act of Congress has been challenged. "The Constitution is the supreme law of the land," he wrote, "ordained and established by the people. All legislation must conform to the principles it lays down. When an act of Congress is . . . challenged . . . , the judicial branch has only one duty,—to lay the article of the Constitution which is invoked beside the statute which is challenged and to decide whether the latter squares with the former." Further, "The question is not what power the federal Government ought to have but what powers have been given by the people."[83] All this was preface to declaring that the Constitution had conferred no powers on the general government to control agricultural production and that a law aimed at that object was of no effect.

Although his legislation was being mowed down by the courts, Roosevelt bided his time throughout 1936, avoiding any public statements about court decisions. There was talk within the administration about proposing constitutional amendments which would provide the New Dealers with clear power to enact the legislation they wanted, but nothing came of these proposals. It was an election year, and the President probably decided against rocking the boat by adding fuel to the flame of constitutional controversy. Moreover, to have stated in blunt constitutional language the powers sought would have been to expose the power grab involved.

Constitutional Amendments of the 1930s

Article XX

[Declared Ratified February 6, 1933]

Section 1. The terms of the President and vice-President shall end at noon on the twentieth day of January, and the terms of Senators and Representatives at noon on the third day of January, of years in which such terms would have ended if this article had not been ratified; and the terms of their successors shall then begin.

Section 2. The Congress shall assemble at least once in every year, and such meeting shall begin at noon on the third day of January, unless they shall by law appoint a different day.

Section 3. If, at the time fixed for the beginning of the term of the President, the President-elect shall have died, the Vice-President-elect shall become President. If a President shall not have been chosen before the time fixed for the beginning of his term, or if the President-elect shall have failed to qualify, then the Vice-President-elect shall act as President until a President shall have qualified; and the Congress may by law provide for the case wherein neither a President-elect nor a Vice-President-elect shall have qualified, declaring who shall then act as President, or the manner in which one who is to act shall be selected, and such person shall act accordingly until a President or Vice-President shall have qualified.

Section 4. The Congress may by law provide for the case of the death of any of the persons from whom the House of Representatives may choose a President whenever the right of choice shall have devolved upon them, and for the case of the death of any of the persons from whom the Senate may choose a Vice-President whenever the right of choice shall have devolved upon them.

Section 5. Sections 1 and 2 shall take effect on the 15th day of October following the ratification of this article.

Section 6. This article shall be inoperative unless it shall have been ratified as an amendment to the Constitution by the legislatures of three-fourths of the several States within seven years from the date of its submission.

Article XXI

[Declared Ratified December 5, 1933]

Section 1. The eighteenth article of amendment to the Constitution of the United States is hereby repealed.

Section 2. The transportation or importation into any State, Territory or possession of the United States for delivery or use therein of intoxicating liquors, in violation of the laws thereof, is hereby prohibited.

Section 3. This article shall be inoperative unless it shall have been ratified as an amendment to the Constitution by convention in the several States, as provided in the Constitution, within seven years from the date of the submission thereof to the States by the Congress.

2. The Election of 1936

It looked as if the Republicans might have a constitutional issue for the campaign of 1936. Indeed, the Republican Platform lashed out at the New Deal in strong terms. Among others, it charged that:

> The powers of the Congress have been usurped by the President.
> The integrity and authority of the Supreme Court have been flouted.
> The rights and liberties of American citizens have been violated. . . .
> It has bred fear and hesitation in commerce and industry, thus discouraging new enterprises, preventing employment and prolonging the depression.[84]

Moreover, some Republicans went on the attack vigorously during the campaign. Herbert Hoover challenged the New Deal to "lay its cards on the table." He raised some questions which he challenged Roosevelt to make "reply in plain words:"

> Does he propose to revive the nine acts which the Supreme Court has rejected as invasions of the safeguards of free men?
> Has he abandoned his implied determination to change the Constitution? Why not tell the American people before election what changes he proposes? Does he intend to stuff the Court itself?[85]

In the main, though, those in charge of the Republican campaign did not feature the more vociferous opponents of the New Deal. The Republicans nominated Alfred M. Landon of Kansas for the presidency. Landon was a Progressive of the old Bull Moose school. Nor had he been a particularly regular Republican, for he had voted for LaFollette in 1924. In a speech, he declared that "I think that as civilization becomes more complex, government power must increase." In 1935 he sounded for all the world as if he were a New Dealer, when he publicly stated, "America bids fair to join the procession of nations of the world in their march toward a new social and economic philosophy. Some say this will lead to socialism, some communism, others fascism. For myself I am convinced that the ultimate goal will be a modified form of individual rights and ownership of property out of which will come a wider spread of prosperity and opportunity."[86] He seemed hardly the man to carry on a crusade against the New Deal. He did criticize the New Deal for wasteful spending, for its failure to balance the budget, and for its multiplication of offices—for poor management in general—, but he did not push for repeal of the programs. Moreover, he was not a spirited campaigner and hardly a match for Roosevelt.

It may not have mattered who the Republicans nominated, however. Not only was much of the population still bemused by the great assortment of New Deal programs but also during the period from about the middle of 1935 to the middle of 1937 there was an economic upswing. Unemployment was still large and the depression lingered, but wages and farm prices were rising. An ongoing credit expansion or increase of the money supply fueled economic activity. Moreover, the WPA hired more people than ever during the period immediately preceding the election. The President placed emphasis on his claim that people were generally better off than they had been four years before. He also launched a harsh attack on big business, whose leaders he called economic royalists. His Social Security and taxing program took much of the bite out of the share-the-wealthers, and his Republican opponent, Alf Landon, never had much bite.

Roosevelt won the election by a landslide. Only Maine and Vermont cast electoral votes for Landon; thus, Roosevelt won in the electoral vote 523 to 8. In Congress, the Republicans were routed. Seventy-five per cent of the Senate was Democratic, and nearly 80 per cent of the House. The New Deal appeared to be invincible.

Roosevelt Takes the Offensive

With so large a portion of the electorate apparently behind him, President Roosevelt took the offensive once again. His Second Inaugural was a call to arms, so to speak, to the work of further reform and completing the new order that he had visualized. In the address, he made it clear that he had embarked on a course, not simply of dealing with an emergency or patching up the old system but building a permanent edifice, a new order. The center of his message was in the picture of deprivation he painted that he said existed in "a great nation, upon a great continent, blessed with a great wealth of natural resources." In the midst of this, he said:

> I see millions of families trying to live on incomes so meager that the pall of disaster hangs over them day by day.
>
> I see millions whose daily lives in city and on farm continue under conditions labeled indecent by a so-called polite society half a century ago.
>
> I see millions denied education, recreation, and the opportunity to better their lot and the lot of their children.
>
> I see millions lacking the means to buy the products of farm and factory and by their poverty denying work and productiveness to many other millions.
>
> I see one-third of a nation ill-housed, ill-clad, ill-nourished.[87]

What did he propose to do about this situation? "We are determined," Roosevelt continued, "to make every American citizen the subject of his country's interest and concern. . . . The test of our progress is not whether we add more to the abundance of those who have much; it is whether we provide enough for those who have too little.''[88] In short, the government must somehow take from the haves and distribute it to the have-nots.

Before proceeding with that project, however, Roosevelt wanted to remove the judiciary obstacle to his programs. It would be futile to pass the legislation and then to have it overturned by the courts, as had been happening.

1. Court Reorganization Plan

Roosevelt did not draw the obvious conclusion from what had happened, that the main thrust of the New Deal was unconstitutional. Instead, he concluded that the judges who had ruled against his programs were misguided at best and ignorant at worst. He did not personally single out those he thought to be worst but rather contented himself with general observations about what was wrong. Others were not so restrained. The core of the opposition to the New Deal measures consisted of four men: Justices Willis Van Devanter, George Sutherland, James C. McReynolds, and Pierce Butler. These were the four most often pilloried by critics. For example, Reed Powell of the Harvard Law School made this *ad hominem* attack on them:

> The four stalwarts differ among themselves in temperament. I think that Mr. Justice Butler knows just what he is up to and that he is playing God or Lucifer to keep the world from going the way he does not want it to. Sutherland seems to me a naive, doctrinaire person who really does not know the world as it is. His incompetence in economic reasoning is amazing when one contrasts it with the excellence of his historical and legal. . . . Mr. Justice McReynolds is a tempestuous cad, and Mr. Justice Van Devanter an old dodo.[89]

Such personal attacks served to divert attention away from the issue of constitutionality as well as emphasize the supposed importance of the outlook of the men, which was an important part of the new theory of legal realism. Justice Owen Roberts, who often sided with these men, was not usually so disparaged. Chief Justice Hughes wavered back and forth in the mid-1930s, apparently more concerned in holding the Court together than with any clear view on the Constitution.

In any case, Roosevelt did not assault the personalities of the members of the high court, or directly even their philosophy. Instead, he moved with indirection by focusing attention on the advanced age of some of the members. In February, he presented Congress with a Court Reorganization bill. The bill was prepared by the White House staff in secret. Hours before he sent it to Congress, Roosevelt called a special meeting of the cabinet and congressional leaders, presented the proposal to them for the first time, and without significant discussion dismissed them. The bill provided that when a Federal judge reached the age of 70 and did not retire that an additional judge could be appointed. For the Supreme Court, the additional members that might be appointed was limited to six; thus, the membership of the Court could be no more than 15. If a judge did retire at the age of 70, he would simply be replaced, of course, and no additional member would be appointed.

The bill was immediately dubbed a "court packing scheme," which it surely was. Age was an accidental factor; Justice Brandeis, who was nearing 80, usually supported New Deal legislation in the Court. Even so, the men who were a thorn in Roosevelt's flesh could for the most part have their influence negated by additional members appointed by him. Roosevelt was not getting a favorable response from Congress, so he made a public appeal in a Fireside Chat early in March. That age was incidental becomes clearer from some of his remarks. He argued that the present Supreme Court "has been acting not as a judicial body, but as a policy making body." It was some of the men on the Court, he alleged, that were making difficulties. "Our difficulty with the Court today," Roosevelt said, "rises not from the Court as an institution but from human beings within it. But we cannot yield our constitutional destiny to the personal judgment of a few men who, being fearful of the future, would deny us the necessary means of dealing with the present."[90] In short, the President's policies were being thwarted by the Court, and he proposed to get enough men on the bench to alter the character of the decisions.

Roosevelt's plan was rejected by Congress. The majority of the Senate Judiciary Committee declared that the only argument for additional judges "which survives analysis is that Congress should enlarge the Court so as to make the policies of this administration effective." The Committee not only recommended rejection but also made a resounding declaration "that we would rather have an independent Court, a fearless Court, a Court that will dare to announce its honest opinions in what it believes to be the defense of the liberties of the people, than a court that, out of fear or a sense of obligation to the appointing power, or factional passion, approves any measure we may enact. We are not the judges of the judges. We are not above the Constitution."[91]

Roosevelt lost the battle but he won the war. The Court had apparently begun to change its stance on New Deal legislation even before congress had rejected the reorganization plan. Justice Roberts apparently succumbed to Roosevelt's intimidatory pressure on the Court and changed sides. Chief Justice Hughes went along with him to form a new majority on the Court. In March 1937, this majority sustained a Washington minimum wage law, reversing its position in a New York case made a year earlier. In April, the

William O. Douglas (1898–1980)

Douglas was a lawyer, jurist, conservationist, and writer. He was born in Minnesota, raised in Washington, graduated from Whitman College, and Columbia Law School. After several years of teaching on the law faculty at Yale, Douglas came to Washington D.C. to serve as a member of the Securities and Exchange Commission. Roosevelt appointed him to the Supreme Court in 1939, the youngest man ever to have become a justice of the high court. His appointment came at a time when Roosevelt had the opportunity as a result of the death or retirement of several members to place on the court a majority of New Deal sympathizers who would interpret the powers of the general government broadly. Douglas served him well in that office, consistently pushing for the increase of the power of both the federal government and the Supreme Court over his many years on the bench. He wrote many books, both about travel and politics.

high court sustained the National Labor Relations Act. And, in May, accepted challenged portions of the Social Security Act. Death and resignation soon removed the conservative judges, and they, along with others, were replaced by such New Dealers as Hugo Black, Felix Frankfurter, William O. Douglas, and Frank Murphy. By 1941, Roosevelt had named seven new justices to the Supreme Court. New Deal legislation went through the Court without difficulty after 1937.

2. More Welfare Legislation

Congressional resistance to court reorganization resulted in new coalitions between some Democrats and Republicans to oppose New Deal measures. Thus, despite the landslide victory in 1936, Roosevelt never again had such easygoing for his programs as during the early years. Congress did pass the National Housing Act in 1937, which set up the United States Housing Authority. This organization was authorized to make long-term loans to local governments to build low-cost housing projects and subsidize rents for low income families. The Farm Security Administration was also set up that year. Mainly, it extended credit to tenant farmers and those seeking to buy small farms. But when Roosevelt called Congress into Special Session late in the year, asking for an assortment of new welfare measures, he came away empty handed.

In 1938, however, the President succeeded in getting some major bills passed. The Agricultural Adjustment Act, which had earlier been declared unconstitutional, was re-enacted. The new act did not contain a tax on processors, which had been the focus of challenge to the earlier act. Otherwise, many of the compulsive features were reenacted. (These had also been condemned by the earlier court.) The act contained such features as marketing quotas, acreage allotments, the attempt to maintain parity, and storage by the government of crops that could not be sold at the parity level. The other major act was the Fair Labor Standards Act. It established minimum wages and maximum hours for many of those in industrial employments. The maximum hours for a week was 40, and work above that amount had to be paid at one and a half times the regular work. This act also forbade the employment of children below 16 years of age in factories, and the like, and the employment of those below 18 in hazardous jobs.

By 1939 most of the New Deal reforms had been enacted or rejected, and the main lines of the Welfare State were in place. Many of the changes had begun to take on an appearance of permanence, though such building programs as those of the WPA were abandoned during the war. World War II brought a host of new government regulations and controls, a story to be told in its place, but these had a different occasion and impact. The government was still, however, bent on redistributing wealth, as some of the wartime measures will show.

Evaluation of the New Deal

The New Deal, coming as it did in the midst of a prolonged depression, wrought great changes both in government and Americans. The role of government, especially the federal government, was greatly expanded. It took on much of the formal responsibility for the well-being of Americans, especially their material well-being. Power was centralized in Washington and concentrated in the executive branch. The government was treated as an extension of the will of the President: he prepared the legislation and pushed its passage; even the courts were eventually brought around to doing his will. Americans became more or less dependent upon government, dependent upon the payments they received from government and upon the programs which were set up for relief, for farmers, and for industrial workers.

Underlying these changes was a fundamental change in the view of political, social, and economic reality. The Founders had believed and stated that man had certain natural rights, that these were gifts of the Creator, God. They were rights which government was restrained from violating in an appropriate constitutional system. Under the New Deal, a new scheme of rights was being subtly advanced. Roosevelt came closest to stating the idea in 1944, when he described an Economic Bill of Rights. He put it this way:

> In our day these economic truths have become accepted as self-evident. We have accepted, so to speak, a second Bill of Rights under which a new basis of security and prosperity can be established for all—regardless of station, race or creed.

Among these are:

> The right to a useful and remunerative job in the industries or shops or farms or mines of the nation;
> The right to earn enough to provide adequate food and clothing and recreation;
> The right of every farmer to raise and sell his products at a return which will give him and his family a decent living;
> The right of every business man, large and small, to trade in an atmosphere of freedom from unfair competition and domination by monopolies at home or abroad;
> The right of every family to a decent home;
> The right to adequate medical care and the opportunity to achieve and enjoy good health;
> The right to adequate protection from the economic fears of old age, sickness, accident and unemployment;
> The right to a good education.

Where do these alleged rights come from? They are not natural rights, for nature does not endow us with adequate medical care, a decent home, or protection from the fears of old age. They are not God given rights. If they are rights at all—which can only be conceived by perverting the language—, they are rights bestowed by government by taking from the productive and giving to the less or nonproductive. To believe in this way is to believe that one has a right to what others have produced. It is this belief that was engendered by the New Deal.

In evaluating the New Deal further there are three aspects to be considered: the political impact, the short term economic effects, and the long term economic effects. It is not enough to evaluate the New Deal in terms of what occurred in the 1930s; the programs, policies, and outlook engendered by the New Deal did not end with that decade or even with the death of President Roosevelt. They set the political and economic tone of an era and the end is not yet. That is the reason for according the New Deal such a large place in this book. While the factual discussion must end with the 1930s, the lines of extension into later decades must be alluded to.

The New Deal was very nearly an unqualified political success. It was a political success for President Roosevelt personally. He was elected for an unprecedented third term in 1940, and for another unprecedented term in 1944. In effect, he was elected for life, for he died of natural causes while still in office. It was a political success for the Democratic Party; between 1932–1968, Democrats occupied the presidency for all but two terms. The

Harris & Ewing

Felix Frankfurter (1882–1965)

Frankfurter was a longtime confidant and adviser to Franklin D. Roosevelt, was appointed by him to the Supreme Court, and had earlier been involved in a number of radical causes. He never was elected to political office but served in several appointive positions under both Wilson and Roosevelt. He was born in Vienna, Austria, came to New York at the age of 12, graduated from the City college of New York and Harvard Law School. Between political appointments he taught on the law faculty at Harvard. On Wilson's War Labor Board, he defended the members of the I.W.W. who were accused of violence. In the 1920s, he was involved in such liberal or radical activities as the formation of the American Civil Liberties Union, the publication of *The New Republic,* and the push for a new trial in the case of Sacco and Vanzetti. Roosevelt appointed him to the Supreme Court in 1939, and he championed the cause of "judicial restraint," i.e., that the courts ought to be restrained in the use of their power in curbing the Congress or the executive branch. That suited Roosevelt well. However, in the 1950s, when the Court began to assert its powers by legislating, in effect, along liberal lines, Frankfurter still was in favor of judicial restraint.

Congresses have been predominantly Democratic from 1932–1980, as have governors. The New Deal showed the way to what looked for a time as perpetual incumbency for a political party. It was to buy the votes of a substantial portion of the electorate with taxpayers' money. It was to promise benefits and promise benefits, spend and spend, and elect and elect. Many Republicans climbed on the tax-and-spend-and-get-elected bandwagon over the years as well.

The New Deal did not simply tax and spend and elect, however. It introduced an even more ominous practice: deficit spending. Taxes are not popular, not with those on whom they fall, but deficit spending conceals the hidden tax involved in devaluating the currency or deferring the payment for future generations. In March, 1933, the national debt stood at $20.9 billion; by 1940, it reached $43 billion. The practice of deficit spending, begun in the last two years of Hoover's administration, has gone on at various paces ever since. Credit expansion, a related and equally devastating practice, has become standard practice also, though it was initiated well before the New Deal.

The New Deal programs did not end the Great Depression; they delayed recovery and prolonged it. Economically, there is but one route to prosperity, and that is through freedom of enterprise, productivity, and competition. The New Deal hampered enterprise and competition. Production was discouraged by such devices as acreage allotments for farmers, shorter hours of work in industry and reducing the number of people in the labor force. Enterprise was hampered by diverting capital from private hands and spending it for public employment and public enterprises. The proof of the pudding came in the period 1937–1939, when in the midst of prolonged depression, the depression deepened. The stock market crashed again in 1937, though not so loudly. Unemployment rose, until in the course of 1938 it reached the highs of 1933, despite such programs as WPA and the CCC. According to some surveys, it reached 11 million in this period. Higher wages resulting from government encouraged unionization and wages and hours legislation contributed to the deepening depression.

To show how the New Deal programs prolonged depression and worsened the situation, it may be helpful to examine a little more closely the fate of the farmers. These measures were often supposed to save the family farm and even increase the number of people in farming. If anything, they worked the other way. About 25 per cent of the population lived on farms in 1933; this had fallen to 23 per cent in 1940 and to 15 per cent in 1950, when most of the programs were still in effect. As for tenant and sharecroppers, who were supposed to be special objects of consideration, the comments of two historians are in order. One says, "The AAA brought benefits to almost all commercial farmers. But in limiting acreage and providing the strongest possible incentive for more efficient land use, and thus for better technology, it forced sharecroppers off the land and worsened the plight of farm laborers."[92] Another says, "New Deal policies made matters worse. The AAA's reduction of cotton acreage drove the tenant and the cropper from the land. . . ."[93] They prolonged the agony of leaving the farm, with the usually small government checks, but by limiting acreage to money crops they sealed the fate of many farmers.

The New Deal concentrated much attention on raising wages and farm prices. To foster this, it adopted monetary and fiscal policies which brought in later years the scourge of inflation, the destruction of savings, and a society bent on somehow holding on to a portion of what has been earned. The long-term result to this date has been the progressive destruction of the dollar. That, too, is a legacy of the New Deal.

It is often alleged that World War II brought the United States out of the depression. It is true that there was full employment during World War II, full employment because there were so many men in military service and so many workers were needed to produce war goods. But it would be nearer the mark to say that World War II only spread the deprivation by rationing and other controls. No one could buy a new automobile after early 1942. A measure of real prosperity only returned after World War II, as the emphasis shifted to an increasing production of consumer goods to supply the pent-up demand from the war years.

Chapter 5

The Coming of World War II

Japan recognizes and respects the leadership of Germany and Italy in the establishment of a new order in Europe.

Germany and Italy recognize and respect the leadership of Japan in the establishment of a new order in Greater East Asia.

—German-Italian-Japanese Pact, 1940

I address this letter to every man and woman in America who is opposed to our country's entry into the European war. I write because we are being led toward that war with ever-increasing rapidity and by every conceivable subterfuge. While our leaders have shouted for peace, they have constantly directed us toward war, until even now we are seriously involved.

—Charles A. Lindbergh, March, 1941

Yesterday, December 7, 1941—a date which will live in infamy—the United States of America was suddenly and deliberately attacked by naval and air forces of the Empire of Japan. . . .

I ask that Congress declare that since the unprovoked and dastardly attack by Japan . . . , a state of war has existed between the United States and the Japanese Empire.

—Franklin D. Roosevelt, 1941

Chronology

1931—Japan seizes Manchuria

1935—
- August—Passage of Neutrality Act
- October—Italy invades Ethiopia

1936—
- March—German troops occupy Rhineland
- July—Beginning of Spanish Civil War

1938—
- March—Germany occupies Austria
- September—Munich Conference

1939—

March—Germany dismembers Czechoslovakia
April—Italy invades Ethiopia
August—Nazi-Soviet Pact
September 1—Germany invades Poland
September 3—Britain and France declare war on Germany
November—Soviet Union invades Finland

1940—

June—Fall of France
August-October—Air Battle of Britain

1941—

June—Germany invades Soviet Union
December 7—Japan attacks Pearl Harbor
December 11—Germany and Italy declare war on United States

Only twenty years after the Treaty of Versailles, which ceremonially brought World War I to an end, a new and more devastating war broke out in Europe and spread in its impact to much of the rest of the world. World War II was total war fought to unconditional surrender. It was a war fought with virtually all civilized restraints removed: war fought not simply among combatants on battlefields but against whole populations, as bombs and artillery rained on young and old alike, on women and children as well as men. Cities, reckoned to be the very seats of civilization, bore the brunt of much of the destruction. Many cities on the continent were absolutely devastated—wrecked or trashed may capture what happened better—, such cities as Berlin, Leningrad (formerly St. Petersburg), Warsaw, Hamburg, Dresden, Stalingrad, London, and many, many more. Paris was spared extensive destruction, as was Rome. War raged across Europe and Asia, most of the great and small islands of the Pacific, North Africa, and threatened to expand to engulf the whole world.

If was as if Western Civilization was under some demoniac urge to destroy itself. Better still, it was as if the technology spawned by that culture—trucks, airplanes, tanks, artillery, submarines, battleships, machine guns, and the like—had broken loose from their makers, as in some science fiction nightmare, and was bent on destroying the people and culture that had spawned them. Frankenstein's monster had become self-directed toward destruction, so to speak. Of course, this did not happen literally, but there is a sense in which something analogous to that did take place. Many of the restraints upon power and its exercise had broken down in the interwar years; the technological development within the civilization proceeded apace, but the religious, moral, and political restraints were being overridden or cast aside. Even more directly to the point, powers were emerging that were directly opposed to Western Civilization, who wished to see its institutions, its culture, its religion, and its way of life destroyed.

Soviet Communists were the most committed opponents of Western Civilization, but Nazism in Germany and Fascism in Italy were hardly less so. Japanese militarists also were thrusting for power in Japan, and these were intent on domination of the Pacific and driving Europeans and Americans out. The Japanese were outsiders to Western Civilization and, though they had mastered Western technology, they would gladly have destroyed other Western influence. (Indeed, it may be well to emphasize that the hatred of Western culture was nowhere accompanied by any significant hatred of Western technology.)

Had the opponents of Western Civilization formed a unified front there is good reason to suppose they could have crushed it in Europe, Asia, Africa, and possibly the South Pacific. Indeed, during the dark days of 1940, there was talk of a Rome-Berlin-Moscow-Tokyo Axis, and as the air Battle of Britain raged in the latter part of that year the possibility of Britain moving its government to Canada and the development of a Fortress America was discussed. The ultimate unification of the opponents of our civilization did not occur, of course. Instead, in 1941 the conflict took on an altered character, especially in Europe. Instead of an all out assault on Western Civilization, World War II became a socialist conflagration at its center. After the German invasion of the Soviet Union in June of 1941, the war became a titanic contest between the two main representatives of revolutionary socialism—Nazi Germany and Soviet Communism.

The Anglo-Americans did not view it in that light, of course, nor have historians done much since to penetrate the haze surrounding the central conflict. Nor did the manner in which the war had developed help in distinguishing the central thread. The war had broke out in the wake of the Nazi-Soviet Pact in 1939. The main combatants became the British and French Allies arrayed against Germany. Moreover, Hitler contributed to the confusion by turning to the West after his conquest of Poland: attacking Norway and Denmark, and then France by way of Belgium, the Netherlands, and Luxemburg. Most of the ancient centers of Western Civilization were now under siege. When Fascist Italy entered the fray, it looked very much as if it would be a war between Fascist totalitarians and Western democracies. That, however, was but a prelude to the main conflict, as it turned out.

When Germany invaded the Soviet Union, the main event was at hand. An old contest was renewed, renewed with the unleashed fury of revolutionary socialism, with one species of that persuasion ranged against the other. The central contest, as it turned out, was over the control and domination of Eastern Europe. It was a life and death struggle for dominion between Nazi Germany and Soviet Communism. Everything else became peripheral until this issue was settled, though the British and Americans might be excused for not seeing the matter in this light. Apparently, Stalin grasped the issue clearly enough, and Hitler was never much in doubt about it.

Not only did the Soviet Union and Germany both covet much of the same territory in Eastern Europe, but they were ideological enemies as well. A goodly amount of the European portion of the Russian Empire had been cut away as a result of World War I. The Soviet Union wanted to restore that territory to the Soviet Empire as well as dominate its nearest neighbors. Moreover, Germany was the great prize in Communist mythology. Karl Marx had focused much of his attention on Germany and predicted that it was in line to become communist. To Stalin, Nazism, usually referred to generically as "Fascism," was the last and most aggressive stage of capitalism. It was the mortal enemy of communism come to life and moving on the world stage. On the other hand, Communism was the essence of much that Hitler hated. He loathed the Slavs, who were the dominant element in Russia, considered them inferior people and only worthy to be slaves. Communism was, he proclaimed, the heart of the "Jewish conspiracy" thrusting to domination in the world. By most accounts, the conquest of the Soviet Union was Hitler's deepest and most abiding ambition, along with ridding Europe of Jews. As for Eastern Europe, Nazi ideology held that the Germans needed *lebensraum* (more living space), and to expand eastward would provide such space near at hand.

The most direct evidence that the eastern front was the central struggle of World War II is the scale of contest and the size of the armies involved. The war was fought on a front stretching for 2000 miles from Leningrad in the north to Rostov in the south. The size of the armies has probably never been matched in all of history. The Germans invaded the Soviet Union in June of 1941 with 135 divisions of their own and 13 Finnish and 15 Rumanian divisions. (In modern warfare, a division typically comprises 10,000 to 20,000 troops.) The Russians brought to bear 136 divisions of their own at the outset. At a later date in the war, the Germans claimed to have identified 360 Soviet divisions fighting against them, and still later there was talk that the Russians had over 500 divisions more or less in combat. By contrast, the United States had 60 divisions on the western front in the spring of 1945—the largest American army ever assembled. Some measure of the ferocity of the fighting on the eastern front can be found in the number of casualties. The Soviet Union reported that in the course of the war it lost seven and a half million personnel killed or missing. German military personnel killed or missing in the war has been reckoned at 2,850,000 though not all of these were on the eastern front. By contrast, the United States lost 292,100 in all theaters of operation, and the British Commonwealth somewhat over half a million.

The ferocity of the war on the eastern front can best be illustrated by examples. Leningrad was placed under siege by the Germans for 900 days. As one history describes it, "Without light or fuel, the inhabitants of the beleaguered city depended upon supplies hauled across Lake Ladoga. . . . Enemy bombardment, starvation, and disease cut down a million citizens;

the dead at times were heaped up in streets littered with refuse and excrement."[94] One of the reasons the Germans never took Leningrad was that Hitler did not want his armies bogged down in the house-to-house fighting of a large city. Even so, it happened in one of the decisive battles of the war, the battle for Stalingrad in the winter of 1942–43. Stalingrad was a key industrial city on the lower Volga river with large oil refineries and other industries. In the late summer and early fall of 1942, German armies swept into the city, but were stalled and eventually surrounded within it. "The closest and bloodiest battle of the war was fought among the stumps of buildings burnt or burning. From afar Stalingrad looked like a furnace and yet inside it men froze. Dogs rushed into the Volga to drown rather than to endure any longer the perils of the shore. The no less desparate men were reduced to automatons, obeying orders until it came their turn to die. . . . The Germans were on half rations from the end of November. . . . Some 70,000 Germans died during the siege, many of them from exposure or starvation, some by suicide. . ."[95]

As should be apparent by now, World War II was not only an assault upon life—not merely those of combatants but of civilians as well—but also upon liberty and property. Millions of conquered people were imported to Germany to work as forced laborers. Hundreds of thousands of German soldiers disappeared in the Soviet Union, many never to be heard from again. Slave labor camps were already widespread in the Soviet Union. The destruction of property occurred on a scale that had never taken place before in the history of the world, by bombing, by artillery, and by massive armored vehicles. Indeed, the callousness toward boundaries and property was epidemic throughout the war. Time after time invasions of nations occurred without warning or declaration of war. All this fit both the pattern of barbarization and what might be expected in a socialist conflagration. After all, socialism proceeds on the thesis that private property is an evil, and no property nor life is secure without it. These are themes to which we must return throughout this chapter. It must be followed now in the course of developments that led to war and in the course of the war.

War Comes to Europe

The outbreak of World War II was not so unexpected as had World I been. The war clouds had been thickening throughout the 1930s, and as war approached its coming was fearfully anticipated. A dress rehearsal, so to speak, had already taken place in the Spanish Civil War (1936–1939). There were four aggressively expansive centers of the threat to the peace: the Soviet Union, Fascist Italy, Nazi Germany, and imperialistic Japan. They were all either totalitarian countries, or well on they way to being by the mid-1930s. The Soviet Union and Italy were totalitarian already in the 1920s. Hitler had consolidated his power in Germany by 1934, and Japan had taken on the familiar earmarks of totalitarianism in 1937 under the leadership of Prince Konoye.

The Soviet Union's territorial ambitions only came out in the open in 1939–1940. Prior to that time, however, Moscow had been the center for the spread of communism around the world. The organ for that effort was the Communist International (the Comintern). It acted by international subversion within countries, not by territorial conquest. The Comintern fostered the formation of communist parties within countries, parties which were not independent but rather directed and controlled from Moscow. These parties, along with sympathizers, fomented discontent within countries, provoked clashes with police, and worked to undermine established governments and to infiltrate institutions. They were, therefore, a continuing threat to domestic peace and harmony, and, to the extent that they were successful (not much, in the 1930s) could lead to civil wars.

Japan was the first of these countries to become territorially aggressive in the 1930s. By all indications, Japan was a peaceful country in the 1920s. It had joined the League of Nations and had participated in the Washington and London naval conferences. Moreover, Japan had a parliamentary system of government modeled on that of the British and universal suffrage. The country had, however, several elements, most notably, the military, who became increasingly disaffected in the 1930s. Japan depended heavily on foreign trade, and this was hard hit by the Great Depression and the decline in foreign markets. If the Japanese could not prosper by foreign trade, there was considerable opinion that the country must expand its sphere of influence and control in Asia and the Pacific. In 1931, the military forces stationed in Manchuria took over that country by driving the Chinese out. Government leaders in Japan were subjected to a reign of terror by elements within the country, and such government as survived eventually accepted the conquest of Manchuria. In 1937, Japan launched a large scale undeclared war against China. At about the same time, totalitarian one party rule was established in the country. Japan occupied considerable territory in China, but the war continued until it became a part of World War II.

The next to make aggressive territorial moves was Benito Mussolini in Italy. Italian armies invaded Ethiopia in October of 1935. Ethiopia was an independent country under the rule of Emperor Haile Selassie at the time, but for all the pomp of his rule, his forces were no match for those of Mussolini. By the spring of 1936, the fighting was over, and Ethiopia became a colony in the Italian empire.

Meanwhile Adolf Hitler was preparing for future military exploits. Germany had been virtually disarmed by the Treaty of Versailles, prohibited to have either the arms or personnel for a major army or navy. This did not deter Hitler for long, and by 1935 he was taking the steps toward restoring German military power. In 1936, he dispatched troops into the Rhineland to occupy territory demilitarized by treaty. War broke out in Spain in 1936, offering both Hitler and Mussolini opportunity for further military adventures. The combatants in this civil war are usually referred to as Republicans versus Falangists (or Fascists, as they were sometimes called). In the general elections of 1936, an assortment of radical parties and unions gained a majority in the legislature and formed a government. In the ensuing contest, they were usually referred to as Republicans. The radical activities of those in power provoked a military revolt led by General Francisco Franco. The Soviet Union gave financial support to the Republican (especially the Communists within it) cause, and volunteers from many countries, usually Communists, or sympathizers, formed an international brigade. Italy and Germany provided munitions and other aid to Franco's forces. Both in the nature of the contestants and in the brutality of the conflict, the Spanish Civil War was a prelude to World War II. Franco's forces emerged victorious in 1939. Meanwhile, Hitler marched into Austria in 1938, bringing that country under his control.

Historians have usually blamed, in varying degrees, Britain, France, the United States, and the League of Nations for not taking stern action to stop or punish aggression as the activities of the totalitarians became more threatening in the 1930s. Aside from taking a stronger stand against it or adopting more effective embargoes against belligerents, it is not entirely clear what they might have done. The most obvious occasion for intervention by Britain and France, especially France, was offered by Hitler's remilitarization of the Rhineland. This was a definite treaty violation, and it would have been appropriate for France to send an army into the Rhineland and drive the German army out. France considered the move, but in the absence of support from Britain, did not act. Ethiopia's appeal to the League of Nations for assistance in 1935 resulted in a partial embargo on war materials but had no great effect on events. Britain and France did make an effort to shut off foreign intervention in Spain, though it was not entirely successful.

In any case, there was little will in France, Britain or the United States (nor, for that matter, the League of Nations) to take strong action.

In fact, there was little will to resist aggression during these years or to risk war with expansionist powers. Pacifist movements were prominent in the United States and other free countries in the 1930s. The Conservative Party, which had a majority in Commons for most of the 1930s in Britain, generally preferred coalition governments to party rule. That is a way of saying that the party leaders did not wish to take full responsibility for the directions taken by the government. France had a succession of governments, usually afflicted with the pacifism of the milder varieties of socialism. So far as foreign policy was concerned, the French had what has been called a "bunker mentality," that is, they preferred to dig in and hope no enemy invaded. They built the Maginot Line, basically underground fortifications, along the French and German border. This approach was prompted by the fact that World War I had entailed mainly trench warfare, and if France was going to fight Germany again, they wanted to have the biggest and best trenches. The temper in the United States was best illustrated by the neutrality acts that were passed in the mid-1930s. These acts were ably designed to prevent World War I, according to prevailing notions of how the United States had got drawn into that war. Senator Gerald P. Nye of North Dakota conducted a lengthy investigation, beginning in 1934, of the role of the American munitions industry in getting the United States into World War I. The conclusion from the hearings was that they had played a prominent role. The Neutrality Act of 1935 authorized the President to act when war broke out anywhere by proclaiming a state of war, prohibiting the export of arms and munitions, and forbidding American citizens to travel on belligerent vessels. The act was reenacted in 1936, and it contained as well a provision by which loans could be prohibited to belligerents. When the Spanish Civil War broke out, Congress extended these prohibitions to civil wars. An even more thoroughgoing act was passed in 1937. Anti-war sentiment had been rising in France, Britain and America as the totalitarian countries were gearing up for war.

The height of the spirit of appeasement was reached at the Munich Conference in late September, 1938. Since the heads of the major European powers, except the Soviet Union, met there—Hitler for Germany, Mussolini for Italy, Prime Minister Neville Chamberlain for Britain, and Premier Édouard Daladier of France—it was what nowadays would be called a Summit meeting. The issue was the proposed annexation by Germany of a portion of Czechoslovakia with a heavy Germanic population. Hitler had been carrying on a vigorous propaganda against the Czech government's alleged mistreatment of Germans for months. Chamberlain made two hurried flights to Germany to meet with Hitler and try to dissuade him from any attack on Czechoslovakia. When Hitler persisted in his demands, the others agreed to meet at Munich. Czech representatives were excluded from the conference; Hitler refused to meet with them. The meeting was really to no avail; Hitler pressed his demands and demanded an immediate reply. Chamberlain, Daladier, and Mussolini agreed that Germany could have the Sudeten portion of Czechoslovakia.

Even so, the leaders claimed a major success because they supposed they had averted war. Chamberlain told the crowd that came out to greet him at the airport on his return from the conference, "I believe it is peace in our time."[96] The House of Commons voted to approve what was done at Munich 366 to 144, and the French Chamber gave an even more enthusiastic margin by its vote of 543 to 75. Euphoria was widespread.

Actually, Hitler hardly waited to catch his breath before renewing his campaign against the Czech government. In March of 1939, Hitler forced the Czech government to submit to German control and made his triumphant entry into Prague. Although France, Britain, and the Soviet Union as well had vouched for the independence of Czechoslovakia, none took any action. A wry saying at the time had it that Hitler wanted peace: a piece of Austria, a piece of Czechoslovakia, and a piece of Poland. In April, Italy invaded and subjugated Albania. In the face of what had happened, France and Great Britain agreed to defend the independence of Poland, as well as several other small European countries. Chamberlain and Daladier had got their backs up finally and began to make preparations for war.

Hitler was making even more definite plans for war. Poland was already marked as the next target. On May 22, 1939, Hitler and Mussolini entered into a firm military alliance which served as the basis of the two Axis powers during World War II. The next day Hitler called together his senior military officers and told them that war was inevitable. "There is no question of sparing Poland," he declared, "and we are left with the decision: To attack Poland at the first suitable opportunity. We cannot expect a repetition of the Czech affair. There will be war."[97]

Aside from mustering his armies, one thing remained to be done. Hitler was determined, if at all possible, to avoid a two front war. The best means open to him at the time was to come to some kind of agreement with the Soviet Union. Stalin paved the way for negotiations by removing Maxim Litvinov as foreign minister (since Litvinov was Jewish, negotiations with him would have been distasteful to Hitler) and replacing him with V. Molotov. The final negotiations were conducted in Moscow August 23–24, 1939 between Molotov and the German foreign minister, Joachim von Ribbentrop. The agreement is usually described as the Nazi-Soviet Pact.

There was an open agreement and a secret agreement. Openly, it was a non-aggression pact, by which each of the countries agreed not to start a war against the other. Secretly, it was an agreement to divide much of Eastern Europe between the two countries. Poland was to be divided between the Soviet Union and Germany. It was agreed that Finland, Latvia, Lithuania, and Estonia would be in the Soviet sphere. When the Soviet Union expressed an interest in Bessarabia, a part of Rumania, Germany indicated it had no interest there. Even the revelation of the open treaty sent shocks around the world. Those who were most shocked were Communists and their sympathizers around the world. Fascism (including Nazism) had been pictured as the most dangerous enemy of Communism throughout the 1930s. Communist fronts had been organized against Fascism, and Hitler had been pictured as public enemy number one. Then suddenly, without warning, the Soviet Union had become virtually an ally of Nazi Germany. From the other side, Japan was astounded, for it had entered into an anti-Comintern pact with Italy and Germany. Undoubtedly, Stalin welcomed the opportunity to defer if not avoid war. Even more certainly, he was pleased with the prospect of expanding the Soviet sphere in the Baltic and possibly in Southeastern Europe. As for Hitler, he judged that he must secure his rear and flanks before moving against Russia.

On September 1, 1939, a massive German army invaded Poland from three different angles. For the first time, the world got a preview of a new kind of war, a war of movement—*blitzkrieg,* the Germans called it, lightning war. The contrast between this new lightning war and the trench warfare of World War I could hardly have been greater. Attacks were usually preceded by bombing and strafing and accompanied or supported by tanks and other armored vehicles and troop carriers. Armies could move so swiftly that they could readily cut lines of communication and spread confusion among the enemy. The German armies outnumbered the Poles more than two to one and were incomparably better trained and equipped than they were. France and Great Britain declared war on Germany on September 3. But they had no forces in Poland, and no attack on Germany from the West was launched. By September 27, Warsaw had surrendered and organized resistance in that country ended. Meanwhile, Soviet armies had invaded Poland from the East (on September 17), and Poland was crushed between two massive armies. According to plan, Poland was then divided between Germany and the Soviet Union.

There followed in the fall and winter of 1939–40 what was called a "phony war" on the Western Front. French forces, joined by a British Expeditionary Force, took up positions along the Maginot Line. German forces were concentrated along their own line of fortifications, the Siegfried Line, and neither went on the attack. This lull in the war lasted until April.

Meanwhile, the Soviet Union, freed from German pressure, continued on a course of aggression begun in Poland. First, in late September and early October, the Soviet Union sought and obtained the rights to set up military bases in Latvia, Lithuania, and Estonia. When Finland rejected similar overtures, the Soviet Union went to war with and invaded Finland in late November, 1939. Although Finland had only a small population and army, it earned the admiration and sympathy of much of the rest of the world by holding the Russians at bay. Eventually, however, superior force told, and the Finns accepted the Soviet terms by ceding part of their territory to the Russians. In early August, 1940, Latvia, Estonia, and Lithuania lost their remaining independence and were incorporated into the Soviet Union. A similar fate befell Bessarabia in June of the same year. Before all this had taken place, the western Axis powers were on the move once again.

Nazi Conquest of Western Europe

Although Hitler was eager to press the attack on France once Poland had fallen, at the urging of his generals he held off until the spring of 1940. When spring arrived, Hitler secured his right flank in the Scandinavian countries before attacking the main goal. On April 9, 1940, German forces marched into Denmark and took that country without resistance. On the same day, an all-out attack was launched against Norway, which fought back as best it could. English and French forces were brought in a week after the invasion to reinforce the Norwegians, but they were too little and too late and had to withdraw even before the fighting ended. Norway had been conquered by June 10, and the king and his cabinet took refuge in England.

On May 10, German armies invaded Belgium and the Netherlands without warning. Four days later, the Dutch army surrendered, and the government escaped to London. The main event for western Europe was now at hand. France had placed virtually its total reliance on the Maginot Line. That line of fortifications had not been extended along the borders of Belgium and Luxemburg, however. (To have done so would not only have been unfriendly but also have signaled an intent not to seriously defend these countries if they were attacked.) The German armies simply bypassed the Maginot Line by attacking through the Low Countries. The British and French sent forces into Belgium to fight alongside the Belgian armies, but within a week after the invasion German armies were in France. The Belgian armies continued to fight until May 26, when they were summarily ordered to surrender by the king. Their unexpected surrender cut the bulk of British forces and some of the French off from the main army. In early June, the British were evacuated from Dunkirk by boats from England, though they left their heavy equipment behind. The German armies were now thrusting through France almost at will. On June 10, Italy declared war against France and Great Britain and launched an attack into southern France.

On June 16, barely five weeks after the invasion, a beaten French army was surrendered by Marshal Petain, who had become Premier of France. Technically, Petain had asked for an armistice, and a few days later the terms were signed. The French forces were disarmed, and Petain agreed that Germany should occupy and control about three-fifths of French territory. The government had moved from Paris to Vichy, and that portion of France which retained some residues of independence was thereafter known as Vichy France. General Charles de Gaulle began the difficult task of assembling a French army in England from remnants he could gather. After the British sunk (to keep it out of Axis hands) or captured the French fleet, Vichy France broke off diplomatic relations with them in July.

In the ensuing months, Germany and Italy moved to secure areas of potential resistence in Southeastern Europe. Hungary and Bulgaria joined the Axis, as did the remains of Rumania after it had been partially dismembered by the Soviet Union, Hungary, and Bulgaria. Yugoslavia and Greece were eventually subdued by Italy with German aid. The Axis stood astride the continental land mass of Europe, except for the European portion of Russia; all countries were either subjugated, allied, neutral, or friendly (as in the case of Franco's Spain) with the Axis.

Great Britain stood alone against the might of Germany and the more questionable strength of her allies. (The British Commonwealth of Nations supported Britain in the war, but they were remote from the scene of the conflict.) Winston Churchill replaced Neville Chamberlain as Prime Minister when Germany invaded Belgium, and it fell to his lot to rally the British for continuing the fearful conflict. Churchill's resolve was well expressed in a reply made to the King of Sweden about rumors of a German peace overture in the summer of 1940:

> These horrible events [Hitler's conquests on the continent] have darkened the pages of European history with an indelible stain. His Majesty's Government see in them not the slightest cause to recede in any way from their principles and resolves. . . . On the contrary, their intention to prosecute the war against Germany by every means in their power until Hitlerism is finally broken and the world relieved from the curse which a wicked man has brought upon it has been strengthened to such a point that they would rather all perish in the common ruin than fail or falter in their duty. They firmly believe, however, that with the help of God they will not lack the means to discharge their task.[98]

Nor did Churchill ever retreat an inch from this resolve in the ensuing months and years.

The United States in the Face of World War

The New Deal had followed a course generally of non-entanglement in world affairs, especially those outside the Western Hemisphere. The neutrality acts passed in the 1930s were about as thoroughgoing as any ever enacted. Moreover, the Tydings-McDuffie Act passed in 1934 looked to the future reduction of American presence in the Pacific. It provided for eventual Philippine independence after a period of preparation for self-government. As for Europe, the United States did not participate cooperatively in any major conferences with powers there. The coming of World War II to Europe did not immediately alter this policy which was isolationist in tendency. When war broke out, President Roosevelt proclaimed the neutrality of the United States, though unlike Woodrow Wilson he did not propose that Americans remain neutral in thought as well as in deed. He did proclaim that the arms embargo was in effect, as he was required to do by law.

There was strong sentiment in the United States at the time for taking all measures to stay out of any European war. So far as was known in the fall and winter of 1939–40, Roosevelt shared these sentiments. After Japan extended its war in China in 1937, Roosevelt did make a "Quarantine the Aggressor" speech, calling for collective action to halt aggression. He did not specify what action, and nothing came of it, nor was American policy altered in the wake of the speech. In a radio address September 3, 1939—the day France and Great Britain declared war on Germany, Roosevelt made a radio address in which he declared: "I have said not once but many times that I have seen war and that I hate war. I say that again and again." "And," he continued, "I give you assurances that every effort of your Government will be directed toward that end."[99]

After the Nazi conquest of Norway, Belgium, the Netherlands, and the fall of France, opinion began to shift in America. There was increasing

Winston Churchill (1874–1965)

Illustrated London News

Churchill was Prime Minister of Great Britain during World War II. He rallied the British people behind the war effort when the Axis powers swept across Europe and did all in his power to maintain the British position in the world. A man of boundless energy, he was (more like Theodore Roosevelt than anyone else who comes to mind), a man of many vocations and avocations: soldier, politician, military strategist, biographer, painter, historian, statesman, and orator—as the occasion arose. Churchill was born in Oxfordshire, England, son of a British lord and an American-born mother, educated at Harrow and Sandhurst, which served as the springboard for his early military career. He was elected to the House of Commons in 1900, and was usually a member of that body for most of the rest of his long life. He also served in a number of cabinet positions over the years before becoming prime minister in 1940. Perhaps his best known writings are his multi-volumned *History of the English Speaking Peoples* and *History of World War II*. He was an advocate of the British Empire and labored to hold it together as long as he could. His flair for the dramatic and vision of geo-political activity contributed to his pre-eminent position as a statesman in the 20th century.

alarm, both at the swiftness of the conquests and the range of them. The alarm mounted as Germany unloosed an all out air attack against Britain, preparatory, most likely, to an invasion. There was still outspoken and considerable opposition to getting involved in the war, however. The most outspoken were those in the America First Committee, an organization formed in September 1940. It was chaired by Robert E. Wood of Chicago, but its most vigorous spokesman was Charles A. Lindbergh, famed for making the first solo flight across the Atlantic and drawn to the hearts of Americans when his child was kidnapped and murdered in the early 1930s. The main aim of the committee was to have the United States defend itself and this hemisphere from foreign invasion, but not go overseas and fight. As Lindbergh put it in a speech:

> There is a policy . . . based on the belief that the security of a nation lies in the strength and character of its own people. It recommends the maintenance of armed forces sufficient to defend this hemisphere from attack by any combination of foreign powers. . . . This is the policy of the America First Committee today. It is a policy not of isolation, but of independence; not of defeat, but of courage.[100]

This sentiment was concentrated in the Midwest, and some members of Congress from that region stood ready to defend the position.

There is little reason to doubt that Roosevelt was prepared to give as much aid as he could to Britain by mid–1940, if not before. However, he moved with caution in that direction, because 1940 was an election year, and as nomination time approached it appeared that he would be a candidate for an unprecedented third term. As it turned out, however, foreign affairs posed less of a problem or obstacle to his re-election than he might have feared at first. The Republicans held their convention first. The leading candidates for the presidential nomination were Robert A. Taft of Ohio, Arthur H. Vandenberg of Michigan, and Thomas E. Dewey of New York. Taft and Vandenberg were outspoken opponents of getting involved in the European war, and Dewey was only less so. When the convention was unable to agree on any of these candidates, it proceeded to nominate Wendell Willkie. His nomination signalled a shift away from the moderate conservatism of Republican candidates in the 1920s and 1930s by nominating what came to be called a Liberal Republican. Both Willkie and the Republican platform accepted the main lines of the New Deal legislation, though they were critical about how it was being administered. In foreign affairs, Willkie was barely distinguishable from Roosevelt, and soon after Roosevelt won the election he began using him as a personal representative on foreign missions. In any case, Roosevelt won the election handily by an electoral vote of 449 to 82 for Willkie.

With the election out of the way, Roosevelt moved as quickly as he could to give aid to Britain. Indeed, he was already moving in that direction from mid-1940 onward. To give a bipartisan character to the undertaking, he appointed Republicans Henry L. Stimson to the War Department and Frank Knox to the navy. Large new appropriations for the army and navy were obtained. The neutrality act was modified to enable the United States to sell war goods to Britain on a "cash and carry" basis. The British were suffering from submarine warfare, and Roosevelt traded Britain 50 older destroyers in return for leases on military bases in British territory. The form Roosevelt used in this transaction was to do it by "executive order." No

Charles A. Lindbergh (1902–1974)

Lindbergh gained national and international fame for his solo flight from New York to Paris in 1927. He left Long Island on May 20 at 7:52 A.M. and arrived in Paris on the next evening at 10 P.M., local time. After returning to the United States, he toured the country as a hero. Lindbergh was born in Detroit but grew up in Minnesota. He studied engineering for three semesters at the University of Wisconsin but left to attend flying school. After that, he enlisted in the army as a flying cadet and became an officer upon graduation. The military service did not hold him long, however, for he left it to become a pilot in commercial mail delivery. It was this experience that prepared him for his daring long distance exploits. (He had flown from San Diego to New York before setting out on his first transatlantic flight.) He married Anne Morrow, who became well known for her poetry and other writings. Their first child was kidnapped and murdered, and the Lindberghs became the focus of national attention once again. Lindbergh's opposition to United States involvement in World War II brought criticism from some quarters, but when the United States entered the war, he supported the war effort.

power is granted in the Constitution for Presidents to take such actions by executive order; indeed the prescribed form would be by treaty. No doubt Roosevelt would have pled emergency if he had been challenged, but he was not. Also, in the fall of 1940, Congress passed a Selective Service Act, which authorized the first peacetime draft in American history.

But with the election behind him, Roosevelt moved much more directly. In December, he made his "Arsenal of Democracy" radio address. "We must," he said, "be the great arsenal of democracy. For us this is an emergency as serious as war itself. . . . The people of Europe who are defending themselves do not ask us to do their fighting. They ask us for implements of war, the planes, the tanks, the guns, the freighters. . . . Emphatically we must get these weapons to them in sufficient volume and quickly enough. . . ."[101] In his annual message to Congress in January, 1941, Roosevelt reiterated the point: "They do not need man power. They do need billions of dollars worth of the weapons of defense. . . ."[102] In the following March Congress passed the Lend-Lease Act which authorized the President to provide weapons on just about any basis he could work out with Britain and her allies. During the course of the war in the next several years, the United States extended lend-lease aid to the extent of $51 billion.

Nor did the United States wait long before it was doing more than simply providing aid for those who sent ships for it. In April the United States occupied Greenland with the consent of the Danish government-in-exile and began to patrol the seas part way across the Atlantic. In the course of the year, the United States became more and more belligerent toward the Axis powers: in September, the President ordered naval vessels to shoot German submarines on sight; in September, the navy began to convoy merchant ships as far as Iceland, and in November merchant ships were armed. The United States was, in effect, engaged in an undeclared naval war against the Axis.

The Axis Powers Invade Russia

On Sunday, June 22, 1941, Hitler launched a massive assault into the Soviet Union, supported by assorted allies, including Italy. Sunday was the chosen day for surprise attacks, and the timing of this one was a surprise, though other countries had sought to warn Stalin that it was coming. In the ensuing weeks, Axis forces (mainly German) drove deeply into Russia, and before the advance was halted by the onset of winter, German forces were virtually on the outskirts of Moscow.

Hitler had cleared the decks, so to speak, in Europe before he launched the assault on the Soviet Union. Britain was hardly in a position to open up a front on the continent, and no other power would conceivably do so in the time frame that Hitler expected to overwhelm Russia. There is little reason to doubt that all Hitler's other conquests had been preludes to this main event of conquering Russia, as noted earlier. On the day before the invasion, Hitler wrote to Mussolini, announcing the forthcoming invasion and summarizing the situation as he saw it. In conclusion, he explained: "Since I struggled through to this decision, I again feel spiritually free. The partnership with the Soviet Union, was . . . often very irksome to me, for in some way or other it seemed to me to be a break with my whole origin, my concepts, and my former obligations. I am happy to be relieved of these mental agonies."[103] Hitler obviously underestimated the tenacity and ferocity of the Russians, but even as the war lengthened into years rather than the months which he had hoped, he never changed his mind about who his number one enemy was.

Churchill wasted no time in forming such alliance as he could with the Soviet Union. Roosevelt announced, too, that he would extend lend-lease aid to Russia, the prelude to the eventual alliance. That Britain, and eventually the United States, should form an alliance with the Soviet Union was, to say the least, strange. It was understandable, of course, that Britain should want allies, given the dire situation in Europe and the threat of invasion hanging over her. Indeed, Hitler's armies were on a rampage, and any port in a storm might seem to apply. But, on any larger view, there was little to choose between Hitler and Stalin and the systems they imposed. Walter Winchell, a staccato-voiced radio newscaster, may have had the best suggestion on the Sunday evening of the German invasion of Russia. He suggested that the two should be given every opportunity to destroy one another, while the rest of the world more or less sat on the sidelines. On a scale of 1 to 10 for totalitarian structure, oppression, and aggression, both would rate a 10. There were differences, of course, between Soviet Communism under Stalin and Nazi Germany under Hitler, but they were differences of ideology and tactics, not differences in their assault upon civilization. The immediate threat of the conquest by the Nazis was greater, but the long range threat of Communism was hardly less, and in view of the immense patience of the leaders more likely to be of an enduring variety.

In any case, the Western democracies compromised their own cause by aligning themselves with a totalitarian power, and unequally yoked themselves to rulers whose purposes and ways were barely akin to their own. The Soviet designs and aims were unaltered by the alliance, and many of the consequences of this wartime alliance are still with us.

Pearl Harbor

The conquest of the Netherlands and the Fall of France in the early summer of 1940 changed the power situation in the Pacific greatly. For the aggressive-minded Japanese, it looked as if French Indochina and the Dutch East Indies might be up for grabs. With the German pressure on Britain, another European presence in the orient was weakened. The British (to the extent that they still did), the United States, and the Russians were the only remaining restraints on the Japanese. In September, 1940, the Japanese succeeded in extorting from Vichy France the rights to bases in Indochina and a few days later entered into a military alliance with Germany and Italy, thus consolidating a Rome-Berlin-Tokyo Axis. This gave the Japanese a free hand in the Pacific as far as the other Axis powers were concerned. When Germany invaded Russia, that shifted Russian attention away from the Pacific, as the Soviet leaders were in a desperate fight to survive.

Meanwhile, relations between the United States and Japan progressively deteriorated from 1940 onward. The United States had opposed the Japanese operations in China all along. In the middle of 1940, the United States banned the shipment of scrap metals and aviation gasoline to Japan. This country also entered into talks with the British and Dutch with a view to holding the line against Japanese expansion and gave increased aid to Chiang Kai-shek's Chinese government. Early in 1941, the Japanese foreign office warned the American government that it would have to change its policies or take the consequences. During the early part of 1941, however, Japan also offered some terms for settlement that contained concessions. They were unacceptable on a variety of grounds, but mainly because they would destroy the independence of China. The occupation of French Indochina in the middle of the year by the Japanese pushed the United States almost to the point of breaking relations. On July 26, 1941, the United States embargoed all oil shipments and froze Japanese assets in this country.

Hideki Tojo (1884–1948)

Tojo was a Japanese general and premier of Japan during World War II. He attended the Imperial Military Academy and became a commissioned officer upon graduation. He rose through the ranks to become commander of an army in China in the late 1930s. In 1940, Tojo was appointed minister of war in Prince Konoye's cabinet, in which he was one of the militant expansionists. When Konoye's cabinet fell in the middle of 1941, Tojo became premier, a position which he held until mid-1944. After Japan surrendered, Tojo tried to commit suicide, but he failed and was nursed back to health to face trial for war crimes before a United States tribunal. He was found guilty and hanged.

Exchanges and discussions between the two countries continued, but neither side made any concessions. A new government was formed in October, headed by General Hideki Tojo. Tojo was the leader of the militant expansionists, and after he became head of the government an expansion of the war in the Pacific became a virtual certainty. Who it would be a against was never so certain. To cover their plans, the Japanese had negotiators in Washington, presumably earnestly seeking a settlement. While this was going on, the Japanese fleet put to sea secretly in late November. By December 1, Roosevelt was sufficiently well informed to know that war was imminent and was virtually certain that it would come by a surprise attack. The bulk of the Pacific fleet was at Pearl Harbor in Hawaii, at great distance from Japan and in a port unlikely to be attacked.

Early on Sunday morning, December 7, 1941, a surprise assault was launched against Pearl Harbor by a combined Japanese submarine and airplane force. The airplanes had been brought within flying distance by aircraft carriers. They swooped down upon the ships in harbor, strafing, dropping bombs, and launching torpedoes. They attacked surrounding military installations as well. The attack came in two separate waves and lasted a little less than two hours. It had a devastating impact. Eight battleships, three cruisers, and nearly 200 aircraft were destroyed or severely damaged. There were 3500 casualties on the American side. The main body of the Pacific fleet had been put out of action indefinitely. On the same day, the Japanese made assaults on the Philippines and Guam and on British forces at Hong Kong and on the Malay Peninsula.

The next day, President Roosevelt asked for a declaration of war against Japan, and Congress obliged with only one dissenting vote. On December 11, Germany and Italy, in keeping with their commitments, declared war on the United States. The United States was now a full-fledged belligerent in World War II.

A Postscript to Pearl Harbor

There is no reason to doubt that President Roosevelt had followed a course of increasing involvement in World War II, beginning in 1940 and intensifying throughout 1941. The United States was engaged in an undeclared, though somewhat limited, naval war against Germany for much of 1941. More broadly, there is no doubt that Roosevelt's sympathies were with Britain and her allies and opposed to Axis expansion. Opinions may differ as to the rightness of this course, but Americans generally and the Congress in particular was leaning in the same direction during the year or so before war came. There were charges at the time, however, and controversies have arisen since, over whether or not Roosevelt maneuvered the United States into war.

The most vigorous of these controversies has surrounded the attack on

Pearl Harbor itself. These were sparked by charges that Roosevelt enticed the Japanese to attack at Pearl Harbor by concentrating the fleet there and withheld information from military commanders there that would have led them to prepare for the assault. For example, Rear Admiral Robert A. Theobald charged (in 1954 in a book published after his retirement) that Roosevelt "applied ever-increasing diplomatic-economic pressure upon Japan . . . ; terminated the Washington conference . . . , which gave Japan no choice but surrender or war; retained a weak Pacific fleet in Hawaiian waters, where it served only one diplomatic purpose, an invitation to a Japanese surprise attack; furthered that surprise by causing Hawaiian Commanders to be denied invaluable information from decoded Japanese dispatches. . . ."[104]

In later years following Pearl Harbor, several investigations were held on the facts surrounding the event. President Roosevelt appointed a commission which concluded in 1942 that Admiral Husband E. Kimmel and General Walter C. Short, the military commanders in Hawaii, had failed to take necessary defensive measures despite repeated warnings from Washington. In 1944, the Army and Navy departments held their own investigations. They concluded both that the commanders had not been fully warned and that they had not sufficiently alerted their own forces, but that there were no valid grounds for court-martial charges to be placed against either Short or Kimmel.

Beginning in 1945, a joint Congressional committee held an extensive investigation which lasted for several months. The committee findings were stated in a majority report and a minority report. The central conclusion of the majority was that "The committee has found no evidence to support the charges . . . that the President, the Secretary of State, the Secretary of War, or the Secretary of the Navy tricked, provoked, incited, cajoled, or coerced Japan into attacking this Nation in order that a declaration of war might be more easily obtained from the Congress. . . ." More, "The ultimate responsibility for the attack and its results rests upon Japan, an attack that was well planned and skillfully executed."[105] However, the majority went on to state that the War and Navy departments did not sufficiently alert commanders in Hawaii, but that the commanders did not take the warranted precautions dictated by information available to them.

The majority report attempted to exonerate high officials in Washington, including the President from any responsibility for the disaster at Pearl Harbor. The minority report, by contrast, charged that the President was responsible in the failure to fully evaluate and convey what was known to the commanders in the field. Neither report alleged any conspiracy in high places specifically, though the minority report cites indications that the Administration had decided to wait to be drawn into the war. The full-fledged conspiracy theory was a scenario devised after the fact. It assumes that what did happen could have been known—indeed was known—by the

Administration beforehand. No evidence that has come to light proves that this was the case. Nor is it likely that President Roosevelt would have deliberately chosen to sacrifice the Pacific fleet in order to go to war. The Navy was, after all, his favorite branch of service, and his connections with it went back to World War I. Surely, the basic plan was made and executed by the Japanese, not in Washington.

Chapter 6

The United States in World War II

The war cannot be ended by driving Japan back to her own bounds and defeating her overseas forces. The war can only be ended through the defeat in Europe of the German armies. . . .

—Winston Churchill, 1941

The governments of the United States of America, United Kingdom, the Soviet Union and China: United in their determination . . . to continue hostilities against those Axis powers with which they are respectively at war until such powers have laid down their arms on the basis of unconditional surrender.

—Moscow Conference, 1943

The Teheran decision [by Roosevelt, Churchill, and Stalin] . . . led to the domination of Eastern and Central Europe by Russia and the postwar upset in the European balance of power which has been so obvious since the war.

—Hanson W. Baldwin, 1950

Chronology

1942—

May—Philippines fall to Japan
August—United States launches Pacific offensive at Guadalcanal
November—Anglo-American offensive in North Africa

1943—

July—Anglo-American invasion of Sicily
November—Teheran Conference

1944—

June 6—D Day, Allied landing in France
September—Liberation of France and Belgium
December—Battle of the Bulge

1945—

February—Yalta Conference
May 8—Victory in Europe
August 6—Atomic bombs dropped on Hiroshima
August 14—Japan Surrenders

The United States became a major participant in World War II following the declaration of the war. There was no illusion that it could be otherwise, as there was in 1917, that the United States could simply provide the war materials, send a token military force, and depend upon allies to win the war. The truth was that there was only one power on the Eurasian land mass in late 1941 that might conceivably have conquered the Axis—the Soviet Union. But the Soviet Union was not at war with Japan then (and would not go to war with that country until a few weeks before the end in 1945) and was in a desperate struggle with Nazi Germany for survival. Not even Stalin believed very strongly in late 1941 that the Russians could turn the tide against Germany, much less take on the Japanese.

Moreover, the situation worsened for the United States and her allies in the weeks and months that followed Pearl Harbor. The British Crown Colony at Hong Kong fell quickly to the Japanese, nor did it take them long to overcome the heavily fortified Singapore. The Japanese already had hold of French Indochina and occupied Burma, thus cutting the land connection between India and China and threatening India itself. Meanwhile, they launched an all out attack on the Philippines. General Douglas MacArthur attempted to defend that American possession with a small combined Philippine and American army, which was greatly outnumbered by the Japanese. He made his stand on Bataan Peninsula, but in March, 1942, he was transferred to Australia, vowing as he left that he would return. General Jonathan Wainwright was left in command of such forces as were left in the Philippines, and he surrendered his remnant in May, 1942. Guam and Wake Island had already been seized. The Japanese swept through the Dutch East Indies and islands of the South Pacific until they were in New Guinea, within flying distance of Australia.

The European Axis powers had already consolidated their hold on continental Europe and during more than half of 1942 were extending their reach into North Africa. Their threat to the Suez Canal was mounting, and the prospect might well be that India would fall to the Japanese and Germany would thrust into the Middle East to consolidate their hold on southern Asia. Only two powers on the Eurasian continent opposed them: the Soviet Union and China. Japan continued the war in China, and, as already noted, the Germans started another massive offensive in the Soviet Union in 1942.

It was clear almost from the outset, then, that the United States must play a major role if the Eurasian land mass, North Africa, at least, and most of the territory bordered by the Pacific was not to be conceded to the Axis. A supplementary role by the United States might fail. The United States might have concentrated on defeating Japan, of course, and offered only as much of war materials as could be spared to Britain and Russia. But, as we shall see, the strategy of President Roosevelt involved a quite different course.

Mobilization for War

The Roosevelt Administration proceeded as quickly as it could toward full-scale mobilization after Pearl Harbor. It did so within the framework already established by the New Deal, of government regulation and control over the economy, of deficit spending, of progressive taxation, of government planning, of redistribution of the wealth, and of the concentration of political power in Washington. Indeed, all this was greatly accelerated during the war. The welfare state was not abandoned; instead, it was advanced as necessary for the war effort, a real war this time. Constitutional restrictions on the powers of the federal government were generally ignored, especially as they related to control over economic matters. There was no organized opposition to the war effort, as there had been during World War I. Communists were technically behind the effort, since the war was being fought in alliance with the Soviet Union. Socialists were either supportive of the war or remained quiet. Thus, the government actions usually went unchallenged except by such "loyal opposition" as existed in Congress. In short, the tremendous growth and expansion of power of the general government, and especially the presidency, had little effective opposition.

Partial mobilization had been begun and was underway for over a year before Pearl Harbor. The peacetime draft had been authorized in 1940, and the service of those had been extended for six months in 1941. At the time of Pearl Harbor, there were already 1,600,000 men in the military services. After war had been declared, Congress approved the registration of all men between the ages of twenty and forty-four for military service. Actually, few men over the age of thirty-eight were ever drafted, and in practice the draft age was reduced to 38. In November, 1942, the draft age was lowered to 18. General Lewis B. Hershey directed the draft as Selective Service Director. Local volunteer boards classified those who registered, exempting or deferring calling up those who were in certain categories, and filling their quotas for draftees from those otherwise available. All told, 9,867,707 men were drafted into the armed forces during World War II, and their ranks were swelled by volunteers, so that over 15 million served during the war. In addition, women volunteers were accepted in the army and navy, in the army as WACs and the navy as WAVEs. These performed such non-combat functions as office work, jeep drivers, and the like.

A vast construction and production effort was required to outfit and supply the American armed forces as well as to send the large quantities of aid to allies. Much of the productive activity of Americans was diverted from production for domestic consumption to production for war. The armed forces required not only uniforms, rifles, warships, tanks, artillery pieces, war planes, submarines, ammunition, and every sort of weapon of war but also housing, airfields, trucks, construction equipment, and a vast assortment of supplies. An assortment of offices was created to coordinate this giant productive effort, but the most important was the War Production Board under the direction of Donald Nelson.

Many methods were devised to obtain the diversion of productive effort, ranging from patriotic appeals to threats to government controls of one sort or another. Workers were induced to go where they were wanted and to stay by higher wages, exemption from military service, and being prohibited to

Douglas MacArthur (1880–1964)

U.S. Army

MacArthur was one of the military heroes of World War II. He was military commander in the Pacific, administered the occupation of Japan after the war, and was a successful commander of United Nations forces in Korea until President Truman dismissed him from command. He was born in Arkansas, the son of a professional army officer, graduated from West Point first in his class, and followed a military career for most of his life. MacArthur served in France during World War I, as superintendent at West Point for several years, and gained a variety of other valuable experience during the 1920s. In 1930, he was appointed Chief of Staff of the Army, went on later to become military adviser to the Philippines, where he retired from the army to take up a command there. He was recalled to active duty with the United States Army in 1941 and was soon engaged in the desperate attempt to defend the Philippines against the Japanese with a combined Philippine and American army inadequate for the undertaking. Afterward, he commanded Allied forces in the South Pacific, led the forces that wrested the Philippines from the Japanese, and prepared for the invasion of Japan. During the Korean conflict, MacArthur sought to win the war, but this got him into difficulty with President Truman, and he was dismissed. He returned to the United States to receive a hero's welcome.

leave employments without permission. All automobile production for private sale was brought to a halt early in 1942. The 1942 models had come out and a number of cars were produced and sold, but after production was halted no more new models were introduced during the war, and none were sold in the markets during the war. A limited number of the 1942 models continued to be produced during the war for government and military use. Rubber for the building of tires was soon in short supply, since the main sources of raw rubber had been occupied by the Japanese. Tires were then allocated to the civilian market by a system of rationing. A crash program for developing synthetic rubber got underway, and during the course of the war large quantities were produced both for the civilian market and the armed services.

The manner in which the war was financed affected many of the other programs of government control, so that it should be discussed at this point. A part of the cost of the war was paid by the increase of taxes and expansion of the base for the income tax. First, the tax base for the income tax was greatly broadened. In 1939, only about 4 million people paid tax on incomes, and even in 1941 after the expansion of defense production had occurred, only about 17 million fell under the income tax. By the Revenue Act of 1942, 50 million people were required to pay income taxes. This was achieved by lowering drastically the minimum income taxed as well as by rising wages. The base tax rate was increased from 4 to 6 per cent, and the graduated tax (or surtax) from 13 per cent on the first $2,000 up to 82 per cent on income in excess of $200,000. It also incorporated an "excess profits" tax which virtually confiscated all income above a certain level. The corporate tax was greatly increased, as were assorted excise and inheritance taxes.

The war provided the occasion for introducing withholding taxes from payrolls. Before World War II, most employees did not pay income taxes, indeed, were not accustomed to setting aside the money to pay taxes at the end of the annual tax period. Collection of taxes from all these new taxpayers promised to be a heavy burden for the government. A financier, Beardsley Ruml, proposed the system of payroll deductions that was adopted. Undoubtedly, this method made collection easier for the Internal Revenue Service, but it rather clearly took the property of the taxpayer without what was theretofore due process of law. That is, it evaded the restraint on government contained in the Fifth Amendment to the Constitution (to say nothing of the fact that it made employers into tax collectors). Under the system of payroll deduction, the taxpayer never actually receives the amount that is deducted. In consequence, he cannot hang on to the money and make the government collect it by due process through the courts, if that is his wish. Due process for the collection of taxes is short circuited, so to speak, by payroll deduction.

Even with the broadened base for income tax and the much higher rates, a large portion of the war costs were not covered by revenue from taxes. The national debt increased from $49 billion in 1941 to $259 billion by 1945. An extended effort was made to borrow money from Americans generally through the sale of war bonds. If individuals bought bonds, the effect of the rising government debt would not be inflationary, i.e., would not result in an increase of the money supply. But the large sales of war bonds to individuals were not sufficient to make up for the government deficit. The government made up the difference by selling securities within the banking system. "In effect," as one historian says, "the banking system monetized this part of the federal debt."[106] To put it another way, the banking system expanded the credit greatly on the basis of these government securities. To cover the greatly increased spending the Federal Reserve increased the currency in circulation from approximately $8 billion to just under $27 billion during the war years. There was, then, a large monetary inflation during the war.

With the large amount of new credit and money entering the economy, the natural result was rising prices. Prices would normally have risen in any case, but with so much of production diverted to war production (there was more money chasing less goods, as some economists say) prices could be expected to rise dramatically. To counteract this, the government adopted an assortment of price and wage controls. The Office of Price Administration (OPA) became the most familiar of government agencies during the war. It had been set up in 1941, but had little authority. The authority was considerably increased in January, 1942, by act of Congress, but the administrator, Leon Henderson, still had difficulty in holding the line on food prices. Thus, Roosevelt asked for, and got, much more comprehensive legislation later on in 1942. Congress authorized the President to "stabilize" wages, prices, and salaries at their level as of September 15, 1942. Roosevelt added the Office of Economic Stabilization to his list of economic control organizations, appointed James F. Byrnes of South Carolina to head it, but continued the OPA for related functions. Actually, prices and wages continued to rise somewhat during the war; most of them were never frozen for long. The major labor union organizations adopted a "no-strike pledge" for wartime, but this hardly prevented a goodly number of strikes from taking place. There were nearly 15,000 strikes in the course of the war. For one thing, the War Labor Board encouraged unionization, and for another the wage controls were arbitrary. John L. Lewis called a general strike of coal miners in 1943. Roosevelt seized the mines; the workers continued to work temporarily, but very shortly struck again. The President then threatened to ask Congress for power to draft the miners, but even that only briefly delayed the making of concessions to keep the miners at work.

Price ceilings that keep prices below what they would be on the market result in shortages. Wage ceilings below market levels tend to result in a shortage of workers. Indeed, such shortages of goods were common during the war; some were so scarce that they could rarely be obtained except on the black market (another development which usually accompanies price controls). To equalize the shortages, the government turned to rationing of goods reckoned to be essential. Thus, automobiles, tires, gasoline, sugar, shoes, fuel oil, and coffee were rationed. Many other types of goods were often unavailable.

It is often alleged that World War II brought an end to the Great Depression in the United States. It is true, of course, that significant unemployment ended with the war effort. With millions of men in the armed forces it is likely that unemployment would have disappeared even if there had been no great increase in production. It is true, also, that people generally had much more money during the war than during the 1930s. It does not follow, however, that the depression had ended. A much better explanation is that the government had shifted the direction of its exercise of power and that the ongoing character of the depression had changed accordingly. The thrust of the government programs in the 1930s had been to raise prices and wages. The economic consequence of this effort was a surplus of goods and manpower. During the war, the government attempted to impose a ceiling on prices, wages, and rents. The result was shortages of goods, manpower, and housing. In like manner, the diversion of productive effort from making consumer to war goods aggravated the shortages. The depression of surpluses was replaced by a depression of shortages during World War II. The greatest shortage was of new automobiles. They were neither produced for the civilian market nor available during World War II. Many other goods were in varying degrees either in short supply or frequently not available. Construction for civilian purposes was drastically curtailed during the war. The shortage depression was largely over by or before 1947, and that may be a better date for the ending of the Great Depression than the ones usually given.

Grand Strategy for War

The United States was involved in a war that extended from the frigid Aleutian Islands to the balmy South Pacific to the China-Burma-India theater to North Africa to Europe to Eurasia. If the war at sea be included, it was truly a global war, leaving no ocean or continent untouched. Huge quantities of materials and vast numbers of men were deployed over large portions of the world: great armies, large fleets, and many thousands of aircraft. At the strategic level, the basic decisions for this vast effort were made by a handful of men with their military advisers and diplomats. The broadest and most far-reaching decisions for the allies were made by three men: Winston Churchill, Franklin D. Roosevelt, and the man known as Joseph Stalin. For the European Axis, the broad decisions were made by Adolf Hitler, though, until 1943, Benito Mussolini had a hand in some of the decisions. The Japanese made their own strategic decisions, and for most of the war, decision making was in the hands of Hideki Tojo. Chiang Kai-shek of China was sometimes consulted by the allies, and leaders and diplomats from other countries played minor roles. In the main, though, it was Churchill, Roosevelt, and Stalin on the one side and Hitler, Mussolini, and Tojo on the other.

Although many decisions were made that made up the grand strategy of the war, three of them at least had broad and long range consequences. They were: to concentrate on the European war and relegate the war against Japan to second place; to require the unconditional surrender of the Axis powers; and to concentrate British and American forces on a cross-channel invasion of the continent by way of northern France.

The Soviet Union had little choice but to concentrate on driving the Germans off Russian soil, for they had planted themselves deep into Russia. The British had a pressing interest in the early defeat of the Germans as well, since only the English Channel separated them from the might of the German armies. The decision for the United States, by contrast, was not nearly so obvious. The Japanese had clearly started the war with the United States, had struck at American forces, and were clearly the number one enemy. There was no direct threat to the United States or any of its possessions by the European Axis. It is true that the United States had been largely peopled by immigrants from Europe and that cultural ties were closest to Europe. On the other hand, except for Wilson's aberration from it during and immediately after World War I, America's long-term commitment had been not to become entangled in European wars and internal affairs. The concentration of American forces in Europe set the stage for the postwar entanglement in Europe.

Be all that as it may, there is no evidence that Roosevelt agonized greatly over this decision. He was probably as good as committed to it by the time the United States entered the war. Churchill and Roosevelt had already held meetings and were in close contact from 1940 onward. They had met and proclaimed the Atlantic Charter which set forth their idealistic aims for the world of the future. Churchill held that Hitler was the number one enemy and that the defeat of Germany should be the number one priority. As and when Stalin exerted influence, it was toward getting all the forces that he could focused on Hitler. Roosevelt agreed with them, and the American force had the top priority of defeating the European Axis.

The decision to require unconditional surrender of the Axis powers had been reached as early as the Casablanca Conference between Roosevelt and Churchill in January, 1943. At any rate, in a radio address to Americans following the conference, Roosevelt said "that the only terms on which we shall deal with an Axis government or any Axis factions are the terms proclaimed at Casablanca: 'Unconditional Surrender.' In our uncompromising policy we mean no harm to the common people of the Axis nations. But we do mean to impose punishment and retribution in full upon their guilty, barbaric leaders. . . ."[107] As a result of a conference in Moscow in October, 1943 between Cordell Hull for the United States, Anthony Eden for Britain, and V. M. Molotov for the Soviet Union, a joint declaration was issued, committing their nations, plus China, to continue hostilities until the Axis had "laid down their arms on the basis of unconditional surrender."[108] The foreign secretaries also gave publicity to a declaration of Roosevelt, Churchill and Stalin "that at the time of granting any armistice to any German government, those German officers and men and members of the Nazi party who have had any connection with atrocities . . . in countries overrun by German forces" would be turned over to those countries to be punished according to their laws for crimes committed.[109]

The requirement of unconditional surrender and the threat of punishing those who had been in power virtually guaranteed that these people would hold out to the bitter end, as indeed the German rulers did, and the Japanese almost did. These positions undoubtedly contributed to the ferocity of the war on both sides. Many of the Allied bombing raids of German cities could best be justified, if at all, on the grounds that all inhabitants were somehow guilty and should be punished. Moreover, it left the Germans with no recognizable government at the end of the war and left all the defeated countries powerless. In short, it made World War II a total war in a different dimension, a war to the point that one side had been destroyed.

The third decision—to concentrate Anglo-American forces for a cross-channel invasion into northern France—may need some further background. As early as 1942 Stalin was insisting that the Western Allies open up a "second front" on the continent of Europe. When Churchill informed Stalin in mid-1942 of the decision of the Western Allies to undertake an invasion of North Africa, Stalin replied in terms that suggested he had been betrayed. He declared "that the refusal of the Government of Great Britain to create a second front in 1942 in Europe inflicts a mortal blow to the whole of Soviet public opinion, which calculates on the creation of a second front, and that it complicates the situation of the Red Army at the front and prejudices the plan of the Soviet command. . . ."[110] Stalin not only wanted the Western Allies to open a second front in Europe but he also wanted a second front across the English Channel into France, not just any second front. In short, he wanted to specify the general location of the front.

In fact, Stalin was suspicious of the West, or pretended to be. Indeed, Stalin was paranoid about people in general, according to a vast amount of direct and indirect evidence, and was always employing the secret police to gather evidence of conspiracies against him and his regime. Western leaders would have done well to be much more suspicious of him and his intentions than they were. That the Soviet Union had territorial ambitions, especially in Eastern Europe, was hardly a secret. The Nazi-Soviet Pact and the Soviet expansion which followed it provided evidence enough of these ambitions.

Further demands for expansion were made for territory in Eastern Europe when Anthony Eden went to Moscow in late 1941 to work out details of an Anglo-Soviet Alliance. Moreover the alliance itself was a very one-sided affair. One history says that the Russians "resisted close coordination of the Allied war effort and often acted unilaterally in matters of diplomacy and military strategy."[111] That understates the case, however; the Russians were downright uncooperative. The United States sent billions of dollars of lend-lease aid to the Soviet Union during the war. The Soviet Union even contributed to making delivery of this aid difficult by designating and restricting ports to which it could be delivered and severely limiting air flights over Soviet territory. The Soviet Union did dissolve the Comintern under Allied pressure, but it was of little consequence, for spying and subversion in Allied countries continued to be directed from Moscow. There were no joint military operations between the Western Allies and the Soviet Union, nor did the Western Allies have any direction over Soviet strategy.

By contrast, Stalin wielded great influence on British and American strategy. He did this in a way that greatly altered the course of events in pressing for an Anglo-American invasion into France to open up what he was pleased to call a "second front." The decision for this was confirmed at the first meeting of the "Big Three"—Roosevelt, Churchill, and Stalin—in December, 1943 at Teheran. The clamor for a "second front" went on apace from 1942 until the actual invasion in 1944. It was not only pushed officially by the Soviet Union government but also by numerous Communists and sympathizers in other lands. That the Allies had already opened a second front in Europe months before Teheran by the invasion Italy was ignored by Stalin and his claque of supporters. They had decided that there could only be one second front in Europe by the Western Allies, and until such a front had been opened in northwestern France there was no second front in their vocabulary.

Why was this decision so crucial? Because the fate of the people and countries of eastern Europe depended on where the Axis were defeated and by whom. That may not have been so clear in 1943 as it has become since 1945, but there is good reason to believe that Stalin was clear about what he intended. Winston Churchill grasped, too, something of the geopolitical significance of Anglo-American strategy. One of the proposals that Churchill still favored as late as the Teheran Conference was an invasion through the Balkans, through the "soft underbelly of Europe," as it was sometimes called. Churchill described his idea this way: "Alternatively [to an invasion through southern France], I preferred a right-handed movement from the north of Italy, using the Istrian peninsula . . . , towards Vienna. . . . If the Germans resisted, we should attract many of their divisions from the Russian or Channel fronts. If we were not resisted, we should liberate at little cost enormous and invaluable regions. . . ."[112] What Churchill did not say was that such a move, if it were a major effort, might keep the Soviet armies out of most of non-Soviet Europe. According to his later account, however, Churchill did not envision a major invasion through the Balkans.

Whether he did or not, it was certainly a live possibility for 1944. When the Big Three met at Teheran, much of the Anglo-American force was in Italy and the Mediterranean. The possibility of conquering most of Italy loomed on the horizon, and after that they could move in several directions. The cross-channel invasion would require, as indeed it did require, the moving of much of that force back to Britain. American forces that were eventually moved from the United States to Britain for the cross-channel invasion might as easily have gone to the Mediterranean. Assaults could have been launched both through the Balkans and southern France. A successful operation through the Balkans would have knocked out the remainder of Hitler's allies and taken away such vital resources as the Rumanian oilfields. It would both have relieved pressure on the Soviet armies and provided an opportunity for many of the countries of eastern Europe to retain or regain their independence. Nor need it have precluded a cross-channel invasion, if enough of German forces were occupied elsewhere.

The Balkan invasion was not to be, of course. Stalin continued to press throughout for the cross-channel invasion. The reasons why he did so are easy enough to surmise. It placed the bulk of the Anglo-American forces at a great distance from eastern Europe, with Germany between them and the prize he sought. It would also keep the Anglo-American forces far removed from any of the countries adjoining Russia. On these strategic questions, Roosevelt showed no great interest and little resolve, except for the cross-channel invasion. Churchill says that "the President was oppressed by the prejudices of his military advisers, and drifted to and fro in the argument, with the result that the whole of these subsidiary but gleaming opportunities were cast aside unused. Our American friends were comforted in their obstinacy by the reflection that 'at any rate we have stopped Churchill entangling us in the Balkans.' "[113] Actually, Churchill appears to have been more interested in luring Turkey into the war and securing some islands than in the Balkans. As for Roosevelt, he went out of the way generally to placate Stalin.

One scholar has pointed out that "The Teheran Conference determined the future map of Europe when the decision was made for an Anglo-American invasion from the west and a Russian attack from the east. Of all the wartime conferences, this one had the most lasting effect on the political outlines of Europe."[114] His meaning was this. The countries of eastern Europe that were occupied by the oncoming Red armies—Poland, Czechoslovakia, Hungary, Bulgaria, Rumania, Yugoslavia, and Albania—became satellite states of the Soviet Union. This occurred because there was no Western presence in this area, and the decision not to invade that area became final at Teheran.

It has often been argued that Poland and, to a lesser extent, other countries in eastern Europe were betrayed at Yalta in February, 1945. Actually, the fate of most of these countries was already almost sealed when the Big Three met at Yalta. Churchill summarized the situation this way on the eve of Yalta: "Romania and Bulgaria had passed into the grip of Soviet military occupation, Hungary and Yugoslavia lay in the shadow of the battlefield, and Poland, though liberated from the Germans had merely exchanged one conqueror for another."[115] The most that Churchill and Roosevelt could do at Yalta was to make some effort to restrain the Soviet appetite for additional territory.

What went on at Yalta does illustrate, however, the awesome power in the hands of a few men during World War II. This was particularly apparent in their discussion of the boundaries of Poland after the war. The Soviet Union insisted upon, and got, considerable territory in eastern Poland. To compensate Poland, Stalin proposed that Poland have territory in Germany. This would involve the relocation of several million Germans. Churchill explained his position this way: "I replied that the question was whether there was room for them in what was left of Germany. . . . I was not afraid of the problem of transferring populations, so long as it was proportionate to what the Poles could manage and to what could be put into Germany. But it was a matter which required study, not as a question of principle, but the numbers which would have to be handled."[116] The audacity of this discussion may need to be highlighted. There were no representatives of either the Poles or the Germans involved at Yalta. Stalin presumed to speak for Poland, though his only claim to do so was based on military occupation. No thought was even given to allowing Germans to participate in any discussions or negotiations; the implication was that the German people as well as the military forces were the enemy. The central point here, however, is that three men with their advisers were discussing the disposition of millions of people and large chunks of territory without regard to the wills and rights of those involved. Churchill and Roosevelt, at least, were presumably civilized men, yet they did not draw back in horror from what they were doing. They had become acclimated to the exercise of vast power on which the restraints had been removed.

Weapons, Tactics, and Commanders

World War II was a war of movement, of mobility. Not only was this so because of the vast intercontinental scale of the war but also because of the dominant tactics. No longer could large armies be concentrated and battles be fought with them in a confined area. Machine guns could wipe out concentrated forces; artillery could bombard them, and in World War II, aircraft could demolish them with machine guns and bombs. They had to disperse and keep moving to survive. Communication has always been essential to the control and direction of military forces, but under the conditions of World War II, radio and telephonic communication played a major role. Indeed, it made possible the control over widely dispersed forces.

The airplane came into its own during World War II as a weapon of war. The only aircraft used extensively during the war were heavier than air and propeller driven. Jet propulsion was still mostly in the experimental stage, and the helicopter was still an experimental device. The Germans were further along with rocket development than the Allies, and they did some long-range bombing with their V-1 and V-2 rockets. The workhorse of American aircraft was the single-engine P-47, which was relatively slow, but heavily armed with 50-caliber machine guns and bombs on the wings. The B-17 was the basic heavy bomber during most of the war. One other airplane needs special mention for its role during the war—the Piper "cub"—which served extensively as observer for artillery. These were light single-engined planes, had no armament, and were slow, but they did an amazing job of spotting enemy artillery and calling down fire on it. Airplanes served as troop support, as fighter protection from enemy aircraft, and most devastatingly as bombers. Since the range of most planes was quite limited, aircraft carriers were used extensively, and to good effect, against the Japanese especially.

Although air superiority was undoubtedly crucial in many battles, battles were won and territory taken by foot soldiers, the Army infantry and the Marines. Although tremendous effort was put into the bombing of cities and factories, it is easy to exaggerate the extent to which these efforts altered the course of the war. The bombing of cities night after night was often a war of nerves on civilians; the barbarity of it from whichever side can hardly be exaggerated; but it had less impact on winning the war than might be supposed. Nor was its effect on war production as decisive as it was hoped. Production was dispersed or put underground so that it continued after otherwise devastating air-raids. Even "blockbuster bombs," as they were called, produced no surrenders. The atomic bombs dropped on Hiroshima and Nagasaki hastened the Japanese surrender, but it could probably have been obtained earlier on the terms that were actually accepted.

In the final analysis, it was riflemen, usually equipped with M-1 rifles, who won the battles and took territory. They were supported by light machine guns and mortars, men carrying Browning Automatic Rifles, grenade launchers, and the like, within their companies. In addition, each infantry battalion had a heavy weapons company which provided heavy machine guns and mortars. Regiments had their own artillery companies and other support forces. These infantry troops made the breakthroughs usually, though tanks often played an important role, won the battles, and captured the prisoners. Against the Japanese, flamethrowers were used against personnel in dug-in positions, but in Europe hand grenades were the main weapon employed in such circumstances. One new weapon developed during the war was of major assistance to the infantry when confronted by tanks. It was the bazooka, a rocket launcher that required only two men to fire, and it was portable.

Among the new devices placed in operation during the war, perhaps radar had the most widespread and large-scale use. The British developed effective radar equipment first, and it enabled them to locate and detect German airplanes coming in for raids during late 1940 and to make these raids too expensive for Hitler to continue on a large scale. Radar could not only detect and locate airplanes early but also submarines. Used in fighters and bombers it greatly increased their effectiveness. The most extensive research and productive effort, however, was put into developing the atomic bomb. Much of this effort was spurred by the fear that the Germans would develop such a bomb first and use it to conquer the world. Professor Niels Bohr told American physicists in 1939 that the Germans had made a major breakthrough toward such a bomb. Between 1939 and 1943, physicists solved the main technical problems toward making an atomic bomb. The task of building the bombs was given to General Leslie R. Groves, and the work was done in secret at plants located at Oak Ridge, Tennessee and Hanford, Washington.

Although the United States had only a small army in the interwar years, some remarkable men emerged from it to lead the huge armies of World War II. The work at the highest levels dealt almost exclusively with broad

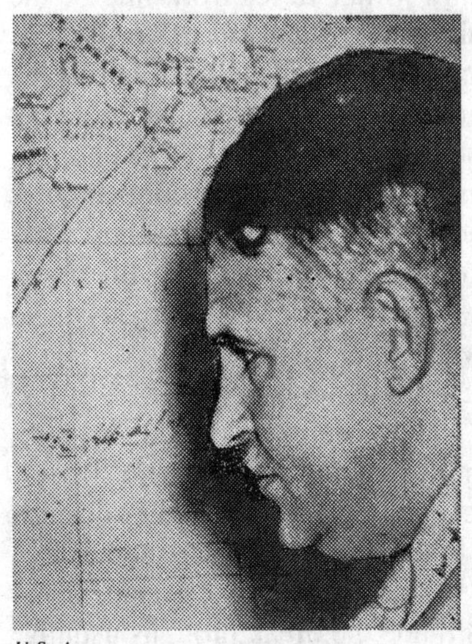

U.S. Army

Leslie R. Groves (1896–1970)

Groves was an army officer who headed the Manhattan Project for developing the atomic bomb. He was born in New York, graduated from West Point, trained as an engineer, and became head of military construction. When the decision was made to proceed with research toward developing an atomic bomb, he headed the top secret research project in which scientists solved the problems surrounding making and exploding an atomic bomb. It was a battle against time, since there was the possibility that the Germans might develop one first. Groves retired from military service after the war and went into private industry.

strategy and organization. Indeed, the organization and coordination of assaults involved hundreds of thousands of men, numerous specialties and skills, and often billions of dollars worth of equipment. Any given assault would be likely to involve the coordination of air attacks, artillery, perhaps naval support and all the various supply units. General George C. Marshall served as Chief of Staff of the Army during the war and probably occupied the single most powerful position. Roosevelt relied heavily on Marshall, who was reputed to have great organization skill. Admiral Ernest J. King was Marshall's counterpart for the Navy. Since the most extensive naval operations were in the Pacific, some of the commanders in the field there were better known than Admiral King. Commander for the Pacific was

National Archives

George C. Marshall (1880–1959)

General Marshall was Army Chief of Staff during World War II, organized the vast military undertaking that sent American soldiers and supplies to the far corners of the world, and was Roosevelt's leading military adviser. President Truman leaned even more heavily upon him after the war, for he appointed him head of a mission to China, appointed him Secretary of State, and then Secretary of Defense in that newly created position. Marshall was born in Pennsylvania, graduated from Virginia Military Institute, and entered the infantry as an officer. He served in France under Pershing during World War I and held several commands in the interwar years, usually in an executive position. In 1939, Roosevelt appointed him chief of Staff, a position which he held throughout the war years. His mission to China embroiled him in controversy, though he won the Nobel Peace Prize for his efforts. Chiang Kai-shek's Nationalist government was involved in a civil war with Mao tse Tung's Communist guerrillas. Marshall tried to get them to form a coalition government. He never succeeded in that, but he weakened the Chiang government by cutting off military aid, thus paving the way for the Communist takeover.

Admiral Chester W. Nimitz, and the best known of his admirals was William F. ("Bull") Halsey.

General Dwight D. Eisenhower was selected to be supreme commander of allied forces making the cross-channel invasion of Europe in 1944. He had earlier been in command in the Anglo-American invasion of North Africa and in other operations in the Mediterranean. Since he was to be in command of British, Canadian, French, and other foreign forces, Eisenhower was chosen as much for his diplomatic ability as for military prowess. Eisenhower was a genial man, courted popular favor, and achieved considerable success in mediating disputes between commanders. General Douglas MacArthur was the supreme commander in the Southwest Pacific. He was probably the most experienced general officer in the service, was a man of large vision, and had a dramatic flair both in expression and action. General Mark Clark became the American commander in Italy after Eisenhower left for England to make preparations for the cross-channel invasion of France. Among the army commanders, the most flamboyant was General George S. Patton. He was most famed for his preference for mobile tank warfare and the driving energy he imparted to his forces. He was a field commander in the invasion of North Africa, Sicily and Italy, and played a major role in the taking of France and the conquest of Germany.

Early Stages of the War, 1942–44

The most pressing military problem when the United States entered the war was keeping the sea lanes open to Europe and to the South Pacific. The transport of troops and supplies was almost completely dependent upon shipping, since air transport was not yet well enough developed even to supplement to any significant degree surface shipping. The most immediate threat to American shipping was the German U-boat (submarine) operating in the Atlantic. But sea transport to the South Pacific was also threatened by the much larger Japanese navy. The Japanese had some of the largest battleships in the world, a large fleet of cruisers, fast powerful destroyers, and twice as many large aircraft carriers as the United States. Japanese torpedoes, whether launched from the air or by submarines, were much more effective than those of the United States.

Shortly after Germany declared war on the United States, the U-boat commander, Admiral Karl Doenitz, shifted most of his underwater fleet to the American coastline from Cape Cod to the Caribbean. Most American destroyers were busy protecting shipping across the ocean, and coastal shipping had almost no defense. The U-boats traveled in what were called wolfpacks, preying on shipping in bunches. During the first six months of 1942, something close to 400 American ships were lost to this assault. Many of the ships sunk were oil tankers, and this threatened the vital supply of oil

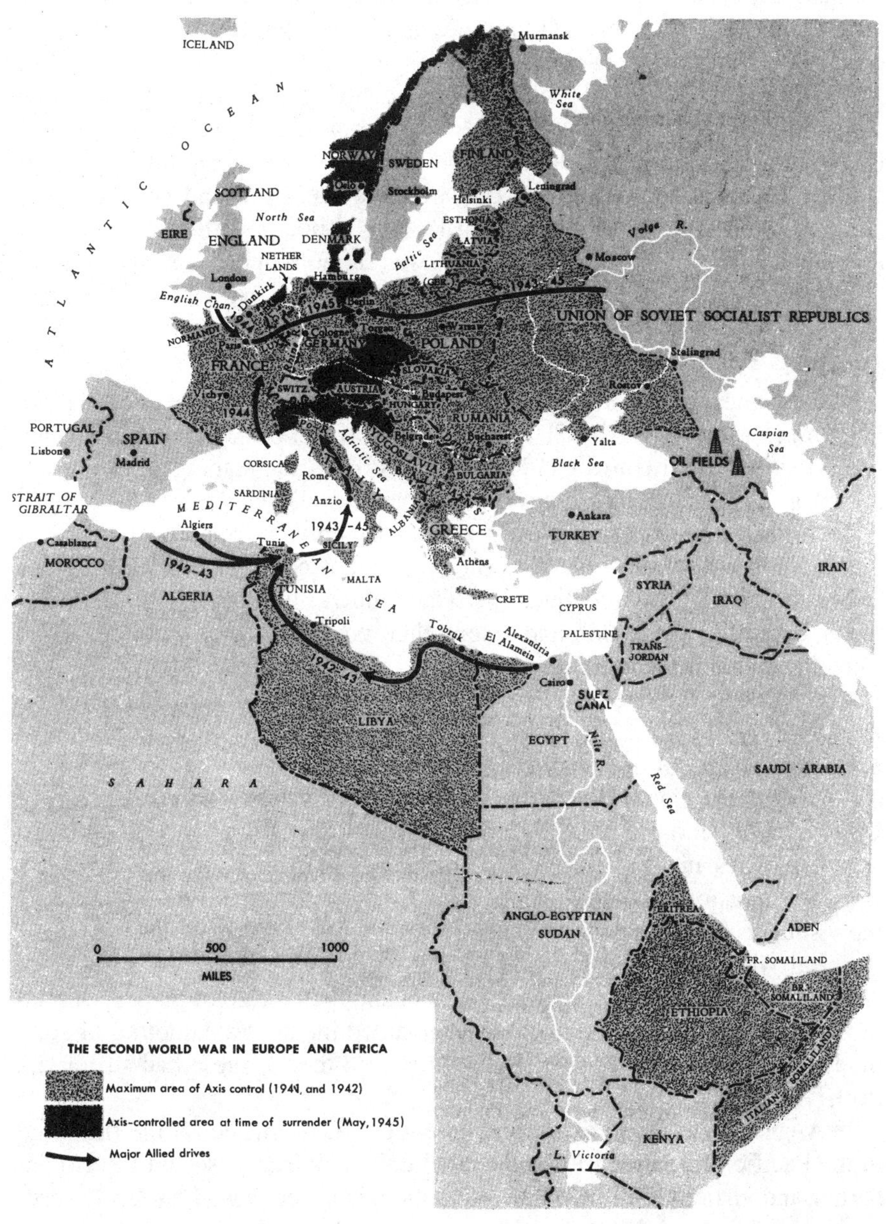
ICELAND
ATLANTIC OCEAN
Murmansk
White Sea
NORWAY
SWEDEN
FINLAND
Oslo
Stockholm
Helsinki
Leningrad
SCOTLAND
North Sea
ESTHONIA
LATVIA
LITHUANIA
Baltic Sea
Volga R.
EIRE
ENGLAND
DENMARK
NETHER LANDS
Moscow
London
Hamburg
Berlin
English Chan.
Dunkirk
1945
1943-45
NORMANDY
Paris
Cologne
GERMANY
Torgau
Warsaw
POLAND
UNION OF SOVIET SOCIALIST REPUBLICS
Stalingrad
FRANCE
SLOVAKIA
SWITZ.
AUSTRIA
Budapest
HUNGARY
Rostov
Vichy
1944
RUMANIA
Bucharest
Belgrade
YUGOSLAVIA
Danube
Yalta
Caspian Sea
PORTUGAL
SPAIN
Lisbon
Madrid
CORSICA
Adriatic Sea
ITALY
Rome
BULGARIA
Black Sea
OIL FIELDS
SARDINIA
Anzio
STRAIT OF GIBRALTAR
MEDITERRANEAN SEA
1943-45
ALBANIA
GREECE
Ankara
TURKEY
Algiers
Tunis
SICILY
Casablanca
MOROCCO
1942-43
Athens
IRAN
MALTA
SYRIA
IRAQ
ALGERIA
TUNISIA
CRETE
CYPRUS
Tripoli
Tobruk
Alexandria
El Alamein
PALESTINE
TRANS-JORDAN
1942-43
Cairo
SUEZ CANAL
LIBYA
EGYPT
Nile R.
Red Sea
SAUDI ARABIA
SAHARA
ANGLO-EGYPTIAN SUDAN
ERITREA
ADEN
FR. SOMALILAND
BR. SOMALILAND
ETHIOPIA
ITALIAN SOMALILAND
KENYA
L. Victoria
0 500 1000
MILES
THE SECOND WORLD WAR IN EUROPE AND AFRICA
Maximum area of Axis control (1941, and 1942)
Axis-controlled area at time of surrender (May, 1945)
Major Allied drives

for military operations in Europe. Admiral King pressed for a crash program to build many more destroyers and develop new techniques for combatting submarine warfare. The Germans were building them much faster than they were being sunk in 1942, and they were harrying shipping not only along the coast but elsewhere throughout 1942.

It was well into 1943 before the United States and their British Allies began to turn the tide against the German U-boats. This was accomplished by building many destroyer escorts, developing superior depth bombs, and the use of radar for detection. Between May and the end of 1943, the Germans built 198 U-boats and lost 186. The U-boat remained a menace to the end of the war, but the threat was now reduced to manageable proportions.

1. The Struggle for the South Pacific

The Japanese were not finished with their visions of conquest in the Pacific in the spring of 1942. They hoped to finish the conquest of islands and possibly cut off Hawaii and Australia as bases and staging areas for any efforts at reconquest. Their naval superiority should have enabled them to make further conquests, for they were opposed only by the enfeebled United States Navy with such support as the Australians could give. The Japanese hoped to complete the conquest of New Guinea, build bases in the Solomons, take Midway Island, and extend their position in the Aleutians. They were thwarted in all these undertakings.

The first battles were naval battles. The Battle of the Coral Sea occurred in early May, 1942. Although it was a naval battle, the ships involved did not come in sight of one another. Instead, airplanes taking off from carriers did most of the fighting and the damage. Both sides suffered losses, the United States more, but the Japanese withdrew from their attempt to establish bases in southern New Guinea, and Australia was saved from a possible invasion. Admiral Yamamoto, the Japanese naval commander, then sought a showdown engagement with the American Pacific fleet. Admiral Nimitz obliged him. The result was the Battle of Midway. The Americans destroyed the Japanese carriers and their cargo of planes, though most of the rest of Yamamoto's fleet remained intact. Yamamoto withdrew his fleet, minus much of his strking force, and the Japanese had suffered a decisive defeat.

In August, 1942, American forces went on the offensive for the first time in the Pacific. A marine division landed on Guadalcanal, seized the crucial harbor and airfield. But the contest for the island see-sawed back and forth in the ensuing weeks and months, punctuated by indecisive naval engagements and hard fighting in the jungles on land. At last, the Japanese gave up the whole island in February, 1943. Americans had also blunted the Japanese offensive in New Guinea, and with Australian aid turned them back. Thereafter, the United States began the process of fighting to gain the most accessible islands, "leap-frogging" the most heavily defended, and moving slowly toward a position from which they could attack Japan more directly.

2. The Struggle for the Mediterranean

The Mediterranean is the vital warm water link between Europe, Africa, and Asia. The vast population centers of western Europe and southern and eastern Asia are linked by way of the Mediterranean by the slender thread of the Suez Canal. By the middle of 1941 the western portion of the Mediterranean was well on its way to becoming an Axis sea. It is true that Vichy France still occupied and held colonies overlooking this portion of the Mediterranean, but that country's independence was hardly more than a technicality, since it existed at the pleasure of the Nazis. The British presence in the eastern Mediterranean was threatened and precarious, as was the Suez link to Asia.

It is not surprising, then, that Churchill should give high priority to driving the Axis from the Mediterranean. Roosevelt, and especially General Marshall, would have preferred to make a cross-channel invasion into France and establish at least a beachhead there in 1942. They had high hopes of striking at the German heartland in 1943. With the battle for control of the oceans and the seas still far from won, it was hardly possible to take on the Axis armies head-on in 1942. Thus, it was agreed in July, 1942 to launch an assault into North Africa later in the year. Indeed, though this would strike only at the periphery of Axis expansion and strength, it took much doing to prepare the forces for this attack.

British forces were already in North Africa, of course. In late October, the major British force under Field Marshal Bernard Montgomery launched an assault against German General Rommel's troops. General Eisenhower was placed in command of both British and American forces which landed in three North African ports on November 7–8. The only organized force to oppose them initially was the French fleet which barred the way at Casablanca. Admiral Jean Darlan, second in authority to General Petain in the French government, happened to be in North Africa when the landing was made, and Eisenhower persuaded him to give a cease-fire order to all French forces. (As a result of this action, the Germans moved in and occupied Vichy France.) The Germans dispatched reinforcements to Africa, and the Germans and Italians did offer major resistance. The war there was fought over the broad area of northern Africa for the next several months. But on May 13, 1943, the Germans and Italians surrendered the remains of their forces, and the Allies had reclaimed North Africa.

By the time that fighting ended in North Africa, if not well before, it had become clear no major cross-channel invasion of France could be made in

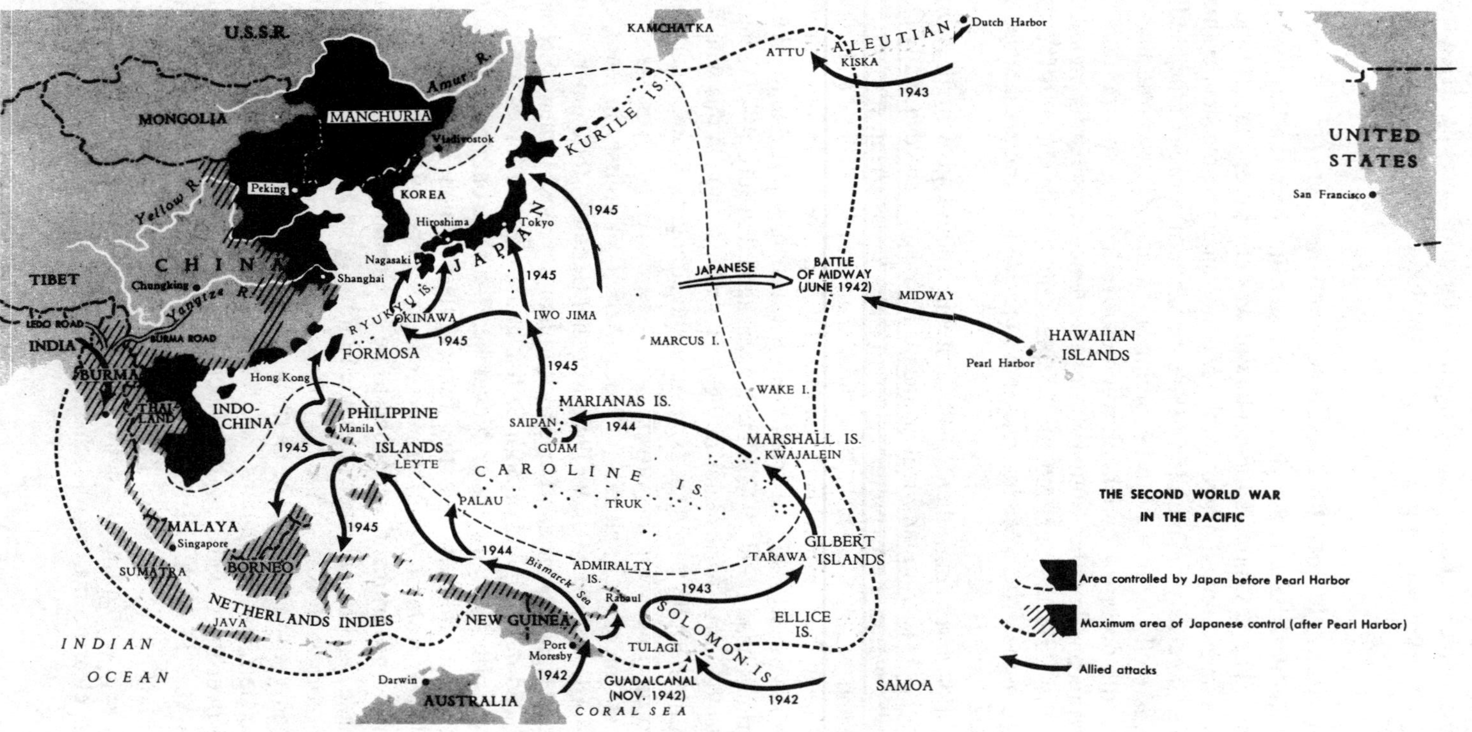
THE SECOND WORLD WAR
IN THE PACIFIC
Area controlled by Japan before Pearl Harbor
Maximum area of Japanese control (after Pearl Harbor)
Allied attacks
U.S.S.R.
MONGOLIA
MANCHURIA
Amur R.
Vladivostok
KAMCHATKA
KURILE IS.
ALEUTIAN
ATTU
KISKA
Dutch Harbor
1943
UNITED
STATES
San Francisco
Peking
KOREA
Yellow R.
TIBET
CHINA
Chungking
Yangtze R.
Shanghai
Hiroshima
Tokyo
Nagasaki
JAPAN
1945
RYUKYU IS.
OKINAWA
IWO JIMA
JAPANESE
BATTLE
OF MIDWAY
(JUNE 1942)
MIDWAY
HAWAIIAN
ISLANDS
Pearl Harbor
MARCUS I.
WAKE I.
LEDO ROAD
BURMA ROAD
INDIA
BURMA
THAILAND
FORMOSA
Hong Kong
INDO-
CHINA
PHILIPPINE
ISLANDS
Manila
LEYTE
MARIANAS IS.
SAIPAN
GUAM
1944
MARSHALL IS.
KWAJALEIN
CAROLINE IS.
PALAU
TRUK
MALAYA
Singapore
SUMATRA
BORNEO
NETHERLANDS INDIES
JAVA
Bismarck Sea
ADMIRALTY
IS.
Rabaul
NEW GUINEA
GILBERT
ISLANDS
TARAWA
ELLICE
IS.
SOLOMON IS.
TULAGI
Port
Moresby
1942
GUADALCANAL
(NOV. 1942)
CORAL SEA
SAMOA
Darwin
AUSTRALIA
INDIAN
OCEAN

1943. The decision was made, then, to continue to clear the western Mediterranean by attacking Sicily and then Italy. The invasion of Sicily was accomplished in July, 1943; a large amphibious landing placed the American 7th Army under General Patton and the British 8th Army under Field Marshal Montgomery on the island. Patton's mettle had already been tested in North Africa in a tank confrontation with Rommel's forces in North Africa, and he had proved equal to the task. There was nothing on Sicily that could delay him for long, and his mechanized force swept across the island quickly. In little more than a month after the landing, the Germans and Italians gave up the defense of Sicily.

The Italians were losing their enthusiasm for the war. Even before Sicily had actually fallen, the king forced Mussolini to resign. Marshal Badoglio became prime minister in his stead, and he began negotiations with the Allies to end the war in Italy. Unfortunately, the negotiations went on for a month or so, giving the Germans time to move in and take over in Italy. In consequence, when Anglo-American forces landed in early September of 1943, they met increasingly heavy resistance from the Germans. Indeed, it

Signal Corps

George S. Patton (1885–1945)

General Patton was an outstanding field commander of American forces during World War II. He was born in California, attended Virginia Military Institute, and graduated from West Point, receiving his commission as a cavalry officer. He served with General Pershing in Mexico and then in Europe during World War I. From the time that it was invented, Patton was interested in the possibilities of the tank in warfare, established a tank training school during World War I, and was a vigorous advocate of tank warfare in the interwar years. He was the master of mobile warfare and of aggressive and unexpected tactics and was the American commander most feared by the Germans. He commanded in the invasion of North Africa, Sicily, and northern France, always distinguishing himself by the drive of his forces. At the end of the war in Europe, Patton was promoted to full general, but he was killed shortly afterward in a vehicle accident.

is most likely that the Germans made a much more effective resistance than the Italians would have done in defending their own country. Allied forces took Naples quickly, but after that they had rough going against stubborn German resistance through difficult and often forbidding terrain. German forces occupied mountain heights which were not only difficult to reach but almost impossible to capture when they were well defended. An assault force which landed at Anzio in January could do no more than maintain the beachhead until May, 1944. It is only 100 miles from Naples to Rome, but it took Anglo-American forces nearly eight months of hard fighting to cover that distance and take Rome in June, 1944.

The fighting in Italy continued until the end of the war in Europe. The decision at Teheran, however, had taken away most of the strategic importance of the war in Italy. Forces were shifted from the Mediterranean and concentrated in Britain for the cross-channel invasion. British and American forces in Italy were denied the necessary men and materials to make the landings to isolate German forces, cut communications, and supply lines. They were left to slog along in campaigns which had to move much too slowly to win decisive victories.

Victory in Europe

In January, 1944, General Eisenhower was shifted from the command in the Mediterranean to England to command all forces in the forthcoming cross-channel invasion through France. His directive was, "You will enter the continent of Europe and, in conjunction with other United Nations, undertake operations aimed at the heart of Germany and the destruction of her armed forces."[117] In the ensuing months, he assembled the armies and other forces with which the invasion was to be accomplished. The exact date for the invasion could not be picked until a day or so in advance. Eisenhower made the decision on June 4 that it would proceed on the night of June 5–6, 1944, and June 6 has since been known as D-Day. The whole operation was known by the code name "Overlord." It was probably the most extensive coordinated landing ever made on enemy-defended shores. The landing was preceded and accompanied by aerial bombing and strafing by several thousand warplanes. Three airborne divisions were dropped by parachute behind enemy lines before the landing. Nearly 5,000 ships and landing craft brought in 176,000 men and supplies for the landing. Three distinct beachheads were established on June 6, the most difficult to establish at Omaha Beach. During the first week, they gained control of seven miles of beaches and extended inland anywhere from 5 to 15 miles. The German commanders defending Normandy were Field Marshals Erwin Rommel and Karl von Runstedt, two of the most astute leaders in the German army. The battle for Normandy had been won before the end of July; Rommel believed the situation was hopeless and prepared to negotiate a surrender to Eisenhower. Hitler got wind of it, had Rommel arrested, and shot. American and British armies started major offensives designed to gain France in late July. On August 15, the American 7th Army invaded from the south of France. Paris was liberated on August 25. By early September, the Germans had been virtually cleared from France, and Allied armies stood poised near the borders of Germany. The Russians had initiated a massive offensive shortly after D-Day, and they, too, were rolling back the German armies through eastern Europe.

As fall approached, however, the Allies were facing difficult supply problems. Not only were the supply lines getting longer, but the Allies badly needed good ports for landing them closer to the armies. General Patton wanted to strike through the south of Germany with an armored spearhead, confident that he could end the war in 1944. Field Marshal Montgomery was equally confident that given the supplies he could strike through the north of Germany to victory. Eisenhower deemed it essential to maintain a broad front, rather than using his limited supplies on one concentrated push, whether by Montgomery or Patton, but he did give Montgomery enough gasoline to make an ill fated attempt to take Arnhem by the use of paratroopers. Instead, during October and November, the armies slugged away at more limited targets on the periphery of Germany.

1. The Election of 1944

There was never much doubt that Roosevelt would run for a fourth term in 1944. Many Americans had become used to the growth and concentration of power in the federal government and to Roosevelt at the helm. Wartime patriotism made it seem almost un-American to oppose him. He occupied the spotlight of newspaper, radio, and newsreel during these years as commander-in-chief of the armed forces and chief diplomat in a world war. Criticism was muted in the midst of an atmosphere of sacrifice, concentration on war production, and winning the war. There was even talk of either dispensing with the election entirely until after the war or perhaps all parties nominating Roosevelt. The Republicans were not of that mind generally, and not to have had the election would have involved suspension of the Constitution.

There was considerable doubt, however, as to the Democratic nominee for Vice-President. Henry Wallace had served from 1941 during Roosevelt's third term, but as Roosevelt visibly aged during the war years, there was increasing doubt that he would live through a fourth term, and less and less enthusiasm for Wallace as his successor. Roosevelt decided to dump him in favor of Senator Harry S Truman of Missouri. The Republicans nominated Governor Thomas E. Dewey of New York as presidential candidate and Senator John Bricker of Ohio as his running mate. Dewey got a great deal of support, though he did not challenge deeply the direction of the President's policies. Roosevelt won by an impressive electoral vote of 432 to 99 for Dewey. The popular vote was much closer: 25,602,000 to 22,006,000. For Americans generally, it was almost as if the election had never been held.

2. The Battle of the Bulge

In mid-December the Germans mounted a major counter-offensive against the Western Allies. The effort was directed by Field Marshal Runstedt. The Germans struck through the Ardennes through thinly manned American lines on December 16. It was a runaway rout at first as Americans abandoned their heavy equipment and fled before what power the Germans could concentrate in a last major thrust. The Germans drove 50 miles into France, almost reaching the Meuse river in a few days. They were halted by the heroic defense of Bastogne during what was for people in more remote circumstances the Christmas season. The 101st Airborne reinforced the small American force at Bastogne, and they held out until Patton's Third Army rushed to their aid and an armored division broke through to rescue them.

What followed, for the rest of December and a good portion of January is known as the Battle of the Bulge. Allied forces returned to the offensive and closed the gap early in 1945. They pressed onward during February toward the Rhine, through the remains of the Siegfried Line to the river that was the last major natural obstacle to the conquest of central Germany. Most of the bridges had been destroyed, but on March 7, American forces took a bridge at Remagen that had escaped destruction. A pontoon bridge suitable for vehicular crossing was swiftly erected below the old bridge, and in the ensuing days the First Army thrust across it for a breakthrough into central Germany.

3. The Sweep through Germany

Hitler had gained the admiration of his military chieftains and much of the German population by his military genius at offensive warfare in the period 1939–1941. He lost it by his blundering stubbornness on the defensive in 1944–1945. If his object had been to defend at all cost the German homeland from invaders, he refused to follow the strategy which might have enabled him to do so. He was confronted by a large-scale war on two fronts from the mid-1944 onward. His only hope, such as it was, was to reduce his perimeter drastically through strategic retreats. Instead, he stubbornly clung to every inch of territory and refused time after time to follow the advice of his officers to retreat. By the time the Russians and Western Allies passed the German frontiers, the German forces were so badly depleted that they could no longer maintain any sustained defense against the attacking forces anywhere.

Beyond the Rhine, the British and Americans met only sporadic pockets of resistance. Once the Rhine had been crossed at Remagen, other crossings were made, and American forces encircled the industrial Ruhr valley. On April 18, the last major German army surrendered in the Ruhr. On April 25, the Russian and American forces met, severing what remained of Germany under Hitler's control. On April 30, Adolf Hitler gave up the personal battle in a bunker in embattled Berlin. He married Eva Braun, with whom he had consorted for years, made a suicide pact with her, shot her and himself. His bodyguards had great difficulty collecting enough gasoline to burn the bodies, as Hitler had requested. Two days before, Italian partisans had captured and killed Mussolini. The body was hung upside down in front of a gas station in Milan. So ended the lives of the vaunted leaders of the Axis in Europe.

Hitler designated Admiral Doenitz as his successor, but the only thing left for him to do was to try to arrange the best terms of surrender that he could. He tried to arrange a unilateral surrender to the West, but Eisenhower refused. On May 7, General Jodl signed an unconditional surrender for German forces at Allied headquarters at Rheims.

Victory against Japan

Although the war in the Pacific had taken a back seat to the struggle against Germany, American forces had continued on the offensive during 1944. After the Japanese were cleared from New Guinea and the Marianas, President Roosevelt, General MacArthur, and Admiral Nimitz met in Honolulu in July. They decided to retake the Philippines next, on the motion of MacArthur, who had spent several years in the Philippines in the 1930s and wanted nothing more than to wrest them from the Japanese. On October 22, naval forces entered Leyte Gulf and landed the 6th Army on Leyte. On the afternoon of the landing, General MacArthur and the president of the Philippines splashed ashore; MacArthur made an impassioned speech in which he announced "I have returned," which he had promised to do.

The Japanese, however, had other plans. They would dispatch the Japanese fleet to Leyte, overwhelm the American navy with vastly superior force, and isolate MacArthur one more time in the Philippines. What followed was the Battle of Leyte Gulf, the "greatest sea fight of this or of any other war."[118] The Japanese did have superior naval fire power and the large fleet, but they reckoned without American ingenuity and the greater effectiveness of American planes. The Japanese divided their force into three parts, which ultimately enabled the Americans to knock them off one by one. In a single day the Japanese fleet was so badly routed that it no longer amounted to a major threat to the conquest of the Pacific.

The war in the Philippines continued until Japan surrendered, but Manila fell on March 4, 1945, and thereafter it was a matter of clearing the

Chester W. Nimitz (1885–1966)

Nimitz was commander of naval forces in the Pacific during World War II and is credited with winning the crucial Battle of Midway. He was born in Texas, graduated from the Naval Academy, and remained under commission for the rest of his life. During World War I, Nimitz was engaged in submarine warfare. Between the wars, he commanded cruisers and battleships. By the time World War II came, he was chief of the Bureau of Navigation, but during the war he distinguished himself as a master of maneuver and placement of ships. Since the navy and marines played such a large part in the Pacific warfare, and since he commanded naval forces there, he shared much of the command credit for the defeat of the Japanese with MacArthur. In 1944, Congress named Admiral Nimitz to a new rank, that of fleet commander. After the war, he served as chief of naval operations and had a hand in unifying the armed forces.

numerous smaller islands. Meanwhile, American forces elsewhere focused on taking islands nearer to Japan to serve as air bases for bombing and possibly staging points for an invasion of Japan. The first of these islands taken after Leyte was Iwo Jima. Marines landed on Iwo Jima in February, 1945 and had taken it by the middle of March. On April 1, four army divisions landed on Okinawa and began the conquest of that Island.

On April 12, 1945, President Roosevelt died as a result of a stroke in the Little White House at Warm Springs, Georgia, where he had gone for a rest shortly after his return from Yalta. He was the second President to die of natural causes while in office since Zachary Taylor. The war was winding down in Europe as Harry Truman succeeded him, and the buildup and offensive was underway in the Pacific. Truman simply continued with the plans that were in operation at the time and spent his early months familiarizing himself with as many of them as he could.

During the late spring and summer of 1945, a great buildup got underway preparing for the invasion of Japan. That it would be a fearful undertaking no one familiar with the fight to the death of the Japanese on remote islands doubted. Surely, they would be even more highly motivated in defense of their homeland. When Allied military chieftains had met at Quebec in September, 1944, they estimated that it would take at least a year and a half after the defeat of Germany. That it might well cost the lives of a million Allied soldiers, probably most of them Americans, was not considered a wild prediction. Meanwhile, full scale bombing of Japanese cities by B-29 long-range bombers was causing devastation to buildings constructed to withstand earthquakes, not incendiary bombs.

On July 16, 1945, an atomic device was exploded in New Mexico. The United States now had a destructive weapon of a new dimension. On July 26, Truman and Churchill sent a joint ultimatum to the Japanese government, demanding full surrender, submission to Allied occupation of Japan, and the return of all Japanese conquests since 1895 to their former possessors. If they did not, they were warned, there would be "prompt and utter destruction." In preparation for this possible alternative, Truman had two atomic bombs shipped to the air force stationed on Saipan. When Prime Minister Suzuki did not accept these terms, the air force dropped an atomic bomb on Hiroshima on August 6. The reason for the choice of this city was that it was the second most important military center in Japan. The bomb wiped out four square miles of the city, killing over 60,000 people, including all members of the Second Japanese Army. On August 9, the Soviet Union declared war on Japan, and a few hours later an atomic bomb was loosed on Nagasaki.

Even after those two fearful bombings plus the modification of terms to allow Emperor Hirohito to continue to reign, the Japanese were not all convinced they should surrender. Hirohito had to overcome the objections of his military advisers and avert a military takeover of the government. The emperor accepted the terms for surrender on August 14. On August 28, an advance party flew to Tokyo to prepare for the surrender. The formal signing took place on September 2, on the battleship *U. S. S. Missouri* in Tokyo Bay. General MacArthur was there, of course, as were officials from Great Britain, China, the Soviet Union, Australia, Canada, New Zealand, the Netherlands, and France.

The fighting of World War II was at an end. The forbidding, perhaps impossible, task of putting a humpty-dumpty world together again was now at hand.

Chapter 7

The Cold War

From . . . the Baltic to . . . the Adriatic, an iron curtain has descended across the Continent. Behind that line lie all the capitals of the ancient states of Central and Eastern Europe. . . . [A]ll these famous cities and the populations around them lie in what I must consider the Soviet sphere, and all are subject . . . to Soviet influence . . . and, in many cases, increasing measures of control from Moscow.

—Winston Churchill, 1946

The peoples of a number of countries of the world have recently had totalitarian regimes forced upon them against their will. . . . The very existence of the Greek state is today threatened by the terrorist activities of. . . armed men, led by Communists, who defy the Government's authority. . . .

In addition to funds, I ask the Congress to authorize the detail of American civilian and military personnel to Greece. . . .

—Harry Truman, 1947

The Congress hereby finds and declares that the Communist Party of the United States, although purportedly a political party, is in fact an instrumentality of a conspiracy to overthrow the Government of the United States.

—Act of Congress, 1954

Whereas the peace of the world and the security of the United States . . . are endangered by . . . the establishment by the Sino-Soviet powers of a military capability in Cuba. . . . Now, therefore, I, John F. Kennedy, do hereby proclaim that the forces under my command are ordered . . . to interdict . . . the delivery of offensive weapons and associated material to Cuba. . . .

—John F. Kennedy, 1962

Chronology

1946—Churchill's Iron Curtain speech at Fulton, Missouri

1947—United States aid to Greece and Turkey

1948—Berlin Blockade

April, 1949—NATO formed

November, 1949—Communist rule established in China

1950—Korean conflict begins

1953—Armistice ends war in Korea

1955—Bandung Conference of Asian-African nations

1956—Revolts in Poland and Hungary

1959—Castro establishes Communist rule in Cuba

1960—U-2 Crisis

1962—United States becomes deeply involved in war in Vietnam

1963—Nuclear atmospheric test ban

1967—Glassboro Summit

1972—Nixon goes to Peking

1973—Cease-fire in Vietnam—United States withdraws

1979—Vienna Summit—Salt II Agreement

1983—Soviets shoot down Korean Air Lines passenger plane

Winston Churchill called the last volume of his multi-volumed history of World War II, *Triumph and Tragedy*. His reason for choosing that title he covered in a single sentence: "I have called this Volume *Triumph and Tragedy* because the overwhelming victory of the Grand Alliance has failed so far to bring general peace to our anxious world." Churchill's brief statement is clearly an understatement of what he has called a tragedy. It is not simply that struggles and wars within and between nations have occurred since World War II. They have, of course, but in themselves they have been only the tip of the iceberg. The tragedy, if that is the right word, is that the guns of World War II were hardly silent before a world wide struggle was underway. It was the struggle between an expansive Communism and the remains of Western Civilization. This struggle, though variously grasped, has been most commonly referred to as the Cold War. The phrase has fallen out of favor in intellectual circles over the past decade or so, but the struggle to which it refers goes on, even if the resistance to Communism has weakened.

Indeed, Churchill was well aware of the struggle well before he wrote *Triumph and Tragedy*. In the speech which he made at Fulton, Missouri in 1946 (*Triumph and Tragedy* was published in 1953), in which he introduced the phrase, "iron curtain," he made a good summary of Soviet Communist expansion going on at that time. He meant by "iron curtain" that when the Soviet Union took over a territory, it shut off normal communication and interchange with the rest of the world. By early 1946, that was already happening, or had happened, in Poland, Hungary, Bulgaria, Rumania, and Albania. In other countries on the periphery of the

Soviet Union, the pressure by the Soviets was being strongly felt. In Italy and France, there were strong Communist parties thrusting toward political power. Moreover, "in a great number of countries far from the Russian countries, far from the Russian frontiers and throughout the world, Communist fifth columns are established and work in complete unity and absolute obedience to the directions they receive from the Communist centre. Except in the British Commonwealth and in the United States where Communism is in its infancy, the Communist parties or fifth columns constitute a growing challenge and peril to Christian civilization. These are sombre facts for anyone to have to recite on the morrow of a victory. . . ."[119]

The situation was ripe for Soviet (and communist) expansion at the end of World War II, and in the ensuing years. Western Europe, which had long been the major center of power and influence radiating outward on the world, was virtually a power vacuum. Germany had been totally crushed, had not even a recognized or *de facto* government at the end of the war. It was completely disarmed, much of its industrial potential either destroyed by bombing or carted away by the Russians, and divided into four zones of occupation. France had been exposed as an ineffective minor power by the Nazi armies within a period of a few weeks during World War II, and was probably incapable of resuming its role as a major power for decades. Italy neither was, nor had been, a power of consequence in the whole modern era. Eastern Europe had been overrun by Soviet armies, which only loosened some of their grip as governments dependent upon Moscow were installed.

England maintained its posture as a world power during World War II, but many of its weaknesses were exposed. Britain had never been a major military power by land, and it had only been able to regain the initiative against the Axis with the aid of allies. The British navy retired from the Pacific as a force in the face of the Japanese offensive, and its tenuous position in the eastern Mediterranean was seriously challenged. After the war, Britain visibly retreated from world status power and quickly became a minor power, in all but name. This change was accelerated by socialism. Elections were held shortly after the defeat in Germany in 1945, and the Labour Party won. Churchill, the symbol of British determination and even bellicosity, was replaced by Clement Atlee, a man committed to socializing the British economy. Within two years of headlong nationalization of industries, Britain had become a land of grave shortages of goods and was seeking loans to survive. Democratic socialists are well known, as well, for their opposition to an assertive role in international affairs; they are often pacifists, and almost invariably favor compromise and negotiation. Far from defending the British Empire, Labourites fell all over themselves withdrawing from colonies and protectorates and granting them independence. What remained of the British Empire in the ensuing years was reduced to the symbolic relationship known as a Commonwealth of Nations.

Indeed, in the wake of World War II, colonial empires were generally disbanded. Japan's empire, acquired before and during World War II, was taken away, as was that of Italy in North Africa. The United States granted independence to the Philippines following the war. The French yielded up their empire in the decade after the war, in Indochina, in North Africa, and elsewhere. The Belgians withdrew from the Congo region, and the Dutch gave up their Pacific empire.

These newly independent nations quickly became happy hunting grounds for Communists controlled by Moscow and presented with a virtual power vacuum in Europe. In the late 1940s, it was nip and tuck as to whether or not Communists might not gain control of governments in France and Italy. (The possibility has remained over the years, though its immediate likelihood has diminished somewhat.) Weakness in every part of the world beckoned as opportunity to Stalin and those around him that were bent on spreading communism and expanding Soviet power and influence.

That communism would inevitably triumph in every country on the earth was dogma to which every leader of that persuasion must be committed. Marx had predicted it; Lenin had affirmed it; Stalin had proceeded on the premise, and those who have followed have continued to profess the belief. Nikita Khrushchev, who succeeded Stalin as dictator of the Soviet Union, declared in 1959: "We believe that the idea of Communism will ultimately be victorious throughout the world, just as it has been victorious in our country, in China and in many other states. . . . Our confidence in the victory of Communism . . . is based on a knowledge of the laws governing the development of society. Just as in its time capitalism . . . took the place of feudalism, so will capitalism be inevitably superseded by Communism—the more progressive and more equitable social system."[120]

The Soviet leaders have not, however, been content to let the "inevitable" take place without aid and guidance from them. To the contrary, they have believed that communism will come by revolution, and that these revolutions must be developed, promoted, and directed. Communism has not been advanced merely by military conquest; indeed, the leaders of the Soviet Union have generally avoided getting their country directly involved in war. Russia under Communist leaders has never started war with a major power. Germany invaded Russia, and the Russians only declared war on Japan when victory for their side was certain. They have not been above attacking small and weak countries—Finland, Poland, and Afghanistan—, but they have avoided military undertakings against major powers.

That is not to say that conquests have not played a large role in the expansion of communism. It was the Red Army conquest of countries in eastern Europe that set the stage for installing Communist governments. Communist governments have usually resulted from conquests and seizures of power, but quite often these have been the result of civil wars in which

Communists were supported from Moscow or some other center of communist power. Even in the case of the Red army victories, there were usually some characteristic moves by which Communists grabbed power. There were usually several parties that were more or less sympathetic with the Communists in a country. The Communists usually helped to move these into control of the governments and then to press for sensitive appointments for their people. Historian Hugh Seton-Watson described the process of the takeovers in eastern Europe as going through three phases generally. In the first phase, the governments were formed by a coalition of left-wing parties. In the second stage, the communists had actually gained control of the government. In the third phase, one-party government was established either by absorbing the others into the communist parties or removing them from power. Seton-Watson had this to say about how communists got the crucial positions in government and exercised power:

> Already in the first phase . . . the communists seized certain key positions. The most important of these was the Ministry of the Interior, which controlled the police. . . . The Ministry of Justice, controlling the formal justice machinery, was considered less important, but was held by communists in certain cases. Control of broadcasting was seized at an early date. Great efforts were made to control and to create youth and women's organizations. In industry, communists were placed in key positions in the management of nationalized factories and in trade unions.[121]

Thus, Communists seized power generally when they had the backing of the Red army.

But since World War II, most of the spread of communism has not been accomplished directly by the armies of the Soviet Union or those of other communist powers, as these have emerged. Communists have usually seized power by way of civil uprisings and civil war. Until the 1950s, these were usually promoted, directed, or supported from Moscow. Since that time, other communist nations have got into the act, more or less independently of Moscow, most notably Communist China. The main effort of Communists has been to seize upon any weakness, real or imagined, of any government, to promote disruption, disorder, arouse discontent, galvanize some class into militancy, or do anything that might lead to revolt or revolution in any land.

The first step, of course, is to get sympathizers and supporters, form a nucleus of organized zeal within a country, and then to gain control or influence over as many organizations within a country as possible. Communist parties usually provided the nucleus of organized zeal within a country. The Soviet Union has usually sent in its own agents of control by way of diplomatic personnel or any other way it can get agents into a country. Beyond these things, Otto Kuusinen, one of Stalin's men, described a part of the process this way: "We must create a whole solar system of organizations and smaller committees around the Communist Party so to speak, smaller organizations working actually under the influence of our party. . . ." Willi Muenzenberg, who was something of an organizational genius of the worldwide communist movement, recommended that communists "must penetrate every conceivable milieu, get hold of artists and professors, make use of cinemas and theatres," and spread and defend communist ideas.[123]

These types of activities were going on in every country in the world, by the 1930s, if not earlier. They were carried on more or less undercover, and constituted, as Congress declared in 1950, a conspiracy to overthrow the government in every land in which they existed. This was so whether or not there was much likelihood of any immediate success. Our concern here, however, is that after World War II, there were many new and unstable governments, which were especially vulnerable to these ideas and tactics. Here, the communist tactic was more pointed, to go beyond spreading disorder to use of violence and terror—to create chaos, fear, and promote guerrilla warfare.

Although it is to get somewhat ahead of the story, how the communists operated in Vietnam is instructive. The Republic of Vietnam was organized as an independent country in 1954 after France pulled out of Indochina. (The country was also referred to as South Vietnam.) Communists in Vietnam began pressing for power there, since they were already in power in North Vietnam. Between 1957 and 1959 an organization known as the Viet Cong (Vietnamese Communists) killed sixty-five village chiefs. In 1959, Radio Hanoi (the voice of the Communist government in North Vietnam) proclaimed the desirability of destroying the Diem regime in South Vietnam, and in 1960 a National Liberation Front was organized to "liberate" South Vietnam. In "1960 and 1961 village officials, schoolteachers, and health workers were being murdered by the thousands." As one result, "the Viet Cong succeeded in closing two hundred primary schools in South Vietnam, interrupting the education of more than twenty-five thousand students. And this is when the terror was just beginning to explode with full force, warning of the horrors to come."[124] This was the beginning of the guerrilla warfare which eventually toppled Vietnam into the communist camp.

At any rate, the Communist conspiracy was thrusting outward by a great assortment of tactics into weakened areas after World War II. Civil war had long been underway in China, although the general war had brought it to a temporary halt. The Soviet Union was making demands on Turkey and loomed as a threat in the Middle East, and Communists had a guerrilla war underway in Greece in 1947.

The Failure of the United Nations

The United Nations was envisioned by Franklin D. Roosevelt as the keeper of the peace and settler of international disputes in much the same role as Woodrow Wilson had conceived for the ill-fated League of Nations. Cordell Hull, Roosevelt's Secretary of State, was an advocate of the idea, but Roosevelt was its most vigorous proponent throughout the war. The United Nations Organization officially came into being June 26, 1945, when representatives from 50 nations meeting in San Francisco signed the charter. But the idea of such an organization had been given currency during the war by a variety of actions. In January, 1942, 26 nations at war against the Axis proclaimed themselves the United Nations in this activity. At Moscow, in 1943, representatives of the United States, United Kingdom, Soviet Union, and China agreed to establish an organization for the "United Nations" as soon as possible.

Roosevelt worked to avoid the pitfalls that had helped to keep the United States out of the League of Nations. His hand is clearly apparent in trying to get the name accepted even before the organization had been formed. (Americans continued to refer to their side as the "Allies" during World War II, not the "United Nations," but officially the term was being used anyhow.) The major conferences on the organization were held in the United States: at Dumbarton Oaks (a residence in Washington D. C.) in 1944 and in San Francisco in 1945. In addition, he courted Republican Senators to try to reduce opposition from that side of the isle. His greatest success was in getting Senator Arthur Vandenberg of Michigan, a leading Republican and earlier a vigorous opponent of international entanglements, to support the United Nations idea. Vandenberg served as a delegate to the San Francisco Conference and helped to get ratification of the charter through the Senate with minor opposition.

But the United Nations was built upon a faulty premise. Indeed, it partook of the utopianism which had been implicit in the Rooseveltian vision of the postwar world. In his Annual Message to Congress in 1941, Roosevelt "voiced a fervent hope for a postwar world built upon the four essential freedoms: freedom of speech and of worship, and freedom from want and fear." These Four Freedoms became a symbol in the course of the war of the cause for which the Allies were fighting and of the Brave New World that was supposed to emerge after the war. The premise of the United Nations was that the peoples of the world wanted peace, and that the nations of the world should be drawn together behind this goal of peace. All the nations which joined the United Nations committed themselves to avoid going to war and to settle their disputes by negotiations and compromises.

As a general rule, it may be so that people prefer peace to war, provided they can have it on their own terms and according to their own wills. But whatever people in general may or may not want, they are rarely, if ever, consulted before nations go to war. Indeed, it has become more and more unusual for parliaments or congresses to be consulted before nations go to war. Sudden invasions and undeclared wars have become more the rule than the exception. But the basic fallacy with the United Nations conception went from the general to particular sources of enduring discord. It was the assumption that the Soviet Union (and other Communist lands as communism spread) shared common ground and common goals with non-communist countries. This was not and has never been the case. Communist countries are bent on promoting world revolution. To that end, as already pointed out, they support spreading disorder and uncompromising antagonisms in non-communist countries. World peace can only prevail, in the view of communists, when every challenge to communism has been removed from the world.

Even if it would have been possible to conceive an organization of the United Nations that would take this thrust of communism into account and put it at nought, the charter did not do that. Instead, it vested authority to deal with matters thereatening the peace in a Security Council, composed of five permanent members and six temporary members. The permanent member nations were: the Soviet Union, the United States, the United Kingdom, France, and China. Each of the permanent members was given a veto over any proposed action. That meant that any nation who held permanent membership could prevent action. The situation was further compounded after 1949, when the Nationalist Chinese were driven out of China, yet still held on to their voting powers in the Security Council.

It soon became apparent that the major powers could not agree on any substantial matter. The main obstacle to agreement was the Soviet Union, which expressed its unwillingness by the threat of or actual vetoes. The Soviet Union's determination to establish puppet governments in Eastern Europe was one of the early issues. Ambassador Averell Harriman informed President Truman shortly after the war ended in Europe that the Soviet Union was violating all its agreements with the other allies. Stalin had promised free elections in Poland at Yalta, yet these never took place. So far as Germany was concerned, the Soviet Union was bent upon establishing a puppet government in its zone of occupation and refused to agree to any plan for the unification of Germany. Stalin was bent on carting all the machinery out of the Russian zone of occupation and getting as much as it could from other zones. It became apparent very early that the Russian attempt to destroy what remained of Germany was working against the United States and Britain as well. Millions of Germans had been driven out of the German territory now claimed by Poland, and these took refuge mainly in the American and British zones, where they were having to be taken care of by the occupiers. The Soviet Union pursued its own policies without regard to what the others sought to do.

The initial attempts to use the United Nations as an instrument for aid to suffering peoples was largely a failure. The United Nations Relief and Rehabilitation Administration, supported mainly by the United States handed out several billion dollars worth of aid in 1945–1946. That portion of the aid which went into Russian occupied areas was used by the Soviet Union to bolster the puppet regimes and subsidize the building of communism. By the end of 1946, Congress had had enough and refused to make the appropriations to keep it going.

Symbolically, perhaps the best indication of the failure of the United Nations because of Soviet obstruction was in the matter of control over atomic energy. At the end of World War II, the United States had a monopoly of atomic energy, which at this point was being used exclusively for the making of atomic bombs. The United States, Britain, and Canada joined in proposing that the United Nations be given international control over the development and use of atomic energy. In early 1946, the United Nations authorized a commission empowered to oversee the development of atomic energy. Bernard Baruch presented a plan for international control to it, a plan which was the work mainly of Dean Acheson and David Lilienthal. It proposed to give the United Nations ownership of all mines and production facilities connected with atomic energy. The United Nations commission would be empowered to prevent national development of atomic explosives, to carry out inspections within nations, and to punish violators of its rules. Whatever the merits of this plan (probably utopian and

Illustrated London News

Dean G. Acheson (1893–1971)

Acheson was President Truman's Secretary of State 1949–1953. He had spent several years in the State Department before that appointment, and he became a symbol to many Republicans of the sophistry in the State Department in the early 1950s. Acheson was born in Connecticut, went to Groton School, Yale, and Harvard Law School. After his admission to the bar, he alternated between the practice of law and serving in political positions in Washington. He played a prominent role in implementing the Marshall Plan, in shaping the North Atlantic Treaty, and guided the United States participation in the Korean conflict within the framework of the United Nations.

foolish, in view of what has happened to the United Nations), the Soviet Union blocked its adoption. Instead, that country proposed to ban the atomic bomb and leave enforcement in the Security Council, where the Soviet Union could veto inspection and control. Meanwhile, the Soviet Union was following its own crash program for building an atomic bomb, an undertaking in which it had succeeded by 1949.

That the United Nations could not effectively restrain the thrust of the Soviet Union was clear by 1947. The Cold War's beginnings date from the time that the United States began to act outside the United Nations to follow a different course in international affairs. The most immediate provocation to that in 1947 was the developing civil conflict in Greece. The Soviet puppet states of Bulgaria, Yugoslavia, and Albania were giving arms and providing bases for Communist guerrillas in Greece. The Labour government in Britain notified the United States that it would be unable to defend Greece or the Middle East generally from communism. At this point, President Truman took the lead in proposing American action, and the Cold War had begun.

Tentative Resistance to Communism

President Truman did not for long, if *ever*, share Roosevelt's view about the malleability of Russian Communists. Roosevelt had appeared to believe that Communists were only suspicious about Western motives and that if they could be reassured on this point, they could be brought around to cooperation. Indeed, Roosevelt was a charming man, and he was inclined to the view that he could bring the Russians around by a combination of concessions and presidential charm. Truman was a man of quite different temper than Roosevelt. While Roosevelt was suave, genteel, and manipulative, Truman was a rough and tumble politician, blunt of speech, and scrappy in his approach to dealing with others. In any case, his assessment of the Soviet government soon took on a quite different flavor from that of Roosevelt. In January, 1946, Truman informed his Secretary of State that "Unless Russia is faced with an iron fist and strong language another war is in the making. Only one language do they understand—'how many divisions have you?—'. . . I'm tired of babying the Soviets."[125]

Even so, there was more than a little tentativeness about the Truman resistance to Communism, as there has been generally since World War II. Resistance has been episodic, limited, usually in response to particular provocations, and rarely, if ever, aimed at anything more than aborting some particular move by the Soviet Union or other communist country. The particular approach of the Truman administration was characterized as aimed at containment. The outlines of this approach were set forth for the American government by George F. Kennan in 1947. Kennan maintained that it "is clear that the main element of any United States policy toward the

Harry S. Truman (1884–1972)

Truman was the 33rd President of the United States. He was elected Vice-President in 1944, and when Roosevelt died the next year, became President. He was elected President on his own in 1948, though the polls had predicted that his Republican opponent, Thomas E. Dewey, would win easily. Truman was born in Missouri, grew up on a farm, and received such higher education as he had in a couple of years attendance at night school. Aside from rising in the National Guard before World War I and his military services during the war, Truman had few successes until he went into politics. At various times, he managed his father's farm, worked as a bank clerk, and started a business which failed. In 1934, he was elected to the United States Senate as a Democrat. During World War II, he captured the public attention as head of a committee investigating the awarding of war contracts and was a compromise choice by the Democrats for Vice-President in 1944. His election in 1948 surprised almost everyone but him, and he was generally admired for the pluckiness with which he had stood up to the Communists in Europe, but he lost public favor during his second term.

Soviet Union must be that of a long-term, patient but firm and vigilant containment of Russian expansive tendencies.'' He argued that ''Soviet pressure against the free institutions of the western world . . . can be contained by the adroit and vigilant application of counter-force at a series of constantly shifting geographical and political points, corresponding to the shifts and maneuvers of Soviet policy. . . .''[126] The most obvious weakness of the containment approach was that it left the initiative for much of the action to the Communists. Of equal moment, it did not envision an end to the policy or the ultimate defeat of communism. The Cold War, as conceived by those who favored containment, was a war of attrition that would go on indefinitely.

There is another facet to the American resistance to communism that has weakened and made it tentative. It is a kinship of many American politicians and thinkers with communism through a shared belief in some of the tenets of socialism. There are two varieties of socialism, as pointed out earlier: revolutionary socialism and evolutionary socialism. After the defeat of the Axis powers, Soviet Communism remained as the only revolutionary socialist power. While Americans and Europeans had generally repudiated Nazism and Fascism, they had committed themselves to an alliance with Soviet Communism. They were also widely committed to evolutionary socialism in their own lands, and evolutionary socialism had common roots with communism. Evolutionary socialism made deep inroads in the United States, particularly with the New Deal programs. Those who favored evolutionary socialism and the programs that had grown out of it could rarely bring themselves to make even a full-fledged verbal attack on the socialism of the Soviet variety. To do so would be to tar themselves with the same brush.

Instead of an all-out repudiation of socialist premises, then, those of the evolutionary socialist premises in the United States, who usually refer to themselves as "liberals," have frequently sought to compete with Soviet socialism. They have done so by devising approaches to containing communism that would be in accord with their variety of socialism. The Truman programs had this character from the outset. In his call for military and financial aid to Greece and Turkey in March, 1947, President Truman declared: "The seeds of totalitarian regimes are nurtured by misery and want. They spread and grow in the evil soil of poverty and strife. They reach their full growth when the hope of a people for a better life has died. We must keep that hope alive. The free peoples of the world look to us for support in maintaining their freedoms."[127] In short, Truman held that poverty and the like provided the opportunity and occasion for communist expansion and called for some redistribution of American wealth to some of these lands to deter the expansion. Congress responded with an initial appropriation of $400 million for aid to Greece and Turkey. Additional appropriations were made later.

On the heels of the beginning of aid to Greece and Turkey came a much broader proposal and programs. These are known as the Marshall Plan. General George C. Marshall, who was now Truman's Secretary of State, proposed the plan in a commencement address at Harvard in June, 1947. He declared that many European countries which had been devastated by war were in dire need of aid. "The truth of the matter," Marshall said, "is that Europe's requirements for the next 3 or 4 years of foreign food and other essential products—principally from America—are so much greater than her present ability to pay that she must have substantial additional help, or face economic, social, and political deterioration of a very grave character. . . ." "It is logical," he continued, "that the United States should do whatever it is able to do to assist in the return of normal economic health in the world, without which there can be no political stability and no assured peace. Our policy is directed not against any country or doctrine but against hunger, poverty, desperation, and chaos. Its purpose should be the revival of a working economy in the world. . . . "[128] These programs began a large and expanding foreign aid activity by the United States.

The story of foreign aid will be told more extensively in the following chapter, but it had to be discussed briefly here within the context of the Cold War. Foreign aid grew out of the idea, or was advanced in connection with the belief, that the way to prevent the expansion of communism was to distribute wealth more nearly equally. No doubt, Marxist doctrine holds that the unequal distribution of wealth anywhere is the result of an exploitative economic and political order. There is no doubt, either, that some people have yielded to the cries to revolt because of conditions that existed, though the appeal of communist ideology has usually been much more effective among intellectuals than with the poor. But there is every reason to doubt that communism holds the key either to the production of wealth or its just distribution. Communists seek power and use propaganda to gain their ends. The extending of foreign aid to government programs within countries is more apt to expand socialism than to deter communist expansion. In any case, such programs grew naturally out of evolutionary socialism.

The Marshall Plan resulted in the European Recovery Plan, which received its initial financing by Congress in the spring of 1948. The Communist nations of eastern Europe were initially invited to send representatives to meetings and participate in planning for recovery efforts. However, Soviet pressure prevented them from participating, and indeed the appropriation measure had been pushed through Congress as an anti-communist measure. The Soviet Union became more obstinate than usual in the face of the American initiative in Europe. Czechoslovakia, which was governed by a coalition government for nearly three years after the war, was fully Sovietized in 1948 with a Communist government. (There was nothing particularly unique in this development, since coalition governments usually precede one-party Communist governments as soon as the Communists have control of the major instruments of government.) Stalin was especially provoked when Britain, France, and the United States moved to unify West Germany under a limited German government. Actually, the Russians had refused to cooperate with the West, had instead gone their own way in their own zone of occupation. That being the case, they should hardly have expected to have a hand in affairs in West Germany. No matter, they took the position that they had been squeezed out.

The Soviet Union provoked a confrontation over access to Berlin, beginning in the late spring of 1948. Berlin was deep in the Soviet zone of occupation in Germany; all land access to Berlin is through East Germany. Berlin, since it had been the metropolitan center and capital of Germany, had nonetheless been divided into four zones of occupation, shared by the

Soviet Union, France, Britain, and the United States. Beginning April 1, 1948, the Soviet Union began restricting movement into Berlin of both people and goods. On June 23, they stopped all overland traffic into Berlin from West Germany. The aim was either to drive the Western allies out of Berlin or force them to abandon their plans for the unification of West Germany. The United States took the leadership in countering this Soviet move. Truman was adamant that there would be no retreat from Berlin. He was, however, faced with the large problem of getting supplies to the city and personnel in and out.

One proposal was to use armed convoys to bring goods and people into and out of Berlin. Truman did not want to start a shooting war if it could be avoided, so he rejected this approach. Instead, he proposed to use airplanes for the job, and it was done. The Soviet blockade of Berlin lasted from June, 1948 to May, 1949. During that period the Royal Air Force of Britain and the United States Air Force made 277,264 flights into Berlin delivering nearly 2½ million tons of supplies. On a daily basis, as much as 4,000 tons was flown to the city. The missions were costly, but the airlift did much to turn western Europe against the Soviet Union and toward Britain and the United States. The new Secretary of State, Dean Acheson, said that "the position of the West has grown greatly in strength, and . . . the position of the Soviet Union in regard to the struggle for the soul of Europe has changed from the offensive to the defensive."[129]

As the Berlin airlift was going on, various countries in Europe and North America were forging ahead toward the formation of a close military alliance against aggression. The result was the North Atlantic Treaty, which was signed April 4, 1949 at Washington. It was signed by representatives of the United States, Britain, France, Italy, the Netherlands, Belgium, Canada, Iceland, Luxembourg, Denmark, Norway, and Portugal. The treaty provided an agreement of the parties "that an armed attack against one or more of them in Europe or North America shall be considered an attack against them all;" and that "individually and in concert with the other Parties," they would take "such action as . . . necessary, including the use of armed force, to restore and maintain the security of the North Atlantic area."[130] A North Atlantic Treaty Organization (NATO) was formed with headquarters in Europe, which has since undertaken the preparing for the defense of Europe. Although the United Nations Charter provides for regional alliances such as this, it should be clear that the formation of NATO signaled a major abandonment of any dependence on the United Nations.

The United States Senate ratified the treaty on July 21, 1949 by a vote of 82 to 13. This indicated a major shift in American foreign policy. George Washington warned against permanent or entangling alliances with other nations. Thomas Jefferson, as President, had taken a similar position. Both men were especially concerned to avoid entanglements in Europe. The Monroe Doctrine had explicitly disavowed any American involvement in

European affairs. So far as European policy was concerned, the United States had hewed rather closely to this line until World War II, although Woodrow Wilson had done his best to get the United States into the League of Nations. Of course, the United States became deeply embroiled in the European situation during World War II. The joining of the United Nations might conceivably have increased this involvement, but it had generally been assumed that engagements there following the war were temporary. Now, the United States had clearly joined in a permanent alliance with European powers, and through economic and military aid was deeply entangled with countries there.

On the other hand, it should be pointed out that Soviet expansion in Europe was halted during 1948. Czechoslovakia was the last European country to fall under the Soviet sphere in Europe. Indeed, Yugoslavia, under the leadership of Marshal Tito, effectively withdrew from the Soviet bloc and followed an independent course in international affairs. It remained Communist, but has since played no significant role in international communist expansion.

Communists Take China

Actually, the tentativeness of the Truman administration's resistance to the spread of communism can be seen most clearly in the case of China. There had been a Communist presence in China since the 1920s, and it turned into a civil war in the 1930s. The recognized government of China was that of the Kuomintang, or Nationalist government of Chiang Kai-shek. The Communists were led by Mao Tse-tung and Chou En-lai, who were secretly supported and guided from Moscow. Throughout the 1930s and early 1940s, the Communists were too weak to be anything more than a nuisance to Chiang's government. After the Japanese invasion of China, Chiang tried to place the internal civil war on the back burner as much as possible and concentrate the force of China against the Japanese. After World War II, the communists became an increasing threat to the Nationalist government. They were greatly aided by the Soviet Union, which had taken Manchuria from the Japanese and turned over weapons and other war materials to them which had been surrendered by the Japanese.

The United States took a markedly different position toward the Chinese Communists than it did to the guerrillas in Greece or, indeed, to the threat of Communist expansion in Western Europe. Communist propaganda and infiltration of the Far East sections of the State Department set the stage for this different approach. Propagandists had for years worked to undermine Chiang Kai-shek and the Nationalist government. Journalists and scholars, under the guise of describing and analyzing the situation in China, had repeatedly asserted or planted the idea that the government was corrupt, undemocratic, ineffective, and bound to be replaced by the Communists. By contrast, the Communists were pictured as pure of heart, not Communists of the Soviet variety, and indeed agrarian reformers of the gradualist variety. At the journalistic level, Edgar Snow busily undermined Chiang and built up the Reds over two decades. His best known work, *Red Star Over China*, had a major impact. In such widely circulated publications as *Saturday Evening Post*, Snow kept up a drumbeat for the Communist side. In one such article, he declared that Chinese Communism "won its following chiefly among the peasants, by working out a program of agrarian democracy with Socialism as an ultimate, but, admittedly distant goal."[131]

One of the most influential of the writers on government policy was Owen Lattimore. He wrote many books about and was accepted as an expert on the Far East. Not only did Lattimore present the Chinese Communists in a favorable light but he was, according to much testimony, a skilled user of the Communist line on China. One scholar of the Far East said of him: "He is a specialized operator within the field of Far Eastern studies, Asiatic studies, and particularly, of Chinese studies, and in this field I consider him principal agent for the advocacy of Stalinist ideas."[132] He was in and out of government during the crucial years as an adviser and consultant to the government of the United States on China affairs. Others in government who played crucial roles in providing information on which policy was determined were John Paton Davies, Lauchlin Currie, John Carter Vincent, and John Stewart Service. These men leaned toward the Communists in China and worked in a variety of ways to undermine the government of China.

At the end of World War II, the policy of the United States government shifted definitely toward forcing Chiang Kai-shek to come to terms with the Communists. As Stanley K. Hornbeck, a long term student of the Far East, put it: "It was then, in the year 1945—and not before then—that the government of the United States . . . embarked upon . . . a course of intervention in . . . the conflict between the National Government and the Communists in China. It was then that . . . the Government of the United States . . . brought to bear pressures . . . upon the National Government, pressures which were not 'against' the Communists but were on their behalf, pressures . . . to the disadvantage of the National Government."[133]

General George C. Marshall executed these new policies. President Truman appointed him to head a special mission to China in late 1945. His task, as he saw it, was to bring an end to the fighting in China, to get Chiang Kai-shek to form a coalition government which would include the Communists, and to integrate the Communist army with the Nationalist army. Marshall did not rely entirely upon persuasion to try to get his way. He could and did cut off American military aid to the Nationalists during the period of his mission. He placed maximum pressure upon Chiang to alter his long standing policies toward the Communists.

Chiang was understandably reluctant to attain Communist cooperation and especially to enter into a coalition government. Not only did he have experience of Communist perfidy over more than two decades but also some understanding of how Communists elsewhere had behaved. Communists have almost always come to power by entering coalition governments. But with Communists in them, they do not remain coalition governments for long. Communists move as swiftly as they can to become dominant and to create a one-party government. Moreover, Chiang could see that he was now in position to crush the Communists now that the war with Japan was over. He had five to one superiority over the Communists in troops, virtually all the heavy military equipment in China, and the only air force there. His armies were driving the Communists back before General Marshall arrived.

Even so, under pressure from the Americans, Chiang agreed to a ceasefire and to make efforts to work out a plan for a reorganized government and absorbing the Communists into the government and army. A truce did go into effect temporarily, but nothing was ever accomplished beyond that. Instead, the Communist Chinese began moving into Manchuria to take over from the Soviet armies there and were greatly strengthened by materials handed over to them by the Russians. Chiang attempted to stop the Communist incursion into Manchuria, which was contrary to the terms of the agreement that had been worked out, but before he had achieved his object Marshall again persuaded Chiang to make a truce with the Communists. It was to no avail. Fighting continued sporadically, and negotiations, such as they were, between the Nationalists and Communists came to nothing. The Communists simply bought time by the truces to arm and train their forces.

In early 1947, Truman recalled Marshall and appointed him Secretary of State. The mission had been a failure. Professor Anthony Kubek summed up its consequences this way:

> Marshall's entire mission was one of convenience to the Reds. Before he went to China, the Communists occupied a very small portion of China. Their Army numbered less than 300,000 badly equipped troops. When Marshall returned from China . . . , the Communist controlled areas had greatly increased. The Communist Army had grown from 300,000 badly equipped troops to an Army of over 2,000,000 relatively well-equipped soldiers.[134]

Equally, or more, important, Marshall had by word and deed expressed his lack of confidence in the Nationalist government. That he became Secretary of State made that position virtually the official one of the United States.

In any case, the Nationalist armies never recovered their earlier initiative; much of the spirit went out of them. Morale was low, and the Communists went on the offensive. In early 1947, President Truman sent General Albert Wedemeyer, an experienced China hand, back to China to see what could be done. Wedemeyer pointed out that the danger was imminent of a

Communist victory, and that such a victory would place China in the Soviet orbit. He recommended extensive aid to the Chinese Nationalists as having the greatest possibility of turning the tide. His report was not made public until after the Nationalists had been overwhelmed. Instead, Marshall maintained that there was nothing the United States could do that would succeed in helping "the present Chinese Government capable of reestablishing and then maintaining its control throughout China."[135] In the spring of 1948, the United States did offer limited financial assistance to the Nationalists, but it was too little and too late.

The Communists swept across China in late 1948 and in 1949. In December, 1949, Chiang Kai-shek moved his government to the island of Formosa, and Mao Tse-tung established the People's Republic of China with its capital at Peking. Mao proclaimed his friendship with the Soviet Union, and the Bamboo Curtain fell, shutting off mainland China from much of the rest of the world.

The most populous country in the world had gone Communist.

The Korean Conflict

Although the Far East is remote from the United States, something of the import of events there was making a depressing impact on America. The sweep of Communism was both startling and opened up fearful prospects. In September, before the final fall of mainland China in 1949, the announcement came that the Soviet Union had exploded an atomic bomb. Now all of the East Asian mainland was Communist with one small exception—South Korea. In early 1950, Dean Acheson, now Secretary of State, announced that the United States would continue to defend the Philippines, Japan, and some areas in the northern Pacific, but not on the mainland of China.

This was almost certainly an invitation to the Communists to take South Korea. Japan had controlled Korea for most of the 20th century up to 1945. The Allies, mainly the United States, had determined that Korea should be an independent country once again when the Japanese had been driven out. Russian troops moved into northern Korea in August, 1945; American troops moved into southern Korea in September. By agreement, the Soviet Union then undertook to occupy the zone north of the 38th parallel and the United States the zone south of that line. That was the origin of a separate North and South Korea, though it was no part of the intention of the United States to make such a permanent division. The expectation was that the United States and the Soviet Union would cooperate in establishing a unified government for all of Korea. That was not to be.

The Soviet Union proceeded to install a Communist regime in North Korea and blocked all efforts at unified control. The United States objected to Russia's unilateral action and took the matter before the United Nations

General Assembly. A Commission was appointed and came to Korea in 1948 with the aim of establishing a constitutional government for all of Korea. The Commission was not permitted to enter the Soviet zone. The Commission proceeded to establish a government, and Syngman Rhee was elected President. Although the General Assembly confirmed that this was to be the government for all of Korea, it actually governed only South Korea. In 1949, American occupying forces were withdrawn, and South Korea proceeded on its course as an independent country.

The Soviet Union had trained and equipped an army for North Korea before withdrawing the bulk of its forces. On Sunday, June 25, 1950, North Korea launched a massive, unprovoked, surprise attack on South Korea. That the invasion was done with the advice and consent of the Soviet Union, as well as Communist China, is both a reasonable assumption and as nearly certain as it could be without official confirmation. As soon as word of the attack reached Washington, Secretary of State Acheson took the necessary steps to get an emergency session of the United Nations Security Council. The Soviet Union was at that time boycotting the Council because the representative of Nationalist China still held the seat there, and in the absence of the Russians, the Council voted unanimously to condemn the aggression and demand withdrawal.

John Foster Dulles and another State Department official in Tokyo radioed Acheson: "We believe that it appears the South Koreans cannot themselves contain or repulse the attack. U. S. force should be used, even though this risks Russian counter moves. To sit by while Korea is overrun by unprovoked armed attack would start a World War."[136] Truman ordered MacArthur, the American commander in Tokyo, to employ naval and air forces to aid South Korea. On June 27, the Security Council adopted a resolution requesting that all member nations come to the assistance of South Korea. Following this resolution, Truman ordered General MacArthur to commit combat forces into Korea. He did not ask for nor receive a declaration of war from Congress. Instead, it was styled a conflict, and conducted and technically directed by the United Nations. Actually, most of the United Nations took no active part in the war. Token forces were sent from Great Britain, Australia, Turkey, and the Philippines. Most of the fighting was done by the forces of the United States and South Korea. General MacArthur was appointed supreme commander of all United Nations forces in Korea, including, of course, those of the United States.

The North Korean forces swiftly broke the defenses of the South, driving out the government from Seoul, and sweeping through the south in July. By August, Korean and American forces were precariously holding a shallow perimeter on the southeastern corner of Korea. It looked as if they might be driven entirely off the peninsula. MacArthur issued his "stand or die" order to General Walton Walker, and the lines held. Meanwhile, MacArthur was planning a daring maneuver. He proposed to make a surprise landing at

Inchon, a port city a few miles from Seoul, to cut off the North Koreans from their supply from the north, and to envelop their armies. He met strong resistance from the Joint Chiefs of Staff at first, but MacArthur was determined, and the authorities in Washington finally approved.

The landing at Inchon was entirely successful. United Nations forces swiftly drove the North Koreans from the South. The landing had been made in the middle of September, and by October 1, the North Koreans were driven back to the 38th parallel. Poised to launch an invasion into the North and end the war, MacArthur called upon the North Koreans to lay down their arms and surrender. When he received no reply, he launched his invasion. Within a few weeks, virtually all resistance had crumbled, and MacArthur ordered what he hoped would be an offensive to end the war. Then, suddenly, as the war was apparently moving toward its conclusion with a victory for the forces which had answered the call of the United Nations, the Chinese swept across the Yalu river to intervene in the war. MacArthur had divided his forces for what was to be the final drive, and in mid-November the Chinese forces moved in and took positions between them. In late November, 1950, the Chinese struck in force, first against General Walker's Eighth Army and then the other United Nations' forces. In the ensuing weeks the cream of the Chinese army flowed into North Korea, driving the vastly outnumbered forces of MacArthur back toward and into the South. As MacArthur said, he now had a "new war" on his hands.

From the time in November, 1950 when MacArthur first discovered Chinese units in Korea until his summary dismissal in April, 1951, there occurred one of the strangest developments that has ever occurred. China went to war against United Nations (mainly American and South Korean) forces in Korea. That this was an act of war not only against the United States and the legitimate government of Korea but also against the United Nations generally was patently the case. In all of American history there had never been a more clear cut and unprovoked attack against the United States. President Truman, who had acted with swift resolve and vigor when North Korea invaded South Korea, now became tentative and timid. From the time of the Chinese intrusion and as massive Chinese armies were driving MacArthur's forces southward across the 38th parallel and retaking Seoul, he had only one action directive. It was to resist the Chinese within the bounds of Korea until MacArthur's armies had to be evacuated from the whole Korean peninsula. In early December, 1950, well before the bulk of the Chinese force had arrived on the battle front, MacArthur estimated that his seven divisions were confronted by "approximately 26 divisions . . . in line of battle with an additional minimum of 200,000 to the immediate rear and now in the process of being committed to action. In addition to this, remnants of the North Korean army are being reorganized in the rear, and there stands, of course, behind all the military potential of Communist

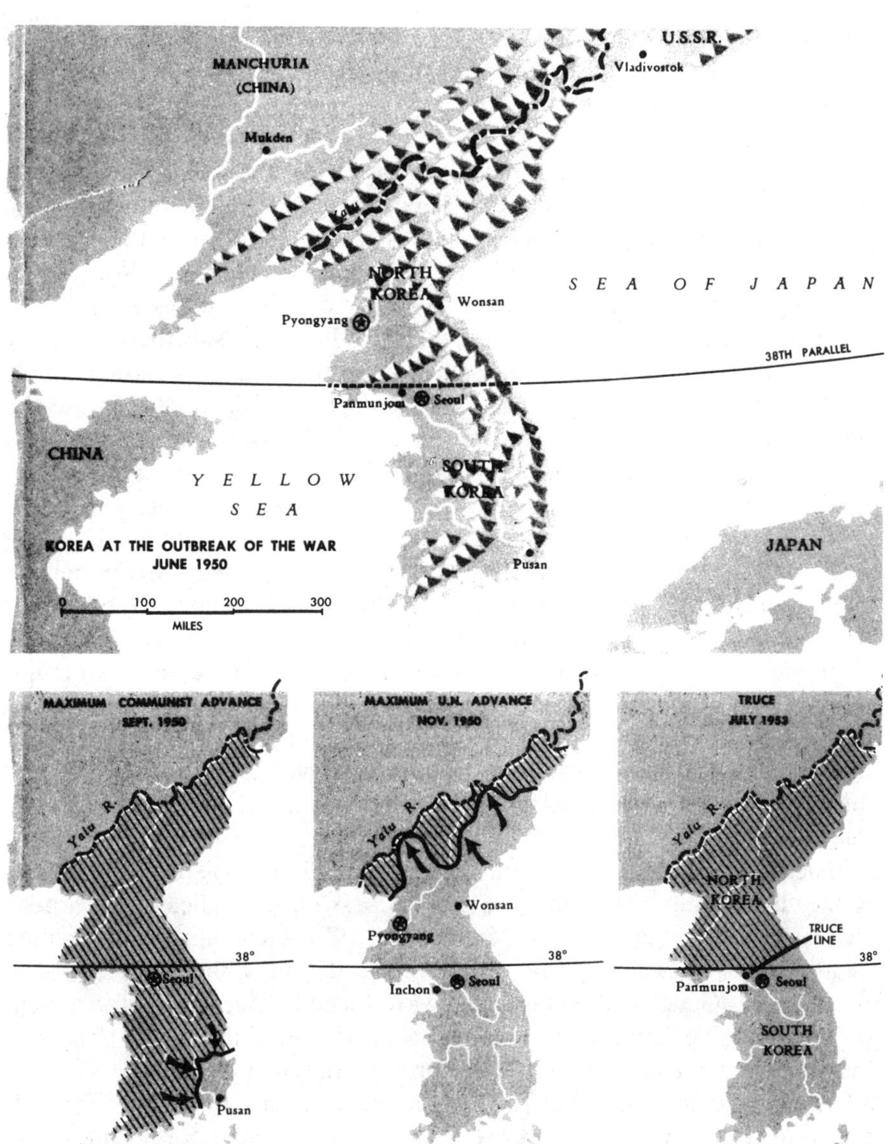
MANCHURIA
(CHINA)
Mukden
U.S.S.R.
Vladivostok
Yalu
NORTH
KOREA
Wonsan
Pyongyang
SEA OF JAPAN
38TH PARALLEL
Panmunjom
Seoul
CHINA
YELLOW
SEA
SOUTH
KOREA
JAPAN
Pusan
KOREA AT THE OUTBREAK OF THE WAR
JUNE 1950
0
100
200
300
MILES
MAXIMUM COMMUNIST ADVANCE
SEPT. 1950
Yalu R.
38°
Seoul
Pusan
MAXIMUM U.N. ADVANCE
NOV. 1950
Yalu R.
Wonsan
Pyongyang
38°
Inchon
Seoul
TRUCE
JULY 1953
Yalu R.
NORTH
KOREA
TRUCE
LINE
38°
Panmunjom
Seoul
SOUTH
KOREA

China."[137] In the face of all this, MacArthur was denied the use of the means at his disposal to effectively retaliate against and punish the Chinese.

When troops began to pour from Manchuria into Korea, his request for permission to bomb the bridges over the Yalu was denied. When MacArthur persisted, he was granted permission to bomb the bridges on the Korean side, but this was tactically impossible. Planes sent in with bombs were subject to attack by Chinese fighters which could fire at the bombers and retire behind their own sanctuary lines unharmed. Nor would Washington permit the attack on any border or other targets in China or pursue Chinese planes. All of mainland China became a sanctuary from any attack. The Nationalists on Formosa had a considerable military force ready to attack the mainland, yet MacArthur's standing orders were to use the Seventh Fleet, if necessary, to prevent any such assault. MacArthur was badly in need of reinforcements in Korea; Chiang Kai-shek was willing to send his crack troops. Washington denied MacArthur authority to use this army. The excuse given was that the small British contingent would object to fighting alongside the Nationalists. Britain had recognized Communist China, and presumably wished to be on the best of terms with that country, despite the fact that the British were fighting them. Nor could reinforcements be obtained as needed from the United Nations. No major mobilization was begun in any timely fashion in the United States, and other nations evinced little concern with coming to MacArthur's aid. MacArthur's frustration was almost unbearable, yet he followed rigorously the restrictive orders placed upon him and continued to do his soldierly duty.

Indeed, MacArthur did much better than might have been expected. Rather than being driven into the sea, as pessimists predicted, his armies stiffened south of Seoul and held in January, 1951. General Walker had died in a freak accident, and MacArthur replaced him with an equally able commander, General Matthew Ridgeway. Indeed, Ridgeway's force went on the offensive, took Seoul once again in March, and in short order had moved back to, and at some points north of, the 38th parallel.

At this juncture, President Truman removed General MacArthur from all his commands on April 11, 1951. He did so without prior warning and summarily; the word came to MacArthur first by radio and then in a cryptic message from the President. There is no doubt that MacArthur's view of the situation in the Orient and what needed doing was coming to differ significantly from that which now prevailed in the Truman administration. Once China entered the war, he held that it was now an entirely different war and should be fought in a different way. On the broadest view, he believed that International Communism had thrown down the gauntlet with the entry of Red China into Korea. It challenged the will of independent countries to resist the expansion of communism. The time was at hand, he believed, to send the strongest message to International Communism that it would be severely punished if it extended its power. That had already been done to North Korea, and Communist China had now invited a similar lesson.

By contrast, the Truman administration had decided that it was to be a war limited exclusively to Korea. A new kind of war was announced, in effect—limited war. It was not to be a war fought to victory, not a war in which aggressors were to be overcome and shown the errors of their ways; instead, it was now to be restricted simply to holding on and allowing whoever would to pour forces into poor Korea. The Truman administration was under pressure from Britain to pursue this limited war. Britain had a Labour (socialist) Government with Clement Atlee as prime minister. A portion of Atlee's party was sympathetic to communism; those who were not were hardly committed to making strong stands against them. The British, and French as well, believed that the defense of Europe was the crucial matter, not war in the Far East. Even Winston Churchill declared that "the sooner the Far Eastern diversion . . . can be brought into something like a static and stabilised [condition], the better it will be. . . . For it is in Europe that the world cause will be decided . . . , it is here that the mortal danger lies. . . . "[138] Also, the British wished to continue good relations with China for trade and other reasons. Truman's own State Department contained some people whose loyalty to America's interest was in doubt, as pointed out above. MacArthur had long been sniped at by elements in the British and American press, and he had been undermined in a variety of ways.

Truman may have had reasons other than those in the Far East for summarily dismissing MacArthur. He was an increasingly frustrated man himself. His control over the American government was tenuous at best by 1951, as his influence and popularity dwindled. His presidency was at a low ebb, from which it never really recovered. Republicans had grown in number in Congress in the mid-term elections and they were meeting with increasing success in discrediting him. Revelations of spies and national disloyalty in his administration plagued him. He relied heavily on World War II military men to give some prestige to him. As his authority waned, he reached out to assert it vigorously and dramatically in an arena where he still could, over the most conspicuous active military leader—General Douglas MacArthur.

None of these things were alleged as reasons for dismissing MacArthur, of course. For several months prior to his dismissal, MacArthur's superiors had taken ever more stringent efforts to muzzle him (and indeed all military leaders). He was to make no public statement which had not been first cleared by authorities directing him. While Truman made no formal charges against MacArthur, he did explain that he had dismissed him because the general had failed to observe the restrictions placed upon him. One instance was a statement he had made in March, which MacArthur characterized as a summation of the situation in Korea. The other was a letter he had written to the Republican leader in the House, Joseph Martin, in reply to his request.

When Martin made the letter public, Truman moved swiftly to dismiss MacArthur.

The issue, as Truman and his apologists would have it, was military subordination to civilian authorities. MacArthur had duly followed the command orders that came down to him, and no evidence was ever brought forward to show otherwise. However, he did not suppose it was insubordination to disagree with the restrictive policies under which he was trying to operate. Nor was any determination made that he had been insubordinate. Instead, Truman dismissed him, removed him from any official position from which he might speak (i.e., officially silenced him), and removed the opportunity for a formal rebuttal of his allegations. Truman tried to shift the issue away from the correctness of the conduct of the war to the bogus issue of civil control over the military. MacArthur had never questioned the authority of the President, only the wisdom of his policies.

If Truman had hoped to silence and discredit MacArthur, the immediate impact was exactly the opposite. The summary dismissal of MacArthur provoked such a furor of opposition to Truman and rallying behind MacArthur as the nation has seldom, if ever, witnessed. The Republicans, under the leadership of Senator Robert A. Taft of Ohio and House leader Joseph Martin, met as soon as they could following the announcement and promised a thorough investigation. "In addition," Martin told newsmen, "the question of impeachments was discussed." Telegrams and letters to the White House came by the bushels, and they overwhelmingly condemned Truman for his action. One history described the widespread immediate reaction this way: "From San Gabriel, California to Worcester, Massachusetts, Harry Truman was burned in effigy. In Los Angeles the City Council adjourned 'in sorrowful contemplation of the political assassination' of the General. In Charlestown, Maryland, a woman tried to send a wire calling the President a moron, was told she couldn't, persisted in epithets, until the clerk let her tell Harry Truman he was a 'witling.' In Eastham, Massachusetts, Little Rock, Houston, and Oakland, flags went down to half-mast. People savored scores of new anti-Truman stories. 'This wouldn't have happened if Truman were alive,' the wisecracks went."[139]

As MacArthur flew from Tokyo to Honolulu to San Francisco to Washington to New York City, he met cheering and sorrowful throngs. In Tokyo, Emperor Hirohito made an unprecedented visit to his quarters to bid MacArthur farewell. A million people lined the streets as he drove to the airport, tearful and silent, waving Japanese and American flags. It had been almost fourteen years since MacArthur had set foot in continental United States, and he had since become almost a legendary figure. The greeting of the crowds in San Francisco was tumultuous. MacArthur had been invited to address Congress, but there was one final effort from the Department of Defense to censor his utterances. He received a message from the Army that he should submit a copy of his speech for approval before delivering it.

U.P.

Robert A. Taft (1889–1953)

Taft was a national political leader from Ohio. He was elected to the United States Senate in 1938 and was twice re-elected to that post. The son of President William Howard Taft, Robert was born in Ohio and educated at Yale and Harvard. He was admitted to the bar in 1913 but was thereafter more often engaged in political pursuits than the law. After World War I, Taft served off and on in the Ohio legislature until his election to the Senate in 1938. In that position, he was an able critic of both the welfare state and international entanglements, which made him the natural leader of the conservative wing of the Republicans after World War II. Twice he sought the Republican nomination for President but failed to get it both times. He came close in 1952, but lost at the convention to the popular General Eisenhower.

MacArthur challenged the authority for this, and the Army backed down.[140] In Washington, he addressed a somber joint session of Congress. The ovation at the conclusion was thunderous. MacArthur had told the legislaters, "War's very object is victory." "In war, there is no substitute for victory."[141] In New York City, famed for its ticker tape parades, MacArthur's turnout may have been the largest ever; the estimates of the crowds ranged from seven to ten million people. In the ensuing weeks and months he traveled over much of the United States to make speeches.

So far as the conflict in Korea was concerned, all this was much ado about nothing. The conflict continued off and on for nearly two more years. The Soviet delegate to the United Nations suggested in June, 1951, that the Chinese and North Koreans might accept a truce. One historian says, "We now know that the strengthened United Nations armies could have cleared the decimated Communist forces from North Korea in the summer of 1951 and that the Russians proposed truce talks chiefly to avert this catastrophe to their cause."[142] But Washington was so eager to come to terms that truce talks were begun in July. After two years of on and off negotiations, an armistice was finally signed in mid-1953. An uneasy peace along the lines as they had more or less existed before the conflict was restored.

Anti-Communism: Popular Fervor vs. Sophistry

Most Americans do not like or want communism. On a scale of one to ten, most would be likely to assign it a one, if they had no option to give a negative rating to it. They do not want communism for their own country. On every occasion when they have had an opportunity to vote for candidates under that name, they have rejected them out of hand. Nor do they favor communism being imposed upon other peoples, though the extent to which they might be aroused by this would vary. Nor is there any reason to suppose that, other things being equal, Americans generally would have any great difficulty in grasping the expansive, subversive, conspiratorial, and tyrannical nature of international communism. Indeed, given the provocation by communist powers (which has rarely been wanting) and the leadership, there have been a number of times in the 20th century when Americans would almost certainly have rallied to make the determined effort to isolate and crush the will to expansion of communism. Certainly, in the early 1950s there was strong popular feeling in favor of much more determined action than the government was willing to take.

Twice in the early 1950s, popular feeling rose to a pitch over American policy toward communism. Both times it was deflected from its course and subsided. The first time was over the conduct of the war in Korea, which culminated in what is known as the Truman-MacArthur controversy. This was deflected from its policy goal by the Truman Administration by raising a bogus issue of civilian control over the military. Attention was thus diverted, eventually at least, from the question of how to deal with an invasion by Chinese Communist subversion. The second time was over internal subversion, evinced itself in the rise of what has generally been described as McCarthyism, and culminated in the censure of Senator Joseph McCarthy of Wisconsin by the United States Senate. The thrust toward the investigation, exposure, and prevention of subversion was deflected from its course by the focus on the methods of McCarthy. Once again, the villain, so to speak, became not the behavior of Communists, their sympathizers, and apologists, but loyal Americans.

During the Cold War, a contest for control of foreign policy has gone on between sophistry and popular fervor. This has been especially the case in dealing with communism, which is what the Cold War has been about. Sooner or later, sophistry has usually won the contest, has stemmed the tide of anti-communism, has deflected popular fervor from its foreign policy object, and has more often than not resulted in the appeasement of Communists. A sophist is one who believes nothing and will argue any side with equal fervor. More to the point, perhaps, sophistry is the art of making the better case appear the worst, of calling forth any argument to discredit the opposition, of muddying the waters, of confusing the issue, of deflecting a devastating argument by focusing on a side issue, and so on. But in the

Cold War the sophistry that has been most widely employed has been in the hands of those opposed to popular anti-communism and in favor of coming to terms with communism. Thus, the sophistry has been used for partisan ends.

The people who usually employ the sophistry would prefer to be called pragmatists. They are commonly "liberal" intellectuals, but they are aided by communists, communist sympathizers, and an assortment of folks, such as those who may see communists as underdogs in America and perversely find pleasure in not conforming to what they take to be the popular view. These modern sophists wield their influence as purveyers of ideas, as professors and teachers, as bureaucrats, as ministers, journalists, in radio and television, in the making of plays and movies or writers of books and novels. Aside from direct influence on government, they are most effective in de-escalating popular anti-communist fervor. They do so, for example, by *not* writing or publishing or favorably reviewing vivid depictions of communist tyranny, and always by sophistical arguments against confronting communism.

A number of developments and revelations contributed to popular anti-communism in the years immediately after World War II. Anti-communism was at a low ebb during World War II. Not only was the United States allied with the Soviet Union but also much propaganda favorable to the Soviets was spread in the United States. Communist expansion in eastern Europe after the war served as a base at the beginning for a revived anti-communism. Soviet belligerence and refusal to cooperate fueled the fire. The fall of China to Communism aroused new fears, and the Korean conflict brought the threat of communism home to many Americans. But there was much else besides. For those who heard or knew of them, the reports of the Senate Internal Security Subcommittee and the House Un-American Activities Committee told a continuing story of infiltration, subversion by Communists within the United States.

Perhaps the most startling of all the revelations of subversion and espionage were those of how the Soviet Union managed to steal atomic secrets which enabled that technologically and scientifically backward country to build an atomic explosive device within four years of Hiroshima. Everything about the atomic project was top secret during World War II, and much remained a secret officially afterward. Where the interlocked projects were located was secret; what scientists were engaged in the work was secret; the design of buildings was secret; the equipment that was assembled or built was secret, and so on and on. The official United States policy was that none of these secrets was to be made known to the Soviet Union, or to any other governments except those of Britain and Canada.

Yet during the course of World War II the Soviet government was able to penetrate the veil and learn virtually everything that it needed to know to duplicate the American and British achievement. Much of this story of espionage was unraveled in court hearings and testimony before congressional committees and the like from 1948–1953. So far as has ever been ascertained, the basic work of turning over secrets was done by those working in the various projects during World War II. Of those who were discovered, they were all more or less Communists, though not in the common phrase, "card-carrying Communists." Once a Communist becomes a spy, he usually breaks all formal connections with the Communist Party, and he would not be caught dead, so to speak, with any identification card or otherwise showing he was a party member. The usual process was that the spy turn over the information to a courier who would then turn it over to a Soviet agent. This was generally the process whether what was involved was atomic secrets, industrial information, military information, or what not. Soviet espionage operations are large; the appetite for information of the Soviet government is huge; and much cloak and dagger activity has long been carried on.

The first inklings of the penetration of atomic secrets to come to public knowledge were revelations by a Soviet defector in Canada, Igor Gouzenko, that there was a large Communist spy network in Canada, the United States, and Britain. Elizabeth Bentley, a former Communist courier, began making revelations of her activities. Allen Nunn May, a British scientist, was caught, tried, and convicted. Klaus Fuchs, a leading scientist who worked on atomic projects both in England and the United States, was caught and something of the large extent of his betrayal became known. The amount of material of one sort or another being shipped from the United States to the Soviet Union—ranging from blueprints of atomic installations to uranium—was suggested by the testimony of George R. Jordan in testimony before the House Un-American Activities Committee in 1949–1950. Jordan had been a major in the Air Force during World War II, had been liaison officer to the Soviet Purchasing Agency at its major shipping point in Great Falls, Montana. He testified that large quantities of strange materials were flown from there, usually concealed in suitcases. He grew increasingly suspicious of these suitcases, and when he managed to open them he found much that had the look of secret papers, blueprints, and the like. He reported as best he could what was going on, tried to get it investigated at the time, but found the State Department, at least, entirely uncooperative even in giving clear answers as to what could go out in what containers under the protection of diplomatic immunity. Of American spies convicted for their roles, there were David Greenglass, Harry Gold, and Julius and Ethel Rosenberg. The Rosenbergs were convicted and eventually executed for treason, though they would no doubt have had their sentence reduced had they confessed. As it was, the trail pretty much ended with them.

The laxity of security, at least so far as people with Communist connections was concerned, at atomic installations is suggested by information elicited over the years from Dr. J. Robert Oppenheimer. Op-

J. Robert Oppenheimer (1904–1967)

Oppenheimer was a nuclear physicist and had a crucial role in building the first atomic bomb at Los Alamos, New Mexico. He was born in New York City, graduated from Harvard, and received his Ph.D. from a German University. From 1929 to 1947 he was on the faculty of the University of California (and a technical institute) and did intensive research on the nucleus of the atom. He took leave from his academic positions in 1943 to direct the atomic laboratory at Los Alamos. After World War II, Oppenheimer served for several years as an adviser to the Atomic Energy Commission. In 1954, he was stripped of his security clearance because of questionable associations with Communists and his lax treatment of security matters. Afterward, he directed the Institute for Advanced Studies at Princeton.

penheimer headed the crucial project at Los Alamos, New Mexico, where the bombs were finally assembled. He was both an atomic scientist and effective administrator during the war years in pushing the project through to completion. After the war, however, he was, after extensive investigation, denied security clearance to work on secret projects, and the investigations revealed how little concerned he was about people around him with Communist backgrounds. He had himself been an enthusiastic supporter of many Communist-front organizations. His wife had been a Communist, and many of their acquaintances—including some who worked at Los Alamos—had Communist connections. Indeed, Oppenheimer was approached on at least one occasion about turning over materials to the Russians; yet he did not report the incident and, even when pressed on the matter, refused to reveal the name of the man. These things are at least suggestive of how widespread and effective the Communist effort may have been.

In any case, there is bountiful evidence that the Soviet Union got the know-how for building atomic bombs through this spy network. Estimates vary as to how long it might have taken the Russians to build an atomic bomb without this explicit information. The task was a huge one for the combined resources of the United States, Britain and Canada, working with the most advanced scientists in the world, with the aid of great corporations specialized in the production of the most sophisticated technology. Some say that it would have probably taken ten years at least, but there is no assurance that they could ever have accomplished it at all, so complex were the problems and so chancy was the likelihood of success. Ralph de Toledano, in his enthralling book on the spy revelations, *The Greatest Plot in History*, had this to say in summary of the achievement of the atomic spies:

> . . . Thousands of words in the precise handwriting of Klaus Fuchs, sketches from David Greenglass, applied theory from the Communist cell at Berkeley, data from Clarence Hiskey, experimental techniques for Pontecorvo, bomb technology from Joan Hinton, invaluable materials from Nunn May, blueprints that funneled through Great Falls—this was the ball game. . . . Every piece of information sped the Soviet traveler down the road hacked out by Western scientific genius. Given this help, the wonder is not that the Soviet Union developed a nuclear device of its own in four years but that it took so long.[143]

There were other exposés and revelations during these years as well, particularly of the influence within American government of Communists and those under their influence. The case that drew the most public attention was the exposure of Alger Hiss by Whittaker Chambers. Hiss was an important second level official in the State Department during and immediately after World War II. He had been an adviser to Roosevelt at the Yalta Conference and played a leading role in forming the United Nations Organization. Thus, when Chambers revealed before the House Un-American Activities Committee that Hiss had Communist connections it created a considerable stir. Even so, nothing might have come of the testimony if a young Congressman from California, Richard M. Nixon, had not pushed the investigation through to completion near the end of it. Hiss denied all charges at first, or that he had ever known Chambers. Chambers did not make a good impression as a witness: he was overweight, a sloppy dresser, and confessed that he had been a Communist in the 1930s and served as a courier for the Party. Hiss, by contrast, had many friends in high places, was then employed by a prestigious foundation, was good looking, and had risen high in government ranks. But Nixon persisted, Chambers brought in more and more evidence, ultimately evidence to support his final charge that Hiss had turned over government papers to him time and again. Hiss was eventually sent to prison for perjury.

There were other, perhaps less dramatic, Communist revelations during these years. The role of Communist sympathizers in the Far Eastern division of the State Department began to come to light. The United States government conducted a lengthy trial of the eleven top Communist Party leaders and won a conviction. This trial was very important because it drove home the point that the American Communist Party was controlled from

Moscow and was an instrument for funding and directing subversive activities in the United States.

One thing that came out of many of these investigations was laxity in government in dealing with those who had been exposed as Communists or sympathizers. Time and time again there were cases of people whose affiliations had been reported but who continued to work in sensitive positions. For example, Roy Cohn, who served as counsel for Senator McCarthy, says that at an earlier time when the eleven Communist leaders were being tried he came across such a case for the first time. The defense called a witness for their side, a man who had held high posts in the government. His name was Doxey Wilkerson. Cohn "remarked to an FBI agent that it surprised me that a man with such an impressive record in government would agree to testify as he did for the Communist leaders. The Agent looked at me and laughed: 'Wilkerson,' he said, 'is not only a Communist himself, but he's one of the top leaders of the party. He's been on their National Committee.'"[144] Cohn expressed his shock that a man with that background should be in government, and the agent told him that he had a lot to learn about what went on. Cohn was later to learn that as early as 1942 J. Edgar Hoover had sent an extensive report of this background to the agency where Wilkerson worked. Far from being removed from office, he was given a higher post in subsequent years. Chambers had reported the background of Hiss to a higher government official long before he testified before Congress, only to have the information ignored. Many times those exposed were kept on in sensitive positions. A large gap existed between what was becoming known and what the government was doing about it.

Senator McCarthy began his move to fill the gap in 1950. He determined to give maximum publicity to the laxness of government agencies to Communists and people under their influence, to put pressure on those in power to act, and to drive people out of office who "coddled" Communists. He began his campaign in 1950 with a speech in Wheeling, West Virginia by claiming that there were ____ people with Communist connections working in the State Department. (The actual number he mentioned has remained in doubt ever since, probably either 205, 57, or 81.) He gave similar speeches elsewhere during the following weeks. He compiled a list of names and sent them to the executive branch. The Senate appointed a special committee under the chairmanship of Senator Millard Tydings of Maryland to investigate "whether persons who are disloyal to the United States are, or have been, employed by the Department of State." It was a partisan committee, since the Senate was controlled by Democrats, and Tydings was a Democrat. McCarthy gave Tydings a list of 110 names of those he claimed were disloyal, 48 of whom were not then employed by the State Department and 62 who were. Instead of making thorough investigations of the charges, Tydings investigated McCarthy, and the

Harris & Ewing

Joseph R. McCarthy (1908–1956)

McCarthy made a concerted effort to drive Communists and those attuned to the Communist line out of government in the early 1950s. He was born in Wisconsin, graduated from Marquette University, and was admitted to the bar. He did not practice law for long before he ran for office as a judge, was elected, and began to become well known. In World War II, McCarthy was with the Marines in the Pacific. In 1944, he sought the Republican nomination for the Senate while he was still in the Marines. He failed in that bid, but ran again in 1946 against Robert M. LaFollette, Jr. and won both nomination for and election to the Senate. In 1950, he began his crusade against Communists in government. He was often blunt in his charges, which probably helped in gaining popularity for his cause but it also earned him some bitter enemies. After his censure by the Senate in 1954, McCarthy lost most of his influence and died less than three years later of a lengthy illness.

majority (Democratic) of the committee concluded that McCarthy's charges were "a fraud and a hoax."

Actually, as was proven by later investigations, there were a goodly number of people on the list whose loyalty to the United States was doubtful. Among them were Owen Lattimore, who the McCarran Committee later described as a "conscious, articulate instrument of the Soviet conspiracy"; William Remington, convicted of perjury for denying his Communist Party membership; John Stewart Service, finally dismissed as a security risk; and John Carter Vincent, who had been identified as a Communist at one time, but was dismissed from the State Department for exercising bad judgment. "There were quite a few (other) similar cases; people with bulging records of pro-Communist activities and associations successfully weathered many departmental security hearings, only to be discharged or allowed to resign under fire later—after McCarthy's charges."[145]

McCarthy was hardly turned away from his anti-Communist activities by

Dwight D. Eisenhower (1890–1969)

Eisenhower was the 34th President of the United States, a professional soldier, and supreme commander of allied forces in the invasion of France in World War II. He was born in Texas, grew up in Kansas, and graduated from West Point. He trained troops in the United States during World War I, and usually served on some higher officer's staff during the interwar years. Although he had never had combat experience and knew military tactics and strategy second hand, Eisenhower was given top command positions in North Africa, Sicily, and France. The skills of getting along with military men which he had honed in the interwar years fitted him well for the diplomacy required in commanding multi-national forces, but the strategy he usually approved bore the earmarks more of the compromises of diplomacy than military genius. After the war, he served briefly as president of Columbia University before returning to Europe to command NATO forces. As President, he showed considerable skill in quieting the political furors which had preceded him, and he was re-elected in 1956 for a second term. He was one of the most popular presidents of the 20th century.

the Tydings report. During 1952, he not only continued to investigate and speak out but also to campaign vigorously against those who were attempting to thwart him. Tydings himself was defeated in this presidential election year, and it is generally conceded that McCarthy's support may have been the decisive factor in the election of several new members to Congress. In any case, not only was the Republican Dwight D. Eisenhower elected President but also a Republican majority now controlled the Senate. Those who hoped that McCarthy would be silenced once the Republicans were in power were doomed to disappointment. McCarthy now headed the Government Operations Committee and a subcommittee under it which he used in his continuing investigation of subversives in government. In 1953–1954, McCarthy investigated the "Voice of America" program and the overseas libraries of the United States Information Service. He then turned to the question of Communists in the armed forces. This aroused the Eisenhower Administration, and McCarthy not only occupied the center stage but also was often put on the spot in the resulting Army-McCarthy hearings in 1954.

Indeed, McCarthy had come under increasingly vigorous and bitter criticism ever since the Tydings investigation. Liberal intellectuals ranged from furious to hysterical about McCarthy, and they did all in their considerable power to destroy him. Above all, they labored to shift the issue away from Communists and subversives in government toward the personal flaws they perceived in McCarthy and upon his tactics. In short, they employed the *ad hominem* attack to discredit him and draw attention away from his revelations. A Washington *Post* cartoonist, Herbert Block, known as "Herblock," published a cartoon picturing McCarthy as a blackener of reputations and referred to the phenomenon as "McCarthyism." The name caught on and became a synonym for one who uses reckless charges, blackens the reputation of innocent people, and swings wildly at those he opposes. The concerted assaults upon McCarthy eventually bore political fruit. In July, 1954, Senator Ralph Flanders of Vermont made a motion in the Senate to censure McCarthy. The committee appointed to investigate recommended that McCarthy be censured for conduct unbecoming a Senator, and a majority of Senators, 67–22, approved the censure resolution in December, 1954. Thereafter, McCarthy's influence waned; he had been effectively silenced.

Something remained, and remains, from all this, however. Liberal intellectuals in general and all those who have a stake in restraining the exposure of Communists, subversive activities, the undermining of American institutions, and the like, have a convenient weapon to beat anyone over the head with who begins to gain an audience for charges against them. It is "McCarthyism." Indeed, they have even succeeded quite often in making it appear that anti-communism is somehow dishonest and tainted. In truth, McCarthy was none too nice in his methods: he was a vigorous prosecuting attorney, so to speak, in his investigations, and he did not state his findings with scholarly precision. Had he exercised the restraint which his critics demanded, however, McCarthy would probably have made no mark at all. The impression remains that his real sin in the eyes of his critics was that McCarthy was a large threat to the world view within which Communists must be tolerated and accepted and eventually accommodated.

Twists and Turns in Cold War

The Cold War did not end in the 1950s; in fact, it has not ended as of this writing. Communist expansion has continued apace from that day to this: in the Middle East (Syria and Afghanistan, for example), Indochina (Vietnam and Cambodia, for example), in Africa (Libya and Ethiopia, for example), and Latin America (Cuba and Nicaragua, for example). Nor has Communist infiltration, subversion, and espionage abated in non-Communist lands. Incidents of Communist barbarity at home and abroad have abounded from 1955 to 1985: the building of the Berlin Wall in the early 1960s and shooting down of East Germans who tried to escape, for one example; the shooting down and hence massacre of 269 innocent passengers aboard KAL 007 in 1983 for another. Communist fomenting of civil wars and gangster takeovers in various countries has continued much as before. Fidel Castro completed his gangster-like takeover in Cuba in 1959, established a dictatorship, drove out large numbers of people, imprisoned and shot others, and proceeded to arm the island with Soviet materials.

The United States got progressively involved in an intensive guerrilla war in Vietnam in the course of the 1960s. Unlike Korea, however, there was never much likelihood that the war would be won. MacArthur's dire predictions of the consequences of appeasement of Communists were fulfilled in what was once known as Indochina. As American forces became deeply committed after the mid-1960s, they operated under such restraints that victory over the enemy was not a possibility. The war was directed and supplied from North Vietnam (aided mainly by the Soviet Union), but neither American nor Vietnamese forces were permitted to invade that country. Not even full scale naval activity against the invaders was permitted, and bombing was limited. No government could be overwhelmed or driven out. Guerrillas could come and go, infiltrate in civilian attire, strike wherever they could, and vanish. It was largely a hopeless war, ambiguous and debilitating.

The Cold War continued after the mid-1950s, but much of the life went out of it after the firing of MacArthur and the silencing of McCarthy. It became amorphous, lost its edge, took on the indirection of diplomatic exchanges, became non-confrontational generally, and had many twists and turns. Stalin died in 1953, and Soviet Communism began to put on a different face to the world, first under Georgi Malenkov, who shortly lost control to Nikita Khrushchev, a clownish dictator who took pleasure in playing to the peanut galleries around the world. Khrushchev denounced the oppressive personal rule of Stalin (in which he played a prominent role) and invited capitalist countries to co-exist with communism.

Changes occurred in the United States as well in the mid-1950s, besides those already noted. Eisenhower became President in 1953, and with a Republican Senate the Republicans were in control of foreign policy. The Democrats were widely suspected of being soft on communism, while the Republicans who had generally talked about being tough were now in power. Initially, the tough talk continued. John Foster Dulles, the new Secretary of State, declared in 1953 that "containing Russia where it now is, is, in itself, an unsound policy; . . . we must always have in mind the liberation of these captive peoples.'' Containment alone, he said, ''is a policy which is bound to fail because a purely defensive policy never wins against an aggressive policy. . . . It is only by keeping alive the hope of liberation, by taking advantage of that wherever opportunity arises, that we will end this terrible peril which dominates the world. . .''[146] In 1954, Dulles announced a policy of massive retaliation against Soviet aggression. Basically, he said, nations and associations of nations would be encouraged to defend themselves. But ''Local defenses must be reinforced by the further deterrent of massive retaliatory power.''[147]

New regional agreements were worked out during the Eisenhower administrations. The Southeast Asia Treaty Organization (SEATO) for mutual defense was formed in 1954. The United States, Great Britain, France, Australia, New Zealand, the Philippines, Thailand, and Pakistan signed it. Other pacts were worked out with particular countries. So far as liberating countries behind the Iron Curtain was concerned, nothing came of it. A rebellion broke out in Hungary in 1956; the Soviet Union sent in armed forces with tanks and put down the rebellion. The United States did not intervene. Nor did it do anything about incipient rebellions in other Soviet satellites. As for massive retaliation, no occasion arose for it, and there is no way to evaluate how effective it may have been.

Whether from the fear of massive retaliation, because of the change of rulers, or for whatever reasons, Soviet policy did change somewhat in the 1950s, though it should be emphasized that a policy change did not indicate a change in the goal of communizing the world. For one thing, a rift developed between the Soviet Union and Communist China. Communism definitely presented a less monolithic face toward the world. The earlier determination of Tito in Yugoslavia to follow an independent course had been the opening wedge in the monolith. Khrushchev even turned loose many of the political prisoners in slave labor camps. There was talk of a thaw in the Cold War, of detente and co-existence between East and West. The idea of competition not only between so-called capitalists and socialists countries but also between different communist centers took hold. This notion received its fullest development in connection with the concept of a Third World.

The Bandung Conference held in Indonesia in 1955 vitalized both the notion of competition (or possibly conflict) and the concept of a Third World. Communist China took a lead in this conference which was attended by representatives of 29 Asian and African countries. What was emphasized there was the view that there were many countries that ought not to be aligned either with the Soviet Union or the West. They belonged to a Third World, a world that was neither Western nor Russian. So far as socialism was the goal, the notion was around that they could move toward neither by the model of Moscow nor the gradualist approach of the West (though they were not much given to using this phrase). They would follow a third approach. India had long been attached to this non-aligned way, and the Bandung Conference was a none too subtle approach by Communist China to form its own configuration of nations. There have been racial overtones to this undertaking as well. The nations involved have usually been yellow, brown, or black predominantly, and that has sometimes been focused upon as distinguishing them from both predominantly white Russia and the West.

In any case, the phrase "Third World" caught on, though it has no precise meaning nor is it necessarily under any particular control of any one power. It has been wooed, however, by several power centers. The United States had been sending foreign aid to some of these countries beginning in the late 1940s and early 1950s. Both Communist China and the Soviet Union extended increasing aid to various Third World countries in the late 1950s and in the 1960s. Among the countries China extended aid to over the years were: Cambodia, Burma, Nepal, Laos, Ghana, Algeria, Nigeria, Chile, and Peru. A Soviet writer made the following claims (probably exaggerated) of Soviet aid through the 1960s:

> The Soviet Union began to establish extensive economic ties with Afro-Asian countries. Alongside the volume of ordinary export-import trade, an important role was played by technical and economic cooperation. . . . . [Today] the USSR is giving economic and technical assistance to 29 Afro-Asian countries.[148]

The Soviet Union has been more distinguished for its aid in establishing Communist regimes than anything else.

Since the mid-1950s a number of highly touted publicity meetings have occurred between Soviet dictators and American Presidents. These meetings are usually called summits by the American media, which usually pushes hard for such meetings to be held. They are supposed to ease tensions between the East and the West by bringing together those who speak for the two major atomic powers in the world. They are more publicity stunts and propaganda mills than conferences which settle the questions at issue between Moscow and the West. President Eisenhower traveled to Geneva to meet the Soviet dictator, Nikita Khrushchev, in 1955. A good time was had by all, but aside from something labeled "The spirit of Geneva," nothing much was accomplished. Khrushchev came to Camp David in 1959, and plans were made for a summit in Paris in 1960. The Paris summit never really got underway, however. Khrushchev had some temper tantrums because the United States had flown high level surveillance planes over Soviet territory, which had recently been proven when the Soviets shot one of them down. Khrushchev's idea of diplomacy was to pull off a shoe and bang it on the table, as he had done on a visit to the United Nations. The newly elected John F. Kennedy met with Khrushchev in Vienna in 1961, and shortly thereafter the Soviet Union began building the wall in Berlin and placing missiles in Cuba. President Lyndon Johnson met with Soviet Premier Alexei Kosygin in an impromptu summit at Glassboro, New Jersey in 1967. This was in the midst of the war in Vietnam, which depended to considerable extent on Soviet arms. A major offensive was launched by the Vietcong against American and South Vietnamese forces following Glassboro. Several summits have been held since, but aside from dubious strategic arms limitation agreements, they have been mostly intermissions between moves by the Soviet Union in its continuing thrust to improve its power position in relation to the West.

The winds of Communism have shifted from time to time over the years. There are those who watch the international weather vane and hail each shift of the wind as portending a basic change in communism. The more it changes, as the French say, the more it remains the same. Thaws, ballyhoo about co-existence, and detentes come and go, but Communist nations remain bent on extending the sway of communism.

Chapter 8

Welfarism at Home and Abroad

I hope for cooperation from farmers, from labor, and from business. Every segment of our population and every individual has a right to expect from our Government a fair deal.

—Harry S. Truman, 1949

. . . So that, although the United States is an old country—at least its Government is old as governments now go today—nevertheless I thought we were moving into a new period, and the new frontier phrase expressed that hope.

—John F. Kennedy, 1961

Building the Great Society will require a major effort on the part of every Federal agency in two directions—First, formulating imaginative new ideas and programs; and—Second, carrying out hard-hitting, tough-minded reforms in existing programs.

—Lyndon B. Johnson, 1964

Chronology

1946—Employment Act

1947—Taft-Hartley Act

1948—Truman elected President

1949—Housing Act

1952—Eisenhower elected President

1953—Creation of Department of Health, Education and Welfare

1956—Federal Highway Act

1960—Kennedy elected President

1961—Kennedy establishes Peace Corps

1963—Kennedy assassinated—Johnson becomes President

1964—Johnson elected President

1965—April—Elementary and Secondary School Education Act
July—Medicare established
September—Department of Housing and Urban Development established

1968—Nixon elected President

The Welfare State became a fixture in the United States in the 1950s and 1960s. The dogmas of welfarism—that the government can and should provide for the material and intellectual well-being of the people, that it should control and direct the economy, that its fiscal policies should be geared to the state of the economy, and that the good life could be achieved in the framework of an all-caring government—were widely believed and acted on. Many of the measures that had been passed by the New Deal in the midst of depression were continued, though sometimes altered or buttressed, in fair weather and foul, in good times and bad. At the same time, the United States became the fount of welfarism abroad. It became a matter of doctrine for most government leaders that not only was the United States government responsible for the well being of Americans, but also, the United States having become a world leader among nations, it should assume a basic responsibility to aid in the well-being of people around the world. This was woven into the fabric of resistance to or containment of communism abroad. So, it was argued, governments of nations must be encouraged and helped to adopt welfare measures in their own lands, lest their people become disaffected and turn to communism.

Welfarism at Home

To say that the Welfare State was established in the United States in the 1950s and 1960s is neither to suggest that it was a completed edifice nor that its programs, and even sometimes its premises, were not challenged. The thrust to new or broader programs continued apace through the period. This appeared most clearly in what has been called in earlier chapters four-year plans. Three of these were set forth in the period under consideration: President Truman's Fair Deal in 1949; John F. Kennedy's New Frontier in 1961; and Lyndon B. Johnson's Great Society in 1965. They were intended to spark new surges of reform and add new dimensions to the Welfare State. Indeed, there was a built-in political drive to increasing the programs of the federal government and to redistribute the wealth more evenly. For one thing, politicians had become accustomed to buying their way into office or to get re-elected by promising new and broader redistribution programs at the expense of the taxpayer. It was not enough merely to continue programs already in effect; benefits must be increased and new ones promised. For another, the thrust toward the welfare state is fueled by the concentration of power in the central government and its exercise by an expanding bureaucracy. More and broader programs keep the process going.

In a sense, too, the Welfare State is a way station on the road to socialism. Socialism is the utopian vision which is supposed to be achieved when society (in practice, democratic government) has gained control over all aspects of the lives of a people. The Welfare State is the result of the gradual movement toward socialism. So far as a completed socialism remained the goal, those who pressed for new programs would be trying to get beyond the Welfare State to socialism. Actually, the vision of socialism was no longer so bright or so certainly propelling the drive for new programs as it had once been.

The thrust toward the Welfare State was countered to some extent by those who challenged particular programs if not welfarism itself. Political opposition was strongest in the late 1940s and was gaining momentum once again in the late 1960s. Much of the political opposition was in the Republican Party, but there were many signs during much of the period that Republicans had accepted the Welfare State and contented themselves usually by opposing some extension or expansion. How far acceptance had gone was signified by the establishment of the Department of Health, Education and Welfare under the first Republican, Eisenhower, elected President since 1932. The raising of "Welfare" to departmental status suggested that it had become a fixture in the government, that providing welfare was as surely one of the functions of the federal government as providing for the common defense.

1. Truman and the Fair Deal

An earlier milestone of the Welfare State establishment had been passed in 1946. It was the Employment Act passed on February 20 declaring that it was "the continuing policy and responsibility of the Federal Government . . . to coordinate and utilize all its plans, functions, and resources for the purpose of creating and maintaining . . . conditions under which there will be . . . useful employment opportunities . . . for those able, willing, and seeking to work, and promote maximum employment, production, and purchasing power." In short, Congress affirmed the responsibility for and intention to follow policies that would assure full employment. To that end, it charged the President to provide it with the information necessary to its task and provided him with assorted instruments, including a council of economic advisers, to help him gather the information and recommendations. It was more than anything an assertion that it was the duty of government to do something believed essential in a Welfare State.

In general, though, the Welfare State was under fire during the period (1945–1949) in which Truman completed the term for which Roosevelt had been elected. The main source of opposition was the Republicans, who had gained control of the Congress following the elections of 1946. They fully expected to win the presidency in 1948 and were running against the New Deal of Roosevelt as well as Truman. One of the long running battles following the end of the war was over price controls. The price and wage controls during World War II certainly bore the earmark both of New Deal and Welfare State thinking. They tried to take the determination of price out of the market and vest it in government. Many Republicans and conservative

Democrats wanted price controls removed at an early date and the government's power over the market curtailed. Labor unions began to strike to break the wage control crunch. When Congress passed a bill which would restrain the price controllers, Truman vetoed it. Following the Republican victory in the election of 1946, Truman removed most of the price and wage controls, accepting defeat on this issue more or less graciously.

With price controls largely out of the way, the market began to assert itself strongly. Goods that were scarce before began to become more plentiful. Prices rose, some more than others, signalling what consumers wanted most, and producers responded to meet the most urgent demands. New automobiles for private purchase had gone back into production in the latter part of 1945—the "1946" models—, but they were difficult to buy for the next year or so. So long as prices were controlled, dealers were reluctant to sell—in a seller's market—at the official price. A few hundred dollars under the table could overcome dealer reluctance, and new cars could be purchased. After price controls were abandoned, however, prices rose, and new cars were available to those who had the money or credit and were willing to pay the price.

One welfarist program which was a legacy of the war did not excite partisan opposition, despite the huge expense involved. It was the "G.I. Bill of Rights," so-called, passed into law in 1944. It provided a cornucopia of benefits for returning soldiers, who became veterans upon their release from service. After past wars, especially World War I, there had been periodic clamorings for a veteran's bonus. What the veterans were usually demanding was a lump sum payment as additional compensation for military service during the war. Congress moved in 1944 to forestall this by passing the G.I. Bill. This time, too, the government would attempt to direct the use of most of the money, not simply hand it out to be spent as veterans chose. Such direction was very much in keeping with the Welfare State idea; the money would be spent on what government believed to be for the well-being of those involved.

The main focus of the G.I. Bill was on subsidizing veterans' schooling. The law provided that the government would pay for tuition and books and provide a monthly stipend for veterans to attend school; the length of the subsidy was apportioned to the length of the veteran's service. The most dramatic use of this program was to attend college, as millions of young men poured into the available colleges in 1946 and thereafter. Some veterans used the G.I. Bill to finish high school; others for vocational training. Although fewer and fewer people were staying in farming, a goodly number of young men took advantage of the G.I. Bill to spend several subsidized years at "on-the-job training" in agriculture. The total expenditures of the Veterans' Administration rose from less than $1 billion in 1944 to nearly $10 billion in 1950. That was the high point, after which expenditures declined.

Although Truman sought to expand New Deal type welfarist programs, the Republican (80th) Congress of 1947–1948 stood athwart his path. Truman vigorously opposed the best known act of these years, the Taft-Hartley Act of 1947. This was an act which tried to counteract the highly privileged position of organized labor under the National Labor Relations Act of 1935. It set forth unfair labor practices which would apply to both employers and labor unions. It forbade the closed shop, an arrangement in which employers were not permitted to hire non-union workers, permitted employers to sue unions for broken contracts and for damages done during strikes, required unions to observe a 60-day "cooling-off" period between the time that a decision was made to strike and actually going out on strike, ended the "check-off system" in which employers collected union dues by payroll deductions, and required unions to make public their financial statements. Truman vetoed the Taft-Hartley bill, and Congress passed it easily over his veto.

Truman was generally unsuccessful in his push for a variety of controls and welfare measures in 1947 and 1948. He did succeed, however, in driving a wedge in his own party by his proposals for new "civil rights" legislation. "Civil rights" is placed in quotation marks here because it was taking on a different coloration from its ancient meaning. For one thing, it had in the hands of its users lost its ancient connection with natural rights. For another, certain rights, such as those to the ownership and control over property were now ignored. For yet another, some things not earlier conceived of as rights at all were now being included. For example, Truman in his message to Congress February 2, 1948 declared that "We believe that all men are entitled to equal opportunities for jobs, for homes, for good health, and for education." In view of the context of the speech, he was declaring that these were rights which government should provide. Moreover, "civil rights" was picking up the connotation of being something which Blacks had been denied and were properly entitled. In short, "civil rights" were being specialized for particular classes of people.

At any rate, in that 1948 message to Congress, Truman called for:

> 1. Establishing a permanent commission on civil rights, a joint Congressional committee on civil rights, and a Civil Rights Division in the Department of Justice.
> 2. Strengthening existing civil rights statutes.
> 3. Providing federal protection against lynching.
> 4. Protecting more adequately the right to vote.
> 5. Establishing a Fair Employment Practice Commission to prevent unfair discrimination in employment.
> 6. Prohibiting discrimination in interstate transportation facilities. . . . [150]

While the proposals had no immediate legislative result, they set the stage for a revolt in the Democratic Party. At the Democratic Convention in 1948, the platform contained a "civil rights" plank. This provoked a walkout by a considerable number of Southern Democrats. A goodly number of these delegates assembled in Birmingham, Alabama to nominate their own candidates for President and Vice President. The new organization was dubbed "Dixiecrat," and Governor Strom Thurmond of South Carolina was selected as the candidate for President. Many Democrats were not enthusiastically in favor of Truman, and there was talk of "dumping" him for some other candidate. There was even talk of nominating General Eisenhower, since it was not known generally what party affiliation, if any, he might have. Nothing came of this move, however; Truman was nominated as the standard bearer of the Democrats, and Senator Alben Barkley of Kentucky as his running mate.

As if Truman did not have enough difficulties with the defection of the Democratic Party in several Southern states, there were difficulties in another direction as well. Henry Wallace, who had been an avid New Dealer and Vice-President (1941–1945) was attempting to revive the Progressive Party as its presidential candidate. Wallace had been dismissed as Secretary of Commerce in 1946 by Truman for making foreign affairs pronouncements contrary to government policy. Wallace did not agree with Truman's policy of resisting Soviet expansion nor his domestic policies. His new party, however, was being manipulated by Communists and their fellow travelers for whom Wallace had become an unwitting spokesman. At any rate, Wallace threatened to draw some of the more radical elements out of the Democratic fold.

Moreover, as pointed out earlier, 1948 had the look of being the year for the Republicans. Thomas E. Dewey was their nominee, and he ran with confidence. Truman, however, was determined not to lose without a fight. He campaigned harder than any incumbent had ever done. Traveling by train, he crisscrossed the country, lashing out at the "do nothing 80th Congress," and giving peppery speeches at every whistle stop along the way. Apparently, his zest carried the day, even though the polls predicted a Dewey win up to election day. Despite all this, and the fact that the Dixiecrats carried South Carolina, Alabama, Mississippi, and Louisiana, Truman won with 303 electoral votes to 189 for Dewey and 39 for Thurmond. Both houses of Congress went Democratic as well.

Even so, Truman had rough going with Congress during the term that followed his re-election. His victory did mean that the Welfare State would not be dismantled, though Dewey's election might not have had that result either. But small Democratic margins in each of the houses of Congress were hardly enough to get much new welfarist legislation passed. Southern Democrats could usually be counted on to vote with most Republicans to turn back any radical new legislation, and they did so often enough to make it clear Congress was no rubber stamp for the President. Truman pushed for a number of new programs in 1949 under the title of his four-year plan, the Fair Deal. Among the programs were: a national health insurance for Americans generally, new "civil rights" legislation, particularly Fair Employment Practices enactments, major new housing legislation, revamping the government farm program subsidies to assure that small farmers were the ones that were helped, repeal of the Taft-Hartley Act, and the expansion in general of welfare programs.

The most notable success of Truman's Fair Deal was the National Housing Act. It placed the government in the inner-city housing business in a big way. The act provided for the construction of over 800,000 housing units over the next half dozen years for lower income families, for government subsidies to reduce the rents to tenants, for slum clearance, and for funds for some rural housing. In the extension of welfarist legislation, Congress voted an increase of the minimum wage to 75¢ per hour, increased Social Security benefits and extended coverage of Social Security to ten million additional people. Congress also increased appropriations for TVA, for electric power and land reclamation in the West, and for the Farmers' Home Administration, which is a government program to provide low interest loans for small farmers.

In the main, though, the Fair Deal programs were rejected. Congress refused to repeal the Taft-Hartley Act, though it showed some willingness to modify the act, but Truman was unwilling to consider compromises. National health insurance was handily defeated, rejected because of the vigorous opposition of the American Medical Association and the realization that it was the prelude to socialized medicine. Truman's modified farm program, known as the Brannan Plan for Truman's Secretary of Agriculture, Charles F. Brannan, failed to pass Congress as well. The Brannan Plan called for paying direct subsidies to farmers rather than driving up the price of farm products when farm income fell below a certain level. It also aimed to make payments to small farmers. Whether it would have worked as billed is uncertain, for it was never tried. Congress rejected it as a dangerous experiment in the direction of full-fledged socialism. Nor was Congress in the mood during the Truman years for extensive "civil rights" legislation nor especially enthusiastic about Truman's efforts to get Federal aid to education. In the mid-term elections in 1950, Republicans made gains in both houses, and the drive, such as it was, went out of the Fair Deal.

2. The Eisenhower Years

The political storms subsided during Eisenhower's two terms in the presidency. When the fighting in Korea ended shortly after he came to office in 1953, World War II and its immediate aftermath began to recede into the past. Communist expansion became less warlike—at least for the remainder

United Nations

Adlai E. Stevenson (1900–1965)

Stevenson was governor of Illinois, twice an unsuccessful Democratic candidate for President, and ambassador to the United Nations. He was born in Los Angeles, moved to Illinois, obtained college training at Princeton and Harvard, and a law degree from Northwestern. His grandfather had been Vice-President, and Adlai soon became interested in politics himself. In the 1930s and 1940s, he worked in several government agencies before his election as governor of Illinois in 1948. His term as governor brought him national attention, leading to his nomination for President by the Democrats in 1952 and 1956. Stevenson was a hit among liberal intellectuals during the campaign for his dry humor and professor-like setting forth of liberal positions, but the voters preferred Eisenhower both times by substantial majorities. He sought the nomination once again in 1960, but Kennedy won with a much more vigorous campaign in the primaries. Kennedy appointed him to head the United States delegation to the United Nations, and he continued in that post under Johnson.

of the 1950s—after the death of Stalin, and took on the coloration more of the extension of influence. The Eisenhower years were generally prosperous, as indeed was the case in the 1950s and 1960s as a period. Americans in general and business in particular had learned to operate within such freedom as could be found within the Welfare State, had regained the productive edge by the use of technology. It was a great era of house building; suburbs grew on the outskirts of cities as more and more of the populations moved outward. More and more people had two-car garages, and when the children in the family reached driving age it became more and more common for them to have motor vehicles as well. The television set had become a necessity for most families by the mid-1950s, and color television was just around the corner. Government still engaged in deficit spending; the Federal budget was rarely balanced, but less and less was said about ever reducing the debt. Liberal economists assured Americans that the debt was nothing to worry about, since we owed it to ourselves. In any case,

Eisenhower was a fatherly figure, and his years in power were relatively calm.

After his bruising battle with Senator Taft for the Republican nomination in 1952, Eisenhower won easily over his Democratic opponent. This could be attributed in part, at least, to the declining popularity of Truman in his last two years. In the polls, his public approval slipped to only about one-fourth of those polled, in the face of the China debacle, the Korean problems, the firing of MacArthur, revelations of corruption in high places, and the televised Kefauver hearings which revealed connections between organized crime and Democratic city political machines. Nor did the Democratic candidate, Governor Adlai Stevenson of Illinois, have any great appeal to Americans. Liberal intellectuals were quite smitten with Stevenson; they found his wit and air of modesty irresistible. But such people were being dubbed "eggheads" by those disenchanted with them in 1952. An "egghead," as described by an insurance executive who may have coined the term, was a person with "a large oval head, smooth, faceless, unemotional, but a little bit haughty and condescending." Louis Bromfield, the novelist, declared that if Stevenson won the election "the eggheads will come back into power and off we will go on the scenic railway of muddled economics, Socialism, Communism, crookedness and psychopathic instability."[151]

However that might have been, Stevenson did not win the election. Eisenhower won by a landslide electoral vote, 442 to 89. Nor did Stevenson's performance improve when he was nominated to run against Eisenhower in 1956. Eisenhower won this time by an electoral vote of 457 to 73 and a popular vote which also increased the margin of victory. In both elections, Stevenson carried only states in the deep South and Border, but the Democratic hold even on the South was visibly slipping. Florida, Virginia, Tennessee, and Texas gave their electoral votes to the Republican Eisenhower in both elections.

Eisenhower's political views were little known at the time he was nominated, nor was it easy during his years in office to pin him down very precisely about them. The appointment of John Foster Dulles as Secretary of State probably indicated that there would be no major shift in foreign policy. Dulles had been in the State Department for several years and had a hand in implementing the policies of Truman. In domestic policy, however, there was at least the possibility of major changes. Eisenhower was the first Republican elected President since the beginning of the New Deal. Also, he had a Republican Congress during his first two years, though by the narrowest of margins in the Senate and with only a few members to spare in the House. Would Eisenhower attempt to roll back or dismantle the Welfare State?

The signals were mixed at the outset. Eisenhower sometimes referred to himself as basically conservative. He did not come into office with a four-year plan to expand government and extend the Welfare State. During

State Department

John Foster Dulles (1888–1959)

Dulles was an American diplomat who served as Secretary of State under Eisenhower. He was best known for his threat of massive retaliation against aggressors and may well have restrained the Soviet Union and Communist China from the direct use of force to expand in the 1950s. Dulles was born in Washington D. C., graduated from Princeton, and received his law degree from George Washington University. He practiced law before World War I and in the 1920s and 1930s, specializing in international law. During World War I, he worked with the War Trade Board. Dulles was a delegate at the San Francisco Conference where the United Nations was organized and served for several years in the United Nations General Assembly. He represented President Truman in Japan in the early 1950s, and was a key figure in the Eisenhower administration.

the campaign in 1952, Eisenhower patched up his differences with Senator Taft, who was decidedly conservative, and until Taft's death in 1953, Eisenhower depended much on his advice. He referred to himself sometimes as being "basically conservative." After he had been in office for a few months, he announced that the Republicans had "instituted what amounts almost to a revolution in the Federal Government as we have known it in our time, trying to make it smaller rather than bigger and finding things it can stop doing instead of seeking new things for it to do." That he opposed the direction things had been going before that, Eisenhower made clear by saying that "in the last twenty years creeping socialism has been striking in the United States."[152] He had indicated during his first campaign to the presidency, also, that he favored a greater separation of powers than recent Presidents had practiced, that he did not think it was the business of the President to initiate and drive legislation through Congress, that the improvement of their well-being was the business of the citizenry without interfering government controls, and that he opposed a government directed and controlled economy.

Eisenhower's cabinet appointments signaled that his administration would not be anti-business, and especially not anti-big business. He appointed the

Ezra Taft Benson (1899–1994)

Benson was a farm leader, Eisenhower's Secretary of Agriculture, a prominent conservative, and is head of the Mormon church. He was born in Idaho, graduated from Brigham Young University, and earned a master's degree in agricultural economics at Iowa State. Afterward, he worked in a number of farm organizations: as county agent, in farm marketing, organized the Idaho Cooperative Council, and served as executive secretary of the National Council of Farmer Cooperatives. He was Secretary of Agriculture during both of Eisenhower's terms. Benson believed that government farm programs drew farmers into uneconomic production quite often and were harmful to taxpayers and consumers generally. Thus, he sought to reduce the government's role in agriculture during his time in office, but Eisenhower did not favor disturbing existing arrangements much. Benson has been an active Mormon for many years, became a member of the Quorum of Twelve Apostles in that church in 1943, and was chosen to head the church in 1985.

man who had been head of General Motors, Charles Wilson, as Secretary of Defense; George Humphrey, president of a large holding company as Secretary of the Treasury; the Postmaster General, Arthur E. Summerfield, and Secretary of the Interior, Douglas McKay, were automobile dealers. Being businessmen did not necessarily mean they were conservatives, but some of Eisenhower's appointments were distinguished by their conservatism. The Secretary of Agriculture, Ezra Taft Benson, was not only an Apostle of the Mormon church but also an outspoken conservative generally. Another notable appointment was that of Dean Clarence E. Manion of Notre Dame law school to head a Commission on Intergovernmental Relations. He was an articulate and conscientious conservative.

Whatever urges Eisenhower may have had initially about dismantling the Welfare State soon spent their impetus. When he was asked in 1953 for an example of "creeping socialism," he answered "TVA." Dean Manion, spotting an opening, publicly proposed the selling of TVA dams to private utilities. Eisehnower backed away from such a controversial proposal, and the good Dean soon left government service. If Eisenhower would not dismantle, he might at least stop the expansion of the "creeping socialism." Benson showed the way by lowering some of the price supports for agricultural products somewhat drastically. When this aroused outspoken resentment, Eisenhower suggested greater caution to Benson. Eisenhower thought he saw a better opportunity to act when TVA asked for funds to build coal fired steam generators at Memphis. Whatever the case for the government's building dams and operating hydro-electric generators in connection with them, Eisenhower did not wish to see further expansion into steam generation by TVA, since this had nothing to do with conservation, water transport, or other development of inland waterways. He ordered the Atomic Energy Commission, a major user of TVA power, to contract for its needs with private utilities in the Memphis area. Eisenhower quickly learned that TVA was a sacred cow, a symbol to liberals of all that was good and holy about the New Deal, and, though they might not say so, they would fight every inch of the way to retain what the New Deal had established. As the controversy raged, Memphis undercut the proposal by deciding to build municipal generating facilities, and Eisenhower backed away once again.

By 1955, if not in the course of 1954, Eisenhower's administration had shifted away not only from any foray toward dismantling the Welfare State but also from vigorously restraining it. Indeed, Eisenhower was detectably moving toward modest extensions if not expansions of welfarism. Eisenhower was not by temperament nor experience either a daring innovator or the holder of stern principles which might isolate him from any large segment of the population. He was more of a "middle-of-the-roader," as he said himself. That had been his way as a soldier, and it had stood him in good stead. He preferred the sustained drive to the daring assault, liked to mass his forces so that he enjoyed massive superiority against the enemy, to take the center position in a dispute and to bring unity by diplomacy. In politics, he wanted to be in the mainstream, and by 1954 it was surely becoming clear to him that did not involve confrontations with the established Welfare State. The mid-term elections in 1954 helped to confirm these conclusions. The Democrats regained control of the Congress, and Eisenhower moved in his own way to accommodate himself to this fact. Sam Rayburn became Speaker of the House and Lyndon Johnson Majority Leader of the Senate. They were both Texans (as was Eisenhower by birth, if not by nurture), used and willing to compromise, and would and did work with Eisenhower if the Welfare State was secure and was at least gently extended.

During the remainder of his first term and his second term Eisenhower followed a course which accepted the Welfare State as a fact, gradually extended its sway, but did not push for any major new welfarist programs. Indeed, by accepting the raising of the Department of Health, Education and Welfare to cabinet level in 1953, he had already tacitly acknowledged the

Welfare State as a fixture. But from 1955 on, he began gradually extending it. Federal aid to education was one area where he moved cautiously toward extension. In 1957, he proposed matching grants to the states for school buildings. In 1959, he proposed aid to states and localities to help with building loans. Both these measures were defeated after amendments were added to them prohibiting aid to segregated schools. An outside spur to Federal aid to education occurred in 1957. The Russians sent a satellite into orbit around the earth; they called it Sputnik. Since this was an achievement well beyond American capability at that time, much ado was made about it by those seeking more money for the teaching of science and mathematics. Marxists argued that "the greatest conquests of the human mind are only possible when the limitations imposed by profit, by decadent capitalism, by the shackles that a decaying system of property relations puts upon science are broken."[153] While Eisenhower had no intention of being stampeded into action by the propaganda claims of the Soviets, he did begin to encourage research efforts in science and mathematics. Defense contracts with universities were increased, and Federal aid at a much increased level went into research facilities.

The most ambitious program of the Eisenhower administrations got under way under the Federal Highway Act of 1956. This act inaugurated the largest road building project in American history—the interstate system. Whether the measure was welfarist in tendency might be debatable, but there is no doubt that it was a major extension of the role of the federal government in road building and management. The Constitution specifically only authorizes the federal government to build post roads (roads on which to transport or deliver mail). Even so, the United States had become involved in interstate road building from time to time in the 19th century, and had provided aid to the states in building United States highways in the 20th century. But this was the first system throughout the United States in which the government proposed to play a dominant and determining role. Initially, the plan called for building 41,000 miles of interstate highways and for spending $32 billion over a period of 13 years. The amount and mileage has been expanded over the years, and the time for completion extended. The highways were to be divided limited access roads, with at least two lanes going in each direction. States were drawn into the program by the payment of 90 per cent of the cost by the federal government. A major argument for the program at the time was national defense—that it would facilitate military movement and the evacuation of population from cities. This argument, if accepted, removed the constitutional objection, though actually the highways have been used thus far mainly for the peaceful transport of people and goods.

In 1954, Congress passed a new Housing Act, initiating major government sponsored developments in towns and cities called Urban Renewal. Over the years a great deal of slum clearance was financed by this program;

lands were cleared within cities and new developments replaced them, quite often high rise apartment and office buildings. By the late 1960s, Urban Renewal could often be more correctly described as "poor people removal" from inner cities, or as some wags said, "Negro removal." Indeed, it was often true that people were driven from the low cost housing of inner cities to build expensive structures on which high rents could be charged. At any rate, the Housing Act of 1954 was justified in welfarist terms, whatever its results.

In 1955, the minimum wage per hour was raised from 75¢ to $1, though the Eisenhower administration had originally sought only 90¢. Under Eisenhower, the coverage of Social Security was extended to farmers, farm workers, domestic workers, and the like. The federal government entered the field of subsidizing hospital, convalescent, and nursing homes. Following discovery of an effective vaccine for polio by Dr. Jonas Salk, Federal funds were provided to make the vaccine available for many children. Thus, the Welfare State grew during the Eisenhower years, not by leaps and bounds, but gradually, and usually as a result of compromises between a more eager Democratic Congress and somewhat reluctant Republican President.

The Eisenhower administrations never came to grips fully with what those who push for government programs call "the farm problem." That there were problems having to do with farm produce in the 1950s, there was no doubt, but that they could be solved by government programs was doubtful. Eisenhower inherited an assortment of New Deal programs, aimed mainly at raising the price of farm products and providing easy credit to farmers. To prevent overproduction, acreage was restricted on certain crops. Even so, production continued to expand—the natural result of higher prices and easy credit—but such controls as were in effect did not prevent the piling up of surpluses. Secretary Benson wanted to lower price supports, and did get flexible supports, but it was not politically feasible to lower the supports enough to accomplish much. A new wrinkle was added with the "soil bank" plan, a program for paying farmers to take land out of cultivation. This was a bonanza for those who preferred letting their land lie idle to cultivating it, but supported prices continued to result in surpluses, even though the prices to farmers did not keep pace with prices generally. The government undertook to give away more farm products through such devices as the food stamp program. The Department of Agriculture remained a huge bureaucracy with an assortment of programs working at cross purposes to one another: trying to raise prices with one hand while giving away farm goods with the other; encouraging greater production and paying people to keep land out of cultivation.

One of the better indicators of the growth of the Welfare State is government expenditures and deficit spending. Eisenhower had come to office advocating frugality in government and a sound dollar. During his terms in office, however, government expenditures continued to mount. In 1950, the federal government had spent $39.5 billion; by 1955 it was $64.4; by 1960, it was $76.5 billion, though there had been some fluctuation over the years between. Between 1950–1960, the national debt rose from $257.4 billion to $286.5 billion. In 1959, Eisenhower had the largest deficit in peacetime history—$12.4 billion. As for the dollar, it continued its decline in value, though not as drastically as in the immediate postwar years. Most likely, it would have declined much further had it not been for developments in technology, which often reduced prices over what they may have been. John Maynard Keynes, the British economist, had recommended deficit spending in hard times, but under Eisenhower it was usually practiced both in good times and bad. Caught between the spending demands of the Welfare State, the popular demand for lower taxes, and the demand for expanding credit, deficit spending became the norm.

3. Kennedy's New Frontier

The discontent of the intellectuals was not so outspoken and raucous in the 1950s as it had been in the 1920s—but it found voices nonetheless. Enthusiasts for Soviet Communism did not usually make trips to Russia and return to proclaim the glad tidings of utopia in action in the 1950s. If Americans had learned nothing else about the Soviet Union, they were at least aware that it was hardly a utopia. Indeed, proponents of Communism were not much in evidence in the 1950s. The conviction of the top Communist leaders in the United States, the execution of the Rosenbergs for spying, the exposure of Communist espionage activity, the establishment of government loyalty programs, among other things, had, if not silenced Communist sympathizers, made them more circumspect. Thus, the discontent of the intellectuals was not so blatant in the 1950s.

But even in the relative prosperity of the Eisenhower years and amidst the general calm that prevailed, liberal intellectuals found cause for discontent. Actually, that may state the matter wrong end to. Liberal intellectuals can find cause for discontent in prosperity, and did in the 1950s, and find reasons to belabor the calm. In fact, some intellectuals described prosperity as unwanted affluence and calm as stultifying conformity. For all that there was peace and spreading material well-being, which are often enough the touchstones of liberal intellectuals, there was something deeply wrong with America and Americans as they saw it. A few of the books which dealt with conformity and affluence which went the rounds in the 1950s will illustrate the point.

Not all the works that dealt with these themes were necessarily simplistic nor wrongheaded, of course. One of the more serious works probing the sources of conformity was David Riesman (and others), *The Lonely Crowd.* According to Riesman, there have been three ways in the course of history in terms of which people have directed their lives. In his terms, they are: tradition directed, inner directed, and other directed. Thus, in earlier societies people ordered their lives by custom, folkways, and traditions, and are tradition directed. Earlier Americans, he pointed out, had come to be much more inner directed, guided by individual conscience and built-in moral and social principles. Now, however, they were increasingly other directed, taking their direction from others, from groups, from fellow workers, from the society in which they lived. If this were so, Riesman might have ascribed this change to collectivism, but he did not probe deeply into the political framework in search of an explanation. He had attempted a serious analysis that might explain the prevailing conformity.

In *The Organization Man*, William H. Whyte, Jr. described corporate and corporation man as being "other directed" by those in the organization(s) to which he belonged. He was a man collectively conforming to the organizations of which he was a part. Whyte said that a social ethic had developed which made "legitimate the pressures of society against the individual. Its major propositions are three: a belief in the group as a source of creativity; a belief in 'belongness' as the ultimate need of the individual; and a belief in the application of science to achieve the belongness."[154] C. Wright Mills, an American sociologist given to Marxian analysis, gave the organizational thesis a somewhat more sinister gloss in *The Power Elite*. He intended to describe those in organizations who had the power to manipulate and control those within the organization. "The power elite," Mills said, "is composed of men whose positions enable them to transcend the ordinary environments of ordinary men and women; they are in positions to make decisions having major consequences. . . . For they are in command of the major hierarchies and organizations of modern society. They rule the big corporations. They run the machinery of the state and claim its prerogatives. They direct the military establishment. They occupy the strategic command posts of the social structure. . . ."[155]

Others focused on how business organizations particularly sell to and manipulate Americans generally. Marvin Mayer focused on the operation of large advertising agencies in *Madison Avenue, U.S.A.* Madison Avenue is a street in New York City on which many of the large advertising agencies are concentrated. Mayer described how these agencies are employed by businesses to conceive campaigns that will alter and shape American buying habits. Vance Packard described in *The Hidden Persuaders* how psychologists and other motivational researchers use packaging, display, color, and setting to sell more goods, or what have you, to the American people. The picture he gave was of a situation in which people only believe they are making conscious choices when they make selections and do their buying. Instead, they are being manipulated by those who know how to call forth the hidden motive forces within us.

John F. Kennedy (1917–1963)

Kennedy was the 35th President of the United States, the youngest ever elected to that office, and the first Roman Catholic either to be elected or serve. He was born in Massachusetts, descended from Irish immigrants of the mid-19th century, attended a private preparatory school, and graduated from Harvard. His senior thesis, *Why England Slept*, was published as a book and sold well both in the United States and England. Kennedy enlisted in the Navy at the time the United States was drawn into World War II and was in combat as a PT boat commander. He was elected to the House of Representatives in 1946 and served three terms in that body. In 1952, he unseated Republican Senator Henry Cabot Lodge and was re-elected to the Senate in 1958 by a large plurality over his opponent. During his convalescence following an operation, he wrote a book, *Profiles in Courage*, an account of men who had served in Congress and had the courage to take unpopular stands. The book was a best seller and won him the Pulitzer Prize. Kennedy won the Democratic nomination for President in 1960, won the election, but was assassinated with more than a year to go in his term.

John Kenneth Galbraith drew much of this into a clearly political framework in *The Affluent Society*. The villain of Galbraith's piece is private affluence, opulence, and wealth, a society whose businessmen are bent on producing more and more consumer goods, then making vast efforts to persuade people that what is produced is what they want so that the goods can be sold. The result is such things as the 1957 automobile, large glittering grill, huge rising fins to the rear, equipped with large gas guzzling engine, an ungainly, costly, and unnecessarily showy thing withal. Galbraith tries to contrast what he conceives as private affluence with public penury. In his imagination, these monsters of automobiles tool down highways at excessive speed, highways poorly maintained, badly built, and for which there is

James Cooke

John Kenneth Galbraith (1908–)

Galbraith was a longtime economics professor at Harvard (now retired), a government bureaucrat, ambassador to India, and popular writer. In the 1950s and 1960s, he was a major source of ideas and justifications for expanding government power and economic planning. He was born in Canada, graduated from the University of California and also received his Ph.D. from that institution. During World War II, he worked in the Office of Price Administration, among other government offices, in Washington. He has been chairman of Americans for Democratic Action, an organization which exercises itself generally in promoting more government involvement in American lives, and president of the American Economic Association, a professional organization. Among Galbraith's better known books are: *American Capitalism: The Concept of Countervailing Power*, *The Affluent Society*, and *The New Industrial State*. Galbraith was prominent among the Harvard advisers to John F. Kennedy.

never enough money. His not so subtle point would seem to be that government needs to direct much more of the disposal of wealth, that economy needs public planning, and that the power over the production and purchase of goods needs to be reoriented.

These and similar writings, analyses, and ideas provided the backdrop for Senator John F. Kennedy's run for the presidency in 1960. His four-year plan, the New Frontier, was conceived in the light of them. America needed to be revitalized, he declared in the campaign, to get hold of a new vision, to "get moving" again. In his acceptance speech after his nomination by the Democratic Convention at Los Angeles in 1960, he announced the New Frontier. "But I tell you," he announced to the faithful gathered there, "the New Frontier is here whether we seek it or not, . . . [here in] uncharted areas of science and space, unsolved problems of peace and war, unconquered pockets of ignorance and prejudice, unanswered questions of poverty and surplus. . . ." America, he declared, was "at a turning point in history," where the choices were "not merely between two men or two parties, but between the public interest and private comfort, between national greatness and national decline, between the fresh air of progress and the stale, dank atmosphere of 'normalcy'."[156] In such phrases as the contrast between "public interest and private comfort" it is easy to see *The Affluent Society* theme. Beyond that, though, the appeal of what he was saying derived its strength from the literary depictions of conformity and opulence.

At 43, John F. Kennedy was the youngest man ever elected President (though Theodore Roosevelt had been younger when he succeeded the assassinated McKinley to the presidency). Nor did he have any administrative experience of consequence. His political experience had been in Congress, where he served first as a Representative and then eight years as a Senator from Massachusetts. Aside from writing a popular book, *Profiles in Courage*, he had done little that captured any national attention. He did make a run for the vice presidency in 1956, but this was at the Democratic Convention, when the presidential nominee, Adlai Stevenson, decided not to name a running mate himself but leave the choice to the convention. Estes Kefauver of Tennessee was the front runner, however, and he eventually won the nomination. In 1960, Kennedy made a vigorous campaign for the nomination, entered many of the state primaries, and won nomination on the first ballot at Los Angeles. He named Lyndon B. Johnson of Texas as his running mate.

The Republicans nominated Richard M. Nixon as their presidential candidate. Nixon had been Eisenhower's Vice-President for two terms and had served in Congress before that. He was well known nationally, had often shared the limelight with Eisenhower, and was clearly his party's choice. Both men conducted spirited races, and the contest was one of the closest in American history. Both were personable candidates, though it may be that Kennedy made the better impression in their televised debates. Kennedy was Roman Catholic; no one of that faith had ever been elected President, and it was generally held to be a political disability. The popular vote was very close: Kennedy got approximately 34.2 million votes to 34.1 million for Nixon. The electoral vote, however, was 303 for Kennedy to 219 for Nixon, with a scattering of votes for Senator Harry Byrd of Virginia.

There was never reason for doubting that Kennedy intended to maintain, extend, and expand the Welfare State. The New Frontier basically was aimed in that direction. It was an amendment, so to speak, to the New Deal, or perhaps an addendum. New Dealers were taken with the idea of legislating for an America for whom the old frontier had ended, no longer filled with the alleged opportunities of the frontier. Kennedy called up the image of opening up New Frontiers by government action. One of Kennedy's biographers says that his advisers "agreed on the same basic principles: that unemployment was too high, that Budget deficits at such times were both unavoidable and useful, and that consumer purchasing power should be more strongly supported by Federal actions than had been true under the previous administration."[157] But Kennedy was soon developing programs in new directions: trying to get medicare for those on Social Security built into the program, Federal aid to education on a much more expanded scale, new civil rights legislation, and the like.

Kennedy was amply aided in his thrust to expand the Welfare State by a variety of intellectuals—a "brain trust" which equalled or exceeded that of Roosevelt. The discontent of some of the intellectuals at least was ended for a time, for they were now a part of the government. How good it was is suggested by the comments of Arthur M. Schlesinger, Jr., who was one of them: "One could not deny a sense of New Frontier autointoxication; one felt it oneself. The pleasures of power, so long untasted, were now being happily devoured—the chauffeur-driven limousines, the special telephones, the top secret documents, the personal aides, the meetings in the Cabinet Room, the calls from the President."[158] In addition to Schlesinger, others were: Theodore Sorensen, McGeorge Bundy, Walt W. Rostow, David Bell, and Walter Heller. John Kenneth Galbraith served first as an economic adviser to the President and then as Ambassador to India; if affluence made him uncomfortable, he made no objection to influence. The cabinet included, among others, the President's brother, Robert Kennedy as Attorney General, Dean Rusk as Secretary of State, and Robert McNamara, a Ford Motors executive, as Secretary of Defense.

The New Frontiersmen were more adept at conceiving programs, however, than they were at getting them through Congress. Congress is much better organized to hack away at, reduce the impact or prevent the passage of large-scale new programs. Nor was Congress inclined to be stampeded by the sparkling rhetoric of the New Frontier. Kennedy did have a Democratic majority in Congress, but a goodly number of the Democrats were less than enthusiastic for drastic change. Older members, of which there were quite a few in positions of power, had seen most of the New Frontier proposals in other forms during Truman's years, and little had happened in between to make them more attractive.

Kennedy could usually get extensions of existing welfarist programs through Congress. The period of time when unemployment compensation could be drawn was extended. Social Security taxes were increased, and additional benefits made available. The minimum wage was raised from $1 to $1.25 per hour. The Food Stamp program continued to grow, and some additional subsidies and price supports for farm products were in effect. The Housing Act of 1961 provided billions more dollars for an assortment of rural and urban housing. Urban Renewal was expanded, and grants could now be made for recreational and historical projects.

But when it came to getting new programs which could be clearly identified with the New Frontier through Congress, these were usually rejected. Congress rejected a bill which would have set up medicare under

Social Security, the proposal for a cabinet-level department of urban affairs, Federal aid to education, and proposals for major tax revisions. Kennedy took the initiative sometimes by simply setting up programs by executive order. The best publicized effort of this character was the Peace Corps, established first by presidential decree and later voted by Congress. Even without costly new programs, the Federal budget continued to increase from $81.5 billion in the last Eisenhower budget to $97.7 in the final Kennedy budget, and the national debt continued to mount.

Not only did President Kennedy fail to get most of his new programs through Congress but his administration was also crisis-ridden and divisive. In both foreign and domestic affairs there were crises and events which tended to divide Americans and bring Kennedy under criticism. One of the first of these was an attempted invasion of Castro's Cuba by CIA-trained Cuban refugees in April, 1961. The invasion was undertaken at the Bay of Pigs, and has since gone by that name. The United States had promised air support, but it was never given. The invasion failed, and Castro's forces rounded up the invaders. Kennedy had been indecisive, neither intervening to call off the attempt nor providing the support that would have been necessary for success. His browbeating of the steel industry executives in the spring of 1962 provoked resentment in the business community. Roger Blough of United States Steel announced a price increase for steel following the making of a new contract with the labor unions. This infuriated the President, who had been involved in getting the unions to reduce their demands. As other steel companies began preparing to raise their prices, Kennedy denounced steelmen in general and declared in a press conference that he was sure that the "American people will find it hard, as I do, to accept a situation in which a tiny handful of steel executives whose pursuit of private power and profit exceeds their sense of public responsibility can show such utter contempt for the interests of 185 million people."[159] The President then moved to have the defense department shift contracts to companies that did not raise prices and ordered an investigation into possible antitrust violations in the steel industry. Roger Blough declared that "never before in the nation's history had so many forces of the Federal Government been marshaled against a single industry."[160] The steel companies backed down and rescinded price rises, but the blunt assertion of government power left enemies behind.

The most serious crisis of the Kennedy administration was the Cuban Missile Crisis in October, 1962. Republican Senator Kenneth B. Keating of New York publicly charged that the Soviet Union was arming Cuba with nuclear missiles, and sites for launching them were under construction. The government confirmed the truth of his allegation and that missiles had begun arriving in Soviet ships in September. President Kennedy went on television and radio to inform Americans about the seriousness of this Soviet action. "The purpose of these bases," Kennedy said, "can be none other than to provide a nuclear capability strike in the Western Hemisphere." He described it as a "deliberately provocative and unjustified" action "which cannot be accepted by this country. . . ."[161] Kennedy warned the Soviet Union in the strongest terms that unless that country removed its missiles from Cuba that he would quarantine all shipments to Cuba and that if any missile were fired upon the United States it would be treated as an attack by the Soviet Union and would be met by massive retaliation. The Soviet Union backed down, and Khrushchev entered into an agreement to withdraw the missiles in return for an American commitment not to invade Cuba. Khrushchev also agreed to withdraw Russian troops from Cuba, though he took his time in doing so.

Whether the Cuban crisis and the way it was handled improved Kennedy's standing with the electorate can only be conjectured. It helped to heighten the feeling that he went from crisis to crisis. But there is no doubt that "civil rights" issues were cutting into his following. The "civil rights" movement was getting into full swing in the early 1960s, and Kennedy took a vigorous stand in favor of Federal help in realizing the aims of the movement. In September, 1962, he sent Federal marshals, and ultimately military force, to protect a black man, James Meredith, entering the University of Mississippi. When Governor George Wallace attempted to bar the way to the admission of blacks at the University of Alabama, Kennedy federalized the Alabama National Guard and sent force to prevent Wallace's intervention. Feeling in some of the Southern states ran strongly against Kennedy.

Kennedy had not been a very effective President during his first two-and-a-half years or so. He had not been able to get what he reckoned to be his major legislation through a Democratic Congress. His administration had in general been crisis-ridden. Foreign action, if any, tended to be decided in the midst of crises, which might not have occurred if his policy had been known in advance. Republicans were becoming more confident that they could win in the presidential election of 1964. Kennedy himself was aware that he had political troubles by mid-November, 1963, and may have known that as matters stood he was coming across as ineffective.

All such questions became moot on November 22, 1963, and in the succeeding days the public estimate of the man and his presidency underwent a seismic change. Lee Harvey Oswald assassinated President Kennedy in Dallas on that day. Oswald fired several shots from several stories up with a high-powered rifle into the presidential limousine, killing Kennedy and severely wounding Governor John Connally of Texas, who was also in the car. Kennedy had come to Texas to try to patch up differences among Democratic leaders there and to shore up his own declining influence. Dallas was one of the cities on his itinerary, and Oswald had probably learned from the newspapers the route the presidential caravan would take. Oswald was captured within hours, though only after he had shot and killed a Dallas police officer, and was charged with the murder of John F. Kennedy the next day.

Kennedy was the first President to die in office since the development of television, and the first to be assassinated since McKinley in 1901. Most American households had at least one TV set by 1963, and television had become an influential medium. How influential it could be in a sustained effort would soon be demonstrated. The assassination of a President is a dramatic, perhaps traumatic, national event in any case. Television coverage magnified the impact of this one over the next several days. The President was shot on Friday afternoon, so that even the timing of the event probably increased the impact of television. At any rate, Saturday and Sunday were coming up; most people would not be at work; and if they chose to watch television they had no choice but to watch the most prolonged eulogy ever given to any person. For four days following the shooting, virtually everything on television was about Kennedy, the assassination, or the surrounding events. Over and over again viewers saw and heard just about everything about Kennedy, with an emphasis upon his youthfulness, his vitality, his zest for living, his charm, his wit, his background, his beliefs, and his accomplishments. All criticism was absent; the setting was funereal; the information told in a highly laudatory frame. Professional football games were cancelled on Sunday, and many schools and other undertakings took a holiday on Monday.

Dramatic events followed one after another during this long weekend. There was the moving scene at the airport in Washington as the newly sworn-in President Lyndon B. Johnson arrived on Air Force One, which also carried the body of the fallen President, on Friday evening. A battery of microphones had been set up for the new President to say something to listening Americans. Johnson turned to walk toward the microphones, suddenly realized he was alone, hesitated momentarily, and then walked resolutely to make his brief speech. The most dramatic further event of all, however, occurred on Sunday afternoon. The Dallas police undertook to move Oswald to the county jail. In the midst of the transfer, he was brought into a room crowded with newsmen and television cameras. Shots rang out in the scene witnessed by millions of television viewers; Jack Ruby, a shady nightclub operator, shot and killed Oswald. Nothing else quite so astounding took place, but television continued to focus on Kennedy for two more days. There was the visit of the dead President's widow, Jacqueline Kennedy, to the Capitol rotunda, where the body lay in state, in company with her brother-in-law, the memorial service in a cathedral presided over by a prince of the Catholic church, the solemn procession of the caisson bearing the coffin followed by the riderless horse down Pennsylvania Avenue, and the lighting of the eternal flame over the grave in Arlington Cemetery.

This sustained television coverage transformed the public perception of John F. Kennedy from a somewhat inept, inexperienced, and at best

Lyndon B. Johnson (1908–1973)

Johnson was the 36th President of the United States and the first from a Southern state to serve in that office since Andrew Johnson did so a hundred years earlier. He was born on a farm in southwest Texas, graduated from public high school, and earned a degree from Southwest Texas State Teachers College. After a brief stint of teaching, he became an assistant to his Congressman, followed by an appointment during the New Deal to be state administrator in Texas for a national youth organization. In 1937, Johnson ran for a seat and was elected a member of the House of Representatives. After 11 years there and a brief tour in the Navy during World War II, he was elected to the Senate. His sure mastery of political maneuvering soon moved him toward the leadership of his party in the Senate. He excelled during the last six years of Eisenhower's presidency as Majority Leader of the Senate. Johnson served as a Vice-President until Kennedy's assassination in 1963, at which time he succeeded him. Johnson got reams of domestic legislation through Congress, 1964–1966, but his determination to fight in Vietnam cut into his following in his own party, so that he left office after having been elected for only one term.

mediocre Chief Executive into an heroic figure who in death loomed larger than life; his weaknesses were now forgotten, and his wishes for America became virtual commands. This had large political consequences, for the next several years at least. The gates to radical reform or major expansion of the Welfare State had been virtually closed during Kennedy's administration. Following his death, the floodgates opened, and welfarist measure after welfarist measure swept through Congress.

4. Johnson and the Great Society

There was more to this, of course, than the television lionizing of an assassinated President. There was Lyndon B. Johnson who played a leading role now, to say the least. Johnson was a Texas-sized Theodore Roosevelt, possessed of Roosevelt's great energy but not his diversity of interests and abilities. Roosevelt spread his activity over many fields; Johnson concentrated his on one—politics. Except for brief periods in jobs as a young man, he was involved in politics virtually his whole adult life. Although in his drive and energy, Johnson calls to mind Theodore Roosevelt, Franklin D. Roosevelt was his hero and model, and once he came to the presidency he sought to emulate him in getting welfarist programs and popularity. As Majority Leader of the Senate, Johnson still had his base in Texas in the 1950s and worked with the proclaimed moderate President Eisenhower. But in the presidency, his base became national, and expanding the Welfare State quickly became his passion.

Undoubtedly, Johnson smoldered with resentment during the period while he was Kennedy's Vice-President. After all, as Majority Leader of the Senate, he had been Kennedy's superior. Kennedy had been a neophyte, and he had been the old hand. Now the positions were reversed. On top of that, the Kennedy people—Harvard people, quite often—could barely conceal their distaste for this nearly uncouth farm boy from Texas. Even so, Johnson took care in the weeks and months following the assassination not to alienate those who were identified with Kennedy. Indeed, he nurtured the Kennedy myth and used it effectively in pushing legislation through Congress. He surpassed the bounds sometimes in renaming places the "Kennedy" this, that, or the other. For example, caught up in the passion for doing this, he attempted to rename Cape Canaveral, Florida to Cape Kennedy. This was too much for some of the residents of the area who correctly maintained that the President had exceeded his authority. Instead, the space launching area was named for Kennedy. Johnson kept the Kennedy cabinet at first, but the Kennedy appointees mostly resigned in the ensuing months.

President Johnson swung into action in 1964, using the impetus from the Kennedy sympathy overlap to get legislation that would establish him as a man of action before the presidential elections of that year. In March, 1964, he sent a message to Congress calling for a War on Poverty. He declared that on "similar occasions in the past we have often been called upon to wage war against foreign enemies which threatened our freedom. Today we are asked to make war on a domestic enemy which threatens the strength of our nation and the welfare of our people." That "domestic enemy," he proclaimed was poverty. "I have," he said, "called for a national war on poverty. Our objective: total victory."[162] Some of the legislation of 1964 was from the Kennedy agenda; some had Johnson's mark on it. He got a Civil Rights Act passed which called for equal treatment in the use of public facilities related to interstate commerce, and even included restaurants and motels. Congress made a billion dollars available for the initial phase of his War on Poverty. Other programs included aid to Urban Mass Transit, housing, and interest equalization.

Barry M. Goldwater (1909–1998)

Goldwater has long been a Senator from Arizona and was the Republican candidate for President in 1964. His nomination was the result of the emergence of conscious conservatism in the 1960s. He was born in Phoenix and educated at Staunton Military Academy and one year at the University of Arizona. His father's death brought to an end his formal schooling because he went to work in the family department store. During World War II, he served in the Air Force, but his political career did not begin until 1949, when he was elected to the Phoenix city council. He ran for election in 1952 as a Republican and was elected to the United States Senate. He broke with Eisenhower's "modern Republicanism" and advocated principled conservatism. His re-election in 1958 to the Senate propelled him into leadership of the conservative wing of the Republican Party, and he won the Republican nomination for President in 1964 on the first ballot. His defeat did not turn him either from politics or conservatism, and he became a fixture in the Senate again from 1968–1986.

The Democrats nominated Johnson as their candidate for President in his own right in 1964. They nominated Senator Hubert Humphrey of Minnesota as his running mate; Humphrey had long been a leading "liberal" in the Senate. Johnson's four-year plan was, not War on Poverty, as might be supposed, but the Great Society. The phrase goes back, at least, to the title of a book by an Englishman, Graham Wallas. Wallas was a Fabian socialist, who lectured at Harvard in the early 20th century and published *The Great Society* in 1914. His argument was a subtle plea for socialist programs that would knit the classes together in a Great Society. Johnson may not have been aware of the origin of the phrase, but he thought it had a good ring to it, and he wanted to use it to identify his administration.

The Republicans nominated Senator Barry Goldwater of Arizona as their presidential candidate. Goldwater had emerged as a leading spokesman for conservatism in the years just before 1964, and Republican conservatives finally managed to nominate their candidate in 1964. It was doubtful that any Republican could win after the assassination of Kennedy, the sustained media eulogy to him, and Johnson's astute propagation of the Camelot legend about him. Goldwater apparently doubted that he could be elected; often, he seemed more concerned with expressing his principles than gaining followers. He would not pander to the Rockefeller wing of the party, and he defended extremism in defense of liberty, which alienated those who thought of themselves as moderates. Moreover, as the campaign wore on, he failed to speak with fire to large enthusiastic audiences. By contrast, Johnson sought to get every vote he could, in the hope that he could exceed the margin of victory of Harding in 1920. Scare tactics were effectively employed on television; Goldwater was portrayed as irresponsible, as a dangerous man to have control over atomic power.

At any rate, Johnson won, and won big. The electoral vote was 486 to 52, not so one-sided as others have been in the 20th century. But the popular vote was approximately 43 million to 27 million, which was a lopsided popular victory. The Democrats, who already controlled both houses of Congress, picked up 38 seats in the House and 2 in the Senate. It was a landslide for the Democrats.

With a lopsided Congress behind him—295 Democrats and 140 Republicans in the House and 68 to 32 in the Senate—, Johnson was ready to press on rapidly to the enactment of his Great Society legislation. Getting acts through Congress was an area in which Johnson was expert. He was not in the least troubled by any constitutional scruples about the separation of powers in dealing with Congress. He chose the legislation that he wanted, designed the bills to his liking, and maneuvered them through Congress by a combination of arm twisting, cajolery, and trades. His vision of his role, one historian who has written of his administration says, was that of a prime minister in a parliamentary system. That may not be literally true, but there is no doubt that he pressed the legislation he wanted through Congress.

The 1965 session of Congress lasted from January almost through November. It approved 89 measures which Johnson's administration had either sponsored or backed. "President Johnson lost only three bills which he had declared to be of any particular significance," an historian associated with the White House says: "the appropriation for rent supplements, home rule for Washington, D.C., and the repeal of Section 14(b) of the Taft-Hartley Labor Act—and it was not at all clear that he really wanted the last."[163] The National Republican Congressional Committee classified it as the "Three-B Congress—bullied, badgered, and brainwashed." A columnist commented that "He's getting everything through Congress but the abolition of the Republican party, and he hasn't tried that yet."[164]

Among the programs inaugurated (or newly funded) in 1965 were: Medicare (passed for the first time); Aid to Education (first large scale federal aid to elementary and high schools); Higher Education (beginning of a general scholarship program for college students); Department of Housing and Urban Development created; Voting Rights Act passed (the first since

Reconstruction); Heart, Cancer, Stroke Program; Law Enforcement Assistance; Federal provision for Mental Health Facilities; Vocational Rehabilitation; Arts and Humanities Foundation; Aid to Appalachia; Highway Beauty; Clean Air; Water Pollution Control; High Speed Transit; Manpower Training; Regional Development; Aid to Small Businesses; Water Desalting; Community Health Services; Juvenile Delinquency Control; and so on and on. Welfarism was now in full flower in the United States. It had gone full circle from depression-originated programs to programs for all seasons and every sort of object which could get some semblance of a group behind it.

A new reformist concern appeared in the 1960s and gave rise to some of the above acts, particularly the Clean Air and Water Pollution acts. In its broadest sense, the idea that gave rise to these acts was called environmentalism. Probably, people have always been more or less concerned about the environment within which they live, but it has usually been left to families and to communities to take action about it. Environmentalists pushed for national, if not international, action to "clean up" the environment, as they were given to saying. It should be noted, too, that the environment comprehends everything, and governments thrusting into this area were limited only by their imaginations as to what they might attempt to prohibit or control. The environmentalists focused upon ecology (which they referred to as a "science"), pollution of air and water by industrial wastes, and by such things as poisonous insecticides. There was more than a little "the sky is falling" stridency about the movement. The comprehensive legislation (the Environmental Protection Act) was not passed until 1970, however—well after Johnson had left office.

Reformers and radicals sowed the wind in the late 1960s and early 1970s, and the country reaped the whirlwind. Much of that story remains to be told in the next chapter. The Johnson welfarist legislation told here was part of that story. Other measures were enacted under Johnson after 1965—the Truth-in-Packaging Act, for example, and Fair Housing Act—, but the steam was going out of this welfarist surge by 1966. Johnson himself was increasingly concerned with the Vietnam War, and criticism of him was beginning to mount, much of it from the area of his greatest support for expansion of the Welfare State in 1964 and 1965.

One economic consequence of the everexpanding welfarism, depending as it did on deficit spending and credit expansion, made its impact between 1967 and 1971. The United States abandoned the last of its backing of the paper money with silver and gold. The half-dollar, quarter, and dime had continued to be made of a silver alloy with monetarily significant amounts of silver in them into the 1960s. Equally, or more, important, silver certificates continued to circulate which were redeemable in silver. By 1967, the paper money had been so inflated and decreased so much in value that the Treasury could no longer maintain them in circulation. The coins were becoming more valuable melted down for their silver, and the silver certificates were all on the verge of being redeemed. Hence, the government began replacing the silver coins with cupra-nickel, made of base metals, and set a date beyond which it would no longer redeem the silver certificates in silver. The United States had also continued to defend the dollar abroad to some extent by exchanging gold for it at a fixed ratio. That was all abandoned by 1971; the price of gold was permitted to respond to the market. There was no longer any formal connection between the dollar and gold. Americans were permitted once again to own gold and to trade in it.

The United States now had a full-fledged fiat money; the currency was money, to the extent that it was, because government decreed that it was the medium of exchange. This set the stage for the vast inflation of the 1970s, for the tremendous devaluation of the dollar that occurred in fact, and for the unnamed depression that lasted at least from the mid-1970s through the early 1980s. It was not called a depression either by the government or the media, but it was. Americans had been taught that government programs had made a prolonged depression impossible, so we had a series of "recessions." The government programs and manipulation of the money supply did alter the character of the depression, but they did not prevent one from occurring.

Welfarism Abroad

Since shortly after World War II the United States has been promoting welfarism abroad as well as maintaining it at home. The main device by which welfarism has been promoted abroad has been by foreign aid, though a variety of international monetary and banking loans which are not usually characterized as foreign aid have played a role in it as well. The foreign aid programs have usually been advanced in the framework of the Cold War, but they need to be discussed as a variety of international welfarism as well. Not all of foreign aid has been welfarist; some of it has been classified as military aid, some as economic aid. Only the economic aid would generally be considered as welfarist.

The following are net figures for foreign aid from the United States for the years 1945–1965. The total for economic and military aid was slightly over $100 billion. Economic aid to countries in western Europe amounted to $23.8 billion, military aid, $16.2 billion. To the Near East and south Asia, $15.4 billion in economic aid, $6 billion in military aid. In the Western Hemisphere, $5.6 billion economic aid, $1 billion in military aid. Since 1965, both military and economic aid have continued, usually to what are referred to as Third World countries. But this has long since been dwarfed by loans from international monetary organizations, to which the United States government has been a major contributor, and by loans from American banks, particularly in Latin America. Technically, loans from American banks are not government aid and are supposed to be repaid with interest. In fact, however, the United States is deeply involved both in American banking and in the manner and time of bank collection. As of this writing, Latin American banks generally are not reducing the principal and show great reluctance even to pay the principal. The United States government is committed to make good to depositors in the banks, should American banks fail due to losses from these loans to foreign countries.

There were two different sorts of foreign aid programs, basically. The first was the European Recovery Program, which grew out of the Marshall Plan. The announced purpose of this program was to aid war-torn European countries to recover from the devastation of World War II. Great emphasis was placed upon cooperation among participating governments from the outset. Secretary of State Marshall said, in his Harvard address in 1947, "that, before the United States Government can proceed much further in its efforts to alleviate the situation and help start the European world on its way to recovery, there must be some agreement among the countries of Europe. . . . The initiative, I think, must come from Europe. The role of this country should consist of friendly aid in the drafting of a European program and of later support of such a program. . . ."[165] As the program developed the emphasis upon economic cooperation among the countries remained a central feature of it.

It is not obvious, on the face of it, why economic cooperation among the countries should have been necessary for American aid. After all, the United States might have extended aid to or within particular countries rather than by some overall plan. Neither Marshall, Truman, nor other spokesmen, made it very clear why such cooperation was necessary. Truman said: "This was our proposal, that the countries of Europe agree on a cooperative plan in order to utilize the full productive resources of the continent, supported by whatever material assistance we could render to make the plan successful."[166] The participating countries made a formal pledge "to organize together the means by which common resources can be developed in partnership. . . ."[167]

There were several things involved, or behind, this insistence on intergovernmental cooperation, matters which it would not have been politically useful to spell out in America. One was the widespread belief, especially in Europe, in government-planned economies. This idea, which gained a considerable following in the 1920s and 1930s, had not yet been so discredited as it would be after the British effort with nationalized industries in the 1940s and 1950s. The planned economy was a socialist idea, of course, and European governments were more or less deeply infected with socialism. The thrust of the Marshall Plan was to extend that planning to the international level. Another reason was that both the welfare state and a government-planned economy tends to make trade among countries difficult. For example, a controlled currency hardly facilitates international exchanges, and socialized medicine paid for by taxation makes goods whose production is taxed too expensive for other markets quite often. Cooperation among governments could overcome some of these difficulties, or so those who favored it hoped. Note, too, that the European Recovery Program described resources of countries as if they belonged to or were controlled by governments. That was socialistic in tendency, and indeed the European Recovery Program did, quite often subsidize socialism. The most glaring example of this was in England, where the Labour Government was swiftly bankrupting the country and was successively bailed out by large loans from the United States.

Thus, the United States promoted welfarism and subsidized socialism in Europe. Historians and other writers often claim that American aid greatly helped Europe recover from the ravages of war. Undoubtedly, the material aid made some of the recovery less painful than it might otherwise have been. It probably served also to prolong the agony of some of the countries wrestling with various socialist experiments, making industries unprofitable and propping up others with subsidies. The Common Market was one of the offshoots of the cooperation under the European Recovery Program. It enables member nations to trade with one another, while shielding them to some extent from the world market. Above all, though, it encouraged European dependence upon the United States, which has still not been broken militarily.

The second sort of foreign aid program in time was the one initiated in 1949 under Truman's Point Four proposal. This was aid to what were then referred to as "undeveloped" countries (since usually called Third World nations). Often, they had been colonies of other nations and were newly arrived, or trying to arrive, at statehood. Truman said that such aid was necessary to "create a firm economic base for the democratic aspirations of their citizens. . . ." He proposed two kinds of aid, basically, technical assistance and capital. Technical assistance "includes not only medical and educational knowledge, and assistance and advice in such basic fields as sanitation, communications, road building, and governmental services, but also, and perhaps most important, assistance in the survey of resources and in planning for long-range economic development."[168] Note here the emphasis by President Truman upon economic planning by governments.

That these programs promoted welfarism is clear both from the justifications that were often offered for them and what they supported specifically. For example, one report to Congress made the following argument:

> No modern self-governing state—and especially no state with a democratic form of government—can maintain itself and develop its potential unless it performs a minimum of public services in the fields of health, agriculture, education, transport, power and communications, industry and overall planning. The countries of southeast Asia . . . are acutely deficient in these public services. . . . The initial step

> in any . . . must therefore be the organization and maintenance of adequate, self-sustaining public services.[169]

More bluntly, another report declared that the United States must assist in the "creation of social and economic conditions and institutions under which the people feel that their basic needs and aspirations are being satisfied by their own . . . governments."[170]

Truman claimed that just such programs were going forward under Point Four:

> A monetary, fiscal, and banking system was introduced in Saudi Arabia. Schools of medicine, public health, and nursing were set up in several countries. A 75,000-acre irrigation project in . . . Haiti got under way. A great multipurpose hydroelectric plant was constructed in Michoacan, Mexico. Irrigation projects in Jordan were started to create 120,000 acres of arable land providing homes and six-and-a-quarter-acre tracts for 21,000 families consisting of 105,000 individuals.

In sum, these governments were being encouraged and aided in providing for the welfare of their people.

Welfarism continued to be promoted abroad in the 1950s and 1960s, and has gone on at one level or another since that time. It has usually been accompanied by military aid to countries that received economic aid. In a sense, promoting welfarism abroad was a reflex of welfarism at home. American politicians had become used to running for public office on the basis of welfare programs they would provide for Americans. Many of them had come to believe, though they might not say so, that groups must be pacified by granting government favors to them and that their loyalty to the country was, or could, somehow be bought and sustained with these programs. In a similar fashion, they supposed that foreign governments could be stabilized and maintained with an assortment of government favors. They even supposed that "democratic" governments, whatever that might mean, could be established and maintained by welfare programs begun with American economic aid. What appeared to be working in Anglo-American countries might also be expected to work in countries with quite different political, cultural, and social backgrounds.

Foreign aid has often led to a sort of caricature of what Americans might have suspected. Many of the aided countries have political heads that are styled "president," or something like that. They have congresses or parliaments, possibly even supreme courts, and they may occasionally hold elections. But their presidents tend to consolidate their power and hold on to it. They often use the economic aid, plus what taxes they can collect, to live on a scale which they have observed in the West. The military appropriations enable them to maintain armies which help them to hold on to their power. If they accept aid only from the United States, they tend to use the threat of Communism to keep the aid coming in. After the mid-1950s, however, as Communist countries began extending aid, they have sometimes played off one side against the other to obtain as much aid as possible. To top it all, many of the countries which have received foreign aid from the United States send representatives to the United Nations to belabor the United States, denounce American foreign policy, and vote against the United States in the General Assembly.

Welfarism at home has tended to centralize government power in Washington and concentrate it in the executive branch. Welfarism abroad has involved the United States in the affairs of countries around the globe, but it has dispersed American power and influence and produced anti-Americanism in many lands.

Chapter 9

A Second Radical Reconstruction, 1960–1975

. . . This Court . . . does not serve its high purpose, when it exceeds its authority *even to satisfy justified impatience with the slow workings of the political process. For when, in the name of constitutional interpretation, the Court* adds something to the Consitution that was deliberately excluded from it. *The Court in reality substitutes its view of what should be so for the amending process.*

—Justice John M. Harlan
Dissent in Reynolds v. Sims, 1964

I firmly believe that a few months of disturbances will be mostly for the good, and that . . . workers, peasants, and soldiers must not interfere with the students in the Great Cultural Revolution.

—Mao Tse-tung, 1966

What happened in Selma is part of . . . the effort of American Negroes to secure for themselves the full blessing of American life.

Their cause must be our cause too. Because it's not just Negroes, but really it's all of us, who must overcome the crippling legacy of bigotry and injustice.

And we shall overcome.

—Lyndon B. Johnson, 1965

All the power to the people! We need some student power and we need some faculty power, whether they want to give it or not. . . . All of you people who are in college, who are trying to decide which way to go, better make up your minds quick because they have pigs who will blow your mind for you, and I mean with a gun. Power!

—Eldridge Cleaver, 1968

Chronology

1954—*Brown vs. Board of Education of Topeka, et. al.*

1955—Bus boycott in Montgomery led by Martin Luther King

1957—Eisenhower sends troops to integrate Little Rock schools

1960—Sit-ins in Greensboro

1961—Freedom Riders to Alabama

1962—*Baker vs. Carr*

1963—Mass Black demonstrations in Birmingham

1964—Berkeley Student Revolt

1965—Watts Riot

1966—Cultural Revolution in China

1967—Black riots in Detroit and Newark

1968—Assassination of Robert Kennedy and murder of King

1969—United States lands man on moon

1970—Kent State riots

1971—Adoption of 26th Amendment

A new reconstruction swept over the United States in the 1960s and the early 1970s. Its antecedents go back at least into the 1950s, though America seemed placid enough at that time, and some of the animus remained after the 1970s. It may be called a reconstruction, for its thrust was to make over, change, and transform the country. It might also be thought of as revolutionary in intent, though technically no revolution took place.

This new reconstruction both resembled and was different from the earlier Reconstruction of the South. It came almost exactly a century after the earlier reconstruction. That one had taken place in the 1860s and 1870s; the new reconstruction in the 1960s and 1970s. The earlier effort focused on reconstructing the South. The reconstruction of the 20th century became an attempt to reconstruct the whole country, though in the early stages it, too, was aimed mainly at the South. Both were led by radicals, though the new reconstruction was ultimately more revolutionary than the first. The new reconstruction had no single occurrence, such as the Civil War which preceded Reconstruction, which brought all the forces involved into focus. Instead, it was propelled by a variety of groups, organizations, movements, and people with causes of one sort or another. The Reconstruction of the South was directed by a radical clique in Congress.

The main governmental body involved in the new reconstruction, at least at the outset, was the Federal courts, and especially the Supreme Court. But much of the thrust to reconstruction was not within the government but outside of it. It came from Black protesters and revolutionists, students, anti-war demonstrators, female liberationists, and so on. There were political assassinations amidst both the earlier and the new reconstruction: Lincoln's assassination and that of both John F. and Robert Kennedy. There were even attempts to impeach and remove Presidents from office in both reconstructions. Johnson was impeached by the House and failed by only one vote to be convicted by the Senate. Nixon resigned from office in 1974 to avoid impeachment and probable conviction. There was a war in the midst of the new reconstruction, a civil war even, the war in Vietnam. There were those who sought to make it the focus and catalyst for all the various radical, reform, and revolutionary movements, but they never succeeded.

But what really linked the new reconstruction to the earlier one was the animating idea of transforming and making over society. The Radical Republicans after the Civil War were determined to transform the South; the radicals and reformers of the new reconstruction were bent on making over the whole country. Many of them were profoundly opposed to all established authority, anarchic in temperament and set to turn all things upside down and inside out. Indeed, most of the similarities with the Reconstruction of the South were rather superficial and accidental. The new reconstruction had closer spiritual ties with the French Revolution and Marxism than with anything that had happened earlier in America. From the French Revolution came both the bent to revolution and zeal for equality. (The emphasis upon equality had been strong also in the Reconstruction of the South.) Marx focused on revolution as the key to transformation. The emphasis upon passive resistance and "peaceful" demonstration owed more than a little to Gandhi of India. The labor union provided the model for organized group demands and assortment of tactics used widely in the 1960s.

There was one difference, however, between the new reconstruction of the 1960s and 1970s and all occurrences and developments in history. It was the role played by and the prevalence of what was coming to be called the media of communication. By the 1960s, as noted in an earlier chapter, television had an almost unique sort of impact on whatever happened, or was reported. Newspapers and journals, which had been around for centuries, might sometimes affect events and developments too. But reading is a silent and individual undertaking, thus limited in its direct impact. Radio added sound and outside voices to news reporting, story telling, and the like. Newsreels brought motion and pictures in darkened theaters to the reporting of a few selected events. But television brought the immediacy of sight and sound to reporting, the intimacy of actually witnessing, as it were, what was going on, and was soon conveying the illusion that its cameras were everywhere anything of moment was happening. For years, Walter Cronkite, the CBS News anchorman, ended his evening news telecast with the announcement: "And that's the way it was." Television people spread the idea that the camera does not lie, which may be literally true, but it ignores the selectivity, the focus upon this instead of that, the angle from which the shot is taken, the role that the presence of television cameras may really play not only in highlighting or ignoring events but also in altering them.

At any rate, the media played a prominent role in the new reconstruction. They gave invaluable publicity to the events and pronouncements of protesters, radicals, and revolutionaries. Often enough, they undoubtedly gave protection to demonstraters from bystanders and the authorities. They explored and reported the alleged wrongs that protesters claimed they wanted to set aright. The media often gave decisive aid to the reconstructers by averting attention away from the often obnoxious doings of protesters and focusing instead on the weaknesses or failure of the authorities. One example will have to suffice at this point.

The Democratic Convention was held in Chicago in 1968. Not only did delegates, candidates, newsmen, and the usual assortment of people who serve such gatherings come to Chicago, but also a motley throng of more or less young people descended upon the city. They came to discredit, disrupt, and, if possible, intimidate the convention and make life miserable for all and sundry. They blocked sidewalks and streets, marched here and there shouting obscenities at the tops of their voices, ripped down and burned the American flag, and made themselves universally obnoxious. When the police proceeded to round some of them up none too gently, many media professed to be horrified. Some of them focused immediately on this question: Did the police over-react? Not were the protesters wild, riotous, disruptive, destructive, but did the police over-react? Newsmen centered virtually the whole of their attention upon the alleged misbehavior of police in the ensuing days. The problem, they would have us believe, was to somehow restrain the police, not to bring the troublemakers to heel. By determining the issue, the media made a major effort to determine the significance of the events. They provided aid and comfort to the disrupters and reconstructers.

An Activist Supreme Court

The new reconstruction began, if such a disjointed development could be said to have a precise beginning, in a setting remote from the riotousness of the streets of Chicago during the Democratic Convention in 1968. It began in the august and dignified courtroom of the majestic Supreme Court building in 1954. The Supreme Court was an unlikely body to spearhead the reconstruction or transformation of America. After all, the powers of the Court had always been understood to be largely negative. Even the power to nullify acts of Congress and of state legislatures was, at best, an implied power. The Constitution does not list such a power for the courts, although it had been understood by at least some of the Founders that in the course of ruling upon cases the courts might refuse to apply particular laws as being contrary to the Constitution. But so far as imposing changes were concerned, all legislative power authorized by the Constitution was vested in the Congress. If transformation was to come, then, few would have conceived as recently as 1950 that the Supreme Court might be the instrument of it.

Moreover, making large-scale changes by government was hardly in the wind at the time. Eisenhower had only recently been elected President, and he was still making conservative noises, of sorts. Eisenhower appointed Earl Warren, former governor of California, to be Chief Justice of the Supreme Court in 1953. Not only was he a Republican but also there was little in his background to suggest that he would turn the court into an instrument for transforming America. Granted, the Supreme Court was still basically that body as it had been shaped by Roosevelt during the New Deal. Four of its members were from the late 1930s, when Roosevelt had succeeded in changing the tenor of the court: Hugo L. Black, Stanley F. Reed, Felix Frankfurter, and William O. Douglas. Roosevelt had added Robert H. Jackson in 1941, and Truman appointed Sherman Minton, Harold H. Burton, and Tom C. Clark. Thus, the court still had about it the flavor of the New Deal; it was hardly surprising that it should be reformist. Warren might have been expected to restrain its reformist zeal. On the contrary, he took the lead in changing the role of the courts.

The Supreme Court broke new ground most dramatically with its rulings in the *Brown vs. Board of Education of Topeka, et. al.*, first announced in 1954. Brown and the Board of Education of Topeka, Kansas were only two of the parties; similar cases from South Carolina, Virginia, and Delaware were considered at the same time. Plaintiffs, acting for minor black children, had brought suits in these states in Federal courts seeking court orders to be admitted to white schools. The cases came to the Supreme Court on appeal, and the basic issue examined was whether or not racially segregated schools were in accord with the Constitution, specifically with the Equal Protection clause of the 14th Amendment. The Supreme Court ruled that they were contrary to the Constitution. Theretofore, courts had ruled on a number of occasions that states could maintain separate facilities for those of different races so long as they were equal. Chief Justice Warren, speaking for a unanimous Court, held that "Separate educational facilities are inherently unequal," and that "the segregation complained of" deprived plaintiffs "of the equal protection of the laws guaranteed by the Fourteenth Amendment."[171]

The complexities of applying this ruling were such, the Chief Justice said, that fuller arguments must be heard before the appropriate orders could proceed from the Court. This was done, and on May 31, 1955, the Supreme Court ordered that since "racial discrimination in public education is unconstitutional . . . , All provision of federal, state or local law requiring or permitting such discrimination must yield to this principle. . . . " Moreover:

> The Courts will require—a prompt and reasonable start toward full compliance—and enter such orders and decrees—as are necessary and proper to admit to public schools on a socially non-discriminating basis with all deliberate speed the parties to these cases. . . . [172]

Earl Warren (1891–1974)

Warren was a lawyer, politician, and Chief Justice of the Supreme Court. He was born in Los Angeles, studied law at the University of California, practiced law, and served in several local political offices. From there, he went on to become attorney general of the state, and to serve for ten years as governor of California. In 1948, Warren ran unsuccessfully as the Republican candidate for Vice-President. He supported Eisenhower over Taft as presidential candidate in 1952, and Eisenhower appointed him Chief Justice in 1953. Under Warren's leadership, the Supreme Court became a kind of super legislature and an annual constitutional convention, making controversial decisions, attempting to resolve questions upon which no national consensus existed, reversing precedents, and laying down ground rules for governments. Some of the most scorching dissents ever written came from members of the high court, but Warren usually managed to get a majority, or go with one. He retired in 1969.

The Supreme Court's decision aroused a major legal controversy, whose reverberations continued for more than a decade, met with widespread resistance, particularly in the lower South, and raised questions about the power of the Court. The national media generally proclaimed the Court's pronouncements were "the law of the land" and should be obeyed, but compliance did not come quickly and public debate continued. The Supreme Court had clearly ignored precedent in its ruling. On a number of occasions, courts had ruled that separate facilities were not, *per se*, unconstitutional. The Court substantially ignored the intention of the framers of the 14th Amendment, since many of the states which ratified it had segregated schools at the time and did not change their policies. (Also, those who had favored the amendment denied that it applied to schools.) It could be, and was, objected that the states maintained the schools and that it was unwarranted interference with their authority for the courts to lay down rules about the managing of them.

But the most serious charge against the Supreme Court was that it had usurped the power of the legislative branch by legislating. In fact, the court did not exactly legislate; it only issued orders as if it had legislated by announcing its opinion that segregated schools were unconstitutional. Thus, in effect, the court legislated. If the court had gone no further than to declare that segregation laws were unconstitutional and that they could not be enforced in the courts, it would have been performing an accepted judicial function. That is, it would have nullified various state laws requiring segregation, but would have left to states the matter of devising any new legislation. The court had not simply refused to enforce compulsory segregation; it had set on a course of compelling integration of state schools. It did so in the absence of any Federal or state laws requiring integration.

That may not have been entirely clear when orders went out in 1955, but it became clear in the ensuing years. Indeed, it might have been clear in 1955 when the court announced that it would send out orders and decrees requiring admission of those students who had brought suit to schools on a non-discriminating basis. In any case, in the ensuing years, the Supreme Court compelled integration in state after state, at first on the basis of particular cases, and then more broadly, in the absence of any law except its decree. One legal historian says that "the Court ordered people" in Alabama, Mississippi, and South Carolina "and other states to fashion legislation of a kind that they had never had on their statute books. . . . "[172] The Court may have expected that states would do that, but it surely did not order them to do so. Some states did take measures to integrate schools in the years immediately following *Brown vs. Board of Education*. The border states did; Kentucky, Tennessee, and Texas made shows of force when integration efforts met with local resistance. Most of the states of the deep South, however, began only hesitant compliance on the basis of court orders to particular schools. When the Supreme Court ordered the University of Alabama to admit a Black applicant, Autherine Lucy, in 1956, she was admitted and then expelled following a riot. When an attempt was made in 1957 to admit Blacks to Central High School in Little Rock, Governor Orval Faubus called out the Arkansas National Guard to prevent their entry. Faced with a Federal court injunction, Faubus withdrew the troops. But when the Black children approached the school a riot broke out. President Eisenhower sent in paratroopers, and the integration took place.

It was well into the 1960s before most of the states of the deep South got full-scale integration. When the courts ordered the admission of James Meredith, a Black, to the University of Mississippi, rioting appeared when he entered the university. President Kennedy sent 3,000 Federal troops to quell the resistance. Open political resistance came to an end in 1963. George Wallace had been elected governor of Alabama in 1962 in a campaign in which he had promised to stand in every schoolhouse door, if necessary, to prevent court integration. When two Blacks attempted to register at the University of Alabama in 1963, Wallace did indeed stand in the door to bar their entry. President Kennedy federalized the National

George C. Wallace (1919–1998)

Wallace has been frequently governor of Alabama and occasionally a presidential candidate. He was born in Clio, Alabama, studied law, and developed an early interest in politics. His path to chief executive of Alabama led through the state legislature and several years as a district court judge. In 1962, Wallace ran for governor and won as a Democrat who stood for segregation, states' rights, and his own variety of the welfare state. Just as Martin Luther King gained national attention for his opposition to legal separation, so Wallace gained prominence—notoriety in some circles—by standing for segregation. He was cocky, outspoken, and had a flair for the dramatic and controversial, coining the phrase, "pointy-headed intellectual." Since his first election, he has been elected governor of Alabama every time the law permitted him to be a candidate. In 1968, he was a presidential candidate on the American Party ticket, and in 1972, he made a vigorous run for that high office by seeking the Democratic nomination before he was shot down while campaigning.

Guard, and Wallace backed down on orders from his own Guard commander. After Kennedy's assassination and Johnson's landslide victory, it became even clearer that the President was determined to enforce integration.

After the mid-1960s, too, any doubt that remained that the courts were bent on compulsory integration was removed. Two examples will illustrate the point. The Alabama legislature adopted what it described as freedom of choice in the public schools. The act left open the possibility of the continuation of predominantly Black or white schools. The parents of students might choose as to whether their children would attend predominantly Black or white schools, as matters stood. Some did choose to change schools, but most children continued to attend the ones they had gone to before. The Federal courts would not have it. They struck down the Alabama law, closed large numbers of formerly Black schools, and oversaw the integration of all of them. If school districts did not conform, the courts laid down or demanded new rules. The other example was the bussing of students. When the court sought racial balance was not achieved by having all children attend neighborhood schools, then numbers were ordered bussed into other districts.

Whether the compulsory integration was judicial legislation or by a strange use of court orders may remain in doubt. Other decisions would follow which made the judicial legislation point better. There was no reason to doubt, however, that a new reconstruction was underway, a reconstruction which altered custom and established ways. As one historian has said: "When to the Segregation decisions are added the later judicial acts extending the new constitutional regime to other places of public assembly, one must acknowledge that judicial orders have required a basic revision of social structure and a root change in human relationships."[173] By other places of public assembly, the author was referring to the integration of restaurants, public transportation, and the like.

The Warren Court, as it was coming to be called, was striking out in other directions by the 1960s. Among the more astounding of the cases were the reapportionment decisions: *Baker vs. Carr*, 1962; *Wesberry vs. Sanders* and *Reynolds vs. Sims*. Many of the new reconstruction decisions were aimed at curtailing and taking away the power of the states. That was the thrust of *Brown vs. Board of Education of Topeka* and the court orders which proceeded from it. But none struck more directly at the independence of the states than the reapportionment decisions. There were two different questions involved in the reapportionment cases. One was the setting up of districts within which state legislators were chosen. The other was the drawing of the lines for congressional districts in which members of the United States House of Representatives were elected. Most states have two houses in their legislatures: usually a senate, styled the upper house; and a house of representatives, or some such body, styled the lower house. Representation in the upper houses was frequently territorial, as one senator for a county, for example, while representation in the lower house was usually based more or less on population. Many state constitutions called for reapportionment of election districts as population shifted. State legislatures sometimes did not get around to doing this so very often, and this was the main occasion for Federal court intervention in the 1960s.

Even so, nothing appeared to be better settled than the constitutional position that the establishment of election districts for state legislatures were matters left to the respective states. The Supreme Court had never claimed jurisdiction in any dispute over such election districts. The Constitution delegates no power to any branch of the federal government to superintend the drawing of lines for election districts for state legislatures. In the absence of the grant of any such power, the Tenth Amendment would appear to have shut the door against any Federal intervention in the matter, for it says that "The powers not delegated to the United States by the

Constitution, nor prohibited by it to the States, are reserved to the States respectively, or to the people." The Constitution does speak, however, on the matter of apportionment of election districts for election to the House of Representatives. But it assigns such authority as it allots to the Congress, not to the courts. The Constitution prescribes that "The Times, Places and Manner of holding Elections for Senators and Representatives, shall be prescribed in each State by the Legislature thereof; but the Congress may at any time by Law make or alter such Regulations, except as to the Places of chusing Senators."[174] During one extended period, the Congress had placed in effect a law on the apportionment of Congressional districts, but the law was no longer in effect in the 1960s. The Federal courts had generally steered clear of intervention, even when a law had been in operation.

Then, suddenly, as it were, the Supreme Court plunged into the whole matter of apportionment, both for the selection of state legislators and for members of Congress. In *Baker vs. Carr*, the Supreme Court held that reapportionment of state legislatures did involve questions which could be decided by the federal courts. Tennessee, the high court held, had denied to its citizens equal protection of the laws in failing to reapportion its legislature over the past 60 years. The Court did not lay down rules—legislate—on how these questions should be settled at this time. Instead, it simply returned the case to the lower federal court for settlement. In *Wesberry vs. Sanders*, however, the Court got around to stating the principles, i. e. legislating. This was a Georgia case and dealt with Congressional election districts. The state would have to realign its districts so that they would be substantially equal in population. The principle enunciated was, "one man, one vote," that is that each man's vote must count as much as any other person's throughout the United States. *Reynolds vs. Sims*, which followed a few months later, proclaimed that both houses of state legislatures must be apportioned on the basis of population.

The most widespread complaint was that the high court had overstepped its bounds, that it had usurped authority belonging to the states (or to the Congress). Moreover, it had laid down rules—legislated—in the absence of any standing law. Nor was it necessary to go beyond opinions expressed in dissent by members of the Supreme Court itself to learn about these complaints. Justice Felix Frankfurter dissented vigorously from the *Baker* case, declaring that it constituted "a massive repudiation of the past . . . , disregard of inherent limits in the effective exercise of the Court's judicial power. . . . "[175] Moreover, he lectured the Court sternly on the dangers of rushing in to offer relief in every sort of case, saying: "there is not under our Constitution a judicial remedy for every political mischief, for every undesirable exercise of legislative power. The Framers carefully and with deliberate forethought *refused to so enthrone the judiciary*. In this situation, as in others of like nature, appeal for relief does not belong here."

Wide World

Hugo L. Black (1886–1971)

Black was a Southern politician, a New Dealer, and an Associate Justice of the Supreme Court. He was the mainstay of the Warren Court in the 1950s and 1960s. Born in Clay County, Alabama, Black studied law at the University of Alabama and practiced it in Birmingham. In 1925, he entered politics in the race for a Senate seat and won. When Roosevelt came in with his New Deal, Black supported it in the Senate and emerged as a prominent New Dealer. When Roosevelt nominated him for the Supreme Court in 1937, the Senate consented, though there was somewhat of a scandal over his earlier membership in the Ku Klux Klan. Black quickly shed his Southern ways to become the leading and most outspoken "liberal" on the bench. He joined with others to cast aside constitutional objections to the government regulation of economic life. Black wrote several of the majority opinions in the crucial decisions of the Supreme Court in the 1960s.

In *Wesberry vs. Sanders*, the majority confronted a larger problem than in the other in devising an opinion to support its ruling. After all, the Constitution had assigned authority for determining electoral districts explicitly, first to the states, and to Congress when it should decide to intervene. The Court could hardly rely on the equal protection clause of the 14th Amendment to buttress its conclusion. Justice Hugo Black, who wrote the majority opinion, turned instead to the records of the Constitutional Convention for a mandate for the Court. Actually, the convention had not explored the question of apportionment of Congressional districts within the states. Nothing daunted, Black attempted to show from what they did discuss that the convention had intended that congressional districts should be equal in population. What the convention had actually discussed was the question of whether one or both houses of Congress should be based on population within the states. In consequence, Black could only impute an intention from the evidence before him. Justice John Marshall Harlan took him to task for his sloppy scholarship. A modern scholar questions "whether Justice Black and the Court majority that supported him . . . had any intention of performing as conscientious scholars.'' He suggests that they had deliberately chosen to misread the evidence, an attitude, which he says ''fairly raises the larger question of whether the Warren Court is any longer entitled to the confidence and presumption of good faith which . . . we accorded past Supreme Courts as a matter of course.''[176]

But it was *Reynolds vs. Sims* which raised the most vigorous dissent and protest. It was inconceivable that a Constitutional Convention which had established the United States Senate based on territory rather than population could have intended that the states should have to base both their houses of their legislatures on population. Nor was there one whit of evidence that the framers of the 14th Amendment had any such thing in mind. In Justice Harlan's dissent, he pointed out that there were many good reasons for assigning a territorial basis for at least one house of the state legislature. Moreover, he said, ''This Court, limited in function . . . , does not serve its high purpose *when it exceeds its authority*, even to satisfy justified impatience with the slow workings of the political process. For when, in the name of constitutional interpretation, the Court *adds something to the Constitution that was deliberately excluded from it*, the Court in reality substitutes its view of what should be so for the amending process.'' Undoubtedly, the Court was doing just that.

Many members of Congress were even more irate. Over 100 bills were introduced in Congress to curb the high court. Representative William Tuck of Virginia introduced such a bill which passed the House, but failed in the Senate. Tuck's bill would have removed state legislative reapportionment from the jurisdiction of the Federal courts. The Congress has the power to define the jurisdiction of Federal courts spelled out in the Constitution. When all legislative efforts failed, Senator Everett Dirksen, Republican minority leader, introduced a constitutional amendment in Congress which would permit a state to ''apportion one house of a bicameral legislature using population, geography, and political subdivisions as factors. . . . '' He was unable, however, to get his amendment through the Senate.

Any attempts to curb the Supreme Court aroused stubborn, vigorous, and successful opposition from ''liberals'' in the Congress, the media, and in the academic world. In their view generally, the high court was finally bringing justice by removing the obstacles to the making over of society by government, and they had no intention of allowing the courts to be restrained. An expression of their attitude appeared in the Washington *Post* in connection with Dirksen's efforts. The paper declared that the Supreme Court's reapportionment

> rulings have unquestionably become the law of the land. It is not the function of Congress to set aside the law, or to thwart its operation. [Dirksen had attached a rider to a bill which would delay the application of the Court's reapportionment decisions until a constitu-

> tional amendment could be considered.] The spectacle of Congress trying to use its legislative power to deny or temporarily nullify constitutional rights which the Supreme Court has clearly upheld is such a serious encroachment upon the orderly division of powers that even the extraordinary measures would be justified to defeat it.[177]

That the Supreme Court could make decisions that broke with all precedent, with no direct foundation in the Constitution, treat their opinions as if they became instantly the law of the land, and in effect incorporate them into the Constitution, clearly did not disturb the editorial writers of the Washington *Post*.

No decisions of the Supreme Court occasioned so much public consternation and long running resentment in many people as those having to do with Bible reading and prayer in the public schools. These decisions came at about the same time as the reapportionment decisions, adding to the resentment, no doubt. In 1962, the Supreme Court ruled in the case, *Engel vs. Vitale*,that a prayer prescribed by the Board of Regents violated the First Amendment of the Constitution. The prayer was non-sectarian, brief, and had the wide approval of clergymen, priests, and rabbis. It was worded this way: "Almighty God, we acknowledge our dependence upon Thee, and we beg thy blessings upon us, our parents, our teachers and our country." While some of the defenders of the decision claimed that it dealt only with state-written prayers, Justice Black, who wrote the majority opinion, had included government sanctioned prayers as well in his description. In any case, the high court did not wait long before extending its ruling.

Two cases came before the Supreme Court in 1963 which, while different in name, fell under the same ruling, the *Schempp-Murray* cases. Both Bible reading and prayer came up for consideration in these. The *Schempp* case was brought in Pennsylvania by a Unitarian; the *Murray* case was brought in Maryland by an atheist. Both objected to the conduct of religious exercises in the classrooms of public schools, even if attendance was not compulsory. The Court ruled that such religious exercises were unconstitutional violations of the establishment clause of the First Amendment to the Constitution. The establishment clause reads, "Congress shall make no law respecting an establishment of religion, or prohibiting the free exercise thereof. . . . "

The Supreme Court had followed a strange and twisted trail to arrive at the conclusion that prayer and Bible reading in state controlled public schools were in violation of this constitutional provision. The most difficult task—that of somehow applying this clause to state-run schools—, the Court almost completely ignored. That is, how does "Congress shall make no law . . . " become, in effect, "States shall make no law respecting an establishment of religion." In 1940, the Supreme Court held that the 14th Amendment "absorbed and applied to the liberties guaranteed by the First Amendment. . . . "[178] No one had supposed this to be the case for nearly a hundred years after the passage of the 14th Amendment, nor is it at all clear how it could have done so. Granted, the amendment does refer to "liberty" when it says that "nor shall any State deprive any person of life, liberty, or property, without due process of law. . . ." But the "liberty" here clearly entails absence of restraint, such as being jailed or imprisoned, and can be avoided by following due process of law. Suffice it to say that the Supreme Court hurdled over such obstacles, with only a sideways glance, to get to what it conceived to be the meat of the matter.

The meat of the matter was that the Court was bent on proscribing religious exercises in public schools. The Constitution had, in the language of one of the justices, erected "a wall of separation between church and state." By prescribing or permitting Bible reading or prayer in the public schools, the states were tending to establish religion. No matter how voluntary the exercises, they were an assault on that wall of separation and must not be permitted to take place. The Constitution had done no such thing, of course. When the Constitution (and the First Amendment) was adopted several states actually had established churches. The First Amendment had simply guaranteed that these might continue, as long as the states so chose, and that no national church or religion would be established.

The prayer and Bible reading decisions aroused an outpouring of resentment from many people and organizations. Former President Hoover said, "This interpretation of the Constitution is a disintegration of one of the most sacred of American heritages." Cardinal Francis Spellman of New York declared that the Court was striking "at the very heart of the godly tradition in which America's children have for so long been raised."[179] Moreover, 70 per cent of Americans, according to a survey, disapproved the prayer decisions of the Supreme Court. When an amendment was introduced in Congress to reverse the impact of the Court's ruling, the governors of the states announced at their annual meeting that they approved "an amendment to the Constitution . . . that will make clear and beyond challenge the acknowledgement by our Nation and people of their faith in God and permit the free and voluntary participation in prayer in the public schools."[180]

None of the amendments that have been proposed in Congress have ever passed muster there. They have met with opposition not only from liberals in Congress but also from leaders of major religious denominations. Many of these latter professed to believe that religious belief would be strengthened by keeping government out of the matter entirely. Many of those who favored an amendment were caught in somewhat of a contradiction, too. If the Supreme Court had erred, as many believed, then the problem was not with the Constitution but the Court. To contrive an amendment that would correct the Court and leave the Constitution intact was more than could be readily accomplished. Widespread resentment remains after the passage of 25 years. Resistance continues as well, since some schools still have prayer and Bible reading. But the position of the Court has not altered.

In the prayer cases, the Supreme Court was not so much legislating as it was making changes by strained constructions of the law. But in its pronouncements about the rights of defendants in criminal cases it not only made farther strides toward the new reconstruction but also as clearly engaged in legislating as it was to come in the 1960s. *Gideon vs. Wainright* was the first of these cases to break new ground. The case was decided by the Supreme Court in 1963. It involved a suit for his freedom by a Florida prisoner, who had been tried and convicted without the aid of counsel. The Court held that Gideon had been denied his constitutional rights because the state had not provided counsel (an attorney) for him. When a new trial was held in Florida, Gideon was found not guilty and freed. In the aftermath, many other prisoners were freed in Florida and other states, when new trials did not take place.

The Sixth Amendment to the Constitution does say that "In all criminal prosecutions, the accused shall enjoy the right . . . to have the Assistance of Counsel for his defense." There are at least two basic questions that this should raise, however. Virtually all criminal prosecutions occur in state courts. Does the Sixth Amendment apply to state courts? The Federal courts had been edging toward the position that it does well before *Gideon*, but they had drawn back from extending it beyond capital cases, so far as assistance of counsel was concerned. Now, the Supreme Court went virtually the whole way of applying it to all felony cases, at least. There was an even more basic question, however. Did the right to assistance of counsel mean that the government had to provide counsel at the expense of the taxpayers, if necessary? Or, did it mean that defendants had the right to obtain counsel and have their assistance in court, if they so chose, provided they could obtain counsel? There is no reasonable doubt that the latter was what the first Congress of the United States meant when it passed the Bill of Rights and what the states understood when they ratified them. The government prosecutes in criminal cases; it hardly makes sense for it to defend as well. The defendant is the one primarily interested in defense.

However that may be, the Supreme Court, having taken the stance that states must provide counsel if the accused cannot, now extended its ruling beyond what happens in the courts. In 1964, the high court held in *Escobedo vs. Illinois* that a suspect is entitled to an attorney while he is being interrogated by the police. To clarify the whole business, Chief Justice Warren set forth the rules that must be observed by police in questioning suspects. He did so in 1966 in *Miranda vs. Arizona*. The Chief Justice held that:

(1) The defendant must have been warned "at the outset of the interrogation process" that he had a right to consult an attorney.
(2) If indigent, the defendant must be assured that the public will provide him with counsel.
(3) The defendant must be apprised of his right to remain silent and if

he "indicated in any manner, at any time prior to or during questioning, that he wishes to remain silent, the interrogation must cease."

(4) If the defendant does give a statement he must be warned that anything he says "can and will be used" against him in court.

(5) Before a waiver of a defendant's rights will be held valid in an interrogation conducted in the absence of an attorney, "a heavy burden rests on the Government to demonstrate that the defendant knowingly and intelligently waived his privilege against self-incrimination and his right to retained or appointed counsel."[181]

Whatever the merits of these rules, the Court surely was legislating by laying them down.

In the ensuing years, the Federal courts frequently enforced the court's rules about obtaining evidence either by throwing out the "tainted" evidence or releasing the prisoners who had been convicted with it. In fact, that was the only method available to the courts. While the police were the violators, in these cases, freeing the prisoners hardly qualified as an appropriate punishment. As the Chief of Police of Los Angeles, W. H. Parker, observed, "I fail to see how the guilty criminal freed constitutes a personal loss to the police officer who has merely attempted to bring a criminal to justice."[182]

There were other decisions during these years that may have broken with the Constitution and tradition as much as some of these, but we must turn our attention now to assessing some of the impact of these.

Impact of the Warren Court

Whether or not the decrees of the Supreme Court constituted desirable or beneficial public policy was not the subject of the above analysis. Instead, the focus was on departures from legal tradition and strained interpretations of the Constitution. In his Farewell Address, George Washington made a point which is the central concern here. He said: "if in the opinion of the people the distribution or modification of the constitutional powers be in any particular wrong, let it be corrected by an amendment in the way which the Constitution designates. But let there be no change by usurpation; for though this in one instance may be the instrument of good, it is the customary weapon by which free governments are destroyed. The precedent must always greatly over-balance in permanent evil any transient or partial benefit which the use can at any time yield." It may be, for example, that integration of the public schools, the prohibition of prayer or Bible reading in the public schools, or other policies were beneficial. If so, however, they were matters belonging basically to the legislative branches of government primarily in the states. The Supreme Court, in most of the above instances, was acting in the absence of legislation or constitutional mandate, thus usurping powers belonging to the people or to other branches of government. It was this that Washington described as productive of "permanent evil" and the "customary weapon by which free governments are destroyed."

The tendency of the Warren Court was to break down the established authority within the United States. Even as the high court was increasing its own power by claiming constitutionality for its every utterance, it was not only undermining the authority of other branches of government but ultimately the foundations of its own authority. The most direct assault was on the authority of state and local governments, on their legislatures, executives, courts, police, and organizations. It was saying, in effect, if there is a wrong to be corrected, it is not necessary to persuade people in local areas and states that it needs correcting, and then electing officials committed to doing it. All that is necessary to do to get it corrected is to go into the federal courts and seek relief. State and local governments administer most of those things which government does that touches the warp and woof of our lives: keeping records and authorizing, where appropriate, regarding such matters as births, marriages, deaths, real property transfers, divorces, court proceedings, and the like. Most crimes are adjudicated in state courts and most of the business of policing is done by state or local governments. State and local governments operate schools and colleges, prisons, jails, mental hospitals, hospitals generally, build and maintain and patrol roads and highways, and oversee much else. They usually conduct all elections and manage their own affairs. They are the seats of popular government in the United States. A concerted assault on their authority is an assault on popular government.

The high standing of the Supreme Court rests on its position as the court of last resort in defending the Constitution. The respect in which the Constitution has been held is the foundation of the Court's authority. To the extent that the high court deviates from the written Constitution and relies on its own assertions to that same extent it is undermining the base of its authority. The Court can make pronouncements about democracy, as it did, for example, in the reapportionment cases, but it is the most remote of all the branches of government from having any popular sanction. The members of the Supreme Court, along with other Federal judges, are appointed by the President with consent of the Senate. The appointments are for life or during good behavior. Pronouncements by the Court without Constitutional backing have no popular base.

To the extent that the Supreme Court rules by its own will, it is rule by an oligarchy. That is, it is rule by a few men—nine to be exact—over the rest. That the court had become exactly that was frequently charged in the 1960s. Indeed, one writer reasoned, with sound logic, that "If it is true that a construction of the Constitution by the Supreme Court . . . is . . . 'the law of the land' . . . ; if it is true that a 'constitutional right' can come into being merely on the Court's say . . . , then, where, in all candor, are we? If a judicial interpretation of the Constitution is, by definition, the *Constitution*, why then we are in the grips of a judicial despotism? That is the meaning of depotism. An unchallengeable authority can be benign, or malevolent, but it is a depotism if the rest of the commonwealth has no practical alternative to succumbing to its will.''[183] Whether the Supreme Court was despotic or not, it was certainly assuming powers formerly belonging to the popular branches of both federal and state governments.

One of the consequences of the assertion of power by the courts for the next two decades has been a tremendous increase in court cases and lawsuits. The courts came to stand for instant justice, so to speak, a place where supplicants could come and solve their problems without having to go through the drawn out process of persuading people generally and legislators or executives to do something about it. In consequence, court cases increased and lawyers multiplied in the late 1960s, 1970s, and into the 1980s. Ironically, Chief Justice Warren Burger, who succeeded Earl Warren in that post, has complained frequently about the overloading of the Federal courts and the impossible case loads of many judges. They asked for it, or so it seems, and they got it.

But the main point to be emphasized here about the impact of the Warren Court was its undermining of governmental authority. Actually, the courts have not yet felt the full weight of the undermining of their own authority. The high court, as well as other federal courts, have continued to enjoy high prestige generally because they have been industriously supported by the major media of communication, Presidents, influential members of Congress, major private institutions, and influential members of the academic world. In short, the ''Liberal Establishment,'' as it came to be called in the 1960s, supported the thrust of the new reconstruction efforts of the courts. The authority of government generally, however, suffered, especially state and local government, and this, along with judicial activism, prepared the way for the radical reformist surge of the 1960s.

Black Activism

Much of the push for radical change in the 1960s did not come from government in general nor the courts in particular. It came from groups and organizations, whose members took increasingly to the streets, engaged in sit-ins, demonstrations, marches, and eventually all sorts of confrontations. The watchword for many of these was ''liberation,'' liberation of Blacks, liberation of colonial people around the world, liberation of students, liberation of women, liberation of children (from the despotism of their elders), liberation of homosexuals, and so on and on.

Black activism was the first of these movements. Indeed, it preceded the others by nearly a decade, paving the way for some of them. The major issue at the outset was legal segregation, and, since it was mostly in the South, the

Roy Wilkins (1901–1981)

Wilkins was the legal strategist of the Black civil rights movement for many years. He headed the National Association for the Advancement of Colored People from 1955 to 1977. The NAACP generally acted through lawyers in bringing court suits and the like, and under his leadership opposed confrontations and illegal activities. Wilkins was born in St. Louis, grew up in St. Paul, and graduated from the University of Minnesota. It was while he was editing a Kansas City newspaper for Blacks in the 1920s that Wilkins joined the NAACP. By 1931, he had come to the attention of the leaders of the organization and was invited to come to New York City to work for it. He remained with the organization for the remainder of his career. He was a lifelong advocate of racial integration and opposed Black separatism.

South was the major scene of Black activism in the late 1950s and early 1960s. Segregation in the schools was only one of an assortment of segregationist issues. In any case, the effort to integrate the public schools was carried on mainly in the courts. The National Association for the Advancement of Colored People was the main organization behind this sturggle. The NAACP was headed by Roy Wilkins. The struggle to end segregation in the schools went on for more than a decade before the logic of *Brown vs. Board of Education* became practice. Meanwhile, there were many other forms of segregation, imposed mainly in the South. Restaurants, hotels and motels, public transportation facilities, playgrounds, sports contests, stadiums, theaters, and much else was segregated, usually by law. Nor was mingling of the races permitted in many employments. Different water fountains and toilet facilities were provided for whites and Blacks in public buildings.

Black activism got underway dramatically in Montgomery in December, 1955; the issue was segregation of city buses. Mrs. Rosa Parks, a Black woman, refused to move to the rear of the bus when ordered to do so. Mrs. Parks was arrested, and angry Blacks moved to start a boycott of the buses. Several Black ministers took the lead in organizing the undertaking: among them Martin Luther King, Jr. and Ralph Abernathy. They formed a Montgomery Improvement Association to collect funds and support the boycott. King emerged as the leader of the movement during the following months as the bus company, the city of Montgomery, and the improvement association clashed. Several things drew attention to King: his home was bombed while the family was absent; he was arrested and tried for his part in the boycott, sentenced, refused to pay the fine (typically), and appealed the case; he championed non-violence. Actually, the boycott did not end segregation on the city buses; the Supreme Court did. The suit to end segregation on intrastate buses had been in the Federal courts for several years before the Parks incident. Shortly after the Supreme Court affirmed a lower court ruling that segregation on intrastate public transportation must end, Montgomery buses were integrated.

Whether the Montgomery bus boycott advanced matters at all is not clear. The boycott had, however, got national attention, and Martin Luther King got the attention which propelled him into the position as a Black leader. In February, 1957, Black ministers from ten Southern states met in New Orleans and organized the Southern Christian Leadership Conference (SCLC). The assembly chose King to head the organization. He was not only a moving speaker, knew the rhythms and emotion-laden tones which could arouse an audience, but also combined these gifts of the preacher with a vision of a transformed society (here on earth). King was, or became, a master of the tactics of non-violence and passive resistance. He said: "I had come to see early that the Christian doctrine of love operating through the Gandhian method of nonviolence was one of the most potent weapons available to the Negro in his struggle for freedom."[184]

Undoubtedly, Dr. King urged his followers not to use violence or to retaliate when attacked, but there was more involved than that. In the early years, he usually went into action by violating some custom or law, usually some law requiring segregation or requiring permits, which his group did not have. This brought him and his followers into confrontation with the authorities, and sometimes with onlookers or mobs. If arrested, he usually refused to pay fines, and he generally ignored the orders of all state and local authorities. In short, he operated in defiance of state and local authorities, as if they had no authority over him and his followers. In effect, King staged these confrontations, left violence to those whom he had provoked, and sought to arouse national indignation against Southern (in the early years) local and state authorities. Quite often, he succeeded. The confrontations were staged mainly for the benefit of national audiences by way of the reporters assembled for the occasion and for television cameras. The confrontations and conflicts were often real enough, of course; people did sometimes get beaten or otherwise beset by authorities and jailed. King undoubtedly hoped for and often managed to get Federal intervention either of the courts or the national executive to get him out of jail or change the local laws and practices.

The next major Black activist undertaking in the South came in

Martin Luther King, Jr. (1929–1968)

King was a Baptist minister and a leader in the "civil rights" movement of the 1950s and 1960s. Born in Atlanta, Georgia, he graduated from Morehouse College and received a Ph. D. in theology from Boston University. Although he was pointed toward a career as a clergyman, following in the footsteps of his father, Dr. King was early drawn into the battle against racial segregation. He understood much better than the militants who were soon drawn into the movement that Blacks were a minority in the United States and that they had neither the numbers nor the means to force their will on the country. He proposed, instead, to dramatize situations by non-violent means, which could often be counted on to provoke violent responses. That way he might be able to arouse the sympathy of those in power to his cause. He helped organize the Southern Christian Leadership Conference, became its head, and devoted full-time to his various speeches and demonstrations from 1960 until his death in 1968. The high point of his career came in 1963 in Washington with his "I have a dream" speech. He received the Nobel Peace Prize in 1964.

1960–1961. The first wave was sit-ins in segregated restaurants in the South. The Congress of Racial Equality (CORE) probably had more to do with initiating these than SCLC. CORE was founded in 1942 and became active in sit-ins in the late 1950s. They published and distributed a comic book entitled *King and the Montgomery Story*, and other materials on the tactics of non-violence. The sit-ins began in Greensboro, North Carolina in early 1960, initiated by two students who had seen these CORE materials. They went into a Woolworth store and took seats at a whites-only lunch counter, along with two other Black students who had joined them. When they were refused service, they continued to sit, and refused to leave. In the following weeks and months sit-ins spread to other Southern towns and cities. As a rule, the sit-ins were in lunch counters, and the like, of national chains of stores, a happenstance which suggests that they had in mind the interstate commerce clause of the Constitution all along. In some places, those who tried thus to integrate restaurants were arrested and convicted, and several cases eventually reached the Supreme Court. Meanwhile, some chains had desegregated their lunchrooms where law permitted. But it was court decisions plus a national public accommodations law that finally ended segregation in such facilities.

A new organization came into being during the sit-ins of 1960 to coordinate the student involvement in the movement. It eventually took the name Student Nonviolent Coordinating Committee (SNCC, pronounced "snick"), but it initially operated under the wing of SCLC. Martin Luther King had participated in some of the sit-in activity and was definitely interested in keeping some control over the student effort.

In March, 1961, CORE announced that it would sponsor "freedom rides" through the South. The object of these was to desegregate waiting rooms and other facilities in bus stations in the South. Although the Interstate Commerce Commission had forbidden segregation in interstate transportation in 1955, states and localities had continued to maintain segregation in station facilities in many places. The "freedom rides" were bus rides that began in the North and were supposed to make their way through much of the Southeast. The first one got underway in May, 1961. It encountered some limited violence in Rock Hill, South Carolina and major trouble in Anniston, Alabama and Birmingham. In fact, no driver could be found who would take the group farther than Birmingham, and there the bus "ride" ended. Later in the month, another "freedom ride" got underway. It very nearly met its Waterloo at Montgomery, where the bus riders met violence and beatings. The Alabama National Guard had to be called out to restore order. Nonetheless, the "freedom riders" proceeded to Jackson, Mississippi, where they were all arrested, tried, and convicted, and when they failed to pay their fines they were sent to prison.

The "freedom rides" had been more nearly stunts than anything else, since it was quite unlikely that the brief visits in any city would alter patterns of segregation. But Black activism was not set back by any temporary failures. Black activism continued to grow and expand in 1962, as James Farmer's CORE became more militant, and SNCC followed an increasingly independent course. There were too many confrontations, marches, and the like, over the next two or three years to deal with in detail. A few need to be mentioned, however, to emphasize the increasing violence and changing moods.

The confrontations and violence in Birmingham was one of these. Martin Luther King and the SCLC targeted Birmingham for a major effort in the spring of 1963. King's leading allies in this undertaking were the Reverends Ralph Abernathy and Fred Shuttlesworth. The campaign opened in early April with marches. While those who headed the effort undoubtedly expected a violent reaction from police commissioner Eugene "Bull"

Connor, it was not immediately forthcoming. For the first few days, demonstrators were simply stopped by police, warned to disperse, and, if they did not do so, were arrested. Then Connor went into court and got a sweeping injunction against all demonstrations. King, with his usual contempt for local courts and law enforcement officials, could not wait to take to the streets. He and the other demonstrators were arrested and thrown into prison, King into solitary confinement. Mrs. Coretta King, his wife, then made strenuous efforts to contact President Kennedy to get him to do something about the situation. Whatever efforts were made on behalf of the President had little effect, for the jailed people remained in jail.

The movement was about to collapse with nothing accomplished, so King posted bond to take charge once again. The decision was then made to use children in the streets to arouse sympathy for the protesters. The first day a thousand school children marched. The police arrested and jailed the children. The next day, 500 more children were sent into the streets. This time, ''Bull'' Connnor accommodated King and his cohorts with the police brutality they had been provoking. High-powered hoses were turned on the children, and as they were knocked down by streams of water under pressure, police waded in with dogs and nightsticks to break up the demonstration. This aroused the wrath, not only of Blacks in Birmingham but of people generally in other parts of the country. Maneuvering by the Kennedy Administration brought at least a temporary end to hostilities. In May, the Supreme Court nullified Alabama's segregation laws, and that might have been that. However, A. D. King, Martin Luther King's brother, had his home in Birmingham bombed by unknown terrorists. ''Within minutes, the black community had picked up the news and had proceeded to act upon it. For more than five hours mobs of angry blacks stormed about the city breaking windows, setting fires, and stoning firemen who sought to put them out.''[185] The police and highway patrol eventually quelled the riot, but in the following summer riots occurred in other cities around the country, the first of five ''long hot summers,'' as they were called, of rioting and disorder.

One other event of 1963 needs to be mentioned—the March on Washington in the late summer. Martin Luther King made a triumphal speaking tour around the country following the ordeal in Birmingham, and the March-on-Washington was the culminating event. Some 200,000 gathered in the Mall before King and other dignitaries in front of the Lincoln Memorial. King gave his most famous speech—the memorable ''I Have a Dream.'' The vision he called up was of a coming day when all people of all colors, all creeds, and all persuasions would join hands as brothers. Then, as he declaimed in his stirring peroration:

> When we let freedom ring, when we let it ring from every village and every hamlet, from every state and every city, we will speed up that

> day when all God's children, black men and white men, Jews and Gentiles, Protestants and Catholics, will be able to join hands and sing in the words of the old Negro spiritual, "Free at last! Free at last! Thank God almighty, we are free at last!"[186]

With legal segregation virtually at an end, due mainly to court action, Black activist organizations turned much of their effort to voter registration drives. Some of them concentrated in the Black Belt of Alabama and Mississippi, though a great deal of Black registration occurred throughout the South in these years. Predictably, some of these groups met with violence, especially in Alabama and Mississippi. The most dramatic development occurred in Selma, Alabama in March, 1965, and King was once again involved. In the face of stubborn and determined white resistance to voter registration, King proclaimed a march from Selma to Montgomery. Alabama authorities went into United States district court and obtained an injunction against the march from Judge Frank Johnson. Shortly afterward, Johnson reversed himself, and enjoined police from interfering with the march, and it took place. There had been considerable brutality and violence during the goings on at Selma, and a woman was shot and killed by Klansmen during the march. But, whatever its purpose or usefulness, the march ended with speeches before the state capitol in Montgomery.

In August, 1965, Congress passed into law an act removing most of the obstacles which had been employed in the South to restrict Black voting. That, with a spate of other "civil rights" legislation during the first two years Johnson was in office, brought to an end most of the occasion for Black activism. Even so, Black activism became more strident, irrational, radical, and violence prone as the earlier goals were being achieved. Indeed, much of the movement and activity changed from 1963 on; a number of the leaders repudiated non-violence and sought more direct action. Some even repudiated integration with whites as a goal and turned toward Black separatism and Black nationalism. Malcolm X was one of the fieriest leaders in this direction, until he was gunned down at a public meeting in 1965. He had been a disciple of Elijah Muhammad, who headed a sect of Black Muslims, until he broke with that group and went on his own. Black Muslim ideology had a considerable impact on Black activism in general in the mid- and late 1960s.

Black power became the slogan of many activists. Adam Clayton Powell, a Black Congressman from Harlem, had used the phrase in an address at Howard University in 1966. Others picked it up, and in the hands of Stokely Carmichael, who became the head of SNCC, it took on ominous overtones. On a march through northern Mississippi in 1966, Carmichael confronted Martin Luther King with his militant attitude. He told King, "I'm not going to beg the white man for anything I deserve, I'm going to take it." At a rally along the way, the New York *Times* described the use of the slogan this way:

> Five times Mr. Carmichael shouted, "We want black power!" And each time the younger members of the audience shouted back, "Black power!" Almost before Carmichael had finished Willie Ricks, who was one of his close associates, leaped to the platform shouting, "What do you want?" The crowd roared back "Black Power."[187]

There were many other ominous signs of spreading militancy, violence, and even claims that revolution was at hand by this time. The thrust toward protest and assault had spread to the colleges and a student revolt was getting underway. But before giving more detailed accounts of the spreading revolt, some further background is in order.

The Great Cultural Revolution

Neither the student nor Black revolt of the latter part of the 1960s occurred in isolation either from a broader cultural context or from what was going on elsewhere in the rest of the world. So-called "liberation" movements were underway in a number of places, especially in Africa, Asia, the Middle East, and Latin America. They were usually Communist inspired, often Communist backed, from the Soviet Union, China, Cuba, or some combination of these, and if the "liberation" occurred a communist government was installed, sooner or later, usually sooner. The characteristic feature of the conflicts was guerrilla warfare. Men who had been or were guerrilla warriors—Fidel Castro, Ché Guevara, and Mao Tse-tung—were often heroes of would-be guerrillas in the United States and elsewhere. Vietnam was the center of such a conflict in the latter part of the 1960s, and that will be discussed below. The main point here, however, is that "liberation" doctrines and ideas that were Communist in origin informed the revolt in America in the 1960s. The new reconstruction graduated into an aborted revolution.

At the heart of the student revolt and Black separatism, women's "lib," and other such movements was an ongoing effort at cultural transformation. This cultural transformation was sometimes Communist inspired but almost always drew sustenance from Communist doctrine and practice. At one level, it is easy enough to see that Black nationalism and students (or women or homosexuals) as an oppressed class drew sustenance from communism. The idea of integrating Blacks into the warp and woof of American society was not communist. It would remove them as a distinct oppressed class whose self-consciousness might spark class warfare. This latter is always grist for communist mills, and they promote such divisions wherever they can. But more broadly the idea of cultural transformation, or, better, destruction, is profoundly Communist.

This can be seen most clearly by looking briefly at what went on in China most vigorously in the late 1960s. The Great Proletariat Cultural Revolution was the name given in China to this undertaking. It got underway formally

Pix Photos

Fidel Castro (1926–)

Castro is the Communist dictator of Cuba, a post he has occupied since 1959. In alliance with the Soviet Union, he has promoted communism in other countries by military aid and otherwise, both in Latin America and Africa. He was born in the Oriente province of Cuba, illegitimately fathered by a prosperous farmer there. Castro attended a Jesuit-run school and studied law at the University of Havana. He was deeply involved in radical politics even as a student, and after Fulgencio Batista took over the government of Cuba in 1952, worked off and on to overthrow his government. Imprisoned for revolutionary activities between 1953–1955, he continued the fight against Batista after his release. In the guerrilla warfare in which he engaged during these years, Castro emerged as the leader. He had disavowed any communist connections until he became dictator, but in 1960 he entered into alliance with the Soviet Union and avowed his Communism. His style is that of a ruffian, guerrilla, and bandit; his rule is by decree.

in 1966, but Mao Tse-tung had been trying without much success to get it going for several years before that. The Great Cultural Revolution was a revolution within a revolution, so to speak. The Communists had come to power over all mainland China in 1949, and had swiftly consolidated that power, brutally, in a brief span of time. Mao made a massive effort to collectivize agriculture and promoted a Great Leap Forward, as it was called, to industrialize. China was driven backward toward the Stone Age with all this feverish activity, accompanied by the liquidation of former landowners, manufacturers, tradesmen, and the like, and the brainwashing of large numbers of those not liquidated. By the beginning of the 1960s, many of the Communists were tiring of Mao's great leaps here and there, mostly downhill, and were quietly working to reduce his role.

Chairman Mao was losing, if he had not virtually lost, his control over the government by the mid-1960s. This was happening at the same time that he was enjoying the adulation of the Chinese generally. He had become a cult figure, or, as one writer describes it, a "semi-celestial being" in the public imagination. But this adulation "at the same time removed him ever further from the daily administration of China, lest mundane cares distract him from planning the transfiguration of mankind. Even when he wished to interfere, his power to do so was severely limited by the institutional structure."[187] Maoists claimed that the bureaucrats had taken over and stalled the revolution.

At any rate, Mao called a plenary session of the Central Committee, the governing body of Communist China, for August, 1966. He had taken care to consolidate his power over the army and other crucial activities well before calling the meeting, and, according to reports, he prevented a goodly number of members from attending the meeting. Even so, the Central Committee appears to have been badly divided. In the midst of the session, Mao publicized these charges: "Some leading comrades from the central down to the local party levels have . . . enforced a bourgeois dictatorship and struck down the surging movement of the great Cultural Revolution of the proletariat. They have . . . suppressed revolutionaries, stifled opinions different from their own, imposed a white terror and felt very pleased with themselves. . . . How poisonous?"[188] Whatever his motives for this piece of propaganda, he succeeded in getting the authority to launch his full scale revolution.

The purpose of the cultural revolution was stated this way in a newspaper in China:

> It is a revolution which will completely eradicate all old ideology and culture, all the old customs and mores, which, springing from exploitive social systems, have poisoned the minds of the Chinese people. In our eyes, the eyes of the proletariat, individuals can find the most profound significance in their lives . . . in immersing themselves in the revolution—in surrendering their . . . individual being to the infinitely splendid cause of Communism.[189]

As the struggle was underway, Mao's journal, *Red Flag*, declared:

> The purpose of the Great Proletarian Cultural Revolution is to completely drag out the persons in power who take the capitalist road after they have wormed their way into our Party. . . . The battle between the two roads of Socialism and capitalism is by no means over. In many areas and in many units of the Party, the struggle between the two lines is still sharp and complex.[190]

Be all that as it may, the crucial point is that the cultural revolution was set on foot to destroy the old culture, customs, and ways. Mao Tse-tung chose the most demonic way imaginable to pursue his programs. He turned the students in colleges, universities, and institutes loose to revolt against teachers, parents, party leaders, bureaucrats, and whoever was in charge of anything in the country. Even the police were not spared from their assault, though the army was. This would have been a devastating approach in any country, but in China the impact was intensified by centuries, if not millennia of cultural patterns. By Chinese tradition, elderly people were venerated; parents were highly respected, and those in authority were obeyed by the young. Mao reversed this, or attempted to, by turning the youth loose on society. Their orders were to destroy the old civilization. These students, these young people, were the Red Guard; they were to be the little generals of disorder. The young were stirred up and emboldened in giant rallies. On one occasion a shy young girl approached Mao and pinned the Red Guard emblem on him. The Chairman asked her name. "'I am called Sung Ping-ping!' she replied." He asked if the name did not mean "refined and gentle?" She agreed, and Mao asked, "Do you not wish to do battle?" She wrote about the experience in this fashion:

> That sentence moved me deeply, and I realized that I was too far removed from what the Chairman wished me to be. Since the beginning of the Cultural Revolution, I had dared too little. When I beheld Chairman Mao and spoke to him . . . , I knew boundless joy and an overwhelming sense of duty. My determination to dare to rebel became overwhelming. . . . I will do battle! I will create disorder! I will carry through the Great Proletarian Revolution to the very end![191]

She changed her name to "Yeo-wu," which means "Will to Battle."

A kind of civil war raged in China 1966–1969. The universities were closed, in effect, and students roamed over the country creating disorder, examining officials, humiliating individuals with posters, subjecting them to slanderous attacks and debasing experiences, and working to unseat many of those in power. Chaos was often the result. Eventually, there were battles, or at least skirmishes, as groups struggled for power in a land where such central authority as there was encouraged a revolt led by youth. Chinese civilization had been vestigial, that is existed in traces and relics, long before the Communists came to power, and the hammer blows of revolution had destroyed most of what remained. The most that the Red Guards could do was to shred the dignity of those holding office. Mao's cultural revolution was a disaster; it worked by destruction, and it could only destroy. Other forces in China eventually succeeded in restoring order.

The above events were remote from the United States, but they were more than a little relevant to what went on here. The remoteness was not due alone to the fact that Chinese culture was poles apart from American culture, nor that the Chinese were Communists, and most Americans were not. The distance was magnified by the anti-foreign spirit which prevailed in China and the lack of direct sources of information as to what was going on. The

United States and China did not have diplomatic relations with one another, and Americans were not welcome there nor under the protection of our government if they went. Such information as reached the United States usually came from countries which recognized Communist China, or from places in the Orient, such as Hong Kong, to which large numbers of refugees from China came.

Even so, there were influences that reached the United States. Mao became somewhat of a cult hero among the radical students in the United States. Many of Mao's sayings were reprinted in English, and some of them were favorites of would-be revolutionaries, such as the one about power coming out of the barrel of a gun. More important, perhaps, the United States was swept by something like a cultural revolution in the 1960s. A profound revolt against authority animated student and Black revolts in the late 1960s. It also seeped through to many others as well. There were parallels, too, between the cultural revolutions in the United States and China. For one thing, the central authority in both countries gave considerable protection to those in revolt and encouraged much of the revolt against local authorities. For another, both countries had cultural revolutions animated by the desire to overturn the older customs and traditions. There was more than a little Marxism floating around in both countries. But most important, it helps to understand something of what was going on in the United States—since that was very poorly conveyed by the media of communication, who were much more intent on displaying and tolerating it than understanding it—by reflecting it through the mirror of cultural revolution in China.

One other major development needs to be discussed briefly before going on to the student and Black revolt.

The War in Vietnam

The war in Vietnam was the occasion, or at least was used as the occasion, for assorted protests in the late 1960s and early 1970s. The ambiguity of American involvement in the war contributed in several ways to make it an occasion for protest. For one thing, it was billed by the Communists and their sympathizers as a war of liberation, and that stirred sympathy for those whom Americans were fighting from more radical students and Blacks. Second, Vietnam was remote from the United States in a little-known country, with whom the United States had little historical connection. Third, Congress never declared war; hence, the enemy was not clearly defined, and the objective was often less than clear.

Vietnam had long been a part of French Indochina. After World War II, a Communist rebellion got underway, led by Ho Chi Minh, a Vietnamese. In 1954, France withdrew, and Indochina was divided into Laos, Cambodia, North and South Vietnam. North Vietnam became Communist under Ho Chi

Minh. South Vietnam became an independent country under the leadership of Ngo Dinh Diem, and received aid during the Eisenhower administration. In 1960, predominantly Communist forces formed a National Liberation Front with a military arm called the Viet Cong, with the aim of taking over in South Vietnam. Although the Viet Cong claimed to be a native uprising in South Vietnam, it was in fact supported by Ho Chi Minh, the Chinese, and ultimately to some extent the Russians.

With the outbreak of this conflict, the United States began sending in military advisers in considerable number to aid South Vietnam. By the end of 1963, there were 17,000 American troops in South Vietnam, as President Kennedy had been gradually stepping up the number of men and extent of American involvement. President Johnson began full-scale involvement in the late summer of 1964. He reported to Congress that a naval assault had been launched against American ships in the Gulf of Tonkin. In August, 1964, Congress passed what became known generally as the Tonkin Resolution, pledging the United States to use force against aggression in Southeast Asia. President Johnson, and his successor, used this resolution as authority for making what was undoubtedly war in Vietnam. General William C. Westmoreland had been appointed military commander in June, 1964, and as his forces were increased the United States took over much of the fighting there.

The war in Vietnam was a strange kind of war. In the conventional sense, it was hardly a war at all. Although Americans at home tended to think of it as similar to the Korean War, that was a quite superficial view. True, there was a North and South Vietnam as there had been (and is) a North and South Korea. It was a limited war, as the Korean War became in its later stages, at least. North Vietnam was Communist as North Korea had been, and the United States sided with South Vietnam as it had sided with South Korea. But there most of the similarities end. Both were presidential wars, in a sense, for Congress did not declare war. But the Korean conflict, or at least American intervention, had been authorized by the United Nations. By contrast, American Presidents entered the war in Vietnam without such sanction. Moreover, the North Koreans, who invaded South Korea, were organized into a regular army, clearly directed by a government (or governments, if the Soviet Union and China be included). By contrast the war in Vietnam was a guerrilla war, so far as the Viet Cong was concerned.

That it was conducted as a guerrilla war by the Viet Cong made a great deal of difference. It meant that there was ordinarily no regular battle lines; the Viet Cong assembled and dissolved at will, attacking first here and then there, appearing and disappearing. Since they were not regular soldiers, they could infiltrate at will and take on the appearance of being part of the general population. They had no capital nor government seat in South Vietnam to be conquered or overrun. The temporary taking of territory meant little; even the presence of soldiers did not keep the Viet Cong from infiltrating. Both security and intelligence were continuing problems throughout South Vietnam.

American forces were prohibited to invade North Vietnam, and neither would they permit the South Vietnamese to invade the country that was supplying the forces they were fighting and offering them sancutary as they needed it. Indeed, North Vietnam also eventually supplied many of the guerrillas who fought there. The United States did bomb North Vietnam occasionally, but that was far from being the equivalent of a land invasion. In short, the United States fought a war with both hands tied behind the back and the feet hobbled, so to speak, a war in which the full enemy was never made clear, a war which went on, more or less, for something like nine years, in which over 50,000 American lives were lost, in which a vast amount of munitions and other materials were expended, but which was not and could not be won on the terms in which it was fought.

From 1965 on the United States poured more men and materials into Vietnam. By 1969, there were more than a half million of American armed forces in Vietnam, and no end of the war was in sight. The draft was the basic means for getting men into the armed services. That was one source of the discontent with the war, but hardly the only one. Communists, of course, fanned the flames of discontent. For the first time in history, actual combat scenes were brought into the home by television. With the best of wills, this had to be a one-sided view, since the atrocities of a guerrilla army could hardly be shown as they were being committed. Ultimately, large numbers of Americans were disaffected from the war. A war of such limited goals for such an extended period, fought under such trying conditions, could hardly be justified.

A concerted effort was made to focus assorted discontents on the war, and to blame the failures in the war on weaknesses in the American system. Thus, the war in Vietnam served as more than backdrop for a widespread rebellion.

Assault on American Civilization

The rebellion which rose to a peak here and there and over and over during the period from 1964 to the early 1970s was nothing else than an ongoing assault on American civilization. The most dramatic episodes in this assault were Black riots in cities and student takeover attempts of universities. But the assault had many facets, ranging from the raucous noise of hard rock music to pornographic movies to the obscenities that now became rampant in much discourse to the peddling of sexism in *Playboy* to the vulgarities of *Hustler* magazine. The assault was the new destruction which followed in the wake of the new reconstruction.

The first of the student uprisings occurred in California, where so many things, good, bad and different, have had their beginnings in the 20th century. This one began at the University of California at Berkeley in 1964. It was led by Mario Savio, a student there. The eruption got underway following an announcement that a place commonly used by outsiders to make appeals to students could no longer be used for that purpose. The word spread that the University was clamping down on "freedom of speech," and a Free Speech movement got underway. The University of California was not exactly notorious for the vigorous exercise of authority. Indeed, it was the epitome of a "liberal" academic university, headed by a paragon of "liberalism," Clark Kerr. It was so unused to asserting authority that when students wanted to mount a revolt against authority, they had to search high and low to find something prohibited. In any case, the Free Speech movement blossomed; students defied the police, and some of them even managed finally to get arrested. In the midst of the Free Speech movement, some of the rebels even tried to establish the right to the public use of profanity and obscenities. Berkeley was the first of these uprisings, but others were to follow.

A "generational revolt," as Professor Lewis Feuer has called it, got underway at Berkeley in 1964, a revolt of the younger against the older, of sons against their fathers, a revolt against "the system," a revolt against all inherited authority. One of its characteristics, as Professor Feuer noted, was the "will to demonstrate, to be disobedient, to 'bring the system to a grinding halt,' to 'lay one's body on the line. . . . ' "[192] But there was much else besides these borrowings from Black activism. There was the adoption of at least the outward forms of the "hippie" lifestyle, the long hair as soon as boys and men could grow it, the ubiquitous blue jeans, flirting with nudity, the experimenting with drugs, the flouting of custom and tradition generally. The fascination with hair was celebrated in an infamous play entitled *Hair*, best known for the fact that its cast made a nude appearance during the performance. Timothy Leary became a sort of guru for a time for his advocacy of use of drugs, most notably "acid," to attain mind expansion. The revolt against authority spread far beyond the campus into countless homes, where children defied their parents, and countless rending breaks between parents and children occurred.

But well before the student revolt reached anything like the frenzy level, Black riots were spreading into the cities of the North. The summer of 1964 was laced with the outbreak of several of these, mostly in New York state. The patterns of these riots generally, not only in 1964 but for the next several years, was demonstrated by a riot in Rochester in July, 1964. Commonly, these events got underway when police attempted to arrest some Black person. So it was in Rochester: Police arrested a Black at a street dance in a Black section. There were shouts of "police brutality," and the crowd became a mob, attacking the police. Rumors swiftly carried the word to other parts of Rochester, and young Blacks took to the streets, rioting, pillaging, and setting fires. The riot went on for three days; one person was killed, 350 injured, and over a thousand people were arrested, before the National Guard finally restored order. Millions of dollars worth of property was stolen or destroyed.

So it was in city after city in the ensuing years. One of the worst riots occurred in Watts, a predominantly Black section of Los Angeles, in 1965. Blacks rioted and pillaged from August 11–17. The National Guard had to be called out in large numbers before the riot was finally contained. Some fifty blocks were systematically destroyed by the rioters; thirty-four people were killed; three thousand were arrested; and property damage was reckoned at close to forty million dollars. Other of the more horrendous of the riots occurred in Newark, New Jersey and Detroit, Michigan, where they took on more of the character of guerrilla warfare as there was widespread sniper fire. Washington, D. C. suffered considerable damage by rioting in 1968, and sometimes smaller cities experienced these semi-rebellions.

Two points especially need to be made about these riots. One, they did not simply occur as the result of some incident, though there was usually some incident to spark them. Blacks were being radicalized, feelings were inflamed, and some leaders were preaching destruction. For example, the riots that took place in various parts of New York City in 1964 were incited by radical groups. One of these riots was sparked by the shooting of a Black boy by a white policeman. The next day the Progressive Labor Movement, a Communist-controlled group, distributed inflammatory leaflets, obviously trying to start a riot. CORE militants spurred a riot in the Bedford-Stuyvesant section of Brooklyn. Clearly, in the case of most riots, there were those ready at hand to spread exaggerated rumors rapidly. Black leaders became more and more violent in their rhetoric, too. H. Rap Brown, who became the head of SNCC, declared that "as counterrevolutionary violence escalates against black people, revolutionary violence will meet it." Malcolm X had said, "Revolution is never based on begging somebody for an integrated cup of coffee. . . . Revolutions are based upon bloodshed. . . . Revolutions overturn systems."[194] Perhaps the most violent of all the groups were the Black Panthers, organized by Huey Newton and Bobby Seale. They wanted to take war to the police, whom they denounced as "pigs," by arming themselves. Eldredge Cleaver joined them, and said this in a speech: "The boot is kept on our necks through violence and we wish to pose revolutionary violence against it. . . . The standing army to the black people is the police, and we want to get them off our backs. But when we move to get them off they use their guns. So we have to get some guns and shoot back."[195] Even the leaders of the more staid Black organizations became more radical in their demands. By 1966, Martin Luther King, for example, was advocating unions of tenants to compel landlords to fix up their buildings. In any case, the riots did not simply occur; there were leaders and groups who set the stage for and incited them.

The other point is this: The Black riots were far and away most destructive

Gerhard E. Gscheidle

Eldridge Cleaver (1935–1998)

Cleaver was a Black revolutionary leader of the 1960s and a Black separatist. He was born in Arkansas, the son of a dining car waiter, attended junior college, but received most of his early "education" on the streets, in reform school, and prison. Most of his prison experience was in California, in Soledad, San Quentin, and Folsom. While serving a sentence at Folsom, he wrote *Soul on Ice*, whose publication brought him to national attention. In 1967, Cleaver joined the Black Panthers, became their minister of information, and was soon deeply in trouble with the police. The temper was such in the late 1960s that a man of such violent temperament with quite a prison record was sought after as a speaker by colleges and was even a guest lecturer at the University of California. He attempted to run for President in 1968 as a candidate for the Peace and Freedom party. Cleaver fled to Cuba in 1969 to escape imprisonment and continued his "exile" in Algiers. While there, he became a Christian convert, has since returned to the United States, and has become a peaceful citizen.

for Blacks themselves. Most of those killed or wounded were Blacks. A large portion of the property burned or destroyed was property inhabited by Blacks. Even when white businesses were burned or plundered, they were businesses which served mostly Blacks. As one writer noted following the Hough riot in Cleveland: "The destruction of the Playmor Auditorium removed a facility for wholesome recreation from the Negro community. Dry-cleaning stores in Hough that were looted, wrecked and closed were stocked full of clothing from the Negro community. . . . The firing of small grocery stores . . . again hurt the Negro, for often as not these same shops were the only ones to extend credit to Negroes between employment or relief checks."[196] There is a related point to be made as well. Most of these riots turned into what has been called "commodity riots." To put it more bluntly, they were looting riots. The riots usually got underway with the breaking of glass out of store windows and then robbing them of their contents.

Televisions were a favorite, as were liquor, guns, and ammunition, but in the midst of riots, with buildings burning, sirens screaming, shots being fired, and every kind of noise and screaming, people were rifling their stores of contents ranging all the way from canned goods to large pieces of furniture. Riots were welfare programs minus the government middle man, a redistribution of the wealth by direct action.

The student revolt was in full swing during the time that Black rioters were burning down their neighborhoods. The Students for a Democratic Society (SDS) was the main student organization, but some Black organizations were also involved. Students generally imitated the early Black movements, except they were not especially committed to non-violence. They usually drew up long lists of demands on the university and declared them to be non-negotiable. Then they might demonstrate, have sit-ins, strikes, occupy college buildings, kidnap deans, boycott speakers or classes, and the like. The thrust of their demands was greater student control over universities and colleges, but they might take on political or other overtones. Among the more raucous of the outbreaks, aside from the initial one at Berkeley, were at San Francisco State, Cornell, and Columbia.

Two outbreaks in the spring of 1970, however, may be discussed both because they may shed some light on these occurrences and because they more or less rung down the curtain on extensive open rebellion among students as well as Blacks. Both took place in May, one at Kent State in Ohio and the other at Jackson State in Mississippi. It should be noted that Richard Nixon, a Republican, came to the presidency in 1969, and his administration was much less favorably disposed to the student or Black rebellion than the Johnson administration. The ardor of the rebellion may have been cooling down somewhat, in any case. In late April, President Nixon had ordered troops into Cambodia, in an incursion to discourage the use of territory there as a sanctuary for use by the Viet Cong. This was taken as a signal for protest by the anti-war movement and was at least used as an occasion for stirring up revolt at Kent State, if not at Jackson State.

On Monday May 4, 1970, a detachment of the Ohio National Guard fired into a collection of students, some of whom were advancing menacingly toward the Guard units, and four students were killed. It was just after noon on a bright spring day. Kent State had about 20,000 students, is located in the small town of Kent, not far from Akron. The fatal shooting followed three days of disturbances, which had begun Friday evening, May 1. The National Guard had been brought in at the request of the mayor of Kent on Saturday night, and they went on the campus following the burning of the ROTC building and general turmoil on the campus. The trouble started on the first night outside a row of bars not far from the campus. Young people shouted "pigs" at a police car that cruised by, rock throwing and window smashing followed, and a full-scale riot appeared to be in the making before city police and sheriff's deputies drove the students back to the campus with tear gas. Attempts to radicalize any disturbance were clearly present both on Friday and Saturday. It was an ugly crowd, probably buoyed up with some outsiders, who burned the ROTC. The mob had such devices as railroad flares, at least one machete, and any number of ice picks, and beset anyone who tried to interfere. Get out of Cambodia signs were painted on store windows; groups chanted the Ho Chi Minh call and "We don't want your ____(obscenity) war."

Indeed, there is considerable evidence to support the view that if the riots were not controlled and directed by some group or groups there were those present who were doing all they could to provoke the kind of revolt and uprising that could only end in some shooting or other episode. Rocks and other missiles were repeatedly thrown at police and National Guard, and they were frequently verbally abused with obscenities. When Governor Rhodes of Ohio visited Kent on Sunday, he pointed out that

> We have the same groups going from one campus to the other and they use the universities state-supported by the state of Ohio as a sanctuary. And in this, they make definite plans of burning, destroying, and throwing rocks at police and at the National Guard and at the Highway Patrol.[197]

There had been at least six radical organizations on the Kent State Campus between 1968–1970, including the SDS and the Young Socialist League. National radical leaders, Mark Rudd and Rennie Davis in 1968, and Jerry Rubin, calling for revolution, in April, 1970. There had been several disturbances in the spring of 1969, provoked by the SDS. Four leaders of this group were convicted of assault and battery and served six months in the county jail. They had been released only two days before the May, 1970 eruption. Whether they had a hand in it has never been proven, though at least one was definitely in Kent during the period. The SDS had been banned in 1969, but some of the ever more radical elements were still seeking recognition at Kent State. Riot fever during the eruptions were surely driven up by radicals.

On the Monday of the shootings, students began to gather on open Commons, presumably for a meeting, though none was permitted. When perhaps 500 had gathered, they were ordered to disperse, but did not obey the order. National Guard units then moved to disperse them by firing tear gas and then to drive them away from the meeting place. As National Guard troops moved on them in a skirmish line that did drive them back they were met with hails of rocks and the screaming of obscenities. When the students had been partially dispersed and driven from their meeting place, the Guard commander ordered the soldiers to withdraw. As the soldiers marched back, they were followed by a throng of students, jeering and taunting them, throwing rocks and other missiles, and moving closer to them. At this juncture, several guardsmen turned back, as if on order, dropped to their knees, and fired live ammunition into the crowd. Four students were killed, and others were injured.

The disturbance at Jackson State took place less than two weeks later, on Wednesday and Thursday nights, May 13 and 14. Jackson State is a predominantly Black college located in the state capital of Mississippi. A major thoroughfare runs through the center of the college, and at night a considerable number of non-students may mingle with the students. The thoroughfare through the center of the campus also brings white motorists through, who are sometimes the targets of jeering and rock throwing. This was the case on the first night of rioting. Jackson police were finally able to bring the disturbance to an end on the first night without bloodshed. It was another matter on Thursday night. The crowds were larger, the revolt more violently inclined, so that both guardsmen and highway patrol were called to the scene. Here are two descriptions of the goings-on around the campus as the uniformed force descended on it:

> The crowd at Stewart Hall grew in size. Students from the dormitory joined the demonstrators in jeering and yelling insults and obscenities. They repeated the references to wives, mothers, and daughters of the officers made the night before. Rocks and pieces of brick were thrown. . . .
>
> . . . Along the fence in front of Alexander Hall, a campus security officer was urging students to disperse. There were jeers, obscene epithets, and a chant of "Pigs! Pigs!" . . . Magee then stepped forward with a megaphone to tell the students to go to their dormitories. . . . Two officers staggered when struck on their helmets by thrown objects; one of them stated he was knocked to the ground. . . . [198]

As the throwing of objects intensified and some reported sniper fire, highway patrolmen and policemen fired in the direction of the dormitory. Two students were killed, and others were injured.

A great furor arose in the wake of these shootings, though much more national attention was focused on Kent State than on Jackson State. Kent State was officially closed for the remainder of the school year, and several colleges and universities dismissed their students for the term. A great hue and cry was raised for investigations, not so much of the student revolt as of the guardsmen and police who had done the shooting. Grand juries were empaneled and a series of investigations were held, including one by a presidential commission headed by former Pennsylvania governor William Scranton. Those who hoped to see guardsmen and police punished suffered a disappointment. They were exonerated by juries, when the matter got that far. Indeed, the pickiness about the use of force by those called to put down riots and restore order, which was so characteristic of the "liberal" press, many academic people, and others in high places, was almost certainly not shared either by law enforcement people or the general public. The superintendent of the highway patrol in Ohio had said in Kent on the day before the shooting: "We have men that are well trained, but they are not trained to receive bricks; they won't take it." The Mississippi grand jury, which investigated what happened at Jackson State, concluded: "When people . . . engage in civil disorders and riots, they must expect to be injured or killed when law enforcement officers are required to reestablish order." The President's Commission on Campus Unrest observed, "That position . . . may reflect the views of many Americans today. It is a view which this Commission urges Americans to reject."[199] There is not much indication that the American public generally took the advice of the commission.

A much more plausible interpretation is that students and others disposed to riot took to heart the lessons implicit in the shootings. Namely, it is dangerous to taunt, jeer at, throw objects at, or otherwise resist or oppose men with loaded guns. In any case, student rioting came to an effective end following these events.

The Revolt against Authority

Most Americans did not, of course, experience the most dramatic of the assaults upon civilization during these days. That is, most did not witness the riots in the inner cities nor the confrontations on college campuses. Even the large changes wrought by court decisions affected many adult Americans only peripherally. Indeed, most Americans were not consciously engaged in an assault on civilization and, most likely, if they had been aware of it would not have approved of it. The revolt against authority, which was the central thrust of the developments described above, did reach through to most Americans. The ongoing revolt against authority touched so many facets of our lives that it could hardly be avoided. It entailed the revolt of the young against the old, children against their parents, the revolt of parents against the responsibilities of parents, of wives against their husbands, of husbands against their wives, and the more general revolt against both civil and religious authority. Divorce was rampant, so widespread that there was talk that the traditional family was on its way out. Women's liberation, so far as it led to divorce or involved divorcees, was much more apt to be the liberation of husbands than of women, since women were often left with dependent children and the necessity of making their own livelihood. There was a widespread revolt against morality during these years. Theologians began to speak of the post-Christian era, and signs abounded of a revolt against God. (Undoubtedly, in all times many individuals are in revolt against God, but the revolt went public in the 1960s, as witness the Supreme Court decisions.)

A widespread revolt against authority is a prelude to or part of an ongoing revolution. It tends to destabilize a society, for it cuts away that sort of acceptance of relationships which make for order and tranquility. As disorder spreads, the way is prepared for the seizure of power by those willing to use the necessary force to impose order when social controls are missing. There is abundant evidence that many of the radicals promoting the revolt against authority were aware both of the revolutionary character of what they were attempting and the potential opportunities which might lie ahead for the seizure of power. Many who participated more or less actively in the revolt against authority were only dimly aware of these things, if at all. Nor was every particular revolt, event, or even development, part of some predetermined pattern. But there were elements in and outside of the United States eager to see the revolt move to full-fledged revolution and the seizure of power from without or within. They were most often identifiable as Marxists, Marxist-Leninists, Maoists, communists in general, and they were aided and abetted quite often by those ranging from "liberal" to revolutionary socialists, wittingly or not.

The revolt against authority reached its political peak in the intimidation and assault on Presidents, aspirants, and other leaders between 1963–1975. During these years, President John F. Kennedy was assassinated; President Johnson was subjected to a torrent of verbal abuse by antiwar people; presidential hopeful, Robert Kennedy, was assassinated; George C. Wallace, a presidential candidate, was shot and paralyzed from the waist down; Vice-President Spiro T. Agnew resigned under charges of taking illegal kickbacks; President Nixon resigned under threat of impeachment; and two different would-be assassins made forays against President Gerald R. Ford. In addition, Martin Luther King was murdered, and while this bore no direct relation to the assaults on the presidency, it was definitely a part of a broader pattern of related events. Only one man was elected to two full terms during the twenty-four years, 1960–1984—Richard M. Nixon—and he did not serve out the second term. There were three different Presidents in both 1960s and 1970s. The office was certainly not exactly stable.

The presidency both symbolizes and is the highest political authority in the United States. Thus, the revolt against authority reaches the summit in assaults on the presidency. Not every one of these events can be closely tied to the general revolt against authority during these years, but as a development they find their nearest common explanation within it.

Lee Harvey Oswald assassinated President Kennedy with two of the three shots he fired from the Texas Book Depository in Dallas, November 22, 1963. That was the conclusion of the Warren Commission, headed by Chief Justice Earl Warren, appointed to investigate the assassination. The Warren Commission also concluded that Oswald acted alone, i. e., was not part of a conspiracy, in planning and executing the assassination, as did Jack Ruby who killed Oswald two days later. About the only thing that has not been a subject of controversy about this case is that Ruby shot Oswald. Extensive scenarios have been devised to prove that there were other shots, and possibly other assassins, in addition to those by Oswald, or instead of them.

This much is known with reasonable certainty (which is not to say that some of it has not been challenged by the spate of books claiming to have discovered a conspiracy of one sort or another). Oswald was a Marxist for several years before the assassination. The extent to which he professed to be a Communist varied from time to time. He defected to the Soviet Union in October, 1959, or at least attempted to do so. He entered the Soviet Union from Finland, renounced, but never gave up, his United States citizenship, and was given a document as a "stateless" person by the Soviet Union. Oswald returned to the United States in mid-1962 with his Russian-born wife and child. During the interval between his return to the United States and his assassination of President Kennedy, Oswald worked at several jobs in Dallas and Fort Worth. He also lived for a short period in 1963 in New Orleans, where he got identified with the Fair Play for Cuba Committee and acted as an apologist for Castro. In late September and early October, 1963, he went to Mexico City. There, he tried to get a visa to enter Cuba, but failed. Someone using his name also visited the Soviet embassy there. Apparently unsuccessful in his efforts there, he returned to Dallas and got a job in the Texas Book Depository.

Whether Oswald acted alone or as a part of a conspiracy remains somewhat of an open question, despite the efforts of the Warren Commission to dispose of the question. If it was a conspiracy, the most probable connection was with the Soviet Union or Cuba, or both. But whether or not it was a conspiracy, communism provided the framework for the assassination. It was a direct assault upon the highest authority in the United States. It would tend to destabilize the government and set the stage for revolution in the United States. Certainly, there were those high in authority in this country, including President Johnson, who feared just this consequence. That it did not happen neither proves that it might not have nor that communists, including Oswald, did not hope for that result.

The vicious verbal abuse of President Johnson reached a peak 1967–1968, as the antiwar (or anti-Vietnamese war) crusade reached a peak. Demonstrators chanted obscenities about Johnson as they marched. A libelous play named *McBird* was produced, a play which was fictional, but clearly alleged that Johnson had Kennedy assassinated and which otherwise held the President up to scorn. The rhetoric of hate had built to such a point by 1968 that Johnson was fearful of appearing in public anywhere except such carefully guarded places as military installations. His birthday occurred during the Democratic National Convention, and the Democrats proposed to honor him with a dinner, but the threat of violence was so great in Chicago that Johnson declined. Whether this public vilification of him played a determining role in his decision not to run again in 1968 is not entirely clear.

He withdrew from the race after the anti-war candidate, Eugene McCarthy, won in New Hampshire. But the torrent of abuse may well have convinced Johnson that the game was not worth the candle.

Johnson had not even left the presidency before the revolt against authority yielded yet another victim. Robert Kennedy, fresh from a primary victory in California on his way toward a probable presidential Democratic nomination, was gunned down by an assassin. Sirhan Sirhan, a Jordanian citizen living in California, was undoubtedly the killer, since the shooting occurred in a room full of people. Sirhan left no doubt in his notebooks that he was revolutionary and a Communist (at least in his commitment). "I advocate the overthrow of the current president of the [obscenity] United States of America," he wrote. Moreover, "I firmly support the Communist cause and its people—whether Russian, Chinese, Albanian, Hungarian or whoever—Workers of the world unite. . . . "[200] So far as was ever discovered, Sirhan acted alone, and he almost certainly did, but it is clear from his notes and background that he believed himself to be acting to advance the Communist cause by undermining or destroying American authority.

Martin Luther King was murdered in the same year, shot down in Memphis, Tennessee. After following a cold trail which led across much of the eastern United States, into Canada, the authorities arrested and charged James Earl Ray with the killing. Ray was a small time criminal and ex-convict who had never shown much interest in politics or ideology, nor was he known to have strong racial feelings. He pleaded guilty and was sentenced to prison in Tennessee. In consequence, if he acted with others or was, for example, a paid killer, the evidence for this has never come to light. There was an attempt, at least, to turn the murder of King into an occasion for advancing the Black revolution; there was rioting in Washington, D. C., which was incited by radical leaders. That is a long way from constituting proof, however, that King's murder was committed to create a convulsion.

The revolutionary spirit among radicals had diminished somewhat by 1972, but the assault on Presidents and presidential candidates continued. George Wallace was shot by Arthur Bremer while campaigning in Maryland on May 15, 1972. Bremer's motives were as obscure as he was, though he was subsequently tried and convicted for the attempted assassination. Wallace was campaigning for the Democratic nomination, and his following was growing at the time. After the shooting, he was paralyzed, had a long convalescence, and was unable to campaign. Whether in consequence or not, George McGovern was nominated by the most radically oriented Democratic Convention in history.

The presidential office reached a new low in public respect over the next two years or so. Vice-President Agnew resigned from that office in October, 1973. Gerald R. Ford of Michigan was elected in Congress to succeed him. Agnew was charged with accepting kick-backs and income tax evasion, and he pleaded guilty to the latter charge to avoid being imprisoned. President Nixon resigned less than a year later, August 8, 1974. The "Watergate Affair" was his undoing. The Democratic campaign headquarters in the Watergate Hotel in Washington was broken into in 1972. The next year it developed that the undertaking had been promoted by the Republican Committee to Re-elect the President (Nixon). Senate hearings under the chairmanship of Senator Sam Ervin got underway in 1973. As the testimony proceeded, it began to appear that "Watergate" involved people close to the President, and eventually Nixon himself. When the House Judiciary Committee approved impeachment, Nixon resigned—the first President ever to have done so.

The travail of the presidency was not quite over. Two attempts were made on the life of President Ford in September, 1975. On September 5, Lynette "Squeaky" Fromme pulled a 45 caliber pistol from her holster and pointed it at Ford. She was wrestled down by guards before she could fire, if that was her intent. On September 22, Sara Jane Moore actually fired a shot at the President before she was taken into custody. Both events occurred in California, the first in Sacramento, the second in San Francisco. Lynette Fromme was a female member of a notorious gang, known as the Manson Family. Charles Manson, the leader, conceived a murky notion or ideology, which entailed vague visions of revolution by way of a community of people which used sex, drugs, and violence indiscriminately. Manson was convicted of having used his malign influence over several members of his "family" to induce them to commit the brutal murders of several people. The Manson "Family" was an offshoot of the revolutionary spirit which reached its peak in the late 1960s; they were undoubtedly "crazies," but only relatively more so than revolutionaries generally. Sara Jane Moore was adjudged to be mentally unbalanced and confined in a mental institution.

The revolt against authority reached its peak, as noted, with the assault on the presidency. Not all of the above events can be closely tied to the revolutionary surge of this period, but most of them were such offshoots as might be expected.

Constitutional Reconstruction

Actually, most of the constitutional changes of the new reconstruction have already been discussed. They were made by court construction of the Constitution and legislative or executive fiat, not by the regular mode of amendment. Ever since the New Deal there had been increasing talk about the flexibility of the Constitution which changed with changing times. The Warren Court went beyond even this doctrine into a judicial activism in which the court laid down rules nowhere else written which were supposed to apply nationally. The notion gained currency that the Constitution consisted not only, perhaps not even especially, of written and formally

THE SECOND RECONSTRUCTION AMENDMENTS

Article XXIII

[Declared Ratified in 1961]

The District constituting the seat of Government of the United States shall appoint in such manner as the Congress may direct:

A number of electors of President and Vice President equal to the whole number of Senators and Representatives in Congress to which the District would be entitled if it were a State, but in no event more than the least populous State; they shall be in addition to those appointed by the States, but they shall be considered, for the purposes of the election of President and Vice President, to be electors appointed by a State; and they shall meet in the District and perform such duties as provided by the twelfth article of amendment.

The Congress shall have power to enforce this article by appropriate legislation.

Article XXIV

[Declared Ratified in 1964]

The right of citizens of the United States to vote in any primary or other election for President or Vice President, for electors for President or Vice President, or for Senator or Representative in Congress, shall not be denied or abridged by the United States or any State by reason of failure to pay any poll tax or other tax.

The Congress shall have power to enforce this article by appropriate legislation.

Article XXV

[Declared Ratified in 1967]

In case of the removal of the President from office or of his death or resignation, the Vice-President shall become President.

Whenever there is a vacancy in the office of the Vice-President, the President shall nominate a Vice-President who shall take office upon confirmation by a majority vote of both Houses of Congress.

Whenever the President transmits to the President pro tempore of the Senate and the Speaker of the House of Representatives his written declaration that he is unable to discharge the powers and duties of his office, and until he transmits to them a written declaration to the contrary, such powers and duties shall be discharged by the Vice-President as Acting President.

Whenever the Vice-President and a majority of either the principal officers of the executive departments or of such other body as Congress may by law provide, transmit to the President pro tempore of the Senate and the Speaker of the House of Representatives their written declaration that the President is unable to discharge the powers and duties of his office, the Vice-President shall immediately assume the powers and duties of the office as Acting President.

Thereafter, when the President transmits to the President pro tempore of the Senate and the Speaker of the House of Representatives his written declaration that no inability exists, he shall resume the powers and duties of his office unless the Vice-President and a majority of either the principal officers of the executive department[s] or of such other body as Congress may by law provide, transmit within four days to the President pro tempore of the Senate and the Speaker of the House of Representatives their written declaration that the President is unable to discharge the powers and duties of his office. Thereupon Congress shall decide the issue, assembling within forty-eight hours for that purpose if not in session. If the Congress, within twenty-one days after receipt of the latter written declaration, or, if Congress is not in session, within twenty-one days after Congress is required to assemble, determines by two-thirds vote of both Houses that the President is unable to discharge the powers and duties of his office, the Vice-President shall continue to discharge the same as Acting President; otherwise, the President shall resume the powers and duties of his office.

Article XXVI

[Declared Ratified in 1971]

Section 1. The right of citizens of the United States, who are eighteen years or older, to vote shall not be denied or abridged by the United States or by any State on account of age.

Section 2. The Congress shall have the power to enforce this article by appropriate legislation.

adopted articles but somehow of all those court opinions and rulings which had not yet been reversed or refined.

Even so, several amendments were proposed during this period and four were ratified. The 23rd Amendment allotted presidential electors to the District of Columbia. Residents of the city of Washington had never been able to vote in national elections before 1961. This amendment may not have grown out of the new reconstruction, but it belongs in it because Black population in the city had been increasing rapidly since World War II. In effect, this amendment enfranchised the Blacks as well as other citizens living there.

The 24th Amendment is known as the anti-poll tax amendment. It prohibited the United States or any state to levy a poll or other tax on voting for either presidential electors or members of Congress. The poll tax was a device used in some Southern states not so much for raising revenue as for restricting the number of casual voters. It was not a discriminatory tax based on race, but applied equally to everyone. However, it was widely characterized as being discriminatory.

The 25th Amendment dealt with the presidential succession by death, disability, or removal from office. The major innovation in the amendment was a provision for choosing another Vice-President when the one in office replaces the President. Since the amendment was not ratified until 1967, it was not utilized until 1973, when Spiro Agnew resigned as Vice-President. Nixon nominated Gerald Ford, and Congress elected him to the post. When Nixon resigned, Ford succeeded him, and Nelson Rockefeller was elected Vice-President. The immediate event which induced Congress to act was the much publicized Kennedy assassination, but it came into use soon as the assault on the presidency mounted. (Ironically, the amendment was adopted in the framework of a trend toward concentration of power in the presidency, not to the decline in the presidential prestige in the ensuing years.)

The 26th Amendment extended the privilege of voting to 18 year-olds, indeed referred to it as the "right to vote." This amendment grew out of the effort to mollify dissident and protesting young people. The phrase had it that if one were old enough to fight in wars he was old enough to vote. Many states also made changes during these years. Twenty-one had long been the customary (and often legal) age when a youth became a full-fledged adult. The age was widely moved back to 18 for such things as drinking alcoholic beverages, becoming legally responsible for debts, marrying without parental consent, and like matters.

One other amendment was submitted to the states for ratification. It was known as the Equal Rights Amendment (ERA) and promised to be the most radical of these amendments. Its main provision reads: "Equality of rights under the law shall not be denied or abridged by the United States or by any State on account of sex." Presumably, the amendment would remove the legal status of those classes of persons known as men and women, but what that might entail, no one could be sure. No matter, there was a flurry of ratifications by state legislatures at first, until the amendment lacked only approval by three state legislatures to become a part of the Constitution. Well before that, however, a reaction had set in, and some states had rescinded their ratification. The failure of this amendment to be ratified owes more to Phyllis Schlafly than any other person.

Chapter 10

The Conservative Response

Already the hour is late. Government has laid its hand on health, housing, farming, industry, commerce, education, and to an ever increasing degree interferes with the people's right to know. Government tends to grow, government programs take on weight and momentum. . . . But the truth is that outside of its legitimate function, government does nothing as well or as economically as the private sector of the economy.

—Ronald Reagan, 1965

So, how do I draw the line between what government should and should not do? I would have government limited *to inhibiting and penalizing the destructive actions; leave all creative activities—without exception, education or whatever—to citizens acting freely cooperatively, competitively, voluntarily, privately.*

—Leonard E. Read, 1975

Civilized man lives by authority; without some reference to authority, indeed, no form of human existence is possible. Also man lives by prescription—that is, by ancient custom and usage, and the rights which usage and custom have established. Without just authority and respected prescription, the pillars of any tolerable civil social order, true freedom is not possible.

—Russell Kirk, 1964

Chronology

1944—Publication of Hayek's *Road to Serfdom.*

1946—Organization of The Foundation for Economic Education. Publication of Hazlitt's *Economics in One Lesson.*

1948—Publication of Weaver's *Ideas Have Consequences.*

1949—Publication of *1984*.

1953—Publication of Kirk's *Conservative Mind.*

1955—Publication of *National Review* begun.

1957—Publication of Rand's *Atlas Shrugged.*

1958—Organization of John Birch Society.

1972—Re-election of Nixon-Agnew.

1973—Arab Oil Embargo.

1974—Nixon resigns—Ford succeeds to presidency.

1974-1982—Extended depression.

1976—Carter elected President.

1980—Reagan elected President.

The landslide victory of Lyndon B. Johnson in 1964 over an avowed conservative, Republican Barry Goldwater, appeared to signify a new era of triumphant "liberalism." In his first two years, Johnson thrust legislation through Congress in a way reminiscent of the New Deal. Yet this new surge toward a more expansive Welfare State was shortlived. Nor was it cut short either because of the unpopularity of Johnson in the last two years of his term or the war in Vietnam. Undoubtedly, the increasing violence and brutality of the student and Black revolts were working to discredit the welfarist approach to solving problems. The welfarist solution is to solve social problems by making concessions to organized groups, especially those minorities supposed to be disadvantaged and to shower them with benefits. That this was not pacifying such groups in the late 1960s was abundantly apparent. The more concessions and benefits some of them received, the more demanding, radical, and even revolutionary they became. The welfarist idea was being discredited by some of its most prominent supposed beneficiaries.

In retrospect, the spate of Johnson Great Society legislation looks more like the last fling of welfarism buoyed up by the sentimentalism that followed in the wake of President Kennedy's assassination than a rebirth of the New Deal. Perhaps "last fling" overstates the case, but there has been a definite winding down of support for welfarist measures since 1968. Much of the edifice of the Welfare State remains in effect in 1985, supported by a residue of belief in its programs, but the initiative has shifted away from reformist "liberalism" and its radical entourage. It has shifted in the direction of conservatism generally and away from government regulation of and intervention in the economy more particularly.

This shift in direction did not simply occur without stimulation and direction from men, ideas, and organizations, of course. Such major changes rarely, if ever, do. Granted, tens of millions of Americans were weary by the late 1960s of revolts, of the trashing of inner cities, of the ingratitude of demanding children and adults, and of accelerating claims of the unproductive upon the income of the productive. The destructiveness, intolerance, and vulgarity of the radicals aroused the disgust of millions of Americans. It would have been expressed much more vehemently, no doubt, if the media of communication had not labored so diligently to defend, make apologies for, and offer explanations for the destructive behavior. But there was much more to the shift than simply a blind reaction to a reformism becoming ever more radical and a Welfare State bloated with ever expanding programs.

A consciously conservative movement had been taking shape ever since World War II. Conservatives had been developing their ideas, becoming adept at depicting the failures of regulation and welfarism, and exposing the shallowness and tyrannical tendencies of the varieties of socialism. Conservatism was not new; the French Revolution had brought an inherent strain in man into focus. But the thrust of Bolshevism and totalitarianism in the 20th century, along with the tremendous growth and centralization of government power in the United States, provided the setting for the development of a much hardier strain after World War II.

The Conservative Movement

A great range of ideas, beliefs, prescriptions, and attitudes comprise what is commonly referred to as conservatism in America since around the middle of the 20th century. Indeed, they are so diverse and some of the groupings so narrow in their focus that some people would question that there is any such thing as a conservative movement. Certainly, there is no single organization which embraces all conservatives, no single leader who is acknowledged in that position, and no authoritative center controlling and giving directions to all the parts. Friedrich A. Hayek, who had been an important influence on American conservatism, once wrote an essay explaining "Why I Am Not a Conservative." Amongst those who have at one time or another been associated with the conservative movement there have been near anarchists and exponents of military power, libertarians and authoritarians, atheists and fundamentalist Christians, interventionists and non-interventionists. While such extreme differences may exaggerate the range, there are at least examples for all of these.

Even so, for the generality of conservatives, there is a common core of ideas, attitudes, beliefs, and predilections widely shared among them. A movement, after all, is not necessarily an organization, though there may be organizations within or clustered around it. It does not necessarily have a single philosophy or even a coherent philosophical unity, such as an individual may have. It is necessary only that it be moving in the same general direction under the sway of similar general tendencies. It is, in this sense, that there has been a conservative movement, increasing in adherents and even in cohesiveness during these years. As for the common core of ideas, these are best described after discussing some of the ideas, men and organizations involved.

1. Men and Books

That many different strains entered into conservatism should become apparent in examining some of the influential men and ideas which went into shaping it. In the years following World War II, conservatism was hardly popular, at least among intellectuals (it still is not), and it was not lightly embraced at first. Some came to it out of disenchantment with the possibilities of utopia, others out of travail over what they perceived lay ahead if the current course were followed, some in the quest for certainty in an intellectual world where relativism held sway, in some, perhaps most, in a more or less deep quest for order. The shattered faith in man brought others to a faith in God, and in groping their way toward something which endures they discovered the Eternal. There were, of course, varying degrees of depth in those who provided the insights, concepts, and visions which went into conservatism, but it must be emphasized that the quest was serious, because in the ensuing years conservatives were frequently mocked and parodied as simpletons. That was hardly the case for most of those discussed below.

One of the first of the influential works in shaping post World War II conservative thought was Friedrich A. Hayek's *The Road to Serfdom*. Hayek was Austrian in background, had lived and gone to school in the United States, and the book was written while he lived in England during the early years of World War II, then published in 1944. It made its first impact near the end of World War II, and its message ran against the grain of the much publicized hopes and expectations of the bright new world that would emerge after the victory over the Axis. The collectivism which had come to the fore in the 1930s in the United States as elsewhere, would come to bountiful fruition after the war. Hayek's thoughtful and carefully reasoned treatise came as a dash of cold water on these visions of a bright collectivist future.

Basically, what Hayek pointed out was that economic planning and controls by government led inevitably to the destruction of individual liberty. "For at least twenty-five years before the specter of totalitarianism became a real threat, we had progressively been moving away from the basic ideas on which Western civilization has been built. That this movement . . . should have brought us face to face with the totalitarian horror has come as a profound shock to this generation, which still refuses to connect the two facts. . . ."

> How sharp a break not only with the recent past but with the whole evolution of Western civilization the modern trend toward socialism means becomes clear if we consider it not merely against the background of the nineteenth century but in a longer historical perspective. We are rapidly abandoning not the views merely . . . of Adam Smith and Hume, or even of Locke and Milton, but one of the salient characteristics of Western civilization as it has grown from the foundations laid by Christianity and the Greeks and Romans . . . , the

> basic individualism inherited by us from Erasmus and Montaigne, from Cicero and Tacitus, Pericles and Thucydides. . . . [201]

Socialism, he was saying, was a root and branch assault on that individualism developed "from elements provided by Christianity and the philosophy of classical antiquity . . . , first fully developed during the Renaissance and has since grown and spread into what we know as Western Civilization. . . . "[202] In the course of the book he showed the connection between the ideas that had produced Soviet Russia and Nazi Germany and those then being applied in Britain and the United States. The horrors of Communism and Nazism were not simply the consequences of evil men coming to power; they were the precise results that followed from the concentration of power to impose collectivist ideas.

The Road to Serfdom is a classic for the conservative movement. Not only did it sell well initially but it also reached a large audience by way of condensation and publication in *Reader's Digest.* Over the years, Hayek produced other works important for conservatism, including *The Constitution of Liberty.*

In 1948, another book brought another strain into conservatism from a quite different background. Richard M. Weaver published what might otherwise be a quite obscure work entitled *Ideas Have Consequences.* Weaver taught English at the University of Chicago, grew up in the mountains of North Carolina, and received his graduate education at Vanderbilt University. Among the influences upon Weaver—besides the Southern ones generally and an ancient Greek, Plato, whose images inform much of his thought—were the Agrarians of Vanderbilt in the 1930s. They were a brilliant group of literary men who perceived the ongoing destruction of a once cohesive society in the South by progressive industrialization. Weaver's enlarged vision extended outward toward the disintegration afflicting a whole civilization.

Ideas, Weaver was saying in this book, *Have Consequences.* He was saying that the prevalent ideas widely accepted in a society or culture, work themselves out in the course of times, not, as some may hope, to reach results that are hoped for, but the full consequences entailed in the adoption of the ideas. If, for example, we secularize education, which we have done, of course, we cut ourselves loose from the ground of all truth. If we no longer respect the past, do not honor and in some manner revere it, we will trample all that is received from it and hate ourselves. Or, take this example, in his own words: "There is bitterness in the thought that there may be no hell; for . . . if there is no hell, there is no justice. When it becomes evident that the world's rewards are not adequate to the world's pain, and the possibility of other reward is denied, simple calculation demands the ending of it all."[203]

What Weaver was maintaining was that Western civilization has cut loose from the great ideas that moved it and substituted lesser or destructive ones in their stead. As he put it at one point: "For centuries now opportunism has encroached upon essential right until certitude has all but banished. We are looking for a place where a successful stand may be made . . . against modern barbarism. It seems that small-scale private property offers such an entrenchment, which is, of course, a place of defense. Yet offensive operations too must be undertaken." Weaver's thought is complex and complicated, woven as it is into a fabric in which reason is only an overlay above profound undergirding visions. Russell Kirk said, "Richard Weaver sowed deep his intellectual seed. . . ."[204] Indeed, he did, but it had impact on the development of conservatism.

Utopian literature had played an important role in acclimating American intellectuals to socialism, as pointed out in an earlier volume. It was appropriate, then, that one of the strains in conservatism was antiutopian. Reformism, as well as more revolutionary varieties of socialist endeavors, has drawn much of its sustenance from an underlying vision of the perfected society, i. e., utopia. It may well be that the utopian vision has grown dim or soured for most American intellectuals—the violence, obscenity, pointlessness, and emptiness which haunts the arts in the 20th century would suggest as much. At any rate, there is a powerful antiutopian strain within conservatism, a considerable willingness to accept the view that human nature is flawed and that perfect societies would not even be desirable if they could be contrived. (Even so, a kind of utopianism continues to inform much of advertising.) In 1949, one of the most effective of all antiutopian novels was published, *1984* by George Orwell.

George Orwell was born in India, educated at Eton in England, and though he was English spent much of his short life in other countries. He was a socialist, sort of, but he was fully aware of Soviet tyranny, for he satirized it in 1945, in the little book, *Animal Farm*. There is no reason to doubt, either, that he had in mind Communism when he wrote *1984,* though it is set in England over 35 years later. His is the picture of a pervasive and absolute tyranny imposed by a "new aristocracy . . . , made up for the most part of bureaucrats, scientists, technicians, tradeunion organizers, publicity experts, sociologists, teachers, journalists, and professional politicians. . . . As compared with their opposite numbers in past ages, they were . . . more conscious of what they were doing and more intent on crushing opposition. This last difference was cardinal. By comparison with that existing today, all the tyrannies of the past were half-hearted and inefficient. . . ." Orwell went on to explain how and why:

> Part of the reason for this was that in the past no government had the power to keep its citizens under constant surveillance. The invention of print, however, made it easier to manipulate public opinion, and the film and radio carried the process further. With the development of

> television, and the technical advance which made it possible to receive and transmit it simultaneously on the same instrument, private life came to an end. . . . The possibility of enforcing not only complete obedience to the will of the State, but complete uniformity of opinion on all subjects, now existed for the first time.[205]

Orwell described the most dreary and debilitated society imaginable. He especially emphasized how these totalitarians had destroyed the language with their "Newspeak" and "Double-think," with their incessant propaganda, and their assault on memory by either wiping out or rewriting history. All the consolations of religion are gone from the society, almost everything distinctly human debased, and the people transformed into virtual automatons. The implicit utopianism of socialism was dealt a severe blow by this work, though unimaginative movie productions and much less than pointed interpretations diluted its impact.

Although it is to take it up slightly out of chronological order, another antiutopian novel had a considerable impact on a part of the conservative movement and may well be discussed at this point. Ayn Rand's *Atlas Shrugged* was published in 1957. It is a massive novel, runs to 1168 pages, and easily dwarfs in size all other utopian and antiutopian novels. Miss Rand had migrated from Europe to the United States after graduating from college there, because, as she said, she chose to live here by choice and conviction. Her novel deals mainly with the imaginary breakdown of the American economy as a result of government intervention and efforts to redistribute wealth to the least productive and unproductive. The focus is upon the breakdown of the rail system under the above government pressures and of the heroic efforts of Dagny Taggart (the heroine) to keep Taggart Transcontinental operating. The heroes of the novel are bold, clearsighted, and efficient entrepreneurs, inventors, and capitalists. The villains are grasping bureaucrats, whining inefficient business people, and assorted parasites on the economy. The heroes and villains are greatly overdrawn—larger or smaller than life—one dimensional, personifications of Miss Rand's concept that people are moved either by a destructive venal selfishness masquerading as altruism or enlightened selfishness which bestows benefits on lesser people without having that as its purpose.

Actually, the novel is both utopian and antiutopian. She describes within the confines of the broader deterioration what is for her an utopia, inhabited by bold entrepreneurs who have fled to an inaccessible mountain retreat in the Rockies. There, they have established their own society where gold is used as the only money, and all exchanges are based on a strict *quid pro quo*. Happily for Ayn Rand, there were no children in this utopia, indeed, neither old nor young who would have to be dependent on anyone else. It is tempting to treat the novel as an allegory or a tongue-in-cheek satire, but the author was devoid of humor as well as the milk of human kindness and insisted that her characters are true to life. It is not that government intervention and redistribution could not produce the results that she depicts—indeed, it tends to do just that—, but rather that her characters and their motivations are more contrived than her melodramatic situations. That is not to deny that Rand wrote with a certain power that could enthrall the sophomoric in both the young and the not so young.

Be that as it may, *Atlas Shrugged,* and Rand's other writings had some impact on the conservative movement. A kind of cult grew up based on her ideas, and her books in paperback sold well in the late 1950s and throughout the 1960s. College students often became what were called "libertarians" during this decade, embracing her cold logic, her atheism, her opposition to all charity and altruism, and her devotion to a rugged individualism larger than life. They were often a thorn in the flesh to conservatives, with whom they shared some of their economic and social views, in parodied fashion quite often, because they tended to be absolutists, as was their mentor, and must have total agreement from others. But as they matured, a goodly number of those who had imbibed Rand's ideas did become conservatives by sloughing off the hard edges of her cold philosophy. Others preferred something nearer purity and formed or joined the Libertarian Party.

To go back to 1949, a major work for American conservatism was published for the first time in English. Yale University Press published a massive tome by Ludwig von Mises, *Human Action.* As Professor Hans Sennholz said of the work: "It was a monumental achievement, the first general treatise on economics since World War I, a magnificent structure built solidly on deductive reasoning and theoretical analysis of human action. It is unquestionably one of the most powerful products of the human mind in our time."[206] Mises was an European, nurtured in the "Austrian" school of economics in Vienna in halcyon days before World War I when that city was not only a cultural center but also the seat of much influential intellectual activity. He had already finished a notable career before he came to New York City to live in the early years of World War II. Though he was 59 years of age by then, he would live many more years during which he taught and wrote in America.

Mises brought his formidable learning to bear over the years in discrediting socialism and interventionist economics and in defending free enterprise—what he often referred to as "capitalism." His first major work published in English was *Socialism,* a devastating analysis of the flaws in that doctrine, published in German in 1922 when socialism was just beginning to triumph in Europe, and published in England in English in 1936. He predicted that socialism must fail in its economic quest because calculation would be impossible in a society organized on socialist principals. But it was his defense of the private ownership of the means of production and free enterprise for which he is best known. Mises contributed

Ludwig von Mises (1881–1973)

Mises was the leading exponent of the Austrian school of economics in the 20th century and a major influence on the American conservative movement. He was born in Lemberg, Austria, educated in Vienna, and received his law degree at the University of Vienna. Mises was economic adviser to the Austrian Chamber of Commerce, 1909–1938, as well as being a lecturer in economics at the University of Vienna 1913–1938. Most influential was his private seminar in which he taught young men who would later be of great influence in their fields: Friedrich von Hayek, Fritz Machlup, and Eric Voegelin. He was lecturing in Switzerland in 1938 when Hitler took over Austria, so that he remained there rather than returning to his homeland. In 1940, Mises moved to New York City and lived in the United States for the remainder of his life. Among his more important and influential works are: *Socialism*, *Human Action*, *Theory and History*, and *The Ultimate Foundation of Economic Science*. He opposed socialism with all his considerable intellectual power during a long career and was a compelling advocate of the free market.

much to the conservative movement both personally and in his writings by his unshaking defense of the free market. Moreover, in his seminars in Europe in the 1920s and 1930s and in the United States at New York University in his later life, he taught many younger men and women in his discipline, some of whom have followed in his steps to become spokesmen for freedom.

In 1951, a major event in the development of conservatism took place. William F. Buckley, Jr., fresh from his student days at Yale University, published *God and Man at Yale*. Much that we would eventually come to associate with Buckley—his wit, his verve, his fascination with long words (quite often archaic ones) and involved sentences, his ability to spear an incongruity and squeeze out the fallacies of an assumption, his sophistication, and the impressive range of his understanding—could be perceived, if at all, only dimly in his first little book. Nonetheless, it made quite a splash, went through nine printings by 1965, and served notice that a controversialist was at hand.

In *God and Man at Yale,* Buckley highlighted three of the strains important to conservatism generally: religious values, limited government, and individual liberty. He says that he brought with him to Yale "a firm belief in Christianity and a profound respect for American institutions and traditions. I had always been taught, and experience had fortified the teachings, that an active faith in God and a rigid adherence to Christian principles are the most powerful influences toward the good life. I also believed, with only a scanty knowledge of economics, that free enterprise and limited government had served this country well and would continue to do so in the future." Thus, he continued, "I . . . looked eagerly to Yale University for allies against secularism and collectivism."

It may be putting it too strongly to say that Buckley's hopes were dashed by what he encountered, but he was surely disappointed and must have felt in some measure betrayed. The burden of the book and the weight of the evidence he cites is to the effect that far from being inoculated against secularism and collectivism students are much more likely to be drawn to it by being immersed in these viewpoints. Buckley did not write in such broad strokes nor level any general condemnation at his *alma mater*. Instead, he examined with great care and fairness the tendencies of professors and the content of many of the books to arrive at conclusions stated with restraint. Even so, he makes it clear that neither Yale nor, by implication, many other institutions were giving wholehearted support to Christianity, religious values, free enterprise, and limited government. His concerns became a part of those widely shared in the conservative movement.

Conscious and distinctive conservatism in America owes much to the publication of Russell Kirk's *The Conservative Mind* in 1953. The subtitle of the book is *From Burke to Eliot,* i. e., from Edmund Burke in the 18th century to T. S. Eliot in the 20th century. It contains the story of the development of conservatism by Anglo-American thinkers told mainly by way of the analysis of the thought of certain thinkers. Kirk focused upon the following: Edmund Burke, Alexander Hamilton, John Adams, Samuel Taylor Coleridge, John C. Calhoun, John Randolph, James Fenimore Cooper, John Quincy Adams, Orestes Brownson, Nathaniel Hawthorne, Benjamin Disraeli, and other 19th- and 20th-century thinkers. It should be noted that Dr. Kirk generally excluded 19th-century liberals from his Pantheon of conservatives and distinguished clearly between liberalism and conservatism, something that many American conservatives of the 20th century find unnecessary. Thus, Kirk emphasized tradition, custom, prescription, yes, even prejudice, as being among the values of conservatism. Nor did he shy away from the values of status and hierarchy, which have

Russell Kirk (1918–1994)

Kirk emerged as the intellectual leader of a reviving conservatism in the early 1950s with the publication of *The Conservative Mind* and *A Program for Conservatives.* He is primarily a man of letters—a writer of biography, novels, articles, reviews, and history. His especial emphasis in conservatism has been traditionalist, an emphasis upon continuity, upon order, and an antipathy to all ideologies. Kirk was born in Michigan, took his bachelor's degree at Michigan State, a master's at Duke University, and a doctorate in letters at St. Andrews in Scotland. He has lectured widely, taught at various times in a number of colleges, but mostly lives and writes in his ancestral village of Mecosta, Michigan. In one sense, Dr. Kirk is certainly an eccentric with a decided preference for old ways, for characters who are far from a common mould, but, in another, he speaks both to a deep American strain as well as a universal sense of awe and wonder before a universe whose most basic feature is its enduring mystery.

been assaulted by 20th-century Liberals so vigorously as to make them anathema to Americans.

Among those things with which conservatives must deal, Kirk said, are: "the restoration of the ethical system and the religious sanction upon which any life worth living is founded . . . ; the preservation of some measure of veneration, discipline, order, and class . . . ," and the following which may well be quoted at length:

> . . . The mass of men must find status and hope within society: true family, respect for the past, responsibility for the future, private property, duty as well as right, inner resources that matter more than the mass-amusement and mass-vices with which the modern proletarian seeks to forget his lack of an object. The degeneration of the family to common house-tenancy menaces the very essence of recognizable human character. . . . To restore purpose to labor and domestic existence, to give men back old hopes and long views and thought of

> posterity, will require the bold imagination which Burke infused into conservative ideas.[208]

Over the years, Kirk would add much more to the vision of conservatism by his concern with education, literature and the arts, but at the outset he provided it with an account of a past and a noble lineage.

Many other books and writers might be discussed—some will be in the following section,—but the main purpose here has been to trace some of the beginnings of contemporary conservatism. One other will be discussed before going on, however, because of its exposition of the American political system. It is Felix Morley's *Freedom and Federalism,* published in 1959. Morley was a journalist and editor, president of Haverford College, and a philosopher by inclination. He had two brothers—Christopher and Frank—and together they hold the distinction of being the only three siblings to receive Rhodes scholarships. All three had distinguished careers afterward, and, as a contemporary writer has said: "Essentially, the work of these brothers was to attempt to stop the growth of the State. . . . The sooner the Morley brothers become household words, the sooner will there be a better appreciation of the value and importance of the individual as opposed to the ubiquitous State."[209] Certainly, Felix showed a high appreciation of the American system of government in *Freedom and Federalism.*

He emphasized anew that a Federal system of government embraces the general government—now misleadingly referred to as *the* "federal" government—and state and local governments. "The United States, as the name implies," he noted, "are a union of sovereign States, federal in nature. . . . The great overriding advantage of the federal system is that it operates to avert the dangers inherent in government by remote control. The essence of federalism is reservation of control over local affairs to the localities themselves. . . . One justifying assumption for such a loose-knit system is that citizens as a body are both interested in, and for the most part competent to handle, local problems. When that assumption is valid there is little doubt that federalism . . . serves admirably to foster freedom without the sacrifice of order."[210]

Morley made other important points, too, than his central one about the Federal character of American governments, the dispersion of power among the governments, and how the various branches and governments might act to restrain one another. He emphasized the importance of having a written Constitution and reminded Americans that it was intended as a reflection of higher laws. "Our whole system of government," Morley said, "is based on the assumption that there *are* certain absolutes, referred to in the Declaration of Independence as 'the Laws of Nature and of Nature's God.'" Further, that "the Constitution, while 'the supreme law of the land,' was in its original form and still essentially remains a valiant attempt to observe as long as they believe in those enduring moral values without which civilization would be impossible."[211] The heart of the conservative movement has been the reassertion of the view that there are enduring truths, that truth is not simply a matter of fashion or changing views, and much of the effort was to make public statements of this belief.

2. Organizations and Publications

It was by no means easy to find anyone to publish works in the conservative vein in the 1950s generally. Indeed, Hayek reported that three publishers in the United States turned down his *Road to Serfdom* before he finally found a publisher. (This was in 1944, which indicates that the condition may have already prevailed.) He wrote that he had supposed that the manuscript was turned down because there were doubts as to a market for it. Later, he discovered that was not the case, that the publishers had disliked his ideas and did not wish to put them in print. In general, throughout the period under discussion, major publishers (mainly located in New York City) did not publish conservative books. Here and there a university press with a favorably disposed editor would publish a conservative writer. Thus, the University of Chicago published Hayek's book and Yale University Press published Mises' *Human Action*. There were two small commercial publishers who did handle conservative books: Henry Regnery Company, headed by Henry Regnery, and Devin-Adair, headed by Devin Garrity. Nor was the world of journals and magazines much more favorably disposed to conservative articles.

In large, this situation was the result of what M. Stanton Evans described as the sway of *The Liberal Establishment* in the United States. "An establishment," Evans said, "is . . . a kind of informal junta by which a community is guided in all those things which matter." He maintained "that such an establishment does exist in America, that it labors to make the ideas of Liberalism supreme in our politics, and that its members do work in concert although not necessarily by pre-arrangement. . . . Establishment members are for the most part products of a Liberal education in the American academy, where they have been taught as right and natural the characteristic Liberal ideas of centralized power, accommodation of our foreign adversaries . . . , the absence of fixed standards of judgment, and the conviction that anyone who does not profess these ideas is an ignoramus."[212]

Liberals occupied the seats of power generally in government, in the publishing businesses, in many of the churches, and in colleges and universities. Believing as they did in the rightness of their views, their initial response to the resurgence of a conscious conservatism was to ignore writers and spokesmen of this persuasion, not to publish their books and articles, not to review their books (certainly not to treat them seriously), not to give conservatives a platform from which to speak, and never to greet their ideas with anything but a sneer. When that did not succeed in silencing conservatives or destroying their public appeal, the Liberal Establishment denounced conservatives with such epithets as "the radical right" and "right-wing extremists." For example, the following are some titles of books that were allegedly about conservatism: Richard Dudman, *Men of the Far Right;* Daniel Bell, ed., *The Radical Right;* Mark Sherwin, *The Extremists;* Harry and Bonaro Overstreet, *The Strange Tactics of Extremism;* and Arnold Forster and Benjamin Epstein, *Danger on the Right.*

Ignored, rejected, or denounced, conservatives found it necessary to set up their own organizations and publications and open up their own channels of communication. A considerable number of such organizations and publications were started over the years, some with broad and others with quite limited purposes. Only a few can be discussed in any detail, and these will generally be selected both to illustrate the range of interests and influence of the conservative movement. They will also be delimited to those founded after 1945 and before 1970, because they have proliferated in number since the latter date.

One of the earliest of the post-World War II efforts was a small magazine, *Plain Talk,* edited by Isaac Don Levine, begun in 1946 and lasting for about four years. It was primarily an anti-Communist effort, devoted to exposing Soviet slave camps, Communist infiltration of labor unions, and Communist tactics generally, though the range of articles was much greater than that might suggest. Despite the modesty of the undertaking, the editor managed to get articles from quite a number of well known writers, such as Eugene Lyons, Harold J. Laski, Margaret Mitchell, William C. Bullitt, and Bertrand Russell. A few titles of articles may convey something of the tenor of the offerings of the publication: "'Gulag'—Slavery, Inc.," "Why Communism is Reactionary," "The Mystery of Our China Policy," and "Inside the Comintern." These brief and pointed articles came in the wake of the wartime collaboration between the United States and the Soviet Union and did much to inform those Americans who consulted about the real nature of communism.

Leonard Read founded The Foundation for Economic Education in 1946 also, an organization of somewhat broader purpose and which had much longer endurance. Mr. Read took on the formidable job of reviving and restoring and understanding of the values of limited government, private enterprise, individual liberty, and the moral and spiritual belief which undergirded them. He called the complex of beliefs which he sought to disseminate "the freedom philosophy." His philosophy was a compound of his American heritage, the teachings of Jesus, an admixture of Ralph Waldo Emerson and Herbert Spencer, much hard-headed economics softened with romantic overtones. Read taught that free men are productive, that government planning must forfeit the great benefits derived from many minds

Leonard E. Read (1898–1983)

Read was the founder of The Foundation for Economic Education and its longtime head. This organization, founded in 1946, has been devoted to explaining the benefits of the "free market, private ownership, and limited government." Mr. Read was born in rural Michigan, had little more than basic schooling, though by wide and extensive reading combined with a keen curiosity he became a learned and wise man. After serving during World War I, he went into the wholesale produce business. In the mid-1920s, however, he moved to California, where he became associated with the Chamber of Commerce. His years with this organization gave him a hankering to form an organization to spread the idea of the free market that would be independent of business as a special interest seeking to use government for its ends. Read was not a political activist; instead, he wanted to teach only those who voluntarily came to learn. He believed he had hold of a better idea for man in society, an idea which could only become actuality as men came one by one to grasp and believe it.

applied to the task when men are free to do so. He never tired of describing with awe the wonders of voluntary cooperative production.

Read's main approach was to revive, bring into being, publish, and circulate ideas on liberty. Before long, he was publishing a monthly journal, called *Ideas on Liberty* at first, then under the title, *The Freeman,* when he bought out that older publication. *The Freeman* contained a variety of articles, scholarly and otherwise, on an assortment of subjects, most often about economics but always on something relating to liberty. Among the books the Foundation circulated widely were Frederic Bastiat's *The Law,* and Henry Grady Weaver's *The Mainspring of Human Progress.* Dean Russell translated *The Law* for FEE. A slim work by a French writer who lived in the first half of the 19th century, it sets forth the case for liberty in terms of natural rights in a straightforward, direct, and logical manner. Read gathered about him men of like mind or similar views, such as F. A. Harper, Orval Watts, and Edmund Opitz, and published or circulated the works of many others, among them Henry Hazlitt, whose *Economics in One Lesson* circulated in large numbers, John Chamberlain, William Henry Chamberlin, and Ludwig von Mises. Through these efforts, plus the weekend and week-long seminars, The Foundation for Economic Education has done much to contribute the economic case for free enterprise to the conservative movement.

Another organization which dates back to 1946 is R. K. Scott's America's Future. Over the years this small organization has provided radio broadcasts, published a newsletter, and circulated many pamphlets. Its main focus has been on schools and education, and in addition to providing many pamphlets for use in the schools, America's Future has commissioned the review of numerous textbooks, mainly in the social studies. The main emphasis of America's Future has been on preserving the American Constitution, freedom of enterprise, maintaining American defense, and opposition to socialism and communism.

Another publication begun in the late 1940s was *Human Events*. This tabloid-sized weekly was begun by Henry Regnery, Frank Hanighen, and Felix Morley, the latter two serving as its first editors. It began as an analytical and thoughtful publication, wedded to a conservatism which had been isolationist in 1930s, or at least opposed to foreign entanglements and military intervention, a long-standing American tradition actually. In view of the threat of Communism, Hanighen believed that the paper should swing its support to anti-Soviet alliances. Morley shortly withdrew, and Frank Chodorov took his place. However, Chodorov, who was, if not the last of the individualists, certainly one of the most emphatic of that persuasion, was soon at odds with Hanighen as well. Hanighen went on to establish *Human Events* as an important conservative influence located in Washington, D. C.

Frank Chodorov conceived and proceeded to get underway a different sort of project around 1950—the Intercollegiate Society of Individualists. He noted in an article that the most significant change of the past fifty years had been "the transmutation of the American character from individualist to collectivist." He went on in a similar vein:

> The replacement of the horse-and-buggy by the automobile is startling enough; but is it as startling as the contrast between Cleveland and Truman? This is not to compare the two presidents, but to point out the remarkable change of the people they presided over. Cleveland's remark that the government could not take care of the people who take care of it was made because Americans thought that way; today, the handout principle of government is accepted by all good Americans, from pauper to millionaire. At the beginning of the century the tradition of individualism that had held up since the Revolution was still going strong; by 1950, that tradition had been washed out by the caustic of socialism.[213]

Chodorov went on to explain how all this had happened, how the ideas of socialism had been planted in the minds of youth, how socialists had got their literature into colleges, sent speakers and formed clubs. Eventually, a generation of young men who had been deeply infected with socialism went out to gain leadership and apply these ideas. What he proposed was that something like this be done on the individualist side, that lecturers be sent to colleges and that individualist clubs be formed. That was very much what the Intercollegiate Society of Individualists did: published pamphlets, organized a lecture bureau, sponsored student clubs, and provided the ammunition for students of a reviving American idea. ISI, as it was called, published a little periodical during the early years called *The Individualist.* Chodorov never administered the organization, and those in charge eventually changed its name and brought it more into accord with what some conceived to be the mainstream of conservatism. Traditionalists, especially, and Roman Catholic thinkers, probably as a rule, did not care overmuch for the idea of individualism. To them, it emphasized too much independence of the individual, even his autonomy, and tended to downgrade community, society, and organizations, perhaps even cooperation. At any rate, the name was changed to Intercollegiate Studies Institute (keeping the same initials), and the regular publication became *The Intercollegiate Review,* with a more scholarly format. But under whatever name, the organization did draw a goodly number of students into the conservative movement.

Another publication, one which sought to become the flagship of conservatism, began publication in 1955 as *National Review.* It was William F. Buckley Jr.'s vehicle from the outset, a biweekly combination journal and commentary on the news. It partook of Buckley's wit, audacity, verve, sophistication, if not always his precise views. (Indeed, Buckley's views were much more often elaborate than precise; they came to the surface from time to time but usually meandered through a thicket of Latin, archaic terms, obscure allusions, punctuated here and there with disjointed syllogisms.) His preferences for staff and writers ran to siblings and/or their spouses, Yale graduates, ex-Communists, Roman Catholics, and anyone who was better known or widely recognized and respected, not necessarily in that order. *National Review* was almost always lively, sometimes entertaining, often informative, and usually controversial. It attracted quite an assortment of writers ranging from Whittaker Chambers to William Rickenbacker, but the main core over the early years consisted of James Burnham, Frank S. Meyer, Russell Kirk, and, of course, Buckley himself.

Buckley was undoubtedly determined to demonstrate not simply that the conservative position was intellectually respectable but that it was superior to Liberaldom. Moreover, he often served as a missionary to Liberalism, ready to welcome any to the table who showed the slightest signs of conversion. *National Review* ranged from contemporary politics to philosophy to literature to debates in writing on controversial issues. The

William F. Buckley Jr. (1925–)

Buckley is the conservative missionary to "liberals," whom he overwhelms with his erudition and woos by ridicule. He is a journalist, publisher, author, occasional politician, and television personality. He was born in New York City, grew up in England, the United States, and France, and graduated from Yale. His biweekly magazine, *National Review*, has been an important voice for conservatism, and a goodly number of people know him for his weekly TV program, *Firing Line*, aired on public television. In addition, he has a regular newspaper column, has written books, including novels, and many articles. In 1965, Buckley even ran for mayor of New York City, but told a reporter that if he won he would demand a recount. He brought humor and literary flair to the conservative movement, something it was sorely lacking before his appearance.

magazine also attempted to serve as arbiter from time to time as to who was and who was not a "real" conservative. Within a few years of its founding *National Review* writers had read Ayn Rand and the John Birch Society out of the conservative movement. "Real" conservatives were more broadly distinguished from others by referring to them as "responsible conservatives." Whether their anathemas made much impact or not is not on the record, but there is no doubt that *National Review* was an important influence in the conservative movement.

Modern Age began publication in 1957, edited by Russell Kirk and published in Chicago. It quickly distinguished itself as having the highest intellectual and scholarly fare of the conservative journals. It was in the mode of scholarly journals, was published quarterly, as they usually are, except for its use of more color on the cover and that its subtitle was *A Conservative Review*. *Modern Age* appeared several years before *Intercollegiate Review*, and though it never attained a large readership served well in providing intellectual prestige and substance to the conservative movement.

Although the John Birch Society may not have added to the prestige of the conservative movement, it became the lightning rod and provided the most aggressively active organization in the movement. It was founded under the leadership of Robert Welch at Indianapolis in 1958. John Birch, for whom the society was named, was a missionary to China, served in the United States Army in the Far East during World War II, and was murdered by the Chinese Communists a few days after Japan surrendered. Mr. Welch was a gentle and kindly man, almost retiring in manner, who managed to put together a tightly knit organization which was often more activist than educational, though it was both. The John Birch Society published *American Opinion,* which was almost certainly the glossiest of conservative journals, and definitely one of the hardest hitting. In addition, the Society sponsored bookstores across the nation, maintained a speaker's bureau, sponsored lecture tours, operated summer camps for young people in several locations around the country, operated a book publishing firm, Western Islands, had a research bureau, and maintained chapters in virtually every town and city in the United States. Members were frequently urged to and frequently did carry out letter writing campaigns on a large scale and served actively quite often in political campaigns.

There were probably two main reasons why the John Birch Society became the lightning rod—i.e., drew much of the fire of criticism from Establishment critics—of conservatism. One was that the aggressive tactics of the Society may have invited some retaliation. Mr. Welch and his followers made arguments, used slogans, and did not try to hide or downplay their contempt for the prevailing Liberal orthodoxy and many of its spokesmen. Robert Welch dissected the highly popular President Eisenhower in a book, *The Politician,* and charged him with giving aid and comfort to the Communist conspiracy. Whatever the merits of the argument, most Americans were not disposed to consider conclusions which were so far removed from their own estimate of the man. One of the Welch sayings which was most widely disseminated read, "This is a republic, not a democracy. Let's keep it that way." The statement was true, all right, but it flew in the face of decades of indoctrination. So, initially, did the admonition to "Get the U.S. out of the U.N. and the U. N. out of the U. S.," though further experience has undoubtedly brought many Americans nearer to agreement with it. At the level of ideas and beliefs, if not otherwise, the John Birch Society was confrontational. Most shocking of all, perhaps, was full-sized billboard advertisements exhorting, "Impeach Earl Warren!"

If the Society was seeking publicity, it succeeded. Both the John Birch Society and, to a lesser extent, Robert Welch became household words. At the peak of the attention given to them, as many as a thousand items a day appeared in newspapers across the United States. But overwhelmingly it was unfavorable; the conception generally purveyed by the media was that reasonable and decent persons would have nothing to do with the John Birch Society. This brings us to the second reason why the John Birch Society became the lightning rod of conservatism. Neither the using of slogans that ran against the grain nor their sloganal confrontations account for the

Robert Welch (1899–1985)

Welch founded the John Birch Society, a tightly knit anti-Communist, pro-American organization, which was the first of the activist conservative organizations on a nationwide scale. He differed from most other conservative leaders in his advocacy of a conspiracy theory to explain the spread of collectivism in the 20th century. Welch was born in North Carolina, was something of a child prodigy, graduating from high school at the age of 12, and from the University of North Carolina at the age when most freshmen enter. He did not take to the academic life after that, however, for he successively dropped out of graduate school at North Carolina, out of the Naval Academy at Annapolis, and out of Harvard Law School. He eventually made good in the candy business and was a notable success in sales. After World War II, he became increasingly interested in world affairs and concerned about the spread of collectivism. This led eventually to his retirement from business and the formation of a variety of active arms of the John Birch Society.

campaign of vilification and denunciation by the media. After all, student and Black radicals in the 1960s made charges that were geometrically more astounding than those made by Robert Welch, and inflamed audiences in ways that John Birchers would neither have conceived nor dared. Yet radical leaders were generally treated with respect and circumspectly defended by the media generally. Their complaints were often aired sympathetically. By contrast, the arguments of the John Birch Society tended to be dismissed without examination and Birchers subjected to ridicule. Actually, media people fatten on controversy; the more outrageous the charges or conduct, the better copy it makes ordinarily. Thus, when they vilify those who might otherwise be grist for their mills, their motives are suspect. The reason is not far to seek in the case of the John Birch Society. The Society had the potentiality of attracting large numbers of followers, of really arousing millions. In terms of the ideology of those dominant within the media, such an effect had to be short-circuited. Birchers must be made into pariahs and their influence nullified. Their assault would also serve to restrain conservatism generally, as many conservatives could be expected to and did distance themselves from the Society, though not always necessarily because of the media attacks.

In general, the principles advanced by the John Birch Society were shared not only by most conservatives but by a great many other Americans of less well fixed philosophy. Robert Welch said in 1978 that the task of the Society was "to bring about a long era dominated by the early and real Americanist philosophy of individual freedom through firmly limited government; of morality and decency restored through a renewed dependence on the family unit; of material abundance and prosperity through free enterprise; and, of an Americanist influence that will be immensely helpful to all the peoples of other nations through exactly the same principles at work as had made our country admired and envied by all the peoples of the world."[214] The approach of the Society mainly was to make available information that would solidify belief in these principles.

Robert Welch was anti-Communist from the outset and placed major emphasis upon conspiracy as the cause of the subversion or undermining of American principles and interests. Indeed, he was fascinated by the part played by conspiracies from time to time in history. The John Birch Society has both published and circulated much literature exposing or alleging conspiratorial activity in many events and developments in the 20th century. The existence of a Communist conspiracy operating around the world has been thoroughly documented by many different individuals, groups, and governments, and much of the evidence is conclusive. Much of it is not known in the West, of course, because the main conspirators have never been brought to trial and convicted, and much of it is in the archives (if it is kept there) of Communist countries. No Communist government that has been long in existence has yet been overturned in the world; thus, their files and archives have never been made public. How high up the Communist conspiracy has extended among government officials and men of influence is simply not known as fact in many instances. But enough has surfaced over the years to make it clear that Communist subversion, disinformation, espionage, stimulated revolts, and influence spread by way of sympathizers have made a major impact on many developments. In one sense, the Liberal media (including fiction writers and publishers and moviemakers) and the academic world, on the one hand, and the John Birch Society, on the other, have been counterparts. The first have understated, underreported, and downplayed the role of conspiracy, as much as it as has been established. By contrast, the John Birch Society has fully reported that which has been established, though greatly limited in the means to publicize it, but has sometimes gone well beyond what could be proved in alleging the extent and persons involved in conspiracies. Conservative writers and thinkers generally could have benefited greatly by sympathetic and constructive criticism from the many able people in the academic and intellectual world more broadly. Instead, they have most often been either ignored, classified by unfavorable terms, e. g., "radical right," or denounced, which has made many of them defensive, to say the least.

In any case, the John Birch Society persevered through the major media assaults of the 1960s, survived, held to its positions, and as the conservative position gained ground in politics, began to get recognition for some of its effectiveness in advancing conservatism. At the time of 25th anniversary of the Society, Senator Steve Symms of Idaho said, "Without any doubt, the educational programs of The John Birch Society over the past quarter century have produced thousands and thousands of politically aware voters who take seriously the responsibilities of citizenship." Of the Society's weekly newsmagazine, Congressman Philip Crane of Illinois said that it "influences public sentiment. It enlightens, educates, and informs in a way we have grown unaccustomed to expecting from most of the media."[215]

In the mid-1960s, the Conservative Book Club was established as a commercial venture. It did much to make conservative books available to a wider audience. Since there were not enough books being published by general publishers to supply its demands, a publishing house, Arlington House, was set up as a publisher of conservative books. Under the leadership of Neil McCaffrey, it increased greatly the number and variety of conservative books in circulation. Arlington ranged all across the spectrum of conservative opinion, ranging from C. S. Lewis, *God in the Dock* to Paul D. Bethel, *The Losers* (an account of the Communist conquest of Cuba) to Henry Hazlitt, *The Failure of the New Economics* to Russell Kirk, *Enemies of the Permanent Things*. Generally, Arlington House did not publish fiction, but a notable exception was Daniel McMichael, *The Journal of David Q. Little*, an anti-utopian novel set in Pittsburgh. The scenario is a Communist takeover of the United States and of the resulting tyranny and breakdown of the society. Works published varied greatly in quality, but some important additions to conservative literature did find a publisher.

There were many other organizations which played some role in the conservative movement. Some of them were of long standing, such as the American Legion, National Association of Manufacturers, and Daughters of the American Revolution. These were not in the conservative movement, *per se*, but they were conservative in tenor and added to the thrust in that direction. Others were newer, and were definitely a part of the movement, such as Young Americans for Freedom and Admiral Ben Moreell's Americans for Constitutional Action. It should be noted, too, that as conservative writers became better known, it became easier for some of them, at least, to get works published by commercial publishers. Another area that began to open up for them in the course of the 1960s was syndicated columns in newspapers. While the national media was dominantly Liberal in the mid-20th century, that was by no means the case with many newspapers, both in small towns and in cities. Many medium-sized cities which had two newspapers would often have one that that was more or less Liberal and another that was more or less conservative. At any rate, as consciously conservative columnists developed, they found a ready market for political columnms on editorial pages especially. Among those who wrote nationally syndicated columns were Buckley, Kirk, John Chamberlain, Ralph de Toledano, and James J. Kilpatrick.

Two other types of organizations deserve some discussion: churches and schools. It might be supposed that churches generally would be conservative, since they look back to a long past for their scriptures and rely more or less heavily on religious traditions, many of which have been in operation for centuries. If for no other reason, it might be supposed that they would be conservative, at least, in their opposition to Communism. After all, Communist regimes are militantly atheist, have quite often confiscated church property, compromised the independence of churches, and persecuted Christians and Jews with greater or lesser vigor from time to time. Yet, the leadership of many of the major churches and synagogues in the United States have often been anything but conservative in this century. Such major Protestant denominations as the Episcopal, United Presbyterian, United Methodist, United Church of Christ, Disciples of Christ, American Baptist, and some Lutheran bodies have been deeply under the sway of the social gospel. (That is, their leaders and many of their clergy have been; their members would, of course, hold widely differing views.) On the matter of Communism, they have tended to favor cooperation with Communist countries and with such subjected churches as exist in their lands. The Roman Catholic Church, which had long been a bastion of religious conservatism and, to some extent, conservatism generally began to shift during the papacy of John XXIII and has since come widely under the sway of a reformist like social gospel.

On the other hand, many of the smaller and now much faster growing churches—fundamental, orthodox, and/or more evangelistic—tend to be conservative on a great variety of issues. The Southern Baptist associations (the largest Protestant denomination in the United States) are governed by their individual congregations, so that generalizations about them are hazardous, but many of them tend to be conservative. The emergence of Jerry Falwell's Moral Majority in recent years attests to considerable conservatism in these bodies.

Numerous private and Christian schools have been organized in the 1960s and 1970s. The compulsory integration of the public schools led to the forming of many private schools in the South during these years. Some Christian schools may also have been formed out of this impetus. But a much broader spectrum of concerns has been behind the forming of many private and Christian schools: the concern about the quality of education in the public schools, the disorderliness in many of them, the presence of a criminal element, especially street gangs and drug pushers, the secularizing of education in the schools, especially the abandonment of prayer and Bible reading, and compulsory courses in humanistic sex education. Independent Baptist churches have been especially industrious in providing schools, but many others have done so as well. Some private and Christian schools have tried to distance themselves from the public schools as far as possible. They have often had rough going in this, however, in many states. State departments of education often claim various kinds of authority over curriculum, instruction, classroom organization, and the like. In effect, states, having adopted compulsory attendance, have claimed that the basic authority over the content of education belongs to them, not to parents. The struggle has gone into the courts in some states, but in general parents have not regained the authority over their own children. To free themselves from the baneful influences of the public schools, some parents have turned to teaching them at home, and a good many states permit this, provided the parents have qualifications satisfactory to the state.

A considerable ferment has been going on in the churches and the schools over the past two decades. In both these, the conservative contingent appears to be growing in number and influence.

3. Common Core of Conservative Ideas

Looked at from the outside, the conservative movement may often appear to consist of small groups of people, far from agreement with one another, often led by eccentric men, and destined to be devoid of much general influence. It looked somewhat that way to Professor Clinton Rossiter when he wrote a book on conservatism in America. In one of his conclusions, he denied

> that Conservatism is a major force in American education—or, for that matter, in American culture and politics. Fix the outer limits of American Conservatism as generously as we possibly can—specifically to include all those men of ideas who admit to profound disenchantment with the assumptions and promises of Liberalism—and we are still left with at most a corporal's guard in contrast to the regiment of intellectuals, not to mention the army of men of affairs, who are comfortably at home with the . . . [the fruits of Liberalism]. Those Americans who speak and write as genuine self-conscious Conservatives are today, as they have been for more than a century, an eccentric minority in the world of ideas, a misunderstood minority in the world of right-wing politics.[216]

Granted, the book was written in 1962, and Professor Rossiter can be excused for not foreseeing the mounting influence of conservatism in the two decades that followed, he still seems to have been off the mark in what he wrote. Much the same could have been said in 1900 about populism and socialist informed progressivism, or in 1925 about what New Dealers would called "liberalism." Ideas do not take hold until the ground has been prepared, the seeds planted, and a period of time elapses for the plants to grow before they bear fruit. What he refers to as "right-wing" politics was little more than the remains of an earlier conservatism not yet enlivened by those who had come to maturity in the conservative movement. These would, and did, eventually enter into politics, get elected to office, and show their connections with that movement.

There was a ferment at work in America in the 1960s, a quiet ferment, usually, on the conservative side. While radicals and revolutionaries occupied the spotlight, conservatives were quietly forming positions and spreading their ideas. Most men are not philosophers, of course, but virtually all of us act upon the basis of assumptions that are more or less philosophical, whether we are aware of them or not. For example, if we believe that it is the business of government to look after our well-being, we will tend to favor political programs that claim to do that. Such assumptions, in turn, rest upon deeper views about the nature of society, the nature of man, and the purpose of life. Conservatives were contending over these years for the minds of Americans. It is undoubtedly true that the ideas of any particular writer and thinker would contain peculiarities particular to him, and some of them would strike others, including other conservatives, quite often as eccentric. That is true of all thoughtful persons, probably even politicians, but they have often disciplined themselves never to say anything that might anger anyone.

But conservatives generally shared a common core of ideas. They would differ in their emphases, differ in the importance they attached to particular ideas and beliefs, and in the extent to which they would press them. Even so, there is a common core of ideas which conservatives generally not only share but also beliefs with which if he is not sympathetic he will not consider himself nor be considered a conservative. Conservatives generally reject the main tenets of socialism and communism. They do not, for example, believe that the Marxian maxim, "From each according to his ability; to each according to his need," describes a just or desirable state of affairs. They oppose communism, not merely because they disagree over tactics or policies followed by Communist governments, but because they reject the basic premises of communism. Nor do they accept democratic socialism—or whatever name it may be called—as a basically just system, including the welfare state form of control and distribution of wealth.

Conservatives generally favor not only the private ownership of personal property but also of the means of production. Some refer to such a system as capitalism, though they are using Marxist terminology when they do so. Generally speaking, they believe that property justly acquired belongs to the owner by right. If they subscribe to the natural law-natural rights philosophy—not all conservatives do—, they believed that private property is a natural right. Conservatives usually do not subscribe to the current doctrine of "human rights" because it is a phrase contrived to leave property rights out of the definition of rights. Conservatives favor freedom of enterprise, though they differ among themselves as to the extent to which it should prevail. They generally tend to oppose both government intervention in enterprise by regulation and control or government engaging in economic undertakings. They tend to favor a free market, oppose the exclusion of foreigners from the American market or the granting of monopolies by government. They differ considerably over the desirability of "antitrust" legislation, but it has been in effect for so long that it rarely comes up as an issue.

As a rule, conservatives are constitutionalists. That is, they believe in limited government. They hold that government is a dangerous instrument, and that it is necessary to take measures to contain and restrict it. The American approach to that has been by having written constitutions. These written constitutions are a contract between the governors and the governed. Generally, conservatives favor a government of laws and not of men, and that the law for the United States government is the United States Constitution. Conservatives do not accept out of hand the notion that the Constitution is what the courts say it is, since it is a written document. They differ somewhat over the extent to which they would accept the view that a written constitution can properly be changed by judicial construction. Traditionalists, who may be in the Catholic or English tradition, would tend to attach greater significance to court precedents than do conservatives in the Protestant tradition. The latter tend to view a written constitution as fixed until it is amended by the regular and prescribed process.

Conservatives tend to be individualists. If the sole issue were the individual versus the collective, as in collectivism, they would be almost invariably individualists. They accept the primacy of the individual, his firstness and lastness, though most believe that in regard to the rights of the individual these are bounded by the necessities of living in society and of cooperation with others.

Conservatives tend to have the greatest respect and attachment for those organizations and institutions nearest at hand to the individual: the family, the church, the local community, the neighborhood school, the local government, as well as customs, traditions, and ways of doing things rooted in locales and regions. Not all conservatives, or those who have some affinity for conservativism, will subscribe to this hierarchy of values. Libertarians and rationalists (those who propose to be governed by reason alone) generally do not.

As a rule, conservatives are not revolutionists, do not favor radical and disruptive change, are not utopians, tend to believe, with Jefferson, that abuses are to be tolerated as long as they are bearable, are not relativists, and tend to believe that in the midst of change there are things that endure or are eternal. They tend to focus upon the fixities, the unchanging, the underlying order, in contrast to thoroughgoing evolutionists. They are more favorably disposed toward order, tradition, and authority, to the nature of things, than are Liberals and the like.

The list could be extended, but the more it is the less there would be who would adhere to the common core. But enough has been said to indicate where that common core may lie. Enough has been said, too, to suggest that conservatism is not something on the fringe of American belief and ways but very much within the frame of the longest established of American traditions.

Conservatism into the Political Arena

The presidential election of 1968 marked a decisive shift in conservative movement influence in national politics. Four years before, Barry Goldwater, "Mr. Conservative" at that time nationally, had been nominated by the Republicans. That he was overwhelmingly defeated only seemed to confirm, what Liberals had held since World War II, that a conservative could not be elected President. Yet four years later, the conservatives had a hand in nominating and electing Richard M. Nixon to the presidency. In his analysis of the Republican Convention in 1968, published in *National Review,* Frank Meyer declared that it was "A Conservative Convention." In support of this contention, he declared that the themes that dominated the convention were conservative, that the Republican platform was subject to conservative interpretation, that the selection of Spiro Agnew as vice-presidential candidate over such Liberal Republicans as John Lindsay, Charles Percy, and Mark Hatfield was a rejection of liberal influence, and Nixon's acceptance speech contained mainly conservative themes. In Meyer's view, the Republican Party in 1968 provided a basically conservative alternative to the contemporary chaos over which the Democrats were trying to preside:

> . . . It has become a stark matter of the survival of the conditions of civilization. Is a great law-abiding, producing people to be held ransom by small minorities of *lumpen* slum-dwellers and *lumpen* students, aided and abetted by Liberal ideologues turned nihilist? The answer of the Republican Convention to that question is a clear and decisive No.[217]

The main point, however, is that in 1968, with the election of Nixon and Agnew, there was a strong shift toward conservatism in the country. This was especially so in presidential elections. Since 1968, the Democrats have elected only one presidential candidate for one term. Even that one exception was almost certainly the result of fallout from the Watergate Affair, and not an indication of any broad change in public preferences. The change in the Congress has been much less decisive. The House of Representatives has remained under Democratic control during this whole period, and the Republicans did not gain control of the Senate until 1980. It must be kept in mind, however, that the presidential election is the only national election in the country, and that it provides the clearest indication of the national temper. The landslide victory of Nixon in 1972, when he ran for a second term, and the overwhelming victory by Ronald Reagan in 1984, when he ran for a second term, suggest that nationally the trend was Republican. And, since Reagan was in the stream of conservatism, the national trend is strongly conservative.

On the other hand, the continuing strength of the Democratic Party in Congress appears to indicate that there is no national consensus as yet, as between liberal and conservative. Two things may help to explain the division that persists, and should at least be noted. One is that the Democrats have long held a registration advantage and that they go into congressional elections with a majority advantage. The main reason for this is the South, which is only slowly moving out of or away from the Democratic fold. The South is now almost solidly Republican in presidential elections, but Democrats still dominate in the House of Representatives. But the shift is underway toward more and more Republicans from the South being elected in the House and the Senate. In 1960, for example, a Republican in Congress was a rare phenomenon. In 1982, half of the Senators were Republican, but somewhat less than a third of the Representatives were.

Even more important nationally, an increasing number of the Republican members (as well as a few Democratic members) of Congress are either highly conscious or movement conservatives. Most of these have come in since 1970, including Senators Jesse Helms of North Carolina (now "Mr. Conservative" in the Senate), Steven D. Symms of Idaho, Gordon J. Humphrey of New Hampshire, John East of North Carolina, Jeremiah Denton of Alabama, William L. Armstrong of Colorado, Don Nickles of Oklahoma, Orrin Hatch of Utah, and Mack Mattingly of Georgia. In the House, they would include Philip M. Crane of Illinois, George Hansen of Idaho, William Dannemeyer of California, Newt Gingrich of Georgia, Phil Gramm (a former Democrat turned Republican) of Texas, Eldon Rudd of Arizona, and Carlos Moorhead of California. The shift toward Republican and conservative has been most pronounced in the Sun Belt (a region including the lower South and westward through Texas, Arizona, and California) but the same has generally been true of the Rocky Mountain states as well.

Even so, there has not yet developed a clean cut and tested conservative consensus in the United States. The acid test of such a consensus would be the adoption of constitutional amendments. Thus far, though a goodly

Richard M. Nixon (1913–1994)

Nixon was a Congressman, served two terms as Vice-President under Eisenhower, and was the 37th President of the United States. He was born in California, graduated from Whittier College, Duke University law school, and practiced law from time to time in the course of his life. After service in the Navy during World War II, Nixon was elected to Congress in 1946 and gained national attention during the Hiss-Chambers hearings. Eisenhower selected him as his running mate in 1952, and following Eisenhower's two terms, Nixon was the Republican nominee for President to succeed him. Nixon was edged out in a close election by Kennedy in 1960 and held no political office between 1961–1969. His presidency marked the onset of an increasing conservative influence at the national level and of Republican dominance in national elections. The Watergate revelations came close to interrupting that development. They did lead to Nixon's resignation in 1974, and since that time he has only occasionally appeared in public.

number of such amendments have been proposed and considered—prayer in the schools, balanced budget, and the like—none has yet received the necessary approval of both houses of Congress, much less three-fourths of the states.

1. The Nixon Years

Richard M. Nixon was not exactly conservative; he was a middling Republican, which made him somewhat conservative, since Republicans generally were more conservative than not. His model for the presidency had undoubtedly been President Eisenhower. The Nixon Administration posited a "Silent Majority" of Americans, people immune to radicalism, not sympathetic to communism, but not so averse to the Welfare State as to favor rushing out and dismantling it. He must have been conscious, too, of how narrowly he had been elected President for his first term. He only got 43.4 per cent of the popular vote in 1968 to 42.7 per cent for Hubert

Humphrey. The electoral vote was somewhat more impressive, 302 to 191, but if George Wallace had not carried five Southern states and got 45 electoral votes, his margin might have been narrower there. The Democrats remained firmly in control of both houses of Congress. In view of these things, Nixon concentrated much of his attention during his first term to increasing Republican strength in Congress and broadening his own following in middle America.

Nixon did make a major conservative push to try to alter the character of the federal courts. He was largely thwarted in having any major impact on the Supreme Court, however. The opportunities were there; four vacancies were filled from 1969 to 1972. In the 1968 campaign, Nixon had criticized the courts, and especially the Supreme Court, for its judicial activism and promised "that he would use his power of judicial appointment to sway them back to 'strict construction' of the Constitution."[218] When Chief Justice Earl Warren retired in 1969, Nixon named Warren Earl Burger of Minnesota to succeed him. Another vacancy occurred the same year when Associate Justice Abe Fortas retired under fire. Nixon nominated Judge Clement Haynsworth of South Carolina to succeed him. Despite the fact that Haynsworth was a highly respected member of a United States Circuit Court of Appeals, the Senate eventually rejected his nomination. The charges against him were piddling ones, mainly that he had not disqualified himself from ruling on a case or so in which he had some small interest, but so much noise was made about these, that the Senate balked and would not confirm him.

Nixon was still determined to have a Southerner, and he nominated next Judge G. Harold Carswell of Florida. Although Carswell had only recently been confirmed by the Senate to a seat on a United States Circuit Court of Appeals, it turned back the effort to get him on the Supreme Court. Much was made by the opponents of his confirmation about racial attitudes Carswell had expressed a couple of decades earlier. In the course of the examination, the level of his intellect also came under attack. Nixon was furious about two of his nominees for the same post being rejected, and declared, "I have reluctantly concluded that it is not possible to get confirmation for a judge on the Supreme Court of any man who believes in the strict construction of the Constitution, as I do, if he happens to come from the South. Judge Carswell, and before him, Judge Haynsworth . . . have been falsely charged with being racists. But when you strip away all the hypocrisy, the real reason for their rejection was their legal philosophy . . . of a strict construction of the Constitution, and also the accident of their birth, the fact that they were born in the South."[219] Undoubtedly, Nixon was right that Southerners were suspect following the "Second Reconstruction," and liberals were doing their best to keep anyone suspected of strict construction off the Supreme Court.

Nixon finally gave ground and appointed Harry A. Blackmun of

Minnesota to the high court. When two further vacancies occurred in 1971, Nixon appointed Lewis F. Powell of Virginia and William H. Rehnquist of Arizona to succeed them. They were speedily confirmed by the Senate. Even with four appointees, however, Nixon had not greatly altered the character of the court. The only one that was in the vicinity of a strict constructionist was William Rehnquist. While Chief Justice Burger was no judicial revolutionary in the mold of Earl Warren, neither was he of the mind to turn the court back to its appointed judicial role. The Burger Court has nibbled away at some of the edicts of the Warren Court, making it a little more restrained here and less obtrusive there, but it has still continued to exercise many of the enlarged powers claimed for it by Warren.

Indeed, Justice Blackmun wrote the majority opinion in *Roe vs. Wade* in 1973. This was judicial activism of the boldest kind (though technically it only nullified state laws) and for many Americans ranks as the most notorious of all decisions by the high court. It was the decision by which the Supreme Court delcared unconstitutional laws in 46 states which prohibited various sorts of elective abortions in the first six months of pregnancy. Justice Blackmun claimed that the question of abortion was covered under an alleged "right of personal privacy" of the mother to dispose of what was allegedly a part of her body. He admitted that "The Constitution does not explicitly mention any right of privacy." But, "In a line of decisions . . . , the Court has recognized that a right of personal privacy, or a guarantee of certain areas or zones of privacy does exist under the Constitution. . . ." Moreover, this "right of privacy . . . is broad enough to encompass a woman's decision whether or not to terminate her pregnancy."[220] That a state was intruding upon a woman's right to privacy when it prohibited elective abortions in early stages of pregnancies was apparently clear enough to Blackmun and his majority.

It might be supposed that the prohibitions against the taking of life without due process of law would have brought the Supreme Court down on the side of the state laws prohibiting abortion. But no, according to Blackmun's view, this matter of whether not an unborn infant was such a "life," entitled to constitutional protection, was too muddled to decide. Blackmun wrote, "We need not resolve the difficult question of when life begins. When those trained in the respective disciplines of medicine, Philosophy, and theology are unable to arrive at any consensus, the judiciary at this point in the development of man's knowledge, is not in a position to speculate as to the answer."[221] Instead of tackling head-on the issue of when life begins, Blackmun retreated to a doctrine of stages of the development of the embryo. These were divided into three, with each corresponding period of pregnancy labeled as a "trimester." During the first "trimester," the Supreme Court solemnly announced, the state could not interfere with the "right" of the female to abort her child-in-embryo. This "right" extended through the second "trimester" as well, though the state might do such things as prescribe who might perform abortions. During the third "trimester" a state was free to prohibit abortions. The distinction the Court relied on was that after the sixth month, the infant could frequently survive if separated from his or her mother.

The carnage that has resulted from this decision has been frightful. As one book says, "As a result of *Roe v. Wade,* at least 1.5 million babies were exterminated each year through 'legal' abortion—15 million or more between 1973 and 1983."[222] The propagandized and indoctrinated American people—taught to believe that every utterance of the Supreme Court was the "law of the land"—were slow to mobilize against this newest assault upon their ways. Nor did they have any ready means at hand to state their horror and to deal with the perpetrators of it. The liberal-dominated media accepted the decision as another victory for women's rights. A further decision in 1976 made this aspect of its decision even clearer. The Court held "that states could not require either the consent of the husband, or—if the woman was an unmarried minor—the consent of her parents, as a condition for terminating pregnancy in the first trimester."[223] In short, any child who became pregnant could dispose of it as *she* chose during the early months. Liberals generally tried to keep such debate over the abortion issue as occurred publicly in the austere framework of "women's rights," and lectured opponents against introducing emotion. Even so, resistance to elective abortion has become increasingly vocal over the years, and there is good reason to expect that it will eventually bear fruit in legal changes.

The war in Vietnam continued through Nixon's first term. Though the youth revolt had been somewhat tamed by the events at Kent State and Jackson State, raucous demonstrations continued. There is no doubt, however, that substantial peace had been restored by the Nixon administration; a major reason for this was that the Nixon Administration gave neither aid nor comfort to the youth who behaved obnoxiously. Nixon himself called student rioters "bums," and explained that "When students on university campuses burn buildings, when they engage in violence, when they break up furniture, when they terrorize their fellow students and terrorize the faculty, then I think 'bums' is perhaps too kind a word to apply to that kind of person."[224]

But it was Vice-President Spiro T. Agnew who took on the noisy disrupters in the most vigorous fashion. Agnew was not well known nationally when Nixon selected him for a running mate. Nor would anyone at the time have identified him with the conservative movement. As Vice President, however, his speeches were laced with conservative ideas, and he emerged as a vigorous controversialist as he made direct assaults on radicalism. He said, in a speech at New Orleans in 1969: "A spirit of national masochism prevails, encouraged by an effete corps of impudent snobs who characterize themselves as intellectuals."[225] A few weeks later, he reaffirmed his position: "What I said before, I will say again. It is time for the preponderant majority, the responsible citizens of this country, to assert *their* rights. It is time to stop dignifying the immature actions of arrogant, reckless, inexperienced elements within our society. The reason is compelling. It is simply that their tantrums are . . . destroying the fabric of American democracy.''[226] He spelled out his meaning this way: ''It is worth remembering that our country's founding fathers wisely shaped a Constitutional republic, not a pure democracy. The representative government they contemplated and skillfully constructed never intended that elected officials should decide crucial questions by counting the number of bodies cavorting in the streets.'' Conservatives began to wonder, at least some of them, if Agnew might not be the right man to follow Nixon in 1976.

As for the war in Vietnam, President Nixon followed at least three more or less intertwined courses. One was the policy known as the Vietnamization of the army. He sought to build up and help to equip a much more effective Vietnamese army. This was accompanied by the progressive withdrawal of American ground forces, though the latter was much easier to do than the former. Second, he kept a strong American presence in Vietnam with a beefed-up Air Force contingent and major naval forces. Third, he sought in various ways, diplomatic as well as military, to negotiate with North Vietnam to end the war.

Although William P. Rogers was Secretary of State, Henry A. Kissinger, Nixon's National Security adviser, was the main architect of broad foreign policy. Dr. Kissinger, formerly a Harvard professor, conceived foreign policy in global terms. Ending the war in Vietnam probably depended on reducing tensions with major Communist countries, and especially Red China. Nixon did this, first, by removing his objection to the admission of Communist China to the United Nations. Second, he made a personal visit to China in February, 1972, to meet face to face with chairman Mao Tse-tung and Premier Chou En-lai. For over twenty years, China had been more or less isolated from the rest of the world, especially the United States. Ever since the Communist Chinese had taken over in China, the United States had held no formal relations with the country, and few formal contacts had been made. Nixon's visit marked the ending of that era and the beginning of closer relations with China.

William F. Buckley was one of the newsmen who went along on the Nixon visit to China. As he reflected in writing on the doings at Peking—the numerous toasts between Nixon, on the one hand, and Mao and Chou, on the other, all the fawning and expressions of goodwill—, he pondered the question of whether or not the world had entered upon a new dark age. He did not answer the question, but rather left it floating in the doubt that it would be possible to know such a thing. Surely, it was less than reassuring to see the President of the United States breaking bread with the men who had beaten perhaps one billion Chinese into abject submission, had reduced them to ant heap lives, and subjected them to one of the worst tyrannies in

UPI

Henry A. Kissinger (1923–)

Kissinger has been a professor of government at Harvard, adviser to Presidents on foreign policy, and Secretary of State under Nixon and Ford. He was born in Furth, Germany and migrated with his family to the United States in 1938 to escape the Nazi persecution of the Jews. After serving in the army during World War II, Kissinger attended and graduated from Harvard and later earned his Ph. D. from the same institution. He published a book, *Nuclear Weapons and Foreign Policy,* in 1957, which brought him to national attention. Kissinger advocated seeking peace through a balance of power, which for him appeared to mean ending the Cold War by coming to terms with the Soviet Union and Communist China. As presidential adviser and Secretary of State he spent much of his time visiting foreign capitals in negotiations and international maneuvering. He was much more successful at altering American than Soviet policy.

all of history. There are many other signs of civilization in disarray in the 20th century, of its paganization by abortion, among many, many more, but certainly dealing with the Red Chinese moves us deeper into the circle of a dark age.

Nixon treated his trip to China as a triumph of personal diplomacy, and the press was generally delighted with it. After only a brief respite, he made another foray into the Communist world, this time to meet with the beetle-browed dictator of Russia, Leonid Brezhnev. While there, the two negotiated treaties both to freeze long-range nuclear missile building for a period of time and to limit anti-ballistic missiles. The deal tended to favor the Soviet Union more than the United States in nuclear arsenals. In addition, Nixon made a deal for the selling of large amounts of grain grown in this country to the Soviet Union.

Tensions may have been relaxed somewhat among the United States, Russia, and China, but it had no immediate impact on the war in Vietnam. Only following massive American bombings around Christmas, 1972, did North Vietnam finally agree to a cease-fire early in 1973. The agreements which followed confirmed the worst fears about the futility of the fighting. American forces were withdrawn, and Communist forces quickly completed their conquest of Indochina.

Nixon's domestic policies were neither especially conservative nor successful. He started out with some resolve to balance the budget. Given the expanding Welfare State he had inherited from Johnson, the continuing war in Vietnam, and large military expenditures, major changes would have had to be made to balance the budget. Nixon had been elected by a minority of those voting and had a Democratic-controlled Congress, which offered him little room to operate. He failed to balance the budget. In addition, it was his misfortune to preside over a currency which was completing its final slide to fiat money. During his term, the government ceased to defend its currency abroad with gold at a set price and allowed Americans to own gold once again. But the government plunged deeper into debt, and as the currency depreciated (with no longer even the remnants of a gold backing), prices rose precipitately. Nixon undertook a short-lived experiment with a government imposed price freeze. Not even Nixon was enthusiastic, and the effort was largely abandoned after his re-election.

Nixon did get one program through Congress worth noting during his first term. It was his revenue-sharing program with cities and other local governments. That the federal government had any revenue to share with any other government was by no means clear. But Nixon dressed this venture out in conservative garb by identifying it as a New Federalism. He claimed that by sharing Federal revenues with local governments, they would gain new life and the Federal system of government would be vitalized. In fact, this plan only made local governments more dependent upon Washington than they had been before, and the deficit-ridden central government went more deeply into debt to pay for it.

Nixon was in reasonably good shape in 1972 for the campaign for re-election. The trips to Peking and Moscow had shown him as a bold and resourceful executive in foreign affairs. The economy appeared to be rebounding. The war in Vietnam staggered on, but many troops were returning home. Even without that, however, the Democrats were setting themselves up for an electoral debacle. The radicals gained control of the party machinery in 1972 and carried their nominee down to defeat. In the primary campaign, Senators Hubert Humphrey and Edmund Muskie managed to eliminate one another; George Wallace, as noted earlier, could not campaign after the attempted assassination of him; the field was left to Senator George McGovern of South Dakota. McGovern almost certainly adopted the most radical posture ever taken by a major party candidate, though his manner belied the posture. He was a slow-talking, laconic Westerner, made statements more like a professor, which he had been, than a rabble rouser. But his anti-war posture sounded as if he would disarm the United States, and his redistributionist suggestions made it appear he would finish the slide toward bankruptcy swiftly. He was more than a little inept and vacillating as well. He chose Senator Thomas Eagleton of Missouri as his running mate. When it was revealed that Eagleton had been treated for mental disorders, McGovern announced that he was behind Eagleton 1000 per cent. As pressure mounted, however, he dropped Eagleton and replaced him with Sargent Shriver.

What completed his undoing was that the Democratic Party had alienated much of its traditional following in the South, among labor union members, and in big cities. This had been accomplished between 1968 and 1972 in the prescription of the makeup of delegations to the 1972 Democratic Convention. In effect, the Democratic National Committee imposed a quota system on state delegations in an attempt to get full representation for women and young people. The Committee sent out a letter in 1971, which said, in part: "We believe that state parties should be on notice that whenever the proportion of women, minorities, and young people in a delegation . . . is less than the proportion of these groups in the total population . . . , [that will] constitute a prima facie showing of violation of the Guidelines. . . ."[228] In order to be accredited, if it was challenged, a delegation would have to show that it had taken vigorous action to achieve such representation, or be discredited. This approach gave power to new people, for the most part. The regular party people were mostly shunted aside, and the radicals had the field to themselves.

McGovern never had a chance, and Nixon won by a landslide. Only one state—Massachusetts—and the District of Columbia cast electoral votes for McGovern. Nixon got 520 electoral votes to 17 for McGovern. The popular vote was crushing as well: over 47 million for Nixon to 29 million plus for McGovern.

2. Watergate and the Aftermath

With a landslide victory behind him, Nixon developed large plans for his second term. Now, he could gain full control of the executive branch, make it responsive to his wishes. Since the adoption of the 22nd Amendment, the notion has gained currency that a President during his second term is a "Lame Duck," that is, since he cannot run for re-election, his influence during his remaining term declines. Nixon had a different notion; he thought the removal of the possibility of re-election, and hence the necessity of mending fences continually, offered possibilities of consolidating political power. He would reduce the cabinet members to the level of functionaries and maintain control within the government by men personally dependent upon and loyal to him. All this he thought he could achieve without requiring congressional action. He visualized much that he could accomplish if he could only make the executive branch fully responsive to him.

Whether his plan would have worked, we will never know. Before he could get much further than forcing some resignations and shifting some men around, he was caught up in a tide of events that would eventually sweep him out of office. Between the spring of 1973 until late summer of 1974, Nixon was increasingly taken up with the Watergate affair. Actually, the break-in of the Watergate Hotel in June, 1972 did not loom so large at the time, or for months afterward. Five men were caught in the act with "bugging" devices in the offices of Democratic headquarters by the Washington police, arrested, and eventually brought to trial in United States District Court. The only immediate problem was that they were in the employ of the Committee to Re-elect the President (Nixon), an operation ultimately controlled from the White House. But in the subsequent grand jury investigation, the grand jury was led to believe that the men were acting on their own initiative, not under the command of the Committee. As the story would eventually unfold, the men most directly involved with control over it perjured themselves before the grand jury, and several hundred thousand dollars was paid to the defendants to keep them from telling what they knew. In short, a major cover-up had taken place, a cover-up which reached all the way to the President himself. But none of this was known at the time. The Republicans went on to their landslide victory without having their involvement known.

In the course of more than a year revelation after revelation came forth: in testimony before the Senate investigating committee, in testimony before trial judge John J. Sirica, and eventually from the release of tapes of conversations in the President's office. It was a sordid and distasteful story: of undercover operations directed from the White House, of bribery, of the abuse of presidential power, of suborning perjury, of "dirty tricks" being played on Democrats, and of conspiracies to harm people who were on the President's "enemies" list. Most distasteful of all, perhaps, was the discovery that the language used by the President and his aides in the highest office in the land was filled with profanity and obscenities. In the midst of these revelations, another shock came when Vice-President Agnew resigned because of charges that he had taken "kickbacks" and was guilty of tax evasion.

It should be clear that President Nixon had no foreknowledge of the Watergate break-in, did not order it, and was reportedly dumbfounded when he learned of it. The man who had been Attorney General almost up to the time, John Mitchell, did not only know beforehand but had approved the operation. He would eventually go to prison for his part in it. John Dean, the president's counsel, was not only involved in the approval but also in the subsequent payoffs to the defendants. Indeed, the President heard about some of these, and the President's chief aide, H. R. Haldeman, was deeply involved in getting the money together. In fact, the President was directly involved in the coverup, because he had requested the CIA (Central Intelligence Agency) to stop any FBI investigation, though this did not come out until the very end. The President alleged to the CIA that national security was involved, yet the only security involved was that of himself and his aides from knowledge of their wrongdoing by the courts, the Congress, and the American people.

As more and more was revealed, Nixon retreated step by step, first denying everything, launching investigations which he controlled, throwing first one and then another of his men to the wolves, so to speak, until the trail finally led back to him. It became apparent by early August, 1974, that the House of Representatives would impeach him and that the Senate would convict him on at least one or more of the charges. The count of heads in both bodies indicated that the President's support had dwindled down to a loyal few. The President finally capitulated and resigned when the situation was made clear to him by the Republican leaders of the House and Senate, accompanied by Senator Barry Goldwater. Nixon was a beaten down and forelorn man as he submitted his resignation to take effect at noon August 9, 1974, while he was en route to his home in California.

Not only was Nixon the first President to resign from office, but also the first to be succeeded by a Vice-President not chosen by regular election. No one outside Congress had voted for him. It was, nonetheless, a constitutional succession, as a result of the 25th Amendment. The man was Gerald R. Ford, long-time Congressman from Michigan. For several years he had been minority leader of the House of Representatives, kept from becoming Speaker of the House because Republicans could not obtain a majority. President Ford exerted an almost immediate calming influence on a government and a city that had been in turmoil for more than a year. He was a calm man, not volatile nor temperamental, recognized for his honesty and integrity. If some measure of tranquility could be restored, he was the man to do it. He was more conservative than not, but he had not made enemies generally, nor were there many sharp edges to his personality. Ford's task was to see to it, too, that Nixon's downfall did not pull down the Republican Party as well, for he was now the leader of the party.

Watergate still cast a shadow across the political landscape, and would continue to do so through the little more than two years of Ford's presidency. Ford did not help matters as far as Nixon opponents were concerned when he gave him a presidential pardon for any crimes he may have committed. Indeed, this pardon was probably one reason Ford was not re-elected in 1976. But the problems with which Ford wrestled had antecedents much further back than Watergate or anything that came up in the impeachment hearings on Nixon. They stemmed from welfarism at home and abroad, and both Nixon and Ford were caught in the backwash. It may be well, then, to put Watergate into perspective before proceeding with a discussion of the Nixon-Ford problems.

In the broader context, those who brought Nixon down were straining at a gnat after having already swallowed a camel. After all, the Watergate

Gerald R. Ford (1913–)

Ford was the 38th President of the United States, the first to come to that high office after having been nominated to the post of Vice-President by the President and elected by Congress. He had served in the House of Representatives for 25 years prior to that, and had for 8 years been Republican leader in the House. Ford was born in Nebraska, grew up in Michigan, graduated from the University of Michigan, where he played football, and from Yale Law School. After practicing law and serving in the Navy, he was elected to Congress in 1948. Ford pardoned former President Nixon, which did not sit well with many people when others involved in Watergate went to prison. On the other hand, he vetoed 48 bills which came before him in his first 21 months in office, indicating a determination to cut down on Federal spending. He succeeded also in establishing some calm following the uproar over Watergate. He lost, however, to the Democratic nominee, Jimmy Carter, in the election of 1976, and retired from the political arena.

break-in and its aftermath had to do with penny-ante crimes committed by inept hoodlums and conspirators in high places. Many of those who denounced these doings with righteous indignation in Congress and the courts had been involved in much broader actions which not only set the stage for Watergate but also were potentially far more tyrannical than anything implicit in Watergate. For several decades before Watergate, Presidents and Congresses had centralized more and more government power in Washington and concentrated it in the presidency. In the decade before Watergate they had piled welfare program upon welfare program for which Washington had become a huge collection center for the wealth of the nation which was then redistributed. They had been piling deficit upon deficit for decades building an ever mounting national debt and destroying the value of the currency to keep the whole thing going. Government had exercised power over and intervened in the lives of Americans in numerous ways, often petty when looked at in terms of a single person or family, but tyrannical in tendency at least. They had plundered the productive for the means to buy votes from the unproductive by promises of benefits from tax money. Many of those in Congress and the courts (and those who had preceded them for several decades, including Presidents) who sat in judgment on Nixon violated their oaths to defend the Constitution by stretching its limited powers beyond all recognition. All these things they justified on the grounds that what they were doing was for the alleged general welfare. They had usurped powers not authorized by the Constitution and abused them by providing for their massive exercise on the people.

Having swallowed the camel of this massive usurpation of power, its centralization in Washington, and its concentration in the vast bureaucracy of the executive branch, they drew back in horror and swatted the gnat of petty abuse of power in the Nixon White House. It was as if it were somehow infinitely worse to sneak around to steal a chicken than go out in broad daylight and plunder the private wealth of a people. This is not to excuse President Nixon, for he was involved in the exercise of power on a grand scale (whether abusive or not) as well as petty abuse of power. The main point in that it was the concentration of power in the executive that set the stage for abuses grand or small. The Democratic leadership in Congress showed only a very limited and highly focused awareness of the problem. They did move in a circumscribed area to limit the exercise of presidential power: reducing his war-making powers, inhibiting the FBI, and restraining the CIA. But they left intact the main source of concentrated power which derived from welfarism at home and abroad and did nothing to restrain the courts and themselves in the continuing usurpation and abuse of government power involved.

What ties all this together was that Americans were beginning to reap the whirlwind of welfarism at home and abroad they had sown in earlier decades in the 1970s. Even before Nixon resigned, a depression of major proportions was getting underway. In the course of 1973, prices were rising precipitately, unemployment was increasing, and interest rates were rising. What aggravated this further was a sudden shortage of oil during the fall and winter of 1973–1974. In October, 1973, Egypt and Syria invaded Israel in what was known as the Yom Kippur War. These Arab countries had been well supplied with Soviet arms and munitions and were threatening to overpower Israel. Israel appealed to the United States for military supplies, and Nixon ordered them shipped in quantity. With these in hand, Israel counterattacked and drove out the invaders. The Arab countries retaliated against the countries that had supported Israel by embargoing oil shipments. Although the Arabs supplied only a relatively small portion of oil used in the United States, the embargo succeeded in making gasoline and fuel oil scarce. The federal government made matters worse by allocating supplies and trying to hold down prices. The embargo was ended in 1974, but OPEC, a cartel of oil exporting countries, mostly Arab, continued in the following years to drive the price of oil upward.

But the basic cause of the depression was not the scarcity nor the high price of oil. The basic cause was that so much of the wealth of Americans was being funneled into government by taxation and borrowing that it was no longer available for enterprise and investment. So much of the wealth of Americans was being drawn off in redistribution to the under- and unproductive that the productive could hardly keep pace. Technological innovation was no longer working its magic of keeping prices down. The deficits mounted throughout the latter 1970s as the federal government borrowed more and more to meet its obligations. Government borrowing drove interest rates higher and higher, to levels never reached before in modern American history. It was a depression, a major one, though different in cause from the one in the 1930s. Some journalists referred to what was happening as "stagflation," i. e., a stagnant economy in the midst of an ongoing inflation. Earlier depressions had usually been caused by some sort of drastic reduction in the money supply. This one was propelled along its path by large infusions of money declining in value.

It was not called a depression, of course, nor was its course or depth clearly described by government economists or the media. There were references from time to time to a recession, but to have called it a depression would have been to admit that a government-managed money supply and widely controlled economy could have a depression. Yet signs abounded of something like a depression. The market for real estate fell drastically, and the construction industry was hard hit. Builders generally built much smaller houses, when they built at all. "Great rooms," so called, tended to replace the more luxurious separate living rooms and family rooms. Three bedroom homes became commonplace once again. Smaller automobiles, often with only four cylinders, replaced the large luxurious six and eight cylinder cars. The price of gasoline was the reason most often given for this, but in reality fewer and fewer people could afford the larger vehicles. Many people bought and lived in mobile homes, tended to give up hope of ever owning a regular house. A host of government programs—unemployment compensation, food stamps, "free lunches" for school children, and welfare—insulated those who could get or would take them against abject poverty. But depression it was.

Establishment economists had little understanding of how to deal with this new kind of depression, even if they had admitted its existence. "We are all Keynesians now," President Nixon had said, which meant most a belief in government manipulation of the money supply, deficit spending in bad times along with increased government spending. It is doubtful that Ford and his economists held a much different view. Ford did, however, oppose new large scale spending programs. The Democratic Congress favored large appropriations for government programs. President Ford vetoed 53 measures that Congress passed, but nine of these were then passed over his veto. He launched a campaign to Whip Inflation Now, issued campaign-sized buttons with the acronym WIN, but it was more the subject of wry jokes than anything else. The depression had not reached its depth as yet, and there were indications that economic conditions were improving by the end of his brief administration.

In foreign affairs, the Ford administration witnessed the conclusion of the Vietnam episode in American history. Vietnam had moved out of the limelight in 1973, when a cease-fire in Vietnam was arranged. Most of American forces were withdrawn as well, and the American presence was greatly reduced. The military draft ended in 1973, and Vietnam was no longer an issue among the young. The Communist conquest was completed in 1975. Large numbers of those identified with the United States were flown out before they arrived, and many others tried to escape later as best they could in boats or whatever transport they could get. Ford generally continued the foreign policies of Nixon, continuing with Henry Kissinger as his Secretary of State. Technically, the United States followed a policy of Détente with the Soviet Union, but the Soviets were rapidly expanding their power base in Africa as elsewhere.

3. The Carter Interlude

In the light of the trend toward conservatism, located politically mostly in the Republican Party, the Carter administration should be considered mainly an interlude. James Earl (''Jimmy'') Carter's election owed more than a little to the still dark shadow of Watergate. By pardoning Richard Nixon, President Ford had, at least in the minds of a good many people, muddied his skirts with the Watergate aftermath. Moreover, he had associated himself with Nixon policies, especially by keeping Kissinger in his cabinet. Even more important, perhaps, Washingtonians—the politicians, that is—had lost caste as a result of Watergate revelations.

There were other factors that help to account for this Democratic interlude under Carter. Mr. Carter was a vigorous and effective campaigner. He spent nearly two years on the campaign trail before the presidential election in 1976. Carter had been governor of Georgia from 1971–1975, and as soon as he left the state house, he began his campaign for the Democratic nomination. The fact that he was a Southerner helped him considerably, both in getting the nomination and being elected. Being Southern had long been a disadvantage nationally, but that was changing. Most Northern Democratic politicians were tarred with the brush of radicalism which had gone down to defeat in 1972. Southern whites were generally believed to be more conservative than their Northern counterparts. Plus, the Democrats needed most of the Southern states for any chance of the victory they got. Then, too, Carter was not at all associated with Washington politics. He made the most of this by describing himself as a Washington ''outsider,'' as one who could act for America rather than the Washington Establishment.

In any case, Carter won the election. President Ford barely got the nomination over Ronald Reagan, who had been waiting in the wings to make a run for election in 1976 (following, he had hoped, a successful second term for Nixon). Carter carried all Southern States, except Virginia, the most populous states of the Northeast, and several in the Midwest. Ford carried the prairie, mountain, and Pacific coast states, and few others. The electoral vote was 297 for Carter to 240 for Ford, and the popular vote was closer still.

The press had a field day with the Carters for the better part of President Carter's term. The Carters were from Plains, a small town in rural southwest Georgia. Carter had a wide toothy grin and a folksy manner. Rather than riding from the inaugural ceremony to the White House, Carter and his wife, Rosalynn, walked hand in hand down Pennsylvania Avenue. But the whole Carter clan, from Jimmy and Rosalynn, to young daughter Amy to brother Billy to Carter's mother "Miss Lillian," were the focus of national attention by way of the media. Billy Carter was especially good copy for the first year or so. He was depicted as a "good ole boy," dashing around in a pickup, running a service station in Plains, and drinking beer in uninhibited quantities with his buddies. A little book was even published on Billy Carter's wit and, most astounding of all, a beer was put out in his name, called "Billy Beer." People rushed out to buy it for a couple of weeks, then it languished in boxes as customers passed it by.

Much the same could be said for the Carter Administration, though it happened less quickly than with "Billy Beer." President Carter rode high in the popularity polls for the first six months or so. He came across as a nice man, a devoted husband and father, a church-going Baptist, and a down-to-earth, all-around good fellow. Perhaps he was, but could he govern? Doubts about this mounted in the course of the first year, and his ineptness became more apparent with the passage of time. As one journalist said, rather harshly, "Rarely in the history of the Republic has there been an occupant of the Oval Office who demonstrated so quickly an inability to conduct even the simplest affairs of the state. . . . He is perceived both at home and abroad as a politician of limited and uncertain talents, a well-meaning man whose power derives far more from the office he lucked into than the qualities of personal leadership he has been able to exert."[229] Carter was adept at running for office, but once there he seemed to be stuck in that groove, nor were those whom he gathered into his administration much more adept at governing.

Carter was the first Democrat to come to the presidency since Grover Cleveland who did not have a four-year plan. That is to say, he did not come to the office with a grand, or grandiose, plan for making over America or the world. He never did quite get a handle on the government, much less give it a clear direction. Rather than being in control, President Carter was more like a man who mounts a bucking horse and is thereafter too busy trying to stay on to worry about the direction of the horse. In domestic affairs, he was confronted by a welfare state whose programmed expansion was already out of hand. He inherited a mounting government deficit, an exploding national debt, and rising budgets. On the foreign scene, he was confronted by a volatile situation in the Middle East, worsening as a result of contending native revolutionaries and the expansion of Soviet power into the area. The African situation generally was hardly less volatile, but less crucial to the American and European well-being.

The appropriations of the federal government rose dramatically in the 1970s. The appropriation was slightly over $222 billion in 1970; in 1980 it was over $690 billion, more than tripling in a decade. The national debt was approximately $533 billion in 1975; in 1980 it was $908 billion. In 1974, the Federal deficit was $4.7 billion (not all the Nixon years had been so good); in 1980 it was $59.6 billion. Social Security was running out of money when Carter came to office; indeed, it could hardly do otherwise since benefits greatly exceeded what recipients generally had paid in. In 1977, Congress applied another poultice to the system by voting raises on the employed that would rise steeply over the next ten years. The runaway deficits and national debt (with its ever mounting interest) produced their bitter harvest of rising prices and interest rates, as government expanded credit and the money supply to finance the spending.

The major expansion of government controls and activity during Carter's term was in the field of energy. Gasoline prices were fairly stable 1974–1978, stabilizing at the pump in the range of 50 to 60 cents per gallon. Then, in 1978 they began to shoot up rapidly, going swiftly from 69 to 79 to 89 cents per gallon, and over a year or so topping out at around $1.45 per gallon depending on local conditions and the kind of gasoline purchased. According to the official line, promulgated by Carter among others, with dire predictions that sounded like the little red hen's announcement that "the sky is falling," the world was confronted with an epidemic fuel or energy shortage. The supply of fuel derived from fossils was being rapidly depleted, they declared. Congress authorized a new cabinet level agency, the Department of Energy, in 1977. Money was appropriated for all sorts of research and experiments in developing new or additional supplies of energy. The government adopted rules and pressured automobile companies to build much more energy efficient and smaller automobiles. The price of electricity shot upward, mainly because many generators were fired with oil. The search was on for alternative fuels for heating.

Actually, the sky was not falling. There was, as yet anyway, no real shortage of fossil based fuels. What happened was that OPEC, a cartel of oil exporting countries, made up of Third World countries, mostly Arab, was controlling the production of oil and driving up the price on the world market. The price of oil rose to around $40 per barrel at its height, a rise of more than 1000 per cent over a few years, thus driving the price of all products derived from oil into the stratosphere. Rather than tackle head on this blatant monopolistic thrust of the Third World nations, President Carter chose to belabor the American people for their use of oil, place restrictions on them, and spend billions of dollars in the futile quest for substitutes.

Indeed, President Carter's general ineptness came through most clearly in dealing with the Iranian hostage situation. The Shah of Iran, an ally of the United States, was driven out of his country by a Moslem revolutionary, the Ayatollah Khomeini. When the United States would not return the Shah to Iran for trial and almost certain death, militant students seized 90 people, including 63 Americans, and held them hostage in the American embassy. Fifty-two of the Americans were held for 444 days from November 3, 1979 until Reagan's inauguration January 20, 1981. When Carter launched a military effort to recapture the hostages on April 24, 1984, the whole thing ended in disaster. The small expedition did not get near Teheran; helicopters could not take off because of faulty parts; and eight of the men were killed. The Carter Administration did work out the agreement under which they were finally released, but only after the much tougher positioned Reagan was elected to succeed him.

President Carter did somewhat better for a while in managing negotiations between Egypt and Israel. President Anwar Sadat of Egypt made an unprecedented trip to Israel in 1977 to meet with Israeli Prime Minister Menachem Begin. The two began talks with the object of settling differences between the two countries. In the absence of their making much headway, President Carter invited Sadat and Begin to Camp David in Maryland for more vigorous negotiations. They never reached agreement on territorial boundaries, but in 1979 Israel and Egypt did sign a peace treaty and resumed diplomatic relations.

In other actions, Carter pardoned most of the Vietnam war draft evaders in 1977. In the same year, the Senate approved turning over the Panama Canal to Panama in 1999. Relations with the Soviet Union worsened during these years. When the Soviet Union invaded Afghanistan, President Carter cancelled grain shipments to Russia and persuaded the United States Olympic Committee to cancel American participation in the 1980 Olympics held in Moscow. The Soviet Union continued to press its brutal war against the people of Afghanistan.

The Democrats renominated President Carter in 1980 to run against the Republican nominee, Ronald Reagan. Carter's chances of election were much slimmer than he had expected. The electoral vote was 489 for Reagan to 49 for Carter. Reagan ran well throughout the country, so that Carter took only Georgia, Hawaii, Maryland, Minnesota, the District of Columbia, Rhode Island, and West Virginia. The Republicans gained control of the Senate and picked up 23 members in the House, though it remained under Democratic control.

Ronald W. Reagan (1911–)

Reagan is the 40th President of the United States, a Republican, and resident of California. He was the first avowed and outspoken conservative to be elected President since the 1920s, and his election signified the coming to maturity of the conservative movement. Mr. Reagan was born in Illinois and graduated from Eureka College in that state. His first employment was as a sports announcer in Des Moines, Iowa, a position he held for five years. In 1937, Reagan went to Hollywood where he became a successful actor in films. Perhaps his best role was in *King's Row,* but he played leading roles in a number of films, most of which have long since been forgotten. He was also a television actor during the first decade or so of television. A "liberal" and a Democrat until the 1960s, Reagan was president of the Screen Actors Guild in the 1940s and 1950s. His shift to conservatism was completed in 1964, when he campaigned for the election of Republican Barry Goldwater in 1964. He served two terms as governor of California before being elected President.

4. Reagan Begins

Ronald W. Reagan of California was the oldest person, at 69, ever to come to the presidency. He was the first professional actor ever to be elected President, though a good case could be made that a goodly number of them have been successful amateurs at acting. With the increasing role of television in American politics, a mastery of the art of projecting one's ideas and personality in the medium has become an important asset. President Reagan is generally conceded to be a master of communication. But there was much more in Reagan's background than being an actor. He had been involved in national politics for more than a decade and served two terms as governor of California, the most populous state in the Union, which was as close as anyone was likely to come to having the experience necessary for the presidency.

Reagan was a conservative as well. If he was not of the conservative movement, he had become the conservative prospect for many conservatives after his speech in the Goldwater campaign in 1964. In his speeches over the years, he confirmed his attachment to contemporary conservative values: individual liberty, limited government, private enterprise, the family and church as primary institutions, and the importance of civilized order. In 1975, for example, he had this to say about a government controlled economy: "The trend today is toward more and more control of the economy by government that goes directly against our traditions, against the ideas of freedom and individual initiative that made us great. . . . There's no question that the self-sufficiency and material well-being of Americans are being diminished by government. We're following England down the road to intellectual and financial destruction."[230]

In his first Inaugural Address, President Reagan affirmed his commitment to limited constitutional government. "Our government," he said, "has no special power except that granted it by the people. It is time to check and reverse the growth of government which shows signs of having grown beyond the consent of the governed." Further, "It is my intention to curb the size and influence of the Federal establishment and to demand recognition of the distinction between the powers granted to the Federal government and those reserved to the state or to the people. All of us need to be reminded that the Federal government did not create the states; the states created the Federal government."[231]

But however conservative Reagan might be, and however personally popular, he headed a government which was far from having a conservative consensus. The Republicans had only the slimmest of a majority in the Senate. Moreover, while Republicans are, taken one with another, apt to be more conservative than Democrats, a goodly number of the Republican Senators were long-term Liberal Republicans. Senator Lowell Weicker of Connecticut, for example, could barely be counted on to vote with the Republicans to organize the Senate. The situation in the house was even more unfavorable for conservative action; the Democrats continued to hold on to a substantial majority there. Thomas P. ("Tip") O'Neill, Speaker of the House, from Massachusetts was decidedly a liberal from what was probably the most liberal state in the Union. As for the Supreme Court, it was little changed from the Nixon years. Warren Burger remained Chief Justice, and while it has been very gradually shifting with the conservative trend, it continues to assert the enlarged powers inherited from the Warren Court. Thus far, Reagan has been able to appoint but one justice, Sandra Day O'Connor, the first woman to sit on the high court.

In the absence of a consensus in government, Reagan has generally moved gradually and cautiously, though generally in a conservative direction. He was confronted with an economic depression which had grown worse in Carter's last years. Reagan acknowledged as much in his first major speech after taking office. "I regret to say," he declared, "that we are in the worst economic mess since the Great Depression."[232] He gave top priority in the following months to getting a major reduction of the income tax burden on Americans. In late July, 1981, Congress passed the largest single tax reduction in history, calling for a 25 per cent reduction over a three year period. The basic idea behind this was that tax reduction would leave more money available for investment, and economic growth would take the country out of the depression.

Although Reagan also called for a balanced budget, to be achieved over the next years, for reductions in spending, and for reduction of the size of inflated government, he has never put the pressure behind these that he did for a tax cut. Indeed, according to a theory advanced by Representative Jack Kemp of New York and others, a tax reduction in itself might do the job without greatly reduced spending. Rising production and income would produce revenues, even at the reduced rate, that would lead to a balanced budget in time, if spending were not reduced greatly.

That theory has not worked in practice. Deficits have continued to mount at what is nearly an exponential rate. They rose from $57.9 billion in 1981 to $110.6 billion in 1982, and reached an all time high of $195.4 billion in 1983, tailing off slightly in the next two years. The national debt mounted from $997 billion in 1981 to $1.57 trillion by the end of 1984. It is now nearing $2 trillion! Spending has continued a moderate rise, and tax revenues are by no means catching up with it, as of this writing. President Reagan has championed tax cuts and tax reform energetically. On the other hand, he has not made any major assault on the welfare state as yet. He has preferred to put pressure on Congress to reduce spending while taking credit for the much more popular tax cuts himself. The Welfare State is still in place, and it is driving the national debt up, up, and up. In 1983, Social Security was in deep trouble once again. The base for Social Security taxes was broadened and rates scheduled for future raises, so that the tax cut was at least partially offset by rises in Social Security taxes.

Even so, a much more favorable atmosphere for business and enterprise generally has emerged during the Reagan Administration. The tax cuts and other incentives did encourage saving and investment. Reagan sent a message to unionists in late 1981 with the firm handling of the Air Traffic Controllers strike. Air traffic controllers are employees of the United States government and are prohibited by law to strike. When large numbers of them defied a government back to work order, those who did were fired, and the government replaced them. For a number of reasons, union membership has been declining, and union leaders have generally considered it unwise to press demands aggressively. Another factor in the favorable business climate has been government deregulation, i. e., reduction, change, or removal of regulations. Some of this had begun during the Carter term and has been continued or stepped up since. The most striking instance of deregulation was of the commercial airlines. Interest rates have fallen gradually but steadily, making credit available much less expensively.

There was not an immediate economic recovery as a result of the tax cut and other measures. Indeed, the depression deepened in 1981–1982. What was going on was a major liquidation, particularly in older manufacturing industries and in farming. Many factories were shut down, sold, or greatly reduced in their activities. In a number of industries, such as steel, American companies had great difficulty competing with foreign imports, often from countries where workers received lower wages. This was especially so for unionized industries with rigid pay scales and stringent work rules. Farmers had overcapitalized in earlier years with the use of easy credit and were now deeply in debt. Many of these faced foreclosure and sales to meet their obligations.

By 1983, however, the recovery began even as the liquidation proceeded. Many of the factories run by union labor closed, were sold, and have since reopened, often with non-union labor. Many factories and other businesses have learned to operate much more efficiently and to compete on the world market. A goodly number of large corporations have diversified, buying other corporations and becoming stronger. Many new businesses are starting, often quite small, but with plans to grow larger. The stock market has been generally on the rise since the latter part of 1985, and the Dow Jones Average has gone to succeeding higher levels in spurts.

President Reagan has apparently succeeded in reviving confidence in America and national patriotism. Flag waving, which was once frowned upon, has become popular again. Nor is this simply a Republican phenomenon, for at the Democratic Convention in 1984, large numbers of small flags were passed out and the conventioneers waved them energetically through much of the proceedings. A part of this may be ascribed to a renewed emphasis on keeping America militarily strong, and highly selective use of military force. Probably the most successful example of this occurred in the invasion of tiny Grenada with a small force to drive out the Communist usurpers. The invasion was successful; local government was restored, and American forces withdrawn. On the other hand, an American force sent into Lebanon to help keep the peace there was eventually withdrawn because of successive terrorist attacks. Communism was still on the march, and terrorism appeared to be worsening, especially in the Mideast, where it was sponsored by Syria and Libya (Soviet-armed countries).

Ronald Reagan won by an even more impressive landslide in 1984 than in 1980. Fritz Mondale, who had been Carter's Vice-President, was the Democratic nominee. Reagan got 525 electoral votes to 13 for Mondale and his running mate, Geraldine Ferraro, the first woman ever to be nominated for Vice-President by a major political party. Mondale carried only his home state of Minnesota and the District of Columbia. Many pundits were saying after the election that if the Democratic Party was to succeed in future national elections, it must move back toward the center—be much less radical, become more conservative.

As Reagan began his second term in 1985, much of what has been called the "Conservative Agenda" had not been achieved. If he intended substantially to dismantle the Welfare State, he had made little progress. The Departments of Education and Energy, which had been targeted for abolition, were still operating. The budget was more gravely unbalanced than when Reagan took office. Not only was there no provision to reduce and eventually pay off the national debt, but it was growing at an ever increasing pace. Little progress had been made in restoring the national government to its constitutional role. Conservatives had not even managed to get a single constitutional amendment before the states, whether to balance the budget, permit prayer in the public schools, or to return to the states the authority to regulate and prohibit abortions. The national media and the college and university professors were still predominantly inclined to liberalism. The Welfare State had a large, sometimes, and often outspoken clientele ready to make loud and sustained protests when their programs were threatened. Probably, there was as yet no national consensus for conservatism, and certainly conservatism in 1985 did not have that dominance that could supplant welfarism.

Notes

1. Edmund Wilson, *The American Earthquake: A Documentary of the Twenties and Thirties* (Garden City, NY: Doubleday Anchor Books, 1985), pp. 181–83.

2. Arthur M. Schlesinger, Jr., *The Crisis of the Old Order* (Boston: Houghton Mifflin, 1957), p. 219.

3. Herbert Hoover, *The Memoirs of Herbert Hoover*, vol. III (New York: 1932), p. 16.

4. Frederick L. Allen, *Only Yesterday* (New York: Bantam Books, 1931), p. 217.

5. Hoover, *op. cit.*, vol. III, p. 17.

6. Allen, *op. cit.*, pp. 231–32.

7. Gene Smith, *The Shattered Dream: Herbert Hoover and the Great Depression* (New York: William Morrow and Co., 1970), pp. 38–39.

8. Quoted in Frederick L. Allen, *Since Yesterday* (New York: Harper & Bros., 1940), p. 38.

9. Herbert Hoover, *State Papers and Other Public Writings* (New York: 1934), p. 496.

10. Herbert Hoover, "Policing the Ether," *Scientific American* CXXVII (August, 1922), p. 80.

11. Herbert Hoover, *The New Day: Campaign Speeches of Herbert Hoover*, vol. II (Stanford, 1928), pp. 101–02.

12. Henry S. Commager, ed., *Documents of American History* (New York: Appleton-Century-Crofts, 1962), vol. II, p. 236.

13. Hoover, *Memoirs*, vol. III, pp. 23–24.

14. *Ibid.*, p. 128.

15. Hoover, *State Papers*, vol. II, pp. 187–88.

16. *Ibid.*, p. 222.

17. Allen, *Since Yesterday*, p. 79.

18. Quoted in William E. Leuchtenburg, *Franklin D. Roosevelt and the New Deal* (New York: Harper & Row, 1963), pp. 4–5.

19. *Ibid.*, pp. 11–12.

20. Allen, *Since Yesterday*, pp. 98–99.

21. Herbert Feis, *1933: Character in Crisis* (Boston: Little, Brown and Co., 1966), p. 82.

22. *Ibid.*, p. 104.

23. *Ibid.*, p. 84.

24. Hoover, *Memoirs*, vol. III, p. 390.

25. The inaugural address is reprinted in Ben D. Zevin, ed., *Nothing to Fear* (New York: Popular Library, 1961), p. 29.

26. Quoted in Arthur M. Schlesinger, Jr., *The Coming of the New Deal* (Boston: Houghton Mifflin, 1958), p. 1.

27. *Ibid.*

28. Eric F. Goldman, *Rendezvous with Destiny* (New York: Vintage Books, 1956), p. 252.

29. Richard Hofstadter, *The Age of Reform* (New York: Alfred A. Knopf, 1955), pp. 300–01.

30. Schlesinger, *The Coming of the New Deal*, pp. 87–88.

31. Leuchtenburg, *op. cit.*, p. 63.

32. William E. Leuchtenburg, ed., *The New Deal* (Columbia: University of South Carolina Press, 1968), p. 44.

33. George L. Mosse, *The Culture of Western Europe* (Chicago: Rand McNally, 1961), p. 378.

34. *Ibid.*, p. 353.

35. Rexford G. Tugwell, *The Brains Trust* (New York: Viking, 1968), p. 527.

36. Leuchtenburg, *Franklin D. Roosevelt and the New Deal*, p. 58.

37. Quoted in Schlesinger, *The Coming of the New Deal*, p. 93.

38. *Ibid.*

39. *Ibid.*, p. 94.

40. *Ibid.*, p. 7.

41. H. L. Mencken, "A Constitution for the New Deal," *Reader's Digest* (July, 1937), p. 28.

42. Quoted in Tugwell, *op. cit.*, p. 172.

43. *The Secret Diary of Harold L. Ickes: The First Thousand Days* (New York: Simon and Schuster, 1953), p. 14.

44. Feis, *op. cit.*, p. 232.

45. Commager, *Documents of American History*, vol. II, p. 263.

46. Quoted in Allen, *Since Yesterday*, p. 95.

47. John T. Flynn, *The Roosevelt Myth* (New York: Devin-Adair, 1956, rev. ed.), p. 57.

48. Quoted in Clarence B. Carson, "Lessons for the Tennessee Valley Authority," *The Review of the News* (June 16, 1982), p. 55.

49. Commager, *Documents of American History*, vol. II, pp. 272–73.

50. *Ibid.*, p. 243.

51. Quoted in Schlesinger, *The Coming of the New Deal*, pp. 114–15.

52. Hugh S. Johnson, "NRA Ballyhoo," Leuchtenburg, *The New Deal*, p. 47.

53. Leuchtenburg, *Franklin D. Roosevelt and the New Deal*, p. 69.

54. Schlesinger, *The Coming of the New Deal*, p. 62.

55. *Ibid.*, pp. 290–91.

56. Harry J. Carman, Harold C. Syrett, and Bernard Wishy, *A History of the American People*, vol. II (New York: Alfred A. Knopf, 1961), p. 670.

57. Quoted in Schlesinger, *The Coming of the New Deal*, p. 186.

58. The quotation is taken from the *Oxford English Dictionary* under the entry, "Welfare."

59. Arthur M. Schlesinger, Jr., *The Politics of Upheaval* (Boston: Houghton Mifflin, 1960), p. 398.

60. James D. Richardson, *A Compilation of the Messages and Papers of the Presidents* (New York: Bureau of National Literature, 1897), pp. 569–70.

61. Commager, *Documents of American History*, vol. II, p. 326.

62. Quoted in Eugene Lyons, *The Red Decade* (New Rochelle, NY: Arlington House, 1970, new edition), p. 173.

63. *Ibid.*, p. 175.

64. Bernard Karsh and Phillips L. Garman, "The Impact of the Political Left," *Labor and the New Deal*, Milton Derber and Edwin Young, eds. (Madison: University of Wisconsin Press, 1957), pp. 107–08.

65. Caroline Bird, *The Invisible Scar* (New York: David McKay Co., 1966), pp. 148–49.

66. Lyons, *op. cit.*, p. 174.

67. Commager, *Documents of American History*, vol. II, p. 326.

68. Quoted in Richard B. Morris, ed., *Encyclopedia of American History* (New York: Harper & Bros., 1953), pp. 352–53.

69. Jane Jacobs, *The Death and Life of Great American Cities* (New York: Random House, 1961), p. 310.

70. William H. Peterson, *The Great Farm Problem* (Chicago: Henry Regnery, 1959), p. 159.

71. Commager, *Documents of American History*, vol. II, pp. 315–16.

72. Fred Witney, *Government and Collective Bargaining* (Philadelphia: J. B. Lippincott, 1951), pp. 229–30.

73. Leland D. Baldwin, *The Stream of American History*, vol. II (New York: American Book Co., 1957), p. 605.

74. Irving Bernstein, *Turbulent Years* (Boston: Houghton Mifflin, 1969), p. 41.

75. Karsh and Garman, *op. cit.*, pp. 97–98.

76. Commager, *Documents of American History*, vol. II, p. 314.

77. Quoted in Schlesinger, *The Politics of Upheaval*, pp. 518–19.

78. Herbert Hoover, *The Challenge to Liberty* (Rockford, Ill.: The Herbert Hoover Presidential Library Association, 1971), pp. 190, 192.

79. *Ibid.*, pp. 197–98.

80. Alonzo L. Hamby, "Introduction," *The New Deal* (New York: Weybright and Talley, 1969), p. 8.

81. Schlesinger, *The Politics of Upheaval*, p. 447.

82. Commager, *Documents of American History*, vol. II, pp. 280, 283.

83. *Ibid.*, p. 459.

84. *Ibid.*, p. 354.

85. Edwin C. Rozwenc and Thomas T. Lyons, ed., *Presidential Power in the New Deal* (Lexington, Mass.: D. C. Heath, 1964), p. 30.

86. Quoted in Schlesinger, *The Politics of Upheaval*, pp. 533–34.

87. Zevin, *op. cit.*, p. 105.

88. *Ibid.*

89. Quoted in Schlesinger, *The Politics of Upheaval*, p. 457.

90. Zevin, *op. cit.*, p. 115.

91. Ray A. Billington, *et. al.*, eds., *The Making of American Democracy*, vol. II (New York: Holt, Rinehart and Winston, 1962), p. 338.

92. Paul K. Conkin, *The New Deal* (New York: Thomas Y. Crowell, 1967), p. 42.

93. Leuchtenburg, *Franklin D. Roosevelt and the New Deal*, p. 137.

94. Arthur J. May, *Europe Since 1939* (New York: Holt, Rinehart and Winston, 1966), p. 76.

95. Peter Calvocoressi and Guy Wint, *Total War: The Story of World War II* (New York: Pantheon Books, 1972), p. 267.

96. Quoted in Eugene N. Anderson, *Modern Europe in World Perspective: 1914 to the Present* (New York: Rinehart, 1958), p. 493.

97. *Ibid.*, p. 497.

98. Winston S. Churchill, *Their Finest Hour* (Boston: Houghton Mifflin, 1949), p. 262.

99. Marvin Meyers, Alexander Kern and John G. Cawelti, *Sources of the American Republic*, vol. II (Chicago: Scott, Foresman and Co., 1961), p. 415.

100. Quoted in T. Harry Williams, Richard N. Current and Frank Freidel, *A History of the United States*, vol. II (New York: Alfred A. Knopf, 1959), p. 541.

101. Meyers, Kern and Cawelti, *op. cit.*, p. 417.

102. Commager, *Documents of American History*, vol. II, p. 448.

103. Billington, *op. cit.*, vol. II, pp. 357–58.

104. Robert A. Theobald, *The Final Secret of Pearl Harbor* (New York: Devin-Adar, 1954), p. 20.

105. Meyers, Kern, and Cawelti, *op. cit.*, vol. II, p. 425.

106. Arthur S. Link, *American Epoch* (New York: Alfred A. Knopf, 1955), p. 516.

107. Commager, *Documents of American History*, vol. II, p. 475.
108. *Ibid.*, p. 477.
109. *Ibid.*
110. Richard W. Leopold, Arthur S. Link and Stanley Coben, *Problems in American History*, vol. II (Englewood: Prentice-Hall, 1966), p. 334.
111. George H. Mayer and Walter O. Forster, *The United States and the Twentieth Century* (Boston: Houghton Mifflin, 1958), p. 614.
112. Winston S. Churchill, *Closing the Ring* (Boston: Houghton Mifflin, 1951), p. 345.
113. *Ibid.*, p. 346.
114. Keith Eubank, *The Summit Conferences*, 1919–1960 (Norman: University of Oklahoma Press, 1966)
115. Winston S. Churchill, *Triumph and Tragedy* (Boston: Houghton Mifflin, 1953), p. 331.
116. *Ibid.*, p. 374.
117. Quoted in Samuel E. Morison, *The Oxford History of the American People* (New York: Oxford University Press, 1965), p. 1030.
118. *Ibid.*, p. 1034.
119. Meyers, Kern and Cawelti, *op. cit.*, vol. II, p. 446.
120. Billington, *op. cit.*, vol. II, p. 405.
121. Hugh Seton-Watson, *From Lenin to Malenkov* (New York: Frederick A. Praeger, 1953), p. 255.
122. Quoted in Lyons, *op. cit.*, p. 47.
123. *Ibid.*, p. 48.
124. Marguerite Higgins, *Our Vietnam Nightmare* (New York: Harper & Row, 1965), p. 14.
125. Quoted in Williams, Current and Freidel, *op. cit.*, vol. II, p. 620.
126. Leopold, Link and Coben, *op. cit.*, vol. II, p. 351.
127. Commager, *Documents of American History*, vol. II, p. 527.
128. *Ibid.*, p. 532.
129. Quoted in Link, *American Epoch*, p. 676.
130. Commager, *Documents of American History*, vol. II, p. 556.
131. Quoted in Anthony Kubek, *How the Far East Was Lost* (Chicago: Henry Regnery Co., 1963), p. 372.
132. *Ibid.*, p. 366.
133. *Ibid.*, pp. 319–20.
134. *Ibid.*, p. 339.
135. Quoted in Link, *American Epoch*, p. 664.
136. Courtney Whitney, *MacArthur: His Rendezvous with History* (New York: Alfred A. Knopf, 1964), p. 322.
137. *Ibid.*, p. 425.
138. John W. Spanier, *The Truman-MacArthur Controversy and the Korean War* (New York: W. W. Norton, 1965), p. 167.
139. Eric F. Goldman, *The Crucial Decade—and After* (New York: Random House, 1960), p. 203.
140. See Whitney, *op. cit.*, p. 483.
141. *Ibid.*, p. 485.
142. Link, *American Epoch*, p. 695.
143. Ralph de Toledano, *The Greatest Plot in History* (New York: Duell, Sloan and Pearce, 1963), p. 187.
144. Roy Cohn, *McCarthy* (New York: New American Library, 1968), p. 25.
145. John Rorty and Moshe Decter, *McCarthy and the Communists* (Boston: Beacon Press, 1954), p. 12.

146. Billington, *op. cit.*, p. 398.

147. Commager, *Documents of American History*, vol. II, p. 610.

148. I. Kapranov, "The USSR and Industrial Development of Newly Free States," *Internationalism, National Liberation and Our Epoch* (Moscow: Novosti Press Agency, n.d.), p. 104.

149. Commager, *Documents of American History*, vol. II, pp. 514–15.

150. Louis W. Koenig, ed., *The Truman Administration: Its Principles and Practices* (New York: New York University, Press, 1956), p. 111.

151. Goldman, *Crucial Decade*, pp. 223–24.

152. Quoted in *ibid.*, p. 243.

153. Harvey Wish, *Contemporary America* (New York: Harper & Row, 1966, 4th ed.), p. 693.

154. William H. Whyte, Jr., *The Organization Man* (Garden City, NY: Doubleday, 1956), p. 7.

155. C. Wright Mills, *The Power Elite* (New York: Oxford University Press, 1956), pp. 3–4.

156. Quoted in Theodore C. Sorensen, *Kennedy* (New York: Harper & Row, 1965), p. 167.

157. *Ibid.*, p. 395.

158. Arthur M. Schlesinger, Jr., *A Thousand Days* (Boston: Houghton Mifflin, 1965), p. 213.

159. Sorensen, *op. cit.*, pp. 450–51.

160. Quoted in *ibid.*, p. 452.

161. Quoted in Frank N. Magill, ed., *Great Events from History* (Englewood Cliffs, NJ: Salem Press, 1975), p. 1889.

162. *Public Papers of the Presidents of the United States: Lyndon B. Johnson*, vol. I (Washington: Government Printing Office, 1965), pp. 376, 380.

163. Eric F. Goldman, *The Tragedy of Lyndon Johnson* (New York: Alfred A. Knopf, 1969), p. 333.

164. *Ibid.*, p. 334.

165. Commager, *Documents of American History*, vol. II, p. 532.

166. Harry S. Truman, *Memoirs*, vol. II, *Years of Trial and Hope* (Garden City, NY: Doubleday, 1956), p. 106.

167. Harry B. Price, *The Marshall Plan and Its Meaning* (Ithica: Cornell University Press, 1955), p. 172.

168. Commager, *Documents of America History*, vol. II, p. 558.

169. Price, *op. cit.*, p. 205.

170. *Ibid.*, pp. 205–06.

171. Benjamin M. Zigler, ed., *Desegregation and the Supreme Court* (Boston: D. C. Heath, 1958), p. 79.

172. Charles S. Hyneman, *The Supreme Court on Trial* (New York: Atherton Press, 1963), p. 199.

173. *Ibid.*

174. Section 4, Article I of the Constitution.

175. Quoted in Theodore Mitau, *Decade of Decision* (New York: Scribner's, 1967), p. 100.

176. L. Brent Bozell, *The Warren Revolution* (New Rochelle, NY: Arlington House, 1966), p. 109.

177. Quoted in *ibid.*, p. 111.

178. Mitau, *op. cit.*, p. 129.

179. Quoted in *ibid.*, p. 125.

180. *Ibid.*, p. 137.

181. *Ibid.*, pp. 174–75.
182. Lyman A. Garber, *Of Men and Not of Law* (New York: Devin-Adair, 1966), p. 183.
183. Bozell, *op. cit.*, pp. 111–12.
184. Quoted in Robert H. Brisbane, *Black Activism: Racial Revolution in the United States, 1954–1970* (Valley Forge, PA.: Judson Press, 1974), p. 35.
185. *Ibid.*, p. 67.
186. Quoted in *ibid.*, p. 72.
187. Robert S. Elegant, *Mao's Great Revolution* (New York: World Publishing Co., 1971), p. 79.
188. Quoted in Edward E. Rice, *Mao's Way* (Berkeley: University of California Press, 1972), p. 252.
189. Elegant, *op. cit.*, p. 178.
190. *Ibid.*, pp. 244–45.
191. *Ibid.*, p. 200.
192. Lewis S. Feuer, *The Conflict of Generations* (New York: Basic Books, 1969), p. 438.
193. Brisbane, *op. cit.*, p. 162.
194. *Ibid.*, p. 181.
195. Gary R. Weaver and James H. Weaver, *The University and Revolution* (Englewood Cliffs, NJ: Prentice-Hall, 1969), pp. 157–58.
196. Saul S. Friedman, "Riots, Violence, and Civil Rights," *National Review*, p. 904.
197. Quoted in *The Report of The President's Commission on Campus Unrest* (Washington: Government Printing Office, 1970), p. 254.
198. *Ibid.*, pp. 424, 428–29.
199. *Ibid.*, pp. 254, 458–59.
200. William F. Buckley, Jr., *The Governor Listeth* (New York: G. P. Putnam's Sons, 1970), pp. 88–89.
201. Friedrich A. Hayek, *The Road to Serfdom* (Chicago: University of Chicago Press, 1944), pp. 12–14.
202. *Ibid.*, p. 14.
203. Richard M. Weaver, *Ideas Have Consequences* (Chicago: University of Chicago Press, 1948), p. 185.
204. "Foreword" to Richard M. Weaver, *Visions of Order* (Baton Rouge: Louisiana State University Press, 1964).
205. Eugen Weber, ed., *The Western Tradition* (Boston: D. C. Heath, 1959), p. 835.
206. Hans F. Sennholz, "Postscript," Ludwig von Mises, *Notes and Recollections* (South Holland, Ill.: Libertarian Press, 1978), p. 161.
207. William F. Buckley, Jr., *God and Man at Yale* (Chicago: Henry Regnery Co., 1951), "Foreword."
208. Russell Kirk, *The Conservative Mind* (Chicago: Henry Regnery Co., 1953), pp. 539–40.
209. Oscar B. Johannsen, "Felix Morley: The Journalist Philosopher," *Fragments*, July-December, 1985, p. 3.
210. Felix Morley, *Freedom and Federalism* (Chicago: Henry Regnery Co., A Gateway Edition, 1959), pp. 1, 4–5.
211. *Ibid.*, pp. 263,275.
212. M. Stanton Evans, *The Liberal Establishment* (New York: Devin-Adair, 1962), pp. 15–16.
213. Frank Chodorov, *Out of Step: The Autobiography of an Individualist* (New York: Devin-Adair, 1962), pp. 240–41.
214. "The Passing of Robert H. W. Welch, Jr.," *The Review of the News*, January 16, 1985, p. 7.

215. John Rees, "Thanks to the Birch Society," *The Review of the News,* December 7, 1983.

216. Clinton Rossiter, *Conservatism in America* (New York: Alfred A. Knopf, 1962, 2nd ed. rev.), p. 234.

217. Frank S. Meyer, *The Conservative Mainstream* (New Rochelle, NY: Arlington House, 1969), p. 306.

218. Raymond Price, *With Nixon* (New York: Viking, 1977), p. 200.

219. Quoted in *ibid.*

220. Congressional Quarterly's *Guide to the United States Supreme Court* (Washington: Congressional Quarterly, 1979), p. 645.

221. Quoted in William F. Buckley, Jr., *Execution Eve* (New York: G. P. Putnam's Sons, 1975), p. 447.

222. Laurel Hicks, *et. al., American Government and Economics* (Pensacola: A Beka Book, 1984), p. 219.

223. *Guide to the Supreme Court, op. cit.,* p. 645.

224. Quoted in Thomas A. Bailey, *The American Pageant* (Lexington, MA: D. C. Heath, 1975, 5th ed.), p. 1049.

225. Spiro T. Agnew, *Frankly Speaking* (Washington: Public Affairs Press, 1970), p. 25.

226. *Ibid.,* p. 44.

227. *Ibid.,* p. 45.

228. Theodore H. White, *The Making of the President, 1972* (New York: Atheneum, 1973), p. 32.

229. Victor Lasky, *Jimmy Carter : The Man and the Myth* (New York: Marek Pub., 1979), p. 11.

230. Charles D. Hobbs, *Ronald Reagan's Call to Action* (Nashville: Thomas Nelson, 1976), pp. 39–40.

231. *Reagan's First Year* (Washington: Congressional Quarterly, 1982), pp. 109–10.

232. *Ibid.,* p. 111.

Glossary

Acreage Allotment—a device by which government prescribes how much land a farmer may plant to particular crops. Such allotments were widely used in the 1930s and 1940s for the purpose of reducing production in certain crops.

Acronym—a pseudo-word made from the initials of other words, such as AAA, from Agricultural Adjustment Administration. Such non-words have come into widespread use with the multiplication of government agencies (though many private firms now use them as well).

Antiutopias—usually novels which depict the unpleasant consequences of the use of government power to try to bring about utopia. Such novels have not been unusual in the 20th century as so many utopian efforts have turned totalitarian.

Appeasement—to seek peace by yielding to the outspoken demands of a country, usually for territory from some other country. The result is the sacrifice of justice for what often turns out to be an illusion of peace. That is what happened at Munich in 1938 when Britain, France, and Italy agreed to Hitler's taking a portion of Czechoslovakia. Appeasement is what parents do when they yield to a child's whims when he is having a tantrum to shut him up. The child only learns to get his way by having tantrums.

Austrian School of Economics—a theory of economics which was developed by Carl Menger and Eugen von Böhm-Bawerk, and brought to the United States by Ludwig von Mises and others. They emphasized the subjective nature of economic value, marginal utility theory, and favored reliance upon the free market for the production and distribution of goods and services.

Axis—an alliance of two or more countries to coordinate their foreign and military policy. It connotes, too, a central alliance into which smaller countries may be drawn. Germany, Italy, and Japan formed an Axis, which several smaller countries joined.

Black Market—the exchange of goods under conditions prohibited by law. A black market is most apt to develop when goods are rationed, as in wartime, or when maximum prices are set below market prices, and goods are difficult to obtain at the fixed prices. A brief black market often comes into being for tickets to entertainment when prices are arbitrarily set low by management.

Brainwashing—being subjected to intensive training aimed at discrediting the beliefs of a person and indoctrination with a new outlook. The Chinese Communists have been the most notorious practitioners of this black art (based on a technique suggested by a Russian, Ivan Pavlov). They have used it on their own people as well as on prisoners of war or aliens who fell into their hands.

Broker Loans—loans made by a broker (salesman) of stocks to buyers of stocks. The stock is used as security for the loan, and the stock is bought with the loan plus whatever portion of the purchase price is put up by the buyer. This is called buying stock on margin and often leads to trouble when large drops occur in the price of stocks.

Cartel—a combination of producers of some good for the purpose of determining terms under which that good will be sold. OPEC is a cartel of oil exporters, but it is made up of nations, mostly Arab, rather than companies.

Coexistence—the idea that Communist and other countries can both exist at peace with one another. In fact, Communists cannot believe in coexistence so long as they continue to believe in a revolution that will eventually encompass the whole world. Communists may find it advantageous from time to time, however, to profess the belief in coexistence in order to gain time.

"Commodity Riots"—those riots in which rioters characteristically plunder stores and take commodities. Most of the inner city riots of the 1960s were of this character.

Common Stocks—ownership shares in a corporation. These are the stocks most commonly quoted on stock exchanges. Each share equals one vote in controlling a corporation, and, when a corporation pays a dividend to common stock holders, each share gets an equal portion with every other share. Common stocks also differ from preferred stocks and other claims on a corporation in that it has no preferred claim on the assets of the corporation.

Confrontation—to stand before those with whom you differ and insist on the rightness of your position. Such confrontations became commonplace in the 1960s—between Blacks and the police, between students and university administrations, between rioters and national guard, and between whatever group claimed it was oppressed and the alleged oppressors. The confrontational mentality has since shifted to the courtroom as litigation has increased by leaps and bounds.

Conscious Conservatism—a discriminating and thought out conservatism, even somewhat of an ideology. To call it conscious is to distinguish it from the unmeditated variety that always exists and is widely shared, that clings to and prefers the ways that prevail and is not readily willing to change. Conscious conservatives are more or less aware, too, of those within society who have and are subverting their values.

Conspiracy—at law, a combination of two or more persons to commit a crime. More broadly, it is defined as a combination of persons for an evil or unlawful purpose. Conspiracies have usually been reckoned to be dangerous and threatening in themselves and made punishable by law. Revolutionaries and others who wish to achieve their ends by the use of numbers have worked diligently to limit and deactivate the application of conspiracy laws. They have had much success in the United States since World War II.

Containment—a policy of confining communism to countries where it was already in power. This notion became American policy in the late 1940s and in the 1950s, but it had only modest successes.

Controversialist—one who deliberately engages in controversy by making provocative statements and denying the validity of widely or deeply held views.

Cooperative—also called a "coop," an undertaking owned and operated by those who use its services. For example, there are cooperative stores, such as agricultural "coops," owned by their patrons. Cooperatives are usually based on the belief that regular commercial stores charge too much in order to provide profits for their owners. In the 1930s, the federal government gave special aid and privileges to electrical and other types of cooperatives.

Counter-Revolution—the attempt to undermine or overthrow a revolutionary government. Marxists tend to interpret all opposition to their rules as being counter-revolutionary and act to suppress it.

Credit Contraction—a reduction of available credit. In the past this usually occurred when large numbers of people withdrew (or attempted to) their deposits from banks and savings institutions. Since the establishment of the Federal Reserve system, however, a credit contraction can be caused by changes in the central bank's rediscount or other policies.

De Facto Government—the actual government of a country when it is different from the one generally recognized by other countries. For example, the Communists ruled in China for years in fact before the United States recognized theirs as the legal government.

Deficit Spending—occurs when governments spend more than they take in from taxes and other revenues. The theory that governments should engage in deficit spending in times of depression is called Keynesianism. Actually, the United States has long gone far beyond that and engaged in deficit spending in good times and bad. The result is a mounting national debt and a currency declining in value.

Détente—a relaxation of tensions, as between nations. This French word became a part of international usage during the Cold War to refer to efforts to reduce tensions between the Soviet Union and the West. Such undertakings as cultural exchanges between the Soviet Union and the United States are a part of a policy of détente.

Devaluation—an official reduction in the value of the currency in relation to others. When a currency is overvalued in international exchange rates, foreigners do not buy as much in the country with the overvalued currency. The valuation of currencies of most countries of the West is now done in the market, so that it would no longer be accurate to say that a currency was overvalued or undervalued.

Disinformation—falsified information presented as fact. It is a technique developed by the Soviet Union into a virtual science. Soviets plant accounts of their version of events in captive or controlled publications, where they are picked up and spread much more widely.

Elective Abortion—an abortion performed by or for the mother without any compelling medical reason. There are spontaneous abortions which happen without human intervention. There are also instances when a pregnancy may be hopeless or such a threat to the life of the mother that a termination of the pregnancy may be medically justified. Most of the abortion controversy centers around elective abortions.

Environmentalism—an emphasis on the impact of land use and pollution on the environment. This became a major issue in the 1960s, leading to such government regulation and control as those on auto emissions and the use of pesticides and herbicides.

Espionage—the act of spying or, more precisely, systematic efforts of a government to get the secrets of another. While some governments have long engaged in some spying, the practice became virtually universal during the Cold War, largely as a result of revelations about the extensive spy networks of the Soviet Union.

Eurasia—refers to the great land mass of Europe and Asia. While these are counted as distinct continents, the line separating them is artificial rather than natural.

Fifth Column—people residing in a country who so sympathize with its enemies that they will aid them when the occasion arises. The phrase was first used in the Spanish Civil War in the 1930s, but it has since found other applications. For example, when Germany invaded Norway in 1940, Nazi sympathizers already provided a helpful fifth column. Communists within countries they do not rule usually provide a highly dependable fifth column.

General Welfare—the well-being of everyone. This phrase occurs twice in the Constitution; once in the Preamble and again as a restriction on the taxing power. New Dealers treated the phrase as if it authorized government spending for the relief of various classes in America. Thus, we now refer to a situation in which a large portion of the population has become dependent upon government as a "Welfare State."

Holding Company—a company which owns stock and controlling interest in other companies. It is a device for centralizing control without bringing all the companies into a single corporation.

Judicial Activism—courts playing an active role in efforts at transforming society. More specifically, the courts take over a portion of the role of legislator and executor, thus, not only ruling on what is the standing law, but actually devising laws and enforcing them.

Lebensraum—a German word meaning living space. Hitler tried to justify his territorial expansion on the grounds that the Germans need more living space.

Liquidity—in economics, to hold a cash position. Liquidation is to turn other assets into cash. Liquidity *preference* is to prefer cash over other types of assets. When that preference is widespread, a liquidity *crisis* may occur causing bankruptcies, because there is not enough cash to satisfy the demand.

Mass Transit—a system for transporting people in large numbers, usually within cities. Commonly, it involves connected cars drawn by a single engine on a track.

Monetary Inflation—the increase of the money supply. This is what used to be meant by the single word, "inflation." Following the New Deal and its monetary policies, however, some politicians and writers began to refer to rises in prices as inflation, hence placing the blame on producers of goods rather than the increase of the money supply by the government. It has become necessary to use the phrase, monetary inflation, to express the correct idea.

New Reconstruction—the extensive effort to reconstruct American society in the 1960s. This distinguishes it from the reconstruction which followed the Civil War.

Parity—means equality and usually refers to prices or income. The term was used widely in the 1930s to justify government efforts to raise prices of farm produce. The New Dealers claimed that farmers should have a parity of income with others in the economy, and that to accomplish this government programs must be introduced.

Planned Economy—shorthand language for a government-planned economy. The phrase is misleading in that it implies that when individuals manage their own affairs economic activity is unplanned. When governments attempt to plan economies, they take away from people their control of their own economic affairs and lose much of the benefit that derives from having many people apply their minds to the solution of problems.

Private Sector—refers to the privately owned portion of the economy. The other sector in this equation is the public sector, i.e., the government-owned and -controlled portion of the economy. These terms, though widely used, are quite misleading, since government intervention often makes government dominant in the alleged private sector and there is, in practice, no clear line dividing government from private activity.

Puppet Government—a government controlled by a foreign government. For example, the Soviet Union set up a puppet government over Poland near the end of World War II.

Purchasing Power—the means to purchase goods. But the phrase actually came into use by those who equated purchasing power with currency, not with the production of goods, which is the real basis of purchasing power. Thus, they acted as if an increase of the money supply or credit actually resulted in an increase in purchasing power. Actually, this is an illusion for as the money supply is increased the value of the money declines, resulting in no increase in actual purchasing power.

Pyramid Scheme—a scheme that usually results in those who are first in line at the top of the pyramid getting the lion's share of the proceeds—a get rich at the expense of others down the line scheme. Laws usually forbid such schemes by private entrepreneurs. On the other hand, the Social Security, operated by the federal government, is a pyramid scheme, because it does not tie benefits to contributions.

Reciprocal Trade Agreements—negotiated trade restrictions between countries. The basic idea is that each country will make concessions to the other in arriving at agreements, thus resulting in reducing trade restrictions. In practice, it tends to shift power over trade restrictions from the legislative to the executive branch and makes trade restrictions a product of negotiation—whether higher or lower or what.

Soil Bank Plan—a government program, in operation in the 1950s, for withdrawing farmland from cultivation. Farmers were paid by the federal government for not cultivating a portion of their land.

Speculation—the buying of a commodity or share of stock in the hope that the price will rise. It is sometimes distinguished from investment, and criticized, because the main object is to benefit from a price rise rather than from profits.

Subversion—the acts involved in undermining institutions and governments. Communists work by subversion so as to bring about the downfall of a government and a revolution. The subversion aims at undermining belief in the loyalty to the institutions of a country, thus removing the support of them.

Terrorism—the practice of using terror to subject or intimidate a people. Terrorism is most often recognized in wanton acts of destruction of property and the killing of people.

Suggestions for Additional Reading

The closer the historian comes to the present the more difficult it becomes to put people, events, and developments into perspective. Indeed, general histories quite often avoid any broad view at all for the last decade or so and simply resort to chronicle with a thin coat of commentary in the manner of columnists. The present work is the only one known to the author which attempts a thematic coverage of the years, 1929–1985, under the title, The Welfare State. While the title strikes the author as both descriptive and obvious, others may disagree. However that may be, one thing should be pointed out: since we are ignorant of what developments and trends may unfold over the next ten or fifteen years, the author may be off base in his treatment of the years after 1970. For example, did the conservative movement come to the fore during these years? Or was it only an abortive interlude? Time will tell. In any case, the reader should be especially aware of biases of those who have written on these years. The "liberal" view has generally prevailed during these years among the most prominent interpreters of the period. Moreover, many of those who have written the history thus far have been involved in the making of events or have taken strong partisan stands. None of us is immune to these things, but the reader needs to keep them in mind so as to discount them as best he can.

There is a bounty of literature on the Great Depression, though it was a development of such impact that it has been difficult to get into perspective for those who can recall those years. Murray N. Rothbard's *America's Great Depression* gives a valuable account of its coming in terms of credit expansion of the 1920s. His judgments on Hoover and his policies are rather harsh, however. Frederick Lewis Allen gives a journalistic account of the coming of and the stock market crash in *Only Yesterday*. John Kenneth Galbraith, *The Great Crash, 1929,* focuses upon the failures of the Federal Reserve Board in dealing with the situation. The broader background, told from a Liberal perspective can be found in William E. Leuchtenburg, *The Perils of Prosperity, 1914–1932* and Arthur M. Schlesinger, Jr., *The Crisis of the Old Order*. For vivid accounts of the depression years of the 1930s, there are: Frederick Lewis Allen, *Since Yesterday;* Caroline Bird, *The Invisible Scar;* David A. Shannon, *The Great Depression,* and Dixon Wecter, *The Age of the Great Depression.*

For Hoover's years in the presidency, his own account is given in *The*

Memoirs of Herbert Hoover (3 volumes). William Starr Myers compiled *The State Papers and Other Public Writings of Herbert Hoover* (2 volumes). Favorable accounts of Mr. Hoover's administration can be found in Ray Lyman Wilbur and Arthur M. Hyde, *The Hoover Policies* and William Starr Myers, *The Foreign Policies of Herbert Hoover*. A much more scholarly account is Gaylord H. Warren, *Herbert Hoover and the Great Depression*.

Roosevelt polarized Americans with his experimental and radical departures from the past. He was the prime architect (or perhaps general contractor is better) of the Welfare State. For an early highly critical evaluation of the New Deal, see Herbert Hoover, *The Challenge to Liberty*. John T. Flynn, *The Roosevelt Myth,* flayed Roosevelt for playing fast and loose with the wealth and political heritage of America. A more restrained, if not admiring, portrayal is J. M. Burns, *Roosevelt: The Lion and the Fox*. Paul Conkin, *The New Deal,* is a somewhat critical evaluation of the New Deal programs. Arthur M. Schlesinger's *Age of Roosevelt* (3 volumes) is favorable to Roosevelt, as is Frank Freidel, *Franklin D. Roosevelt* (4 volumes). On labor unions in the 1930s, see Irving Bernstein, *The Turbulent Years*. For a somewhat broader treatment of unionism, see Clarence B. Carson, *Organized Against Whom?*

On Roosevelt's foreign policy, there is a comprehensive account in Allan Nevins, *The New Deal and After*. On his Latin American policy, see E. O. Guerrant, *Roosevelt's Good Neighbor Policy*. On Roosevelt's relations with the Soviet Union, a critical account is given in George N. Crocker, *Roosevelt's Road to Russia*. Opinions differed greatly over the Roosevelt policies toward the war in Europe during the critical years of 1940–1941. Charles A. Beard, *President Roosevelt and the Coming of the War* and Charles Callan Tansill, *The Back Door to War* blame Roosevelt for deviously manipulating the United States into the war. Basil Rauch attempted to refute Beard's charges in *Roosevelt from Munich to Pearl Harbor*. Pearl Harbor and its background have been equally controversial. For a detailed account of the events of December 7, 1941, see Walter Lord, *Day of Infamy* or Walter Millis, *This is Pearl*. For the charges against the Roosevelt Administration, see Husband E. Kimmel, *Admiral Kimmel's Story*. For a broader perspective, there is Herbert Feis, *The Road to Pearl Harbor*.

Most Americans identified with their country during World War II, but post facto disagreements about unconditional surrender, the military abandonment of Eastern Europe, and other decisions has often been sharp. For war production and the home front, there are: Eliot Janeway, *The Struggle for Survival;* Donald M. Nelson, *Arsenal of Democracy;* and John M. Blum, *V Was for Victory*. On the war itself, see Dwight D. Eisenhower, *Crusade in Europe;* Samuel E. Morison, *The Two-Ocean War;* and K. S. Davis, *Experience of War*. Specialized studies include Gaddis Smith, *American*

Diplomacy During the Second World War; George C. Herring, *Aid to Russia, 1941–1946;* and Lloyd Gardner, *Architects of Illusion.*

Since the Cold War has been an ongoing (on and off, according to some), no complete history of it is as yet possible. The opinion of intellectuals toward it has shifted considerably over the years, however. Up to the 1960s, they generally accepted the view that the Soviet Union was primarily to blame for it; since that time, many intellectuals have viewed it as largely a creature of the United States. Books that deal with the Cold War are: Herbert Feis, *From Trust to Terror: The Onset of the Cold War;* Walter LaFeber, *America, Russia, and the Cold War;* Eric F. Goldman, *The Crucial Decade;* and D. F. Fleming, *The Origins of the Cold War.* On particular aspects, for the fall of China, see Anthony Kubek, *How the Far East Was Lost.* For his own account, Harry S. Truman, *Year of Decision.* Other developments are discussed in Thomas A. Bailey, *The Marshall Plan Summer;* W. P. Davison, *The Berlin Blockade;* R. E. Osgood, *The Entangling Alliance;* Robert A. Taft, *A Foreign Policy for Americans;* and John Foster Dulles, *War or Peace.*

There were hot wars as well as cold wars, most notably in Korea and Vietnam, and there was Communist espionage and other types of conflicts as well. On the Korean War, see S. L. A. Marshall, *The River and the Gauntlet* and Carl Berger, *The Korea Knot, a Military-Political History.* On the Truman-MacArthur controversy, see J. W. Spanier, *The Truman-MacArthur Controversy and the Korean War;* Courtney Whitney, *MacArthur: His Rendezvous with History;* and C. G. Lee and Richard Henschel, *Douglas MacArthur.* An insight into spying and espionage by Communists can be gained by reading Elizabeth Bentley, *Out of Bondage* and Ralph de Toledano, *The Greatest Plot in History.* For the kind of charges leveled against Senator Joseph McCarthy, see Richard H. Rovere, *Senator Joe McCarthy.* For a reasoned examination of the McCarthy affair, see William F. Buckley, Jr. with Brent Bozell, *McCarthy and His Enemies.*

Welfarism at home and abroad must usually be traced from administration to administration in other sources. Frederick Lewis Allen traces some of the changes that have occurred in America over half a century in *The Big Change.* Truman tells his own policies in *Years of Trial and Hope.* On the Truman years, see A. L. Hamby, *Beyond the New Deal: Harry S. Truman and American Liberalism;* Cabell Phillips, *The Truman Presidency;* and B. J. Bernstein, *Politics and Policies of the Truman Administration.* Eisenhower provided memoirs of his years in the presidency in *Mandate for Change* and *Waging Peace.* A more comprehensive coverage can be found in Herbert S. Parmet, *Eisenhower and the American Crusade.* The more extensive accounts of Kennedy's interrupted administration were written in the afterglow of the assassination when anything less than fulsome praise would have been considered *lese majesty* by his admirers. Indeed, those closely associated with him wrote the most extensive accounts, namely, Theodore C. Sorenson, *Kennedy* and Arthur M. Schlesinger, Jr., *A Thousand Days*. Johnson's presidency is as yet incompletely evaluated. Johnson's own memoir, *The Vantage Point,* is marred, as are most presidential memoirs, by a tendency to self-justification. Eric F. Goldman provides an insider's view, written by a professional historian, of the Johnson White House. J. C. Donovan discusses the Great Society programs in *The Politics of Poverty*. His foreign policy is surveyed in P. Geyelin, *Lyndon B. Johnson and the World.*

E. Brent Bozell provides critiques of the major decisions of the Warren Court in *The Warren Revolution.* G. Theodore Mitau surveys the major court decisions from 1954 through 1964 in *Decade of Decision,* along with providing much valuable information on public reaction. On the court's invasion of the legislative domain, see Lyman A. Garber, *Of Men and Not of Law.* A most useful survey of the Black revolt is Robert H. Brisbane, *Black Activism: Racial Revolution in the United States, 1954–1970.* For some insights into the student revolt, see Gary R. Weaver and James H. Weaver, *The University and Revolution. The Report of the President's Commission on Campus Unrest* gives a detailed account of the outbreaks at both Kent State and Jackson State. Many books have been written on the assassination of John F. Kennedy, including the *Warren Commission Report.* For the event itself, see William Manchester, *Death of a President.* On the shooting of Martin Luther King, see Gerold Frank, *An American Death.*

In addition to the works cited in the text on conservatism, see also, Frank S. Meyer, ed., *What Is Conservatism?* and William F. Buckley, Jr., ed., *Did You Ever See a Dream Walking?: American Conservative Thought in the Twentieth Century.* Nixon has written about his presidency in *RN: The Memoirs of Richard Nixon.* Theodore White presented a sobering account of Watergate in *Breach of Faith.* Several of the participants have also weighed in with their versions of it. The Ford, Carter, and Reagan presidencies have not yet proceeded much past the campaign biography stage, and those of Ford and Carter have inspired very little writing. Reagan's presidency is not yet completed, so that complete evaluations are not yet in order.

Index